Treasures Of The
Santa Catalina Mountains

Unraveling The Legends & The History Of The
Lost Mine, Lost City, And The Lost Mission

By
Robert Edward Zucker

BZB Publishing, Inc., Tucson, Arizona
First Edition 2014

Treasures of the Santa Catalina Mountains
Unraveling the Legends and History of the Lost Mine, Lost City, and Lost Mission
By Robert Edward Zucker

Collaboration with William T. "Flint" Carter
With contributions from John Vidal, Roy Roush and Steve Friesen
Reprints from Ron Quinn and Donald Page
Gina Torres-Vanasse, Intellectual Property Assessor
Assistance, Rachele Dakos
Illustrations by Robert E. Zucker. Clip art graphics from Desk Gallery, Zedcor, Inc.

Cover: Romero Ruin at Catalina State Park, Tucson.
Back photo: Cañada del Oro and nugget. Non-credited photos are by Robert Zucker.

First Edition: November, 2014.
ISBN-13: 978-1-939050-05-2
ISBN-10: 1-939050-05-7

A project of the Santa Catalina Historical Preservation Project
of Southwest Alternatives Institute, Inc. (SAI), a non-profit 501(c)(3) Arizona corporation.
Published by SAI, Inc., through BZB Publishing, Inc.
P.O. Box 91317
Tucson, Arizona 85752
520-623-3733

Web: http://emol.org/treasurescatalinas
Web: http://robert-zucker.com

Email: bob@emol.org

Available through Amazon.com and other retail outlets.
Printed in the United States of America by CreateSpace, an Amazon.com Company

Treasures Of The Santa Catalina Mountains

LEARN THE SECRETS OF THE MOUNTAINS
Unraveling The Legends & History Of The
Lost Mine, Lost City, & Lost Mission

The Entire Story Of The Legends
Told For The Very First Time—
Lost Spanish Treasures
The Lost Escalante Mine
The Iron Door Mine
The Lost Santa Catalina Mission

Tucson Gold Rush Of The 1800s
The Canyon Of Gold
'Buffalo Bill' Cody's Mines
Tucson Prospectors

Maps Of Santa Catalina Mountains

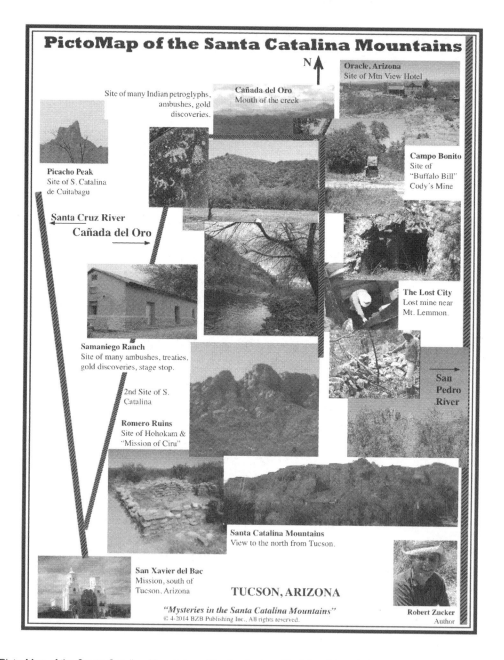

Picto-Map of the Santa Catalina Mountains with sites featured in this edition. Although Picacho Peak is shown on these maps it plays a role in this story although it is not near the Catalina Mountains.

Map of the Santa Catalina Mountains, Arizona. This map is reproduced throughout the book with arrows to mark points of interest in various chapters. The present-day city of Tucson is located south of the Santa Catalinas. Art and photos by Robert Zucker.

This is a specimen of quartz bearing gold and silver from the Santa Catalina Mountains north of Tucson, Arizona. This polished stone is a sample of the precious minerals mined in the Santa Catalina Mountains for centuries. Photo courtesy of William Carter.

"Myth becomes history
as often as history
becomes myth."

Wallace Stegner,
Professor and Western Author [1]

---

[1] "American West Magazine" quoted in "The Durable Frontier Image And Its Place in Urban West," by Robert W. Glasgow, regional editor. *The Arizona Republic*, February 21, 1967. Page 7.

Unraveling The Legends And History Of The Santa Catalina Mountains

The Lost Mine, Lost City, And Lost Mission

The legends Hidden In The Santa Catalinas

ne of the greatest treasures in the world– the Santa Catalina Mountains– is hidden in Tucson's own back yard. More than their beauty, these mountains hold deep secrets and some amazing mysteries.

The famous legend of the Iron Door Mine, a forgotten mission and a lost city somewhere in the Catalinas, has lured prospectors and treasure hunters for hundreds of years. The discoveries of early Spanish placer mining sites, stone ruins, and stories of the mountains only fueled speculation about the riches still left behind. Common knowledge among the locals eventually gained legendary status. Even more surprising was the abundance in gold, silver, and copper etched into the mountains.

These stories became embedded in Arizona's early history and were spun into some sensational legends and featured in numerous literary and film adventures.

How did these legends evolve? Are there buried treasures still to be uncovered? Digging though written accounts that haven't seen the light of day for hundreds of years as well as through the dirt in the mountains has revealed some of the secrets about the Santa Catalina Mountains, Tucson, *and* of Arizona that one probably has never heard.

The folklore about the lost mines and the rich mineral samples collected from the mountains prompted many adventure seekers to risk their lives to prospect the hills and canyons. As they hunted for lost Spanish treasures, they found gold dripping from the Cañada del Oro– the Canyon of Gold. One obstacle that often stood in the way of those aspiring pioneer prospectors was the Apache Indians who guarded the mountains and defended them with blood for hundreds of years.

Once the hostilities were subdued, mining operations sprung up all around the Catalinas. Multi-millions of dollars worth of gold, silver and copper were extracted. Investors, including William "Buffalo Bill" Cody, committed hundreds of thousands of dollars towards massive mining ventures.

Over the last century thousands of men labored in the mountains, established small communities from their campsites, and extracted millions in valuable ore.

This book is a collection of legends, memoirs, and historical events that present a more encompassing story of the hunt for gold– and adventure– in the Santa Catalina Mountains. Comprehensive footnotes are provided for research follow up and more detailed insight.

Explore the Santa Catalinas– both their beauty and history. Then, discover how the legends may have evolved from history.

Learn the stories that lured countless prospectors to riches and failures. Many have taken their secrets to their graves. Yet, some of those secrets can still be revealed.

The Santa Catalina Mountains are not as serene as one might think.

"More gold has been mined from the thoughts of men than has been taken from the earth." [2]

---

[2] Napoleon Hill, American author who lived from 1883-1970. Best selling author of THINK AND GROW RICH. (1970). Aboce graphic drawn by Robert Zucker, at Mt. Lemmon, circa 1973.

Tucson sits in the Santa Cruz valley at the foothills of the Santa Catalina Mountains. Home to nearly a million people today, the valley has been inhabited for centuries. This is a view looking north. It is the most predominate site from almost any part of the city.

L earn the untold legends and history which brought the curious to the Santa Catalina Mountains. Each of three sections uncovers how the mysteries and history played a role in the hunt for treasures and valuable minerals in the mountains.

The first portion, **The Legendary Sites and Ruins in the Santa Catalina Mountains,** explores several infamous locations that have been connected to the legends of the lost city, the lost mission, and lost mine– the Iron Door Mine (or the Escalante Mine).

The second section, **The Legends of the Santa Catalinas,** reveals the stories intertwined with those locations. These legends are examined within the historical events that occurred at the time and how they influenced the hunt for minerals.

The final section, **The Tucson Gold Rush,** describes the successes and failures of prospecting and mining for gold, silver, copper, and other valuable minerals in the Santa Catalina Mountains. Famous Tucson businessmen and lawmen often led the way.

While many pioneers were involved in homesteading and ranching in the Santa Catalinas, those mainly with mining interests in the mountains are featured.

This is where the legends and the history of the Santa Catalina Mountains begin.

The Legendary Sites & Ruins In The Santa Catalina Mountains

Ancient Inhabitants Of The Catalinas
Petroglyphs & Monoliths
Pueblo Viejo

Cañada Del Oro ✦ Las Ventaña
The Romero Ruin ✦ Mission Of Ciru
The Lost City
Searching For *Nueva Mia Ciudad*—
The Fabled Nine Mile City

This view is along the western slope of the Santa Catalina Mountains as it stretches from the Tucson foothills (towards the right side of the photo), follows along the Cañada del Oro river, and ends at the town of Oracle (toward the left). Ancient Indian ruins, petroglyphs, irrigation canals, and evidence of early mining activities are found along the river. In the 1880s, the road from Tucson to Oracle and Camp Grant passed through this valley. There was never a prehistoric mining community without an agrarian culture to support it.

T he Santa Catalina Mountains are shrouded in history and immersed in legends. For thousands of years the mountains have been the source of water, food, and other essentials for many nomadic groups who lived in the valley and foothills.

Over the past few hundred years, the mountains were exploited and bled for their mineral wealth. The bloodstains of natives, Spanish, Mexican, and American settlers who tried, but failed, to extract their riches overshadow those who made fortunes hedging the Catalina's secret lode.

Sky Island Holds A Treasure Story

The Santa Catalina Mountains, north of Tucson, Arizona, have a looming and ominous presence. They are an undeniable landmark to the north of the city– seen for miles in all directions. Their peaceful sentry, however, hides some deep mysteries that continue to lure the risk takers.

The mountain range stretches and shape-shifts across the entire Tucson cityscape. The peak, at Mt. Lemmon, reaches 9,157 feet above sea level. [3] A twenty-plus degree difference in temperature separates Tucson on the desert floor from the village of Summerhaven on top of Mt. Lemmon. Within the Santa Catalina range are several major landmarks: the Cañada del Oro, Ventaña Canyon, the old Indian ruins, Samaniego Ridge and Oracle Ridge.

The Santa Catalina Mountains earn their name as a "sky island" since they jut out in the middle of the Sonoran desert. Named by Father Kino in 1697, they are now under the protection of the Coronado National Forest, and the Oracle and Catalina State Parks.

Besides its beauty, the Catalina Mountains are also the source of mystique, lost treasure legends and a long documented history of precious metal mining. The history of the mountains is also displayed in Indian carvings found on boulders and the ruins near the canyon.

As prospectors, eager to find its riches staked out claims around the mountain range, they learned about the tales of the Santa Catalinas. Those stories became part of Arizona's early history.

Today hikers still find remnants from a long forgotten time– old mining tunnels, abandoned equipment, artifacts, arrastras, and stone ruins. Modern prospectors still hunch over the winding creeks hoping to pan some gold nuggets or even flakes.

The whole Catalina mountain range had been engraved with gold, silver, and copper mostly embedded in quartz veins. A substantial amount of minerals have already been taken from the mountains. Yet, there is still more buried within those rocks.
The daunting mountains may seem quiet now. But there is a lot of forgotten history, as well as many legends, still to uncover.

---

[3] Mount Lemmon Trail #5, U.S. Forest Service, Coronado National Forest.

This view is facing north toward the Santa Catalina Mountains. Beyond Finger Mountain (in the middle of photo) is the "Window"– *La Ventaña*.

"The southern slope of the Santa Catalinas, visible from Tucson, consists of one, single, undivided range, running from the mouth of the Sabino canyon to La Punta de la Sierra on the west, On this range are La Ventaña, The Finger, Rifle Notch, the Clay Banks, and the Church peaks, all visible from Tucson." January, 1884 [4]

---

[4] Arizona Arbors, An Immense Growth of Native Timber. The Santa Catalina Mountains and Their Extensive- Vast Timber Wealth, from Ira Carter, Citizen reporter. From the Weekly Citizen, January 19, 1884.

Naming The Santa Catalina Mountains

Father Eusebio Kino named the Santa Catalina Mountains on his first journey through Pimería Alta– now Southern Arizona– in 1697. [5]

Early Spanish settlers also called the mountains "La Iglesia," the Spanish word for church since the looming mountains looked like a cathedral. [6] One of the near visible peaks from Tucson is Cathedral Peak, resembling church towers.

When Father Kino first circled around the mighty range, he discovered thousands of natives living near its foothills and waterways.

There is a famous legend about Kino's first, and subsequent, expeditions around the mountains. According to this story, and historical documents, Kino traveled with a military group that made several trips to investigate reports of rich minerals in the area. This was the first of many legends tied to the Catalina Mountains.

Close up photo of Finger Mountain. It isn't determined which finger is being used.

[5] Luz de Tierra Incognita, by Juan Mateo Manje, libro ii, 60, Manje. November 10, 1697. English translation in Unknown Arizona and Sonora, 1693-1721. Translated by Harry J. Karns, Tucson, Arizona. Arizona Silhouettes, 1954.

[6] New Mexico and Arizona State Parks: A Complete Recreation Guide, by Don Laine and Barbara Laine. Page 204; and Arizona Place Names, by Will C. Barnes, page 389.

21

Is It Catalina Or Catarina?

The name of the Catalina Mountains has been embroiled in controversy since Americans first arrived. In the 19th and early 20th centuries there was disagreement on the proper name of the mountain range– both Catalina and Catarina were used.

Geologist Edgar B. Heylmun had one theory about the origination of the name. He suggested that Kino named the mountains after his sister, or her patron saint, Catarina. [7] [8]

Early cartographers often used *r*– Santa Catarina [9]– in maps before the 1900s. Newspapers at the time used both names, even in deed records, to describe the same mountain range. This seemed to cause a lot of confusion. [10]

But, in Father Kino's 1699 account of his exploration into Pimería Alta with the Spanish military, he wrote the name of the nearby missionary outpost as "Santa Catalina"– using *l* instead of *r*. [11]

A facsimile of the way Father Kino wrote "Sa Catalina" in his 1699 field diary that recorded his journey to San Xavier del Bac mission and the Tucson valley as far north as Picacho Peak. [12]

---

[7] Guide to the Santa Catalina Mountains of Arizona, by Edgar Heylmun, 1979. Page 4. Also republished in Guide to Arizona's Wilderness, Big Earth Publishing, 1998. Page 217.

[8] Santa Catarina honored Catherina of Alexandria, from Monday Memo, Vol. 2, No. 8, Diocese of Tucson, May 10, 2004. The Church calendar had removed "and suppressed from the cult of saints" the name of Catherina of Alexander in 1969.

[9] Sierra de la Santa Catarina, from Arizona Place Names, by Will C. Barnes. University of Arizona Press, 1960. Page 389.

[10] The Centennial Gazetteer of the United States, By A. Von Steinwehr, 1874, page 825; Memoirs of the Academy of Sciences, Volume 13, by the National Academy of Sciences, 1886, page 463; and repeated in Catalogue of the meteorites in North America, by Oliver Cummings Farrington, 1915, page 463.

[11] Kino writes: "Catalina," from Kino's Report on Exploration, 1699. Page 7. Holographic copies at the University of Arizona Libraries Digital Collection.

[12] Fr. Eusebio Kino Report, 1699, Courtesy of University of Arizona Libraries, Special Collections. Report of an exploration, written at Mission Dolores, Pimería Alta, 1699. Page 7. Written after he

The issue of Santa Catarina or Santa Catalina first came up for public debate in 1881. A Tucson newspaper considered both names to be correct. Since the county line divided the mountain range in half it was decided that the Catarina portion would be in Pinal County, north of the line, and the Catalina portion in Pima County on the south. [13]

The Catalina-Catarina issue came up again later that year when United States Deputy Mineral Surveyor L.D. Chillson wrote a letter to the editor. He requested a solution to a "vexed question." The editors replied with a plea for "some of the fathers of Arizona (to) answer the conundrum." [14]

Chillson owned several mining claims in the Cañada del Oro and used both versions in his various applications. Chillson got his answer a week later when the newspaper declared the proper name to be Santa Catalina, while Santa Catarina was a local corruption of the name. [15] Yet, seven months later, the U.S. Postal Service established a post office near the Cañada del Oro and called it Santa Catarina. [16]

After the beginning of the 20th Century, Santa Catalina became the popular name for the entire mountain range. Depending on the citation, either name is used throughout this book.

returned to his base mission at Dolores on November 18, 1699. This copy is preserved in the library special collections and canbe viewed online at
http://www.library.arizona.edu/contentdm/kino/about.php

[13] ("...and the saints are in heaven."). The Arizona Weekly Citizen, Tucson, A.T., February 6, 1881.

[14] A Mooted Question, by L.D. Chillson, The Arizona Weekly Citizen, Tucson, Arizona Territory (A.T.), September 18, 1881.

[15] The Arizona Weekly Citizen, Tucson, A.T., September 25, 1881.

[16] "Santa Catarina (sic). Santa Catalina. Some early geographers spelled this name wrong. The post office people seem also to have made the same error. P.O. established as Santa Catarina April 26, 1882, Louis Goodman, P.M." from Arizona Place Names, by Will C. Barnes. Page 389.

Graphic of an Indian tribe deep in the mountains.

There are several locations in the Santa Catalina Mountains that have a mystery surrounding them. These sites have drawn the interest among legend seekers, treasure hunters, and historians.

Each of these places played a role in the history and legends about the Catalinas.

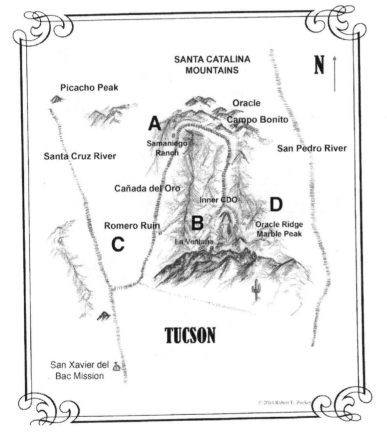

A. **Cañada del Oro**
the Canyon of Gold
and a lost mission site

B. **La Ventaña**
the "Window" and a
lost mission site

C. **Romero Ruin**
in Catalina State Park
and a lost mission site

D. The **Lost City**
ruins by Mt. Lemmon,
near Oracle Ridge

A map of the four legendary sites surrounding the Santa Catalina Mountains.

Early Residents Of The Catalinas

Tucson is one of the oldest, continually inhabited areas in North America.

The Santa Catalina Mountains have been home to humans for thousands of years. Remnants of the lives of some of those prehistoric nomads are still left in the canyons. The most obvious remains are the ancient ruins found in Catalina State Park, along the Cañada del Oro.

The history of inhabitation of the Tucson basin spans over ten thousand years. The ancient canals, stone structures, and artifacts throughout the Santa Cruz Valley provide evidence of Tucson being the longest inhabited "civilization" in North America. [17]

Deep within the Catalina Mountains, there are also signs of human activity. The area has ancient manmade developments, including remains of stone buildings, springs, fences, and pipelines. Archaeological surveys dated the petroglyphs that overlook miles of prehistoric irrigation canals between four to six thousand years old. [18] Archaeological research within the Catalinas has been minimal. [19]

Numerous Native American tribes lived in and around the mountain range thousands of years before the first Spanish explorers passed through in the 1500s. The Spanish Jesuits arrived in the 1680s and later established missions in the valley near the Santa Cruz River through late 1700s.

When they arrived, groups of native Indians were found scattered in small villages around the Santa Cruz Valley. Hostile Apaches used the shelter of the Catalina Mountains to attack the Spanish settlers. The villages were eventually abandoned and fell into ruin. All that is left behind are some ruins, legends, and some long, lost documents.

---

[17] Archaeology in Tucson, Newsletter of the Institute for American Research. Vol. 1, No. 4, Summer 1987; See also, Metropolitan Tucson Convention and Visitor's Bureau. Also, National Trust for Historic Preservation, Travel Itinerary: Tucson.

[18] See upcoming chapters on petroglyphs and monoliths discovered in the Santa Catalinas.

[19] Coronado National Forest Draft, Samaniego Ridge Potential Wilderness Area Evaluation Report. Page 5.

Cañada Del Oro– The Canyon Of Gold

A cactus stands above the dry Cañada del Oro creek– a reminder of the parched desert.

The Cañada del Oro has a long history of Indian aggressions and gold discoveries. This was the first area of the Santa Catalina Mountains reported to contain valuable minerals.

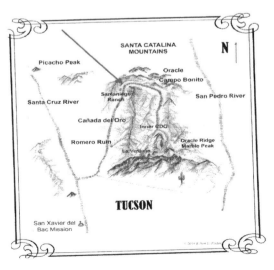

The Cañada del Oro flows north out of the midst of the Catalinas. It winds northwest and turns to the south near pre-historic Indian ruins and eventually joins the Santa Cruz River west of Tucson.

The CDO (as it is nicknamed) is often a dry creek bed except for a few weeks throughout the year. Parts of the riverbed are still favorite spots for amateurs to prospect for gold flakes and grains.

27

The flowing Cañada del Oro after a seasonal rain. Now, the CDO only runs after heavy rains in the Catalinas.

When the Cañada del Oro drains out the Santa Catalina Mountains, it empties into the Tucson valley, eventually joining the Santa Cruz River near Tucson and Marana at the I-10 Interstate. When it flowed regularly, it was a reliable source of life for both animals and humans. Mountain runoff still helps supply drinking water for northwest Tucson residents today. [20] A handful of homes and the sprawling adult-oriented community of Saddlebrooke sit along the edge of the mostly dry arroyo.

Thousands of years before the American, Mexican and Spanish settlers arrived, the Cañada del Oro was home to another group of people who left their mark on the mountains.

---

[20] 2013 Water Quality Report, Metro Main Service Area, Metro Water District, Marana, Arizona. May 2014. Page 1. Marana, north of Tucson and west of the Cañada del Oro gets its drinking water from underground sources.

"Gold placering in Cañada del Oro ("gold gulch") was undertaken in the northern Santa Catalina Mountains by Spaniards as early as the mid-1700's" [21]

The Cañada del Oro riverbed flows out of the Catalinas past remote spots that have not been explored in a long, long time. Gold nuggets and flakes can still be found among the rocks and pooling waters. Not far from this spot a number of large boulders marked with ancient petroglyph drawings were found.

---

[21] Mineral Appraisal of Coronado National Forest, Part 5. Reprinted 1984. Department of the Interior, Bureau of Mines, MLA 25-94, 1994. (1976). USBM_MIA_025-094. Page 24. Source of statement is attributed to Edgar Heylmun.

A petroglyph found in the Cañada del Oro area. Photo taken in the 1980s by William Carter.

Cañada Del Oro Petroglyphs

O n the northwest edge of the Santa Catalina Mountains, overlooking the Cañada del Oro, once stood numerous large boulders etched with petroglyphs.

Several hikers along with a seasoned prospector discovered the glyphs as they explored the rolling hills in the northwest portion of the Catalinas in 1981. [22] Numerous boulders with distinct markings were found on a hill overlooking the valley close to the mouth of the Cañada del Oro.

After the discovery was reported, the Arizona State Museum conducted an archaeological survey on the property. It concluded that the glyphs were authentic and might represent the Desert Culture people who occupied Southern Arizona from 6,000 to 500 B.C. [23]

Several archaeologists from the museum inspected over 80 acres of washes, ridges, and terraces along the Cañada del Oro. Three prehistoric sites and two possible historic sites were noted. Three prehistoric rock art sites were considered to be "sufficient significance to warrant preservation," and a 200-foot radius buffer zone was recommended around the sites to ensure their preservation. [24]

One spot, a one thousand foot by one hundred foot area, had eight to ten boulders with various patterns were packed into a patinated surface. The archaeologists were unable to decipher the glyphs. One of the boulders appeared to have a double Omega sign with a line through it, another had some type of ancient craft and the other had various animals, according to one of the discoverers of the petroglyphs. [25] The site, however, has been disturbed, and the boulders no longer remain.

---

[22] Discovered and reported to the Arizona State Museum by William T. "Flint" Carter and his group in February 1981. The photos of the petroglyphs are the original images from 1981.

[23] Letter to William T. Carter from Sharon F. Urban, Public Archaeologist, Arizona State Museum, University of Arizona. March 11, 1981.

[24] Letter to Richard R. Willey, Coordinator, Academic Conference Center, University of Arizona, Arizona State Museum from John H. Madsen, Assistant Archaeologist, Arizona State Museum, University of Arizona. April 2, 1981.

[25] Interpreted by William Carter, who discovered and reported the find.

One of the Cañada del Oro petroglyphs had images of desert animals.

George Wilson, landowner in the Cañada del Oro between 1911[26] and 1940s, drew maps of the Santa Catalina Mountains where he indicated an "old Indian village" in the northwest and one in the southwest portions of the Catalinas. [27 28] Old Indian ruins were usually called Pueblo Viejo– old village.

_____

[26] Wilson purchased the property in 1911. National Register of Historic Places, Rancho Linda Vista registration for Rancho Linda Vista/Bayless Ranch. Section 7, Page 1. May 1999.

[27] Maps of Rancho Linda Vista, Maps #8 and #47. Page 48. Rancho Linda Vista Historic District. National Register of Historic Places, Rancho Linda Vista.

Close ups of some of the Cañada del Oro petroglyphs. These photographs were taken in the 1980s. The boulders are no longer in their last known location. Petroglyph photos courtesy of William Carter.

[25] This map is reproduced in Canyon of Gold, Tales of Santa Catalina Pioneers, by Barbara Marriott. Chapter 4. "The Days of the Don." Page 65.

Cañada del Oro petroglyph photos courtesy of William Carter.

Looking east towards the Canyon of Gold– Cañada del Oro– where the petroglyphs were discovered. Photo by Robert Zucker.

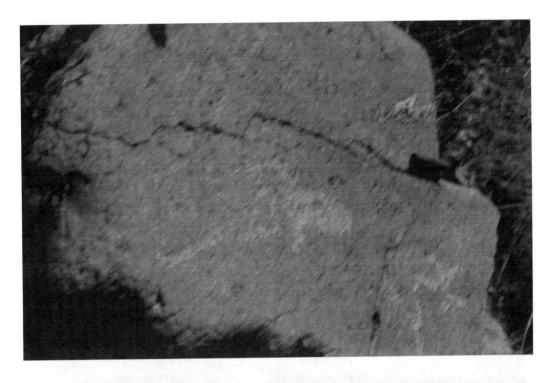

Close up of markings found on another large standing boulder near the entrance of the Oracle Ridge mine. Photo courtesy of William Carter.

Monoliths Around The Catalinas

Located on a small bluff at the entrance of the Oracle Ridge Mine in the Santa Catalina Mountains north of Tucson, Arizona, stood a huge, ancient monolith with unusual markings.

This inscribed boulder was on the opposite side of the Catalinas from the Cañada del Oro petroglyphs. The standing stone had one-inch lines and dots in no obvious order. It was the second largest inscribed boulder in the area. Another ten foot tall monolith was placed at the juncture of Alder Canyon and the San Pedro River. [29] That monolith was bulldozed over during road building. Its exact location is unknown.

Further southeast near Redington Pass, a local news article in the 1880s mentioned monolithic stones set upright and a cave system that holds "fish without eyes." [30] [31]

In 1896, Herbert Brown found two granite, monolithic posts set in the ground on the southern slope of the Catalinas. [32]

A monolith found by William Carter (2nd from right) and friends, outside of the Oracle Ridge mine in the 1980s.

---

[29] Corridor Through Time, by Alice Carpenter, Journal of the Southwest. 38 (3). Pages 279-298. Big Bell Site (AZ BB:6:2 [ASM].

[30] Relics of Antiquity, The Arizona Weekly Star, April 8, 1881 from the Record Union, Sacramento, California, April 1, 1881 (Arizona Historical Society: Arizona Mountains – Santa Catalina)

[31] Old Arizona Treasures, by Jesse Rascoe. Frontier Book Company, Texas, 1968. Page 59.

[32] Prehistoric Relics and Quarrying, by Wm. Blake, Director School of Mines. Arizona Weekly Citizen, March 28, 1896.

La Ventaña-
The Window

"At the Ventaña divide there is a never failing stream that flows down to the Cañada de Oro. This latter canyon opens in the Santa Catalina Mountains above Pueblo Viejo, and trends around to the east and south, heading towards the divide at the north base of Mt Lemmon. This canyon also has three large forks." [33]

One of the most spectacular natural wonders of the Santa Catalina Mountains is Window Rock, also called *La Ventaña*– a natural formed hole in the boulders that juts out from the peak. Besides being a popular hiking destination, this spot has played a role in the mountain's notorious legends.

Spanish for "the Window," La Ventaña was a popular topic of speculation among Tucsonans in the 1880s. Is it a natural hole in the rock or a notch? Does it point to the legendary lost mine?

Tucson dairyman C.G. Jones took a trip to La Ventaña in 1882. He said the granite abruptly rose to a height of thirty feet and the hole is about ten feet in diameter. On one side he could see the entire Tucson valley. When he peered through the north side, he viewed a deeply wooded canyon. A year later, two local hikers tried to find the Window Mountain. They said they saw an elbow projection of granite that was supposed to be the long, lost hole, but they could not reach it. [34]

---

[33] "Arizona Arbors," Arizona Weekly Citizen, Tucson, A.T., January 1, 1884 and January 19, 1884. Canyon de Oro is the spelling used.

[34] "La Ventaña, An Interview With a Party Who Has Been Through the Window Mountain – A Second One," The Arizona Weekly Citizen, Tucson, A.T. October 27, 1883.

A Hole, Or A Notch?

The argument of "Hole vs. Notch" was a popular topic in the 1880s. A reporter in 1883 questioned the appearance of the "aperature (sic) in the Window Mountain that it is no hole after all." There is a "two-fingered shaped projection from the ends of the meeting ridges" and that space between them gives the appearance of a hole, he said. [35]

The issue came up again that year when C.G. Jones, Ira Carter who was an *Arizona Weekly Citizen* reporter, [36] and John Hart all affirmed that La Ventaña is a hole.

But, a newspaper reporter, along with several others who also made the hike up the mountain, contended that it is a notch. Both sides visited the site after a 14-mile buggy ride from Fort Lowell into the mouth of the Pot-hole, or Ventaña Canyon, and an

---

[35] Ibid.

[36] "Arizona Arbors, An Immense Growth of Native Timber, The Santa Catalina mountains and Their Extreme Forests– Vast Timber Wealth," from the Arizona Weekly Citizen, January 19, 1884. Ira Carter was known for his deep exploration of the Catalinas where he had a claim and a cabin. He also ran a sugar camp from the tree sap.

hour climb to the top. [37]

In 1895, Mariano G. Samaniego, who owned a ranch nearby and prospected the Cañada del Oro, said he went to La Ventaña and "the square hole (was) seen through the crest" of the Catalina Mountains. Samaniego said he rode his horse through the hole. He claimed it was nothing more than "two immense granite cliffs" that appear like a hole when standing far away. Judge Scott said it was confirmed to be a hole seen from a telescope at the University in the Tucson valley. [38]

Another trip to the Window in 1896 by University of Arizona students and their professors J.W. Toumey, Forbes, Hoxie and Hall found the landmark "window" but they concluded it was not a window. The telescope that saw the window "must have been off." An old timer from Tucson who approached the group while they were looking at it said it was only "two overhanging cliffs." They found the "window" to be about thirty feet across, fifteen feet high and about ten feet through. [39]

E.M. Tardy, who joined on the trip, remarked that anyone who says they rode a horse through the hole is "talking through his hat." It would be impossible to get a horse in there "unless he had wings." [40]

La Ventaña graphic by Robert Zucker.

---

[37] "Hole vs. Notch," The Arizona Weekly Citizen, Tucson, A.T. December 8, 1883.

[38] "Hole in the Mountain," The Arizona Weekly Citizen, March 28, 1895.

[39] "Trip to the "Window," The Arizona Weekly Citizen, January 4, 1896.

[40] Ibid.

The Santa Catalina Mountains viewed north from Tucson's foothills by Pima Canyon. Sabino Canyon is several miles to the right. Pusch Ridge is to the left.

From *La Ventaña*, You Can See The Lost Mine

"They say if you get to a point in the mountains where you can look through "The Window" and see the San Xavier Mission nine miles to the south that the mine lies exactly in that line."

William Neal, undated. [41]

La Ventaña was often mentioned as a location point for the lost mine in the Catalinas. One clue that author John D. Mitchell gives to the existence of the legendary Iron Door Mine is the *ventaña*– the large natural hole in the rock that resembles a window.

---

[41] "Buffalo Bill Believed In "Lost Mine" In Catalina Mountain's and Organized Company; William Neal Thinks It Really Exists," undated newspaper article, Cody Scrapbook, Arizona Historical Society.

Mitchell, one of the perpetuators of the Iron Door Mine legend in the 1930s, claimed the lost mine is located one league northwest of the *ventaña*. "On a clear day, the miners, when standing at the mouth of the tunnel, could see the light shining through the *Ventaña* near the summit of the mountain in a southerly direction from where they stood." [42] One league is equal to about three miles. A league could be covered in about an hour walk.

Oracle hotel owner and partner of William "Buffalo Bill" Cody, William Neal, told a newspaper reporter in the early 1900s that the earthquake of 1887 might have further eroded any resemblance of a hole and buried any visible tunnels. Before the quake, Neal said they were able to "cut through the Cañada del Oro to Tucson right through where the hole in the mountain– what they call "The Window" is now. The earthquake tumbled all that in." [43]

Neal believed the fabled lost mine did exist, and, if one gets to the point to look through "The Window" they were able "see the San Xavier Mission nine miles to the south that the mine lies exactly in that line." Cody, who had mining interests in the Santa Catalina Mountains in the early 1900s, reportedly searched for the lost mine with Neal numerous times. [44]

---

[42] The Lost Mines of the Great Southwest, including stories of hidden treasures, by John D. Mitchell, 1933. From "The Lost Escalante Mine." Page 44.

[43] "Buffalo Bill Believed In "Lost Mine" undated newspaper article, Cody Scrapbook, Arizona Historical Society.

[44] Ibid. Also, The Lives and Legends of Buffalo Bill, by Don Russell. Pages 434-35.

This is the view east towards the San Pedro Valley from the Santa Catalina Mountains, near Oracle. Numerous Indian villages were found along the San Pedro River, according to Father Kino's journals, maps and other documents of the late 1600s. Ruins of earlier civilizations have been uncovered, including a large monolith. Archaeologists suggest humans have inhabited the valley for thousands of years. Over the past hundred years, miners, ranchers have cleared away any ruins and treasure hunters have hauled off almost all artifacts. As early as 1858, American discovered gold between Tucson and the San Pedro River. [45] While a location was not revealed, the entire mountain range was soon found to contain valuable minerals.

---

[45] Sacramento Daily Union, Sacramento, California. April 14, 1858.

Pueblo Viejo – The Old Village

T he Spanish words Pueblo Viejo means Old Village or Old
Town. There were numerous locations around and within the
Santa Catalina Mountains that were called Pueblo Viejo.

The name often referred to the ruins that natives left behind after they abandoned their
homesteads. There were several spots where they may have settled. Throughout the
Catalinas, dozens of archaeological sites have been uncovered that represented several
cultural periods. [46]

Some of the remaining stone ruins left one the west side of the Santa Catalinas at Catalina State Park, part
of the Romero Ruin site.

---

[46] Archaeology of the San Pedro Valley, by Patrick D. Lyon, Center for Desert Archaeology,
Archaeology Southwest Magazine, Vol. 18, No. 1, Winter 2004.

"Pueblo Viejo" North And East Of The Catalinas

Archaeologists have discovered evidence of human occupancy along the San Pedro River, on the east face of the Santa Catalina Mountains that dates back nearly 7,000 [47] to 13,000 [48] years. One of the first human hunting grounds for mammoths in the North America was in the upper San Pedro River valley.

In the late 1690s and early 1700s, Father Kino described numerous Sobaipuri Indian villages in his diaries and drew several maps with their locations, mostly along the banks of the San Pedro River and Santa Cruz Rivers.

It is possible that Coronado may have passed this way on his route to the Seven Cities of Cibola in 1540. Father Pedro Font, who accompanied De Anza in 1775, described seeing ruins in the area. American investigations of ruins found in the San Pedro valley have been documented since 1852. [49]

About forty miles north of Fort Goodwin [50] old ruins, called Pueblo Viejo, were mentioned in accounts from travelers, the military, and prospectors in 1867 [51] and 1873. [52]

---

[47] Archaeological Survey in Catalina State Park With A Focus On The Romero Ruin, by Mark D. Elson and William H. Doelle. Institute for American Research, Technical Report No. 87-4, 1987. Introduction. Page 1.

[48] Sonoran Desert Conservation Plan, Historic and Cultural Preservation Element. Page 14. And, San Pedro Valley Reserve, Pima County Conservation Report. Page 83. Pima County Government.

[49] Pedro Font description from Hackenberg, 1964; John R. Bartlett, "Descriptions of ruin near western source of San Pedro, 1852; A.F. Bandelier, Descriptions of ruins in Tucson Basin, San Pedro River, Middle Gila," 1982. From "Archaeology of Southeast Arizona: A Class I Cultural Resource Inventory," by Gordon Bronitsky and James D. Merritt. Bureau of Land Management, 1986. Appendix I. Page 345.

[50] Ft. Goodwin was one of the first U.S. military posts in the area, established in June 1864, located about two miles south of the Gila River.

[51] "Notes of a Trip Through Arizona in the Summer of 1866," J. H. Marion, The Weekly Arizona Miner, Prescott, A.T., January 26, 1867.

[52] The Legislature: Those persons who have recently settled on the Gila, above old Camp Goodwin, want a new county created, to be called "Pueblo Viejo," – after some old ruins on the east bank of the Gila, and at the head of the large valley which they have settled, which by the way, is part of Mr. Cochise's reservation." Weekly Arizona Miner, Prescott, Arizona. February 8, 1873.

Unidentified ruins deep within the interior of the Santa Catalinas. This structure is among several, near Oracle Ridge, that have been archaeologically surveyed, but not yet excavated. Photo courtesy of William Carter.

Jack W. Swilling and others began to construct a town in the upper portion of the Gila River in 1872 and called it Pueblo Viejo, named after ruins located nearby.[53] Col Hodge, stationed at Old Camp Goodwin, commented in 1875 that he saw some "hieroglyphics or memorial stones," ruins of houses and pueblos scattered over forty miles on both sides of the San Pedro River in the valley of Pueblo Viejo.[54]

---

[53] "Ho for Pueblo Viejo," The Weekly Arizona Miner, Prescott, A.T., November 2, 1872.

[54] "Letters from Col. Hodge. Old Ruins – Rick Land – Large Products – Telegraph Building," from Old Camp Goodwin, The Arizona Weekly Citizen, October 9, 1875.

"These ruins are at most wholly of stone, and their amount indicates large houses supported in the center by cedar posts, a few of which are yet standing. The ancient town was supplied by water from tanks or fountains on the mesa near by, some of which were circular in form and others nearly square."

Letter from Col. Hodge, October 3, 1875, describing old Indian ruins near Camp Goodwin, north of the Santa Catalina Mountains. [55]

Remnants of ancient stone buildings in the Catalina State Park, on the west side of the Santa Catalinas.

---

[55] Ibid.

Pueblo Viejo's Around Tucson

As American settlers began exploring the desert and mountains around Tucson in the mid 1800s, there were numerous discoveries of old, abandoned structures. One of the earliest published records of ruins discovered in the Santa Catalina Mountains was reported by Tucson merchant and prospector Isaac Goldberg.

In March 1875, both Goldberg and his partner, Mr. Scott, reported finding "an excavation of considerable length, with steps cut in the natural stone walls" about five miles northwest of Tucson. He believed the steps were used to carry ores, or something else, from the excavation spot. Or, he pondered, that it could have been a dwelling at one time. The two had been looking for "fabulous gold mines which were supposed to exist somewhere among the summit peaks." But, they did not find anything else beyond the ruins. [56]

Goldberg relentlessly explored and prospected the Santa Catalinas for decades. He started in 1867 when he accidentally discovered a large ledge of quartz-bearing copper in the Cañada del Oro. But, he lost its location and had searched for it ever since.

Near Tucson, during construction work on the Wetmore ditch, near E.L. Wetmore's ranch, on the south bank of the Rillito River in the spring of 1877, cobblestones were found. Six feet below the surface two skeletons were found sitting in an upright position. Evidence of an ancient ditch that had both served as a dam and furnished water from the Catalinas was uncovered. Hieroglyphs were also found on rocks in the Santa Catalinas. [57]

Another mention of "old ruins on the southern summits" of the Catalinas was buried within a newspaper story about mining ventures near Oracle in 1880. [58] No specific location was mentioned.

There may have been many other spots throughout the Catalinas that had signs of occupations, but they are gone. A few preserved reports provide some clues of their possible existence.

---

[56] "Evidence of old towns…" The Arizona Weekly Citizen, Tucson, Arizona A.T., March 6, 1875.

[57] San Francisco Chronicle, San Francisco, California. September 11, 1899.

[58] The Arizona Weekly Citizen, Tucson, Arizona A.T., January 21, 1880 and "Old Hat District," The Arizona Weekly Citizen, Tucson, Arizona A.T., February 21, 1880.

Stone Building Constructions

There are several structures in the Santa Catalinas that are very old. Whether there is a connection between them is debatable since there is no complete record of their construction. But they were built long before the American settlers arrived.

The most documented site near Tucson is the Romero Ruin (see photo A) on the western slope of the Santa Catalina Mountains. This historic spot, also called Pueblo Viejo, has evidence of thousands of years of human habitation. The last occupant was the Romero family, a Mexican rancher and his wife who fought off the Apaches in the late 1800s. Romero said he built his home on top of more ancient stonewalls. The site is now preserved as part of the Catalina State Park. [59]

There are several stone foundation structures gathered north of Mt. Lemmon (Photo B) that have been covered up with overgrown brush and trees. This Lost City site is located near old mining tunnels and has been surveyed by the U.S. Forest Service.

The southernmost building on the Samaniego ranch, at the mouth of the Cañada del Oro, is a mystery (see photo C). This structure is built on a stone foundation that rises about two feet from the ground. Built on top of that is an adobe frame. The building might be dated much earlier than Samaniego's settlement on the property in the late 1800s.

As a comparison, the east wing of the San Xavier del Bac Mission (see photo D), constructed before 1884, has a stone foundation similar to the others built around this period. Father Eusebio Kino began the foundation of a church site in 1700, but it was never completed. [60] The only other pre-San Xavier Mission building is the Espinoza ruin. The foundation still exists and sits between the actual church and the school to the west. Huge pieces of mesquite beams, taken from the original, much smaller church, were used in the south wing construction which still exists today. [61] There is also a report from the early 1880s of a stone structure with a mosaic floor near Ventaña Canyon. [62] No photos are available and the site has not been located.

---

[59] Archaeological Survey In Catalina State Park With A Focus On The Romero Ruin, by Mark D. Elson and William H. Doelle. Institute for American Research, Technical Report No. 87-4, 1987. Pages 6-7.

[60] A Brief History of Mission San Xavier del Bac, from Mission San Xavier del Bac.

[61] Noted by John Vidal, Facilities Manager, San Xavier del Bac Mission, 2014.

[62] "The Stone Church, A Romance of the Santa Catalina Mountains" The Arizona Weekly Citizen, November 11, 1883.

A. The Romero Ruin in Catalina State Park is built on top of more ancient Hohokam Indian ruins.

B. The remains of one among several stone buildings found near Mt. Lemmon. Photo courtesy of Will Grant.

C. Stone foundation of a home in the Samaniego Ranch property.

D. San Xavier del Bac Mission, first stage of the east wing foundation. Photo by John Vidal, Facility Manager, San Xavier Mission, 2011.

1880: An Old Stone Building

The most famous story about the Iron Door Mine, published in early 1880, told about ruins that were discovered by two prospectors deep within the Santa Catarina Mountains, as they were called at the time.

> *"We came upon a stone building (granite or marble) that was in fair state of preservation excepting for the roof, which had fallen in; the structure was something after the style of the old Cocospari church in Sonora, and we decided that this must have been the place of worship of the people of this once populous city."* [63]

These ruins were part of the hunt for the fabled Nueva Mia Ciudad, the Nine Mile City, located somewhere in the midst of the Catarinas. The story was familiar and "probably all of the old Arizonans in the vicinity have heard the tradition of the Santa Catarinas."

The two prospectors were equipped with a map to the legendary mine with the iron door given to them by one of the grandchildren of a miner who once lived in the ancient city.

After descending down the Cañada del Oro, they found ruins "two miles in width" before they came upon the old church structure. They also brought back "100 pounds of pure gold in nuggets" as proof of their success. [64]

U.S. Mineral Surveyor Solomon Allis, who may have been the correspondent who wrote the newspaper story about the two prospectors, also mentioned seeing "old ruins on the southern summits" of the Catalinas two months before the prospectors discovery. [65]

---

[63] "The Mine with the Iron Door Mine, The Nine Mile City of the Santa Catarinas, The Story as Told to Our Correspondent," Arizona Weekly Star, March 4, 1880.

[64] Ibid. This article is available, on microfilm and typewritten, at the Arizona Historical Society. Also, available at University of Arizona Libraries Special Collections (M9791 Pam4).

[65] "Old Hat District," Arizona Weekly Citizen, February 21, 1880.

1881: Ruins Near Ft. Lowell

"Ruins of a prehistoric race" were discovered throughout Arizona as the Territory became more inhabited. One spot mentioned was "about six miles north of Camp Lowell." This is one of several reports about this site.

At the base of the mountains, where the Rillito River forks join, an ancient town covered about sixty acres, according to one report. Stone foundations were "set up on edge" in various sizes instead of being laid flat. The rooms were about sixteen square feet and faced a plaza or court that was boxed in one three sides. One building had a square front and the rear outer wall was "in the shape of a half circle with a large hall extending through the building." [66]

1881: Many Ruined Buildings Found In the Catalinas

"Many ruined buildings" are found in the Santa Catalina Mountains according to the Sacramento, California *Record Union* on April 1, 1881– April Fool's Day. The article described abandoned "cities" located on the eastern and northern slopes of the Santa Catalinas. [67]

The discoverers found "squares of stone set on end about eight feet by ten feet in size, as well." These squares were spread all about the area. In addition to pottery, stone metates, bowls, stone axes and other relics were scattered on the ground.

The author further described that, "on the slope in a cave we found skeletons of a race of people who when alive were above the stature of the present day." On the northern slope of this same mountain more ruins were discovered along with placer diggings. They

---

[66] "Ruins of a Prehistoric Race," Arizona Weekly Citizen, May 1, 1881.

[67] "Relics of Antiquity," The Arizona Weekly Star, April 8, 1881 from the Record Union, Sacramento, California, April 1, 1881 (Arizona Historical Society: Arizona Mountains – Santa Catalina).

called the town site Pueblo Viejo (Old Town or Old Village). Also, in the mountains near Reddington they reported seeing a lake in the cave that contained "fish without eyes."

There was also mining close to the "placers of Cañada del Oro, where we found shafts that were sunk to the bedrock, drifts run for long distances, and the rich ledges of gold and silver on the same slope proved an industry that must have been remunerative to their workers." [68]

Another reporter in 1881 described ruins of a town north of Tucson, "about six miles north of Camp Lowell, near the junction of the forks of Rillito creek, at the base of the Santa Catalina mountains," where an ancient town covered about sixty acres.

The foundations were "set up on edge, and are of various sizes" unlike the stone masters of the day who laid stone flat. The rooms were about six square feet and faced a plaza or court that was enclosed on three sides. At the end of the enclosure was a large building facing south with a back wall the shape of a half circle. Other foundations and rooms were described among the ruins. [69]

1882: Pueblo Viejo Voting At The Canyon Del Oro

As Mexican and American ranchers began to settle in the Cañada del Oro valley on the west side of the Catalinas, there were enough residents to warrant a polling precinct.

At their meeting on the January 28, 1882, the Pima County Board of Supervisors authorized precinct No. 21 at Pueblo Viejo. Francisco Romero's ranch was set as the voting site. John Zellweger was appointed Inspector. Romero and Miguel Martinez were selected as Judges of Election. [70] This is the area where the ruins of Romero's Ranch and the communities of Oro Valley, Catalina, and Saddlebrooke are now located.

---

[68] Ibid.

[69] "Ruins of a Prehistoric Race," The Arizona Weekly Citizen, Tucson, Arizona A.T., May 1, 1881.

[70] Arizona Weekly Citizen, January 5, 1882.

1883: The Story Of The "Stone Church"

Tucson Judge Charles H. Meyer related an obscure story of an Indian tribe and lost ruins near La Ventaña in an 1883 Tucson newspaper article about the "Stone Church."

The respected local judge told a reporter about a roaming group of Indians who were constantly chased by the Apaches from the San Pedro River into the Santa Catalina Mountains through the Cañada del Oro and back into the Catalina Mountains somewhere near Ventaña Canyon and Finger Rock Mountain, on the south side of the Santa Catalina Mountains. There, they built a polished granite stone church with a stone mosaic floor.

> *"The Judge is very fond of relating stories he has heard from the old people of Tucson, and among others is that of the old stone church. The story goes that many years ago about the time the Pilgrims landed on the rock, there was a thriving Mexican village on the San Pedro. There was wood from the Santa Catalina Mountains and water from the river. The valley's fertile soil produced all the corn and beans they could use. Abundance of mescal grew on the hills. The ledges were rich in minerals. The colony was prosperous and accordingly it was happy. On a fatal day the Apaches made a raid, and massacred a majority of the people. A remnant escaped and came through a long, deep natural cut that goes through the Santa Catalina Mountains and comes out on the western side of the mountains, some twenty four miles north of Tucson."* [71]

Near that location at the north edge of the Cañada del Oro, they established a village and again prospered. There was plenty of water and grass. They worked the mines nearby, as the remains of the old furnaces and the abundance of slag testify, according to Meyer's account. Again, the Apaches descended upon them. Nothing remains of their work but a head of ruins called Pueblo Viejo, the story relates.

> *"A few escaped out of this second massacre and inhabited the mountaintops between the Finger Mountain and La Ventaña. They built a large stone church out of the granite of those mighty hills. The blocks were hewn and polished by their patient toil. The floor was laid in mosaic, and it was honored with an arched roof. Here they worshiped God according*

---

[71] "The Stone Church, A Romance of the Santa Catalina Mountains" The Arizona Weekly Citizen, November 11, 1883. http://chroniclingamerica.loc.gov/lccn/sn82015133/1883-11-24/ed-1/seq-4/

> *to the dictates of their own consciences. What became of them is unknown.*
> *They were probably all killed by a third massacre committed by their*
> *inveterate foes, the Apaches, which had followed them from the San Pedro*
> *to Pueblo Viejo.* [72]

The Apaches may have eventually died out from smallpox. This newspaper article appeared a few years after an 1880 account of two prospectors who said they discovered old stone ruins deep in the Santa Catalina Mountains during their hunt for the legendary Iron Door Mine and Nine Mile City.

There is evidence of natives living along the San Pedro River to the east of the Santa Catalina Mountains and at the Cañada del Oro River on the west side. But this story related by Meyer suggests at one time Indians also occupied land on the south side of the Catalina Mountains near Ventaña Canyon– in the Tucson northern foothills.

The story also mentioned a local Mexican, named Geronimo, who discovered the old stone church while hunting cattle and riding down a canyon between the Finger Mountain and La Ventaña. Some local people knew about the old stone church. He told the local priests and the "matter was referred to Bishop Salpointe just before he left for Rome, and he would attend to it on his return."

> *There are placer diggings near this church, which were worked by these*
> *San Pedro Mexicans.* [73] *In the beginning of the present century a lot of*
> *Apaches broke away from their tribe and settled near the church. They*
> *had a few cattle, and worked the placers. They evinced a desire to be*
> *civilized. The smallpox swept them away in 1861. Two of these Indians,*
> *Colorado and Charco Carbon, were well known in Tucson.* [74]

Judge Meyer said he often saw the gold and silver these Indians brought in for barter. His story was never followed up and became buried in time. [75] There is no record found of Bishop Salpointe's follow up.

---

[72] Ibid.

[73] This is the only instance of the name San Pedro Mexicans used to refer to these people.

[74] "The Stone Church, A Romance of the Santa Catalina Mountains," The Arizona Weekly Citizen, November 11, 1883.

[75] A search, by this author, for any report made by– or sent to– Salpointe has not been found.

1889-1896: More Ruins Seen In The Santa Catalinas

Reports of ruins and remains discovered by pioneer Tucsonans became frequent as more people ventured out to explore the Santa Catalina Mountains. Even close to Tucson, people were discovering remains of ancient civilizations.

In 1889, ancient ruins were reported about four miles northwest of Tucson– where the Rillito and Santa Cruz converge. Early Tucson residents also called this area Pueblo Viejo.

Broken pottery, stone hatchets, and ancient irrigation canals were seen in the area. Seven miles northeast of Tucson at Ft. Lowell ruins and skeletons from an ancient civilization were found lying on the ground surrounded by charred wood and ashes "indicating that they had come to a violent death" on the south bank of the Rillito River. Not far away, in the Tucson Mountains, petroglyphs were found. [76]

Another discovery reported in the early 1890s by an "Editor Prospector" of a local newspaper was that he had found the "ruins of a long, lost pueblo" in the Santa Catalinas years earlier. Next to the ruins he found numerous shafts. After being frightened off by a bear, he attempted– but failed– to find the ruins another time.

The second time he found "an old weather worn iron door leading to a Jesuit mine." The more recent discovery was a flight of stone steps that displayed "ruby and native silver in vast extent, sparkling with gold." The old iron door was found to be an opening to a treasure vault, he claimed. The find was located beneath the earlier discovery of the "lost pueblo." He indicated the spot might be very close to both the Pima and Pinal county borders. [77]

Near Tucson, there was "abundant evidence of what once was a flourishing village," according to local Tucson community leader Sam Hughes. All that is left are the remains of old buildings, a "well defined acequia, and an ancient reservoir." Hughes, an authority on Tucson's history, said that when the Spanish arrived, Tucson was an Indian village.

---

[76] "Ancient Irrigation, Traces of It to be Seen in Vicinity of Tucson – The Old Ditches – Ruins of a Dam – Pueblo Viejo," The Arizona Weekly Citizen, September 7, 1889.

[77] "New Discovery," The Tombstone Daily Prospector, February 17, 1891 and Tombstone Epitaph, Tombstone, A.T., February 22, 1891.

The main portion of the village was in the Osborne addition on the southern line of the town's corporate limits. There was a large town 18 miles northwest of this place, and there was a town "four miles north of Tucson to Santa Catalina." [78] The name was said to be Santa Catalina. All that was left by 1896 were ruins of an old building, a "well defined acequia and an ancient reservoir." The writer speculated it was possibly an old mission on the west bank of the river. [79] The distance from the Tucson presidio eighteen miles northeast is at the Cañada del Oro.

Both places disappeared in the course of time except Tucson, which survived and retained its ancient Indian name, said Hughes. He also reported that the visible ruins of a large house, known as Casa de Padre, was built about the same time as the San Xavier mission. [80]

Herbert Brown made a discovery of two granite monolithic posts on the southern slopes of the Catalinas in 1896. The posts were found at an ancient Indian site and looked like the "Druidical monuments of England," but on a smaller scale. A foot or more of the stone raised above the ground and "cut to five inch squares," according to William Blake, the Director of the School of Mines at the University of Arizona. [81]

Pottery sherds are still visible throughout the Cañada del Oro region.

---

[78] In 1876, Hughes said there was a "town in ruins situated about three miles below Tucson, one mile east due east from what is known as the Casa de Padre." Arizona Weekly Citizen, July 15, 1876.

[79] "Tuc or Tus, Which?" Arizona Weekly Citizen, February 22, 1896.

[80] "The Ancient and Honorable," Arizona Weekly Citizen, February 22, 1896.

[81] "Prehistoric Relic and Quarrying," Arizona Weekly Citizen, March 28, 1896.

The remains of stone walls by the Cañada del Oro close to the Romero Ruin.

"The archaeological department of the territorial museum at
the University has been enriched by the gift from Mr. Herbert
Brown, of Tucson, of two monolithic posts of hard granite,
found by him set in the ground with others, on the site of an
ancient Indian village on the southern slope of the Santa
Catalina Mountains…It would make a good hitching post."

Wm. Blake, Director School of Mines, University of Arizona, 1896. [82]

---

[82] "Prehistoric Relics and Quarrying," Arizona Weekly Citizen, Tucson, A.T., March 28, 1896.

Ruins At Catalina State Park

"The ruins at this site seem to represent four periods of culture (although until excavations are made, I'm not prepared to say that this particular example is not a Spanish building, and if so a church)

Donald Page, "Data Relative to Spanish and Indian Ruins" [83]

O n the west side of the Santa Catalina Mountains, along the Cañada del Oro creek, there is evidence of early Indian, Mexican and possibly colonial Spanish occupation. Numerous stone foundations are scattered on top of a mesa at the foot of the mountains.

Catalina State Park is located on State Highway 77 (Oracle Road) at mile marker 81, just nine miles north of Tucson and six miles north of Ina Road.

These ruins have been excavated and artifacts from numerous civilizations– as early as 450AD– have been uncovered. [84]

Archaeological work on the site in the 1980s suggests there were several other periods of occupancy: early Hohokam, based on the pottery found (1450-1692 AD); early Spanish occupancy (1692-1821); and the more modern

---

[83] Data Relative to Spanish and Indian Ruins, by Donald Page. Donald Page Papers, Arizona Historical Society. Page 1. September 1927.

[84] Archaeological Survey in Catalina State Park With A Focus on the Romero Ruin, by Mark D. Elson and William Doelle. Institute for American Research, Technical Report No. 87-4, 1987. Page 6. Also cited in "Data Relative to Spanish and Indian Ruins," by Donald Page. Arizona Historical Society.

Mexican ruins built by Francisco Romero in the early to mid-1800s. [85]

Ellsworth Huntington, a geographer who visited many sites around Tucson and wrote about the Romero Ruin in 1910, was at first a strong advocate of a Spanish influence on the structure. Later he suggested that some of the ruins might be much older. [86]

> *"The ruins of middle age are those of a Spanish Mission of unknown date. Records of it, however, are found in Mexico. According to the common (but scarcely credible) story, gold ore was crushed here in large quantities, being brought from the mountains. This is possible for there is some ore in these mountains. The small hollow which I took at first for a little reservoir, may possibly be an arrastra, or Spanish mill for crushing ore by turning a big stone like an olive press and catching the gold in mercury filling the cracks. Of course there is a story of treasure buried by the priest when the place was abandoned. One surmises that the mission must be old, and that it was abandoned when the Apaches came into the country."* [87]

Traces of this old stone-built city could be the ruins of a Hohokam village from 500-1450AD, suggested historian Captain Donald Page in the 1920s. Other stones that were laid in mud mortar may be part of an early Spanish type of stone wall in the 1700 or 1800s, Page said. The ruins may represent four phases of culture with round stone pit houses, a rectangular pit house, a single and multi room houses, and a multi-room adobe walled communal building. [88]

There may have been some Spanish occupation at this site, based on one of the architectural styles of a portion of the ruins before they crumbled. [89] The ruins might be

---

[85] Ibid.

Archaeological Testing At Romero Ruin, by Deborah L. Swartz. Center for Desert Archaeology, Technical Report No. 91-2, 1991.

Archaeological Testing At Romero Ruin: Part 2, by Deborah L. Swartz, with contributions by Lisa W. Huckell and J. Homer Thiel. Technical Report No. 93-8, Center for Desert Archaeology, 1992

[86] Archaeological Survey in Catalina State Park With A Focus on the Romero Ruin, Page 8.

[87] Ibid. Page 6.

[88] Data Relative to Spanish and Indian Ruins, by Donald Page papers, Arizona Historical Society.

[89] Archaeological Survey in Catalina State Park With A Focus on the Romero Ruin, by Mark D. Elson and William Doelle. See the chapters in this book on Pueblo Viejo (Old Village) and the history of the

those of the legendary Lost Mission of Ciru, Page suggested. [90] [91] Treasure hunters have damaged the structure and dug up the floor. Any valuable relics have been taken. According to Page, the site was "located close to an early Spanish mining camp that lies on a mesa in a nearly inaccessible part of the mountains" and a "group of mysterious ruins lie on a small mesa east of the lower end of the canyon (Cañada del Oro) may be a link to the lost mine." Page called it Ciudad Nuevo Millas," located "9 miles from Tucson." [92]

There are signs of Mexican construction with paved foundations and floors. In the mid 1800s, Mexican rancher Francisco Romero built his home on top of some of the ruins of the old Hohokam Indian village. The site is now named after him– the Romero Ruin.

The ruins were well known to early Tucson residents many years before Romero moved there. Tucson pioneer Sam Hughes said he first saw the ruins in 1858. Dr. Robert Forbes took some of the earliest photographs of the ruins around 1910. [93] Bishop Salpointe claimed they were the ruins of the Mission of Ciru, according to Page. [94]

An 1880 Territory of Arizona map marks the "Ruins of an old Pueblo" at the spot of the Romero Ruin, just east of the "Gold Cañon Creek." [95]

These ruins are now protected as part of the Catalina State Park, a popular public recreation site. A trail in the Santa Catalina State Park, called the Romero Ruin Interpretive Trail, passes through the ruins. This trail is open to the public. Since this site is on state land, further excavation is not possible at this time.

---

legends. Also, read Data Relative to Spanish and Indian Ruins, by Donald Page. Donald Page Papers. Arizona Historical Society, Tucson, Arizona.

[90] See notes of Donald Page, Data Relative to Spanish and Indian Ruins, by Donald Page.

[91] Also discussed in Archaeological Survey in Catalina State Park With A Focus on the Romero Ruin by Mark D. Elson and William Doelle. Pages 8-9.

[92] Ibid.

[93] Ibid. Page 6. As noted by Dr. Robert H. Forbes.

[94] Ibid. Page 9. Also, see Data Relative to Spanish and Indian Ruins, by Donald Page. January 29, 1928.

[95] Official Map of the Territory of Arizona Compiled from Surveys, Reconnaissance's and Other Sources, by E.A. Eckhoff and P. Riecker, Civil Engineers, 1880." From the David Ramsey Collection, Cartography Associates. Publisher, The Graphic Co. Photo-Lith, NY. Pub. Ref. Stretter 526; P-Maps 123.

The remains of the mud-packed mortar southwest wall of the Romero Ruin, as described by Donald Page. Page believed the famed "Mission of Ciru" was located among these ruins.

The Fabled "Mission Of Ciru"

Donald Page– a local historian, author, and miner– suggested there was a Spanish influence in the Cañada del Oro ruins after he explored ruins in the 1920s. [96]

In the summer of 1927, a local newspaper article had speculated about the Mine With the Iron Door and lost city legend. That next month Tucsonan Glenton Sykes encouraged Page to examine some ruins between Montrose and Romero Canyons on the west side of the Santa Catalina Mountains. They walked up a steep slope to a mesa close to an old black walnut tree by the Cañada del Oro. Several stone lined pit houses, multiple room adobe walls, and a "Spanish type of stone walled building" were found. The stones were laid in mud mortar. They also found the remains of a Mexican type structure. The entire group of buildings was surrounded by the remnants of a stonewall. [97] The Mexican ruins could have been the remains of the Romero building– now called Romero Ruin.

Tucsonan Agustin Tomé told Page when he was eight years old he overheard a conversation by two soldiers at the Tucson presidio. They were discussing the ruins of the mission in the foothills and called it Mission of Ciru. Tomé told Bishop Jean-Baptise Salpointe and showed him the ruins. [98]

Tomé said that in 1902 a man approached him and wanted to know the location of a placer mine near the "Mission of Ciru." Tomé said he heard claims that those were the ruins of the mission. He said he also heard Bishop Salpointe say there were Indian excavations done on top of the hill. [99]

Page suggested that the Mission of Ciru was possibly located at the ruins near the Cañada del Oro on the western slopes of the Santa Catalina Mountains. He asserted that the

---

[96] Data Relative to Spanish and Indian Ruins on Mesa Between Montrose and Romero Canyon Known as the 'Rancho Viejo' or 'Mission of Ciru,' by Donald Page. January 29, 1928. Arizona Historical Society. MS 0641.

[97] Ibid.

[98] Cañada del Oro and the Iron Door Mine, Look to the Mountain, by Suzanne Hensel, 2003. Page 8.

[99] Ibid. "On his notes of June 20, 1915, p 39." Page 3. January 29, 1928. Page writes: "Agustin Tomé [an early Tucson settler living in the Tucson area by at least 1865] ... tells me that the late Bishop Salpointe claims that the ruins were those of the Mission of Ciru."

presence of a Spanish mission near a mine is evidence that the missionaries were complicit in operating the mines.

Page recounted the beliefs that the place was attacked by Indians and burned and that the "padres and the other Spaniards (were) killed." The flames were seen by travelers and reported at the Presidio of San Agustin de Tucson. A relief party was sent to investigate, but arrived too late. [100]

In a 1956 magazine article, Page claimed the lost mine was "located close to an early Spanish mining camp on a mesa in a nearly inaccessible part of the mountains." Page gave further detail: the Jesuits owned the mine and camp and later built a church. The mine was worked until their expulsion in 1767. A "group of mysterious ruins lie on a small mesa east of the lower end of the canyon (Cañada del Oro) may be a link to the lost mine." [101]

Could the Mission of Ciru legend, the "Ciudad Nuevo Millas" (City Nine Miles), be connected to the ruins? Page ponders that it would have to be located nine miles from some specific spot. Tucson was nine miles away at the time and the ruins were over 18 miles from the Presidio site. [102]

---

[100] Ibid. Page 3. No year was given in Page's report, but it could have been the 1751 Pima Indian Uprising.

[101] Lost Jesuit Mine with the Iron Door, by Donald Page. Desert Magazine, October 1956.

[102] Ibid. Page 3. Page doesn't speculate about the use of the word *milla* for mile, instead of *liga* for league. One league would be about three nautical miles. Nine leagues would be twenty seven miles.

Quest For The Mission Of Ciru

The following article about the infamous Mission of Ciru is reprinted from Ron Quinn's book on hunting for lost Spanish treasures in Southern Arizona, SEARCHING FOR ARIZONA'S BURIED TREASURES.

Don Page and several colleagues once visited Cañada del Oro where it winds its rocky way down the western slopes of the Santa Catalina Range. There they discovered a number of old stone ruins on a small flat overlooking the canyon.

Roy (Purdie), our partner, heard the following from Don Page:

They dug and discovered that two different Indian cultures had once lived there before the stone structures were built on top of older ruins. Spanish explorers that were working a mine somewhere in the surrounding vicinity, as several arrastras were found later, undoubtedly erected the dwellings. Don claimed the "Mission of Ciru" once stood at this location. The location of the hidden mine, Don Page felt, was associated with the Cañada del Oro arrastras.

Roy had obtained Don's notes, so we made our own search of the region. We never found the arrastras, but Don had stated they were located east of the ruins. Also, a faint trail led toward the towering mountains, but was lost after a mile or so. Don always believed there was a hidden mine somewhere in the area, and that it was once worked by the residents who occupied the small village. But, he also felt no "iron door" would have covered the entrance.

During our search of the site, we did locate the ruins and the area where Page claimed the small lost mission once stood, but found no trace of its remains. The area is now designated as Catalina State Park, and the ruins and mine, if one does exist, might fall within its boundaries. I believe the ruins do, as the park covers some 5,500 acres and most of Cañada del Oro. No digging or collecting is allowed.

Several years back, the mayor of Kearny, Arizona supposedly found a sealed mine, or a tunnel, in this region. He wanted a permit from the state to excavate the site, as he believed it "might" contain one of the treasures hidden by the Spanish padres. If it was unearthed, he was willing to split with the state 50-50. His request was denied. [103]

---

[103] "Board denies bid to hunt gold cache in state park," Arizona Republic, August 1, 1982.

66

Soon afterwards, a state official said that if there is such a treasure, it should belong totally to the state. Did the mayor discover the Iron Door Mine? We will never know, but he isn't the only one to claim finding a sealed mine in that area. [104]

An enormous 30-foot plus saguaro cactus guards over the Indian ruins near the fabled "Mission of Ciru" in the Catalinas.

---

[104] SEARCHING FOR ARIZONA'S BURIED TREASURES, A TWO-YEAR ODYSSEY, by Ron Quinn (2014). Reprinted by permission. Ron Quinn spent two years with his brother and two friends in the Tumacacori Mountains in the 1950s where they discovered 82 bars of gold buried in the hills.

The Romero Ranch– Built On Top Of Indian Ruins

Francisco Romero and his wife Victoria settled on the west side of the Santa Catalina Mountains in 1823-38, [105] 1844, [106] or after 1865. [107] Romero apparently built his homestead on top of ancient Hohokam Indian ruins. That angered the nearby Apaches who lived in the Catalinas, and they attacked his adobe frequently. [108]

Romero, the grandson of a Spanish soldier who arrived in the 1770s, told his grandson the original ruins of the building were about three feet high. He rebuilt three of the structures and enclosed a wall to protect his wife and himself from the Apache Indians. [109]

Romero eventually moved across the arroyo (of the Cañada del Oro). That new location was called "Rancho Nuevo." The ruins he left were then called "Rancho Viejo." Francisco's grandson, Fabian, often heard his grandfather talk about the Spanish ruins. He believed there was once a Spanish church "located on the east of the buildings at the tip of the mesa, over against the small rock hill."

Fabian said he spent much time searching for the Spanish mine when he lived on the land. He found two arrastras used in grinding stone nearby. That was by a spot where some "vaqueros once found a small lump of gold ore in a niche of the rocks where it had evidently been left and forgotten." A capped well and a concrete base for a water storage

---

[105] Donald Page cites 1828-1838– given by Fabian Romero, Francisco Romero's grandson, in Page's report Data Relative to Spanish and Indian Ruins, from Donald Page papers, Arizona Historical Society.

[106] Arizona State Parks: Catalina: Park History. "Romero is mentioned as establishing a ranch of 160 acres on the west side of the Catalina Mountains in 1844 near the Cañada del Oro, including 320 acres of farmland along the Santa Cruz River west of Flowing Wells and land on Main Street in the downtown Tucson business district."

[107] Reference is made that Romero established his ranch shortly after the Civil War ended in 1865. Archaeology in Tucson, newsletter of the Center for Desert Archaeology. Vol. 11, No. 4, Fall 1997. Page 1.

[108] The Tucson Citizen published an article in April 2008 about the Romero Ruin and the Hohokam people.

[109] Data Relative to Spanish and Indian Ruins, by Donald Page. Arizona Historical Society.

tank are the only remains. [110] Romero and his wife left for Sonora in 1870 because of the constant Apache attacks that made the "Catarinas unsafe for man or beast." [111]

Treasure hunters would often go to the site to locate the church and the Spanish gold mine, Fabian remembered. A fortune in gold bullion was supposed to buried underneath the floor of the old mission when the padres were forced to leave the country in about 1823, according to historian Page. He doesn't cite his source for that date. The Franciscans, however, left in 1821 when the region became part of the new Republic of Mexico following Mexican independence from Spain. [112] [113]

Years later, Page wrote a letter to the director of the Arizona State Museum about the ruins. He suggested they represent four cultural periods, including "the lower courses of their walls being known to be Spanish and the upper portions thereof of Mexican construction."

Page questioned why "South American adobe wall work of Colonial times was of rammed earth instead of adobe brick." Page was unable to find any historical confirmation, but he believed the area might have been a "real de minas (actual mines)." [114] The Museum director placed the date of the earliest ruins not before 700 A.D., and no older than 1200-1400 A.D., at the peak of its population. [115]

[110] Catalina State Park, Arizona State Parks. http://www.stateparks.com/catalina.html

[111] Reference made to *Arizona Weekly Citizen* 1870 article, from "Archaeology in Tucson," Vol. II, No. 4, Fall 1977. Pages 1 and 2.

[112] Mission San Xavier del Bac, http://www.sanxaviermission.org/History.html

[113] Patronato, Mission San Xavier del Bac. History. http://www.patronatosanxavier.org/preservation/history/

[114] Letter to Dr. Emil W. Haury, Director, Arizona State Museum, from Donald W. Page. April 8, 1953.

[115] Letter to Capt. Donald W. Page from Emil W. Haury, Director, Arizona State Museum. April 19, 1958.

Archaeological excavations and reports from prominent Tucsonans suggest that several groups of people have lived on this site over the past few thousand years. The Romero Ruin is among several other remaining stone walls and ball courts.

This is a view towards Pusch Ridge, named after pioneer George Pusch who owned land on the southwestern slope of the Santa Catalinas in the mid-1870s. On the left (outside of the photograph view) is the mouth of the Cañada del Oro creek. Ancient ruins (not pictured) are in this area, now a part of the Catalina State Park.

The Lost City Near Mt. Lemmon

William Carter (left) and Joseph Wilson examines the stone foundation wall among several ruined buildings, possibly the "Lost City," deep within the Santa Catalina Mountains near Oracle Ridge not far from the monolith. Photo courtesy of William Carter.

Hidden among heavy brush in the heart of the Santa Catalina Mountains– near the Reef of Rock and Cañada del Oro river– is another fertile area that has signs of previous human activity. It is unknown how long this area has been inhabited.

The remains of a hidden, previous occupation discovered among ruins of stone structures deep within the Santa Catalina Mountains near Oracle Ridge, north of Tucson, Arizona. Photo courtesy of Will Grant, 2014.

This part of the Cañada del Oro canyon was active at the turn of the 20th Century with numerous mining operations. It remained quiet for decades until a group of prospectors, professionals, and community leaders went into the deep brush and trees to check out reports of a lost city site somewhere near Marble Peak.

At this remote location there is evidence of both human habitation and mining production–scattered stone ruins, some artifacts, mineshafts, and debris.

In 1978 Tommy Thompson, president of the Oracle Historical Society, along with film producer Thomas Perry, [116] prospector William "Flint" Carter, and six others drove to Catalina Camp west of Oracle Ridge. They proceeded on foot to the Reef of Rock in search of the legendary Lost City. They found evidence of old stoves, possibly from the 1880s, but not the fabled Lost City.

---

[116] Perry, an actor, played the holy man in the film The Trial of Billy Jack. He later produced Wanda Nevada, (1979), a story of a gold mine in the Grand Canyon starring Brooke Shields and Peter Fonda.

The lost city site was finally discovered when Carter, with another group, found the ruins near Catalina Camp in 1985. They didn't think it was much because they only found a few old stone foundations and walls. It was anti-climatic. But, it seemed someone was there earlier with a bulldozer, pushed material over the hill, and destroyed any other evidence of the city.

The "ninja crew," as they called themselves, staked mining claims in the area in 1990. Within the corner of one of the buildings, Rich Wong, Dean Chambers, [117] Joseph Wilson and Carter found what they believed was the legendary hatchet that the miners used to carve the gold out of the mountain. The item was turned over to the U.S. Forest Service.

The lost city ruins site deserved further examination. An Archaeological and Historical Site Inventory conducted by the U.S. Forest Service found evidence of at least three, possibly four, multi-room rock wall structures with collapsed roofs. [118]

Glass bottle fragments (some were purple and some were clear), tin cans, and a pocket tobacco tin (marked "Twin Oaks") were among some of the artifacts collected. The purple glass and hole-in-cap tin can indicated the site was used before the 1920s. Activity of a former mining camp was nearby. A systematic survey was not done so other cultural materials may be uncovered, the inventory report indicated. Carter's Claim is still in possession of Carter & Co. through federal mining claims.

Since 1873 through the late 1950s, the areas near the Reef of Rock and Oracle Ridge has been steadily mined. Pioneers Emerson O. Stratton, Robert Leatherwood, and a generation later, Francis Hartman, made dozens of claims around the mountaintops and valleys along the Oracle Ridge. Production records are minimal, but with the restart of the Oracle Ridge Mine recently, there still are enough minerals to make the investment worthwhile after one hundred and forty years of American mining production.

During another expedition in 1995, one of the members of Carter's group included George Mroczkowski, author of the "Professional Treasure Hunter," found an 1812 Mexican coin in front of a caved-in tunnel. Carter staked a claim and got a permit to open the tunnel. But after four years of extensive digging, it turned out to be just a 30-foot exploratory tunnel from the turn of the century. Drill holes were found at the end of the tunnel. Several additional quests were conducted over the years with varying results. A recent expedition in the spring of 2014 with a geologist and crew revealed additional structures and evidence not observed earlier.

---

[117] Dean Chambers was owner of Equestrian Videos in Chicago. Illinois.

[118] Carter's Claim, Archaeology and Historical Site Survey, Site number AR 03-05-05-164, U.S. Forest Service. Coronado National Forest. September 11, 1991.

That hidden area, deep in the Santa Catalina Mountains, is far from the path, covered in brush and trees, and not visible from the Arizona Trail. Nature has reclaimed its space.

The interior of the Santa Catalina Mountain valley, as viewed from Catalina Camp near Oracle Ridge. The Reef of Rock, an elongated range of granite (above left), is where the East and West Forks of the Cañada del Oro merge to flow north out of the canyon. Near this area are ruins and evidence of past and present mining activities.

Onka's Leap Of Faith– An Indian Legend

There are some legends among the Indians who lived in the Santa Catalinas. One tale, published in 1897, told of a brave Indian woman who got her revenge after rival Indians annihilated her tribe who once lived deep in the mountains. [119]

This undated Pima Indian legend tells about a spot in the Catalinas called Onka's Leap. It's located on a narrow ridge running from the base of the peak where the ruins of an ancient settlement lie below. Those ruins run about a mile in distance and end at a cliff that rises 100 feet from the bottom of a rocky gulch.

On one particular rainy night, an old *ve-kol* (grandmother) sat alone amidst the desolation of what once was her home. She was the only survivor of a terrible massacre of her tribe.

The marauders were still there and demanded that she show them the way out of the mountains. She reluctantly led the way while the thunder and lightning pounded around them. The darkness was so intense that it was impossible to see ahead with the relentless rain.

When she approached the edge of a precipice, she stopped and stepped aside. Her followers continued walking, one after another, falling into the deep abyss. Their screams were drowned out by the storm's fury. When the last of her enemies perished, a flash of lightning lit up the sky. Onka let out a scream into the darkness.

"Not yet, not yet will I leave them! The spirit of Onka shall follow to taunt them!" she yelled out with a leap to follow her victims.

Graphic of Onka, from Treasure Land: A Story, Volume 1, by John George Hilzinger.

---

[119] Treasure Land: A Story, Volume 1, by John George Hilzinger, Arizona Advancement Company, 1897. Page 159. Also, printed in the *Border Vidette*, Nogales, Pima County Arizona. September 8, 1898. Page 159.

The History And The Legends Of The Santa Catalina Mountains

How The Legends Started

The Spanish Mines Of Sonora

The Lost Escalante Mine

The Lost Mission Of Santa Catalina

Perpetuating The Legends With Historical Anachronisms

"History has its truth, and so has legend. Legendary truth is of another nature than historical truth. Legendary truth is invention whose result is reality. Furthermore, history and legend have the same goal; to depict eternal man beneath momentary man."

Victor Hugo, "Ninety-Three," First published 1874.

The connection between the Lost City, the Lost Mine, and the Lost Mission is intertwined with folklore and history. Somewhere within those giant mountains of the Santa Catalina Mountains great treasures once were– and may be still– hidden. History gives some clues about their existence.

Several Arizona pioneers [120] who wrote about the new Territory and its mineral riches in the mid-1850s perpetuated the stories about the abundance of gold, silver, and the old mines once operated by the Spaniards. Their repeated stories became ingrained in the imaginations and the historic record of the newly acquired land. Unfortunately, events that were never recorded until after the Americans arrived had clouded the historic records. On careful examination, those stories– collectively, the legends of the Santa Catalinas– were spawned from actual events. But the dates didn't always match the events. Historical anachronisms [121] discredited any grains of truth.

There are two major stories in the hunt for gold in the Santa Catalinas. One story is about the buried treasures supposedly hidden during early Spanish mining activities. The other treasure is about the naturally occurring gold actually embedded in the mountains. Both served as a reason for ambitious people to spend their lives, with and without success, digging around the mineralized deposits.

How did the legends become tangled into these historical anachronisms? Historians.

---

[120] See upcoming articles on Sylvester Mowry, Charles Poston and other sources.

[121] An anachronism is a person or object chronologically out of place– Moses wearing an iWatch, for example.

The Mines, The Missions And The History Of Arizona

"The reports of the immense mineral wealth of the new country, made by the Jesuits, induced a rapid settlement. They are laid down on the map before me, more than forty towns and villages. Many of these were of considerable size. There were a few north of the Gila, and several on the lower Gila, near the Colorado. The Santa Cruz and its tributary valleys teemed with an agricultural and mining population. Thousands of enterprising Spaniards cultivated the rich valley of San Pedro, and scattered settlements flourished at every suitable stream and spring at the foot of the mountains towards the Rio Grande."

From Sylvester Mowry's, Memoir on the Proposed Territory of Arizona, 1857. [122]

Very little was known about the new Territory of Arizona during the mid-1850s. Virtually, all of the early information about the Spanish mines is based on reports of the new acquisition with the Gadsden Purchase. At the time, this account was considered to be the authoritative history of Arizona.

Sylvester Mowry [123] was a U.S. Delegate Elect to the Congress for the proposed Territory of Arizona. He related the above story in 1857, and it was published over and over again for decades. Mowry's major source of Arizona's early history was a century-old Spanish map, drawn by some Jesuit missionaries in 1757, and some accompanying notes. He said he obtained his information from "official data."

This was just after the 1854 Gadsden Purchase added Southern Arizona and southwestern New Mexico to the United States' holdings. The vast wilderness was virtually unexplored by Americans and they were eager to learn about the new land, especially when it was filled with intrigue and mystery.

---

[122] The entire account is stored in the Lillian Goldman Law Library, Yale Law School Avalon Project: Memoir of the Proposed Territory of Arizona, by Sylvester Mowry, USA Delegate Elect. Washington; Henry Polkinhorn, Printer. 1857. This quote is from page 5.
http://avalon.law.yale.edu/19th_century/arizona.asp Book available from Project Gutenberg: https://archive.org/details/memoirofthepropo02382gut

[123] Sylvester Mowry was born in 1830 and died in 1871 in England. He is credited with the founding of Mowry, Arizona, now a ghost mine town. He also had the only printing press in the Territory at the time.

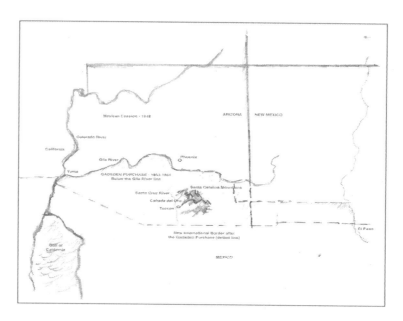

The Gadsden Purchase map showing the new Territory of Arizona and New Mexico.

Capt. Charles Pomeroy Stone, [124] who compiled the original notes about the new Territory in 1857, acquired these documents from the Mexican Government when the United States obtained the new Territory, according to Mowry. [125]

While Mowry's story of Arizona gained the attention of America, there was a military reconnaissance almost a decade earlier in 1848 by George Cook, William Emory, and others as they traveled along the Gila and San Pedro Rivers. They took brief notes about the ruins left by the Spaniards who they suggested had worked the mines after the Indians drove them out. [126] But this observation did not garnish the same attention as Mowry's stories which became the foundation of the legends as we know them today.

---

[124] Charles Pomeroy Stone, born 1824 and died 1887. Capt. Stone had a job directing an extensive mineral survey of Sonora as "Chief of the scientific Commission in the Service of the Mexican Government, for the Survey and Exploration of Public Lands in the State of Sonora, 1857-60." Source: Charles P. Stone, Cullum's Register #1237, Class of 1845.

[125] "Consisting of reports of Col. Emory, Gray, Lieut. Parke, Hon, J.R. Barlett, and others..." Evening Star, January 7, 1858.

[126] Notes of a Military Reconnaissance: From Fort Leavenworth, In Missouri to San Diego in California, by Lt. Col. W.H. Emory, Washington, 1848. (30th Congress, 1st Session, Ex. Doc. 41). Page 582-583. Journal entry: October 23rd.

How The Spanish Mining Story Unfolds

B ased on his notes and the old map, Mowry believed his version was accurate and reliable. [127] One newspaper went as far to say, "No statement is made without apparent full and reliable evidence of its entire correctness." [128]

Mowry described how a Jesuit missionary (unnamed, but presumed to be Father Kino) from Sonora who, in 1687, passed through the valley of the Santa Cruz River to the Gila River, descended along the San Pedro River, and established missions along the way.

The "reports of immense mineral wealth made by the Jesuits induced a rapid settlement," Mowry noted. [129] In one document to the Government of the Viceroy of Spain, Mowry said he found the following language: "A scientific exploration of Sonora with reference to mineralogy, along with the introduction of gold and silver, so marvelous that the result will be such as has never been seen in the world." [130] [131]

Mowry said the notes contained the "names and localities of more than a hundred silver and gold mines which were worked with great success by the Spaniards." The San Pedro mine in 1748 "was worked with extraordinary success," he noted. Among the other mines named included the 'Santa Catarina.' [132]

---

[127] Memoir of the Proposed Territory of Arizona, by Sylvester Mowry. 1857. Page 4-6.

[128] Evening Star, Washington, D.C. January 7, 1858.

[129] Memoir of the Proposed Territory of Arizona, by Sylvester Mowry, Page 4. Henry Polkinghorn, Publisher. Also published in "Geography and Resources of Arizona and Sonora: An Address Before the American Geographical and Statistical Society," by Sylvester Mowry. A. Roman & Company, 1863 and 1864. Page 82.

[130] Ibid. Page 5.

[131] Also, reprinted in The Mining Magazine and Journal of Geology, Vol. 1 edited by William Phipps Blake, 1860. Page 2.

[132] Memoir of the Proposed Territory of Arizona, by Sylvester Mowry, Page 6. Mowry did not specify if this mine was in the Santa Catarina Mountains, as they were called at that time.

When the mineral wealth of the new Territory was described in the 1850s, it was often mentioned with the tales of early Spanish mining operations and the surrounding villages that were destroyed by hostile "savages." The Indians who lived near the missions "were reduced first to obedience by the Jesuits and then to slavery by the Spaniards." They were "forced to labor in the silver mines with inadequate food, and barbarously treated." [133]

Eventually, the Indians rebelled and joined up with the more hostile Apaches. They constantly attacked the missions and settlements until they drove out the invaders. All that was left by the time the Americans arrived were the ruins that were visible everywhere of "extensive and hastily deserted mining operations and the tradition of the country." [134]

Historically, Father Eusebio Kino arrived in northern Sonora on March 12, 1687. [135] He did make several journeys through the land known as Pimería Alta. Father Kino and the military officers who accompanied him on expeditions into the Santa Cruz Valley in the late 1690s wrote some of the preserved letters Mowry had in his possession. But in reality, Kino was not involved in mining activities. His purpose was to save the natives from forced labor.

Over time those journeys became the basis of the early legends of the mountains, but, it was only one part of the whole picture.

---

[133] Ibid. Page 6.

[134] Ibid.

[135] Kino's Historical Memoir of Pimería Alta, Volume 1, By Eusebio Francisco Kino, Edited by Herbert Eugene Bolton, 1919. Page 51. Also see: Missions, Tumacacori, Arizona. National Parks Service. http://www.nps.gov/tuma/historyculture/missions.htm

The Earliest Sources Of The Spanish Mine Legends

In 1757 Father Andres Marcos Burriel, [136] a Spanish Jesuit and historian, published a three-volume set with over 500 pages, maps, and eight copper engraved illustrations titled NOTICIA DE LA CALIFORNIA. [137] This was a revision of an earlier unpublished work written in 1739 by Miguel Venegas, a Jesuit administrator and historian. [138]

Burriel's book was the standard authority at the time on the early history of the missions, California, and the Southwest. It was considered "an accurate" description of the new country in the mid 1750s.

Venegas, the original author, never visited California but compiled his book while in Mexico in 1729. After Burriel acquired the manuscript, he made additions from the Spanish archives, added maps and illustrations, including the map later used by Mowry. It was translated in broken English (1759), Dutch (1761-1762), German (1769) and French (1776-1767). [139]

The first English edition, A NATURAL AND CIVIL HISTORY OF CALIFORNIA, was published in London in 1759. [140] [141] It reproduced Burriel's book with maps, copper plates

---

[136] Andres Marcos Burriel was born in 1719 and died in 1762. Source: archive.org.

[137] Noticia De La California, y Desu Conquista Temporal, Y Spiritual, Hasta El Tiempo Presente, SACADA De La Historia Manuscrita, Formada en Mexico año de 1739. Por el Padre Miguel Venegas, de la Compañia de Jesus, y de otros Noticias, y Relaciones antiguasm y modernas. Published in Madrid, Spain. 1757.

[138] Empresas Apostolicas, by Miguel Venegas. 1739.

[139] The Mineralogy Record– Library, Miguel Venegas, Noticia de la California, 1757, lists all of the publications of each international volume. http://www.minrec.org/libdetail.asp?id=1420

[140] A Natural and Civil History of California Containing An Accurate Description of that Country, Its Soil, Mountains, Harbours, Lakes, Rivers, and Seaports, Animals, Vegetables, Minerals, and famous Fishery for Pearls. The Customs of the Inhabitants, Their Religion, Government, and Manner of Living, before their Conversion to the Christian Religion by the missionary Jesuits. Translated from the original Spanish of Miguel Venegas, a Mexican Jesuit, published at Madrid 1757. London: Printed for James Rivington and James Fletcher, at the Oxford Theatre, in Pater-Noster-Row, 1759."

[141] North American States, 1883, by Hubert Howe Bancroft. Page 281, footnote 5.

and a rough translation of the original Spanish. Herbert Eugene Bolton, who compiled KINO'S HISTORICAL MEMOIR OF PIMERÍA ALTA, the diary of Father Kino in 1919, made reference to Venegas' book [142] and its first English translation. [143] Bolton, an authority on the Spanish conquest, only lightly touched on the subject of the Spanish mines.

The original 1757 edition of "Noticia de la California," and its 1759 translation of A NATURAL AND CIVIL HISTORY OF CALIFORNIA was possibly the first published declaration about the Spanish missionaries, the mines, and forced labor.

In the original story, Father Kino obtained permission in 1686 to convert the Indians and exempt them from being obligated to "work either on the lands or in the mines." He was disappointed when some of those who he baptized were "forcibly dragged from him to be buried in the depths of a mine, whence few ever return." [144]

This statement may have been the foundation of the legends.

---

[142] Printed Works. Venegas, Miguel (Burriel). Noticia de la California, y de su conquista temporal, y espiritual, hasta el tiempo presente. Sacada de la Historia Manuscrita, formada in Mexico ano de 1739, Spain in the West, A Series of Original Documents From Foreign Archives, Volume IV, by Herbert Eugene Bolton, PhD, 1919. Page 286.

[143] A Natural and Civil History of California Containing An Accurate Description of that Country, 1759.

[144] Ibid. Page 296.

The Map Of Spanish Settlements And Mines

In Mowry's report, he provided a map produced in 1757 by the "Society of Jesuits to the King of Spain." The Mexican government certified that the map was authentic and that it was based on Father Eusebio Kino's original map.

The 1757 map, drawn by Miguel Venegas, was stored in the Mexican archives. [145] It had the inscription, "Carte levee par la Societe des Jesuites, dediee au Roi d'Espagne en 1757." ("Map levee by the Society of Jesuits dedicated to the King of Spain in 1757") [146]

Mowry said this map showed more than forty towns and villages. There were at least nine Indian villages along the San Pedro with Spanish names. On the Santa Cruz side, were the missions of S.F. Xavier del Bac, S. Cosmé, S. Augustin, S. Catherine [147] and S. Angelo.

The Sobaypuris, the Indians who lived in the Santa Cruz valley, were labeled in place of the Catalina Mountains. This version is drawn from the original 1687 survey made by Kino. It was reprinted in 1710 with new discoveries and again in 1757, according to Mowry. [148] The map Mowry used was drawn almost fifty years after the death of Father Kino.

---

[145] Memoir of the Proposed Territory of Arizona. Page 2.

[146] A copy of the map was produced in Noticia de la California 1757 and in English in "A Natural and Civil History of California," 1759.

[147] Also referred to as Santa Catalina and Santa Catarina, depending on the date used.

[148] Charles P. Stone, Cullum's Register #1237, Class of 1845.

85

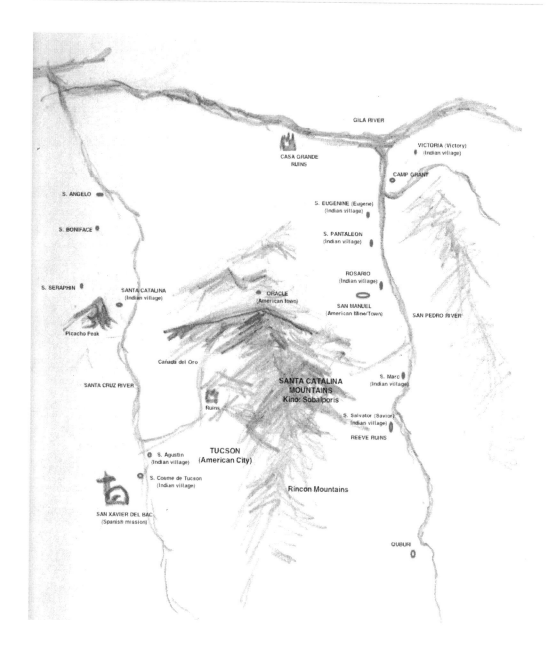

This map shows the approximate locations of the Indian villages along the San Pedro and Santa Cruz Rivers named by Father Kino during his expeditions in the 1690s through early 1700s. [149] It is similar to the map described by Mowry and contains the same villages marked by Kino.

---

[149] Map compiled from *Ex autoptica observatione delineata a R.P. Chino e S.I.*, original map drawn by Father Kino from his 1698 journey. Arizona Historical Review, January 1935. Page 35. Also added are locations of present-day American sites.

Kino's Map Of The New Land

Father Kino's famous 1705 map of the Pimería Alta was the first detailed map of the missions and land known to the Spanish at the time.

The map was inscribed (translated to English) "Passage by land to California discovered by Father Eusebio Kino, a Jesuit; between the Years 1698 and 1701; containing likewise the New Missions of the Jesuits."

This was the first map to demonstrate that California was not an island, but part of the mainland. The first edition of this map was printed in one of the volumes of the Jesuit reports, LETTRES EDIFANTES. [150] Emanuel Bowen drew an English reproduction of the popular map [151] in 1742.

It was reissued in various languages for decades. This map was published in John Lockman's TRAVELS OF THE JESUITS, (Paris, 1762), [152] a NORTH AMERICAN STATES, 1883, by Hubert Bancroft (1883), [153] and an earlier 1705 version in Herbert Bolton's KINO'S HISTORICAL MEMOIR OF PIMERÍA ALTA. (US, 1919). [154]

The other maps, mentioned earlier, were copied from this particular one. They were also translated into English and French. Kino's map shows the earliest location of the lost mission of Santa Catalina, near Picacho Peak west of the Santa Catalinas.

---

[150] Lettres edifantes et curieuses, ecrites des missions etrangeres, chez Nicolas Le Cierc. Paris, 1717.

[151] From Kino's Historical Memoir of Pimería Alta, 1683-1711," by Herbert Eugene Bolton, Volume II from "Spain in the West, A Series of Original Documents from Foreign Archives, Volume I," inside cover. Public domain document.

[152] Travels of the Jesuits, by John Lockman. Volume 1. Paris, 1762. Paris, Page 395.

[153] Venegas Map of the Peninsula, 1757, from "North American States, 1883," by Hubert Bancroft. Page 471.

[154] Kino's Historical Memoir of Pimería Alta, by Herbert Eugene Bolton, Volume II from Spain in the West, A Series of Original Documents from Foreign Archives, Volume I, inside cover.

How The Legends Circulated

There wasn't much known about the new Arizona Territory in the 1850s. People got their basic news mainly from the tabloids and the wild rumors that circulated about recently discovered wealth in the new frontier.

The California Gold Rush had met its peak in the 1860s. Homesteaders and prospectors were searching for new places to stake their claims. The exciting stories of lost Spanish treasures and abundant minerals inspired new hope.

Some of the "official data" that Sylvester Mowry relied on for his 1857 memoir was made available a year earlier from a collection of the Mexico City Department of Foreign Affairs in Mexico. References to these reports were included in a Smithsonian Institute Report [155] and a Congressional Serial Report in 1856. [156]

These materials also contained reports on the conditions of the State of Pimería written by Lt. Cristobal Bernal in 1697 and a letter written by Father Kino describing an expedition with Capt. Diego Carrasco in 1698. The collection also had a letter written by Father Silvestre Veléz de Escalante nearly one hundred years later in 1778. [157] This odd placement of Escalante's letter may have caused confusion in telling the legend another 100 years later– creating one of those historical anachronisms.

Mowry's story spread quickly across the country. [158] His narrative, MEMOIR OF THE PROPOSED TERRITORY OF ARIZONA provided the justification for the new Arizona Territory. It became a part of Arizona's written tradition and its early history. Mowry recited his report in front of many professional organizations. It was published and republished.

---

[155] First published in 10th Annual Report of the Board of Regents of the Smithsonian Institute. Proceedings of the board up to March 22, 1856. Pages 307-309.

[156] Also published later that year in the Congressional Serial Set, 1856, U.S. Government Printing Office. Pages 307-309.

[157] Ibid. "Buckingham Smith, esq, has copies of those in the royal archives in the city of Mexico." Prof. John Henry, Secretary of the Smithsonian Institute.

[158] News article first published his story in *Evening Star*, Washington, D.C. January 7, 1858. Many others followed. See upcoming footnotes for dates and publications.

As soon as Mowry's story began to circulate, tales of the "Old Spanish mines and mineral riches in the new Arizona Territory," were reprinted in newspapers, books, and magazines across the continent. Often, the interpretations would be embellished, but this didn't stop many enterprising entrepreneurs looking to exploit new options.

Mowry's account may have first been published in a Raleigh, North Carolina, newspaper in August 1857 [159] in an article about the new Territory of Arizona. It was repeated in a California newspaper that November, [160] a Washington, D.C. newspaper in January, 1858, [161] and presented by Mowry at an address before the Geographical and Statistical Society in New York on February 3, 1859. [162]

The story was published again that November in several mining magazines [163] and later in 1860, [164] 1861, [165] and 1863. [166] [167] Mowry published the same text in a book in 1864 and 1866. [168]

---

[159] The New Territory of Arizona, Semi-Weekly Standard, Raleigh, North Carolina, August 19, 1857. Also, Weekly North Carolina Standard, Raleigh, North Carolina, August 19, 1857.

[160] Notes upon the New Territory of Arizona, in the Journal of Commerce in the Daily Alta California on November 27, 1857. California Digital Newspaper Collection. Available sources of information about the new territory included notes of Col. A.B. Gray, Major Emory and Hon. John R. Bartlett in their reports and in the appendix to R.A. Wilson's book "Mexico and Its Religions" compiled about his travels through Northern Mexico in 1853.

[161] Evening Star, Washington, D.C., January 7, 1858.

[162] The Geography and Resources of Arizona and Sonora, by Sylvester Mowry, 1859. An Address Before the American Geographical and Statistical Society.

[163] The full article, dated November 1859, included Mowry's accounts and was "compiled for the *Mining Magazine* from the various Reports and Statements of Messrs. Brunckow, Ehrenberg, Poston, Mowry, Park, Emory, Bartlett, Parry, Schott, Gray, Blake, Ward, Wilson and others." The same article is published in "Mining Magazine: Devoted to Mines, Mining Operations, Metallurgy" in 1860, Pages 1-7.

[164] The Mining Magazine and Journal of Geology, Mineralogy, Metallurgy, Chemistry and the Arts, Vol. 12, by Thomas McElrath, Jewett Tenney, William Phipps Blake, George M. Newton. 1860. Pages 2-8.

[165] Arizona or the Gadsden Purchase, from Our Whole Country, or, the Past and Present of the United States, by John Warner Barber, Henry Howe. 1861. Pages 1445-1448.

[166] A second edition published as The Geography and Resources of Arizona and Sonora, An Address Before the American Geographical and Statistical Society by Sylvester Mowry, graduate of the U.S. Military Academy at West Point, Late Lieutenant Third Artillery, U.S.A., Corresponding member of the American Institute, Late U.S. Boundary Commissioner, etc. A New Edition with an Appendix, San

It was reprinted in several Arizona history books that circulated in the late 1860s. [169] Mowry was cited in the Report of the Governor of Arizona to the Secretary of the Interior" and the Annual Report of the Department of Interior of 1899 [170] and reprinted numerous times in the early 20th Century. [171] History became ingrained in the legend.

Col. Charles D. Poston, another Arizona pioneer often called the Father of Arizona, traveled to the new Territory with several others under instructions to explore the area and purchase any of the "old mining ranches, abandoned by the Mexicans." On December 31, 1856, Poston concluded the purchase of the Arizona Ranch, near Tubac." The Mexicans called the ranch "La Aribac," fifteen miles south of west from Tubac. It contained 25 silver mines, with small quantities of gold. They also acquired title to twenty four veins of silver ore in the Santa Rita Mountains, at the south edge of the Catalinas, and the nearby Salero and Ojero mines. [172] The Mexicans worked those before they were ambushed and they hadn't been mined since the Americans arrived in the mid-1850s. [173]

Francisco and New York, A. Roman & Co., 1863. Since his first speech I have made several journeys in Sonora and Arizona, and have resided about a year at my place, the Mowry Silver Mines' in Arizona.

[167] The Geography and Resources of Arizona and Sonora, by Sylvester Mowry. Published by A. Roman & Company, 1863. From an Address Before the American Geographical and Statistical Society.

[168] Arizona and Sonora, by Sylvester Mowry, 1864. Mowry's Address Before the American Geographical and Statistical Society, 1859 was republished.

[169] Some books include: Out Whole Country, or The Past and Present of the United States, by John Warner Barber and Henry Howe, 1861, Pages 1445-1448.

[170] Excerpts regarding the Apache raids and silver mines were cited in the Report of the Governor of Arizona to the Secretary of the Interior, 1899. Part of the United States Congressional Serial Set of Annual Reports of the Department of the Interior for the Fiscal Year ended June 30, 1899, Miscellaneous Reports, Part II, Washington, 1899.

[171] Some publications includes The Loyal West in the Times of the Rebellion, by John W. Barber, 1865; All the Western States and Territories, from the Alleghenies to the Pacific, By John Warner Barber, Henry Howe, 1867; Report of the Proceeding of the Annual Session, Volume 8-10, by the American Mining Congress, 1906.

[172] Report of the Sonora Exploring and Mining Co. to its Shareholders, 1857. Pages 3-5.

[173] "The Silver Mines of Arizona," Evening Star, Washington, D.C. August 18, 1858.

The Word Spreads About Arizona

"Two centuries ago, when the Pilgrim Fathers were struggling with barbarism upon the shores of New England, Spain established an empire amidst her newly-found wealth, and drew millions from the very region where now the Anglo Saxon is erecting a second era of civilization. Years passed, and the civilization of the Jesuit, always superficial and never permanent, faded away. Indian depredations drove those monk miners from their possessions, and we now behold on every hand, the remains of ancient works and old mining establishments, used by the Spaniards when the New World was in its infancy."

The Weekly Arizonian, Tubac, Arizona, March 10, 1859 [174]

One writer exalted that Arizona's silver mines were once a rich source of revenue for Spain, and he speculated some of those riches were thought to still be there. But the hostile Apache Indians made it too dangerous to attempt any exploration by venture seekers.

The author described Sonora and Arizona as "dotted with spots where they are reported to have covered up some awful rich mines. Generally these mines are said to be closed with massive doors, but the first plank has yet to be found." The writer had no doubt that the priests worked the mines, or employed the "idle Indians." He affirmed the common knowledge that the "Mission of the old Jesuits" had been accused of knowing about the mines and that they were accused of hording their immense wealth in Lower California in the 17th Century. [175] This is the earliest mention of old mines sealed with doors.

Mowry promoted the mineral virtues of the new Territory in an 1859 address to the Geographical Society. He added details about the dozen of operating mines throughout the Southwest. Tucson, at the time, had about 1,000 residents– up from about two hundred. The San Xavier del Bac and Tumacacori missions were both deserted, he said.

---

[174] "The Mineral Wealth of Arizona," The Weekly Arizonian, Tubac, A.T. March 10, 1859. Also published in the "Morning Leader," Cleveland, Ohio, March 10, 1859.

[175] "Mining Stories and Realities," The Weekly Arizonian, Tubac, Arizona. July 7, 1859.

[176] The publication of an 1878 overview of the new Territory, called "The Handbook of Arizona," featured hundreds of pages on the minerals and mining opportunities in the new Territory. [177] That eventually piqued the interest of eastern venture capitalists in the next decades. But, the treasures were still out of reach.

Mowry's career was tinged by scandal, however. He was suspected as a Confederate sympathizer and arrested in Tucson. He resigned his commission as second lieutenant in 1858. After he was released, he returned to Tucson and tried to rebuild his Mowry Silver Mines, nine miles south of Patagonia, Arizona. Mowry bought the mine in 1860 for $25,000. Sonoran Mexicans started the mine before the 1850s, prior to the Civil War. [178] [179] In June, 1862, the Mowry Silver Mines was seized, and he was jailed for nearly six months on a "false, ridiculous, and malicious charge," he claimed. His mine was placed into receivership under the Confiscation Act, and he suffered "great loss." [180]

Nevertheless, Mowry's memoirs were the basis of the Spanish mining legends. His account of the early history of Arizona and Sonora became embedded in the public record and imagination.

---

[176] See Arizona and Sonora: the Geography, History, And Resources of the Silver Region of North America, By Sylvester Mowry. Harper & Brothers, New York. 1864.

[177] The Handbook of Arizona, by R.J. Hinton, San Francisco, 1878.

[178] Mowry Mine (Patagonia Mine; Enterprise Mine; Phoenix Mine), Mowry Hill, Mowry Wash, Mowry, Patagonia District, Patagonia Mtns, Santa Cruz Co., Arizona, USA. Mindat.org

[179] Guide to the Sylvester Mowry Letter, Historical Note. Northwest Digital Archives. Sylvester Mowry died in 1871.

[180] Arizona and Sonora, by Sylvester Mowry. 1864. Page 62-63 and footnote. Mowry was arrested June 8, 1862 under order of General Charlton, commander of New Mexico on a "charge of treasonable complicities with the rebels." A board of investigation appointed by Charlton determined that Mowry "had given aid and comfort to the enemy" and there was sufficient reason to try him before a military commission. His property was seized and he was jailed. He was unconditionally released November 4, 1862 from prison under order from the U.S. War Department since there was no evidence presented to the board. Mowry filed a grievance alleging illegal seizure. The property passed from military to the civil authority. There are no documents about the outcome. Mowry went on to start up some new mines, the Olive and the Esperanza, nearby the old Mowry Mines. He blamed "personal hostility" on the part of General Charlton for his misfortune.

The Legends & The History

There Is A Lost Gold Mine
Somewhere In The Santa Catalinas.

Early Spaniards Operated The Mine
And Forced The Natives To Work.

A Mission And A City Were Nearby
Where The Workers Lived.

At The Time Of The Expulsions Of The
Jesuits And/Or Franciscans, The Mine— With Its Bullion—
Was Sealed Off. Its Location Is Still Unknown.

Several legends are merged into the folklore about the Santa Catalina Mountains. The basic storylines have usually been the same and, over time, became woven into a single legend that early Americans heard from local residents. [181] Stories of secret Spanish mining operations and legends of a lost civilization spurred the imagination.

We are left with common folklore, crumbling façades, and some documentation.

According to the saga that most people knew in the mid-1800s, the Spaniards prospected lucrative gold mines after Father Eusebio Francisco Kino pioneered the New World and

---

[181] These legends are published in numerous newspaper accounts since 1880 and repeated by authors Donald Page (1920s); John D. Mitchell (1950s); Jesse Rascoe (1969); Edgar B. Heylmun (1980s); Archaeology in Tucson, newsletter of the Center for Desert Archaeology, Autumn II, No. 4, page 4, Fall 1997; Eugene L. Conrotto (2012), among others.

93

established new missions– like the San Xavier del Bac, located south of Tucson, Arizona. This version of the adventure turns local.

Sometime during this period, oral legends assert, a small community and church were built in the Santa Catalina Mountains. The Spanish conquistadores forced the local natives into slavery to mine the gold from the Catalina Mountains. The details vary with the different versions. The common theme was that the local natives worked the Spanish mines, under the direction of the Jesuits, and then later the Franciscans. But, history points its finger at another group who had more control over the population– the Spanish military.

Other variations of the legend say the mines were probably operated under the supervision of the Spanish military. They mined for gold, silver and copper until either 1751 when the Pima Indians revolted, and/or in 1767 when the Jesuit missionaries were expelled and left behind their riches. Some accounts claim the mines were also worked until the Franciscans were expelled in 1827.

The location of this mine and the mission has not been established. There are plenty of theories. The one detail the storytellers agree on– if a lost city, mission, and mine existed– its remains were somewhere in the Santa Catalina Mountains.

The evolution of the legends, however, developed from some historical facts. Scant evidence and documentation is overshadowed by decades of storytelling. The Iron Door Mine, which became the theme of a popular book and several movies in the 1920-2000s, further perpetuated the legend.

While these legends may be rooted in some truth, a lot of confusion has distorted the true events. There must have been some reason for the start of the rumors.

To envision the entire story, step back a few hundred years when the early Europeans explored the New World and came upon the Canyon of Gold.

Early Spanish Search For Gold

The Legend: Coronado's discovers gold at Cañon del Oro.
The History: Coronado may have passed by the Catalinas.

One of the earliest legends in the search for gold in the Santa Catalina Mountains was part of a debate on Coronado's route during his search for the Seven Cities of Gold (Cibola). His journey apparently ended in failure, but a legend about Coronado adds a twist to the history.

Five years before Francisco Vasquez de Coronado's expedition in 1535, Spanish explorer Alvar Nuñez Cabeza de Vaca, two companions, and a black Moorish slave named Estevan (or Estevanico), all escaped from imprisonment by natives in Florida.

They made their way across the southern land. Along their route they heard tales of cities of gold called the "Seven Cities of Cibola."

While the fabled cities were not found, it sparked the imagination and rumors of extraordinary wealth in the new land.[182][183]

---

[182] The Journey of Alvar Nuñez Cabeza De Vaca, by Alvar Nuñez Cabeza de Vaca, 1542. Translated by Fannie Bandeuer, 1904. Brigham Young University Library.

[183] A History of Mining in AZ, The Mission, Means and Memories of Arizona Miners, Arizona Mining Association website. Page 2. http://www.azmining.com/images/HISTORY_FULL.pdf

Four years after Cabeza, in 1539 Franciscan explorer and Frenchman Fray Marcos de Niza (Nica) [184] passed through the San Pedro Valley, accompanied by Estevan the slave, to follow up on de Vaca's exploration for the Seven Cities of Cibola farther north. Cibola possibly stood at the Pueblo of Zuni on the Arizona-New Mexico boundary.

Subsequent trips by others failed to find the rich cities, but a trail through the San Pedro Valley, east of the Santa Catalina Mountains, became established for many years. A marker was placed near the bridge across the San Pedro at Palominas by the Dons of Phoenix to commemorate Fray Marcos de Niza's passage. [185] Although Niza's group may have only passed by the Santa Catalinas, they paved the way for others who ventured inside.

In retelling the early Spanish stories in the 1930s, one prospector embellished the legend when he included the year 1539 in his history of the Catalina Mountains. C.W. McKee believed a priest named Francist (Niza was a Franciscan friar) enslaved the local natives to mine the Santa Catalina Mountains that year, and they were eventually driven out. McKee, however, was the only one who used that year and name of Francist in his rendition of the legend even though the historical date matched. [186]

Francisco Vasquez de Coronado's Spanish expedition to locate the fabled Seven Cities of Gold between 1540-42 was also a futile search. History says he never found the gold or the riches, and his actual route is still in dispute.

The legend-part of this story has Coronado's group making a stop at the Cañada del Oro in the Santa Catalina Mountains; history is not so clear.

In 1871, General J.H. Simpson, [187] who wrote a book on the expedition, was the first to suggest that Coronado's group stopped at the "Santa Catarina Mountains." [188] It was here,

---

[184] A Relation of the Reverend Father Frier Marco de Nica, Touching His Discovery of the Kingdom of Ceuola or Cibola, Situate about 30 Degrees of Latitude, to the North of Nueva Espanna, American Journey Collection, Document No, AJ-072. Wisconsin Historical Society.

[185] Ibid. Page 12-13.

[186] See series "Romantic Story of Mine With Iron Door Began With Conquistadors and Indians," by Sherry Bowen. Part 1 to 6, The Arizona Daily Star, Tucson, Arizona. December 21, 1932. McKee's story is told later in this book.

[187] See Coronado's March in Search of the "Seven Cities of Cibola, and discussion of their probable location, by Brevet Brigadier General J.H. Simpson, 1871. Contains the Annual Report of the Board of Regents of the Smithsonian Institution for 1869, which includes notes mentioned in these chapters. http://ia600502.us.archive.org/23/items/coronadosmarchin00simpiala/coronadosmarchin00simpiala.pdf

he proposed, where they "descended the stream two days, and quitted it to the right at a foot of a chain of mountains," which they followed for two days. [188]

Twenty-five years later, this story was repeated in a compilation of reports of "The Coronado Expedition." Pedro de Casteñada who was on the expedition originally wrote this translated account. However, it leaves it out any reference to the Catalinas:

> *"From here we went through deserted country for about four days to another river, which we heard called Nexpa, where some poor Indians came out to see the general, with presents of little value, with some stalks of roasted maguey and pitahayas.* [190] *We went down this stream two days, and left the stream, going toward the right to the foot of the mountain chain in two day's journey, where we heard news of what is called Chichiltic Calli."* [191]

Historian Col. Charles D. Poston, considered to be the Father of Arizona, [192] believed that when the Coronado expedition went down this stream for two days, they "stopped here awhile and washed some gold from the sands of the Cañon del Oro [193] on sheep skins." [194]

---

[188] Santa Catarina was the name used at that time for the Santa Catalina Mountains.

[189] Coronado's March In Search of the Seven Cities of Cibola, by Brevet Brigadier Gen. J.H. Simpson, published in the Executive Documents, U.S. House of Representatives, 1871. Page 325.

[190] Interesting Side Note: Maguey is a desert plant like the agave, century plant and aloe that is grown in the Santa Cruz Valley and other parts of the Sonoran desert. Its fibers could be used for clothing, building materials and juices can be fermented to make alcoholic beverages. Today, agave juice is distilled and processed into tequila. The natives would also consume large amounts of pitaya fruit and then remove the seeds after defecation. The seeds were collected, often roasted, and ingested as a "second harvest." There is no mention if the pitaya that the Spaniards received were from a "second harvest."

[191] Translation of the Narrative of Jaramillo, in The Coronado Expedition, 1540-1542,"By Pedro de Casteñada de Najera, Francisco Vasquez de Coronado, Antonio de Mendoza, Juan Camilo Jaramillo. U.S. Government Printing Office, 1896. Pages 585-586.

[192] Charles Debrille Poston (1825-1902) was called the Father of Arizona because of his role to help Arizona gain territorial status. He was one of the first white settlers who arrived in 1853 on a mining trip. He died in near poverty in 1902.

[193] Cañon del Oro was the name used at the time for the Cañada del Oro.

He went on to say that, "the Spaniards, from this experience, remembering the island of Colchis, [195] named Tucson, *Jason*, in Spanish." This is supposedly the first use of the name the city bears today. [196]

Poston, however, is the only one to suggest the gold discovery and this origin of Tucson's name. Because of his status, his statements were taken as fact. Since then authors have repeated this story without any attribution.

The argument is still whether the Nexpa River could be the Santa Cruz River or the San Pedro River; the Cañon del Oro lies in between.

Juan Camilo Jaramillo, who also chronicled that expedition, mentioned the Nexpa River twice in his account. His original report is no longer accessible except for an English translation of a faulty French version. Friar Marcos' earlier description suggests that it was the Santa Cruz River over the San Pedro River. [197]

Most historians disagree, or even acknowledge, if Coronado ever found gold or ever was near Tucson or the Cañon del Oro. Poston didn't cite his source and none of the translations of the expedition mention such a discovery or name the location. His story, though, is similar to a finding in the same spot a few hundred years later by another military officer.

Dr. Freeman suggested in 1917, that if Coronado's team traveled along the Santa Cruz, they must have passed the site of the San Xavier mission and the future site of Tucson. When they realized they were going off course, they left the Santa Cruz and went along the western base of the Catalina Mountains, then north until they reached Casa Grande. [198]

---

[194] Published in Building A State in Apache Land, by Charles Poston, President of the Arizona Historical Society, from articles in the Overland Express Monthly and the Out West Magazine, July-December (August) 1894. Page 205.

[195] Colchis (Mingrelia), was one of the locations where Jason, the Phoenician took his expedition from Greece to Colchis in Argos. From A History of the Precious Metals, from the earliest times to the present, by Alex Del Mar, M.E., 1902. Page 7.

[196] Building A State in Apache Land, by Charles Poston. Page 205.

[197] "Chichiticalli," from the Bulletin of the American Geographical Society, Volume 40. 1913. Pages 268-269.

[198] Coronado's Expedition in 1540, address before the Arizona Archaeological Society by Dr. Merrill P. Freeman. March 19, 1917. Bancroft Library, University of California, Berkeley.

Freeman does not specify if they went through the Cañon del Oro, but it is on the western slope and does lead to the San Pedro River on the eastern side. The San Pedro eventually leads to the Gila River and then to Casa Grande. The other theory is that after crossing a four-day uninhabited area, the Coronado expedition only went along the San Pedro River on the east side of the Santa Catalina Mountains. [199] [200]

A few years later, "Calling their finds the 'Seven Cities of Cibola' in 1582, Antonio de Espejo reported on the richness of the region and the discovery of mines in what is today central Arizona." [201] He didn't mention specific locations.

If Coronado, or his group, ever did scoop up gold from the Cañada del Oro, there is no surviving account. It would take another hundred years for another tale to become merged into the Catalina Mountains' history.

Graphic of a Spanish conquistador in Pimería Alta, by Robert Zucker.

[199] This theory is advanced by Bolton 1949; Flint and Flint 2005; Reff 1981, 1997; Riley 1987, 1997; Seymour 2007a, 2008. http://www.seymourharlan.com/My_Homepage_Files/Page2.html

[200] The Conquest of Mexico in "The Spanish Settlements Within the Present Limits of the United States," by Woodbury Lowery. Page 299. "...ascended the Sonora and descended the San Pedro Valley, and turning eastward where the lower course of the stream becomes impassable, went through or around the rugged chain of the Santa Catalina Mountains which skirt the eastern side of the San Pedro."

[201] "A History of Cochise County, Arizona," By Carl Trischka, reprinted in *The Cochise Quarterly*, Vol. 1. No. 3, September 1971. "The Coming of the Spaniards," Page 9-12. http://www.cochisecountyhistory.org/uploads/Vol1_3.pdf

Next Wave Of Spanish Conquest

The Legend: In 1698 Father's Kino and Escalante sought minerals reportedly discovered in the Santa Catalinas by the Indians.

The History: In 1698 Sgt. Escalante, accompanied by Father Kino, sought minerals reportedly discovered in the Catalinas by the Indians.

In the late 1600s and early 1700s, thousands of natives were living in the Santa Cruz Valley and the nearby mountains. They hunted and had a nomadic life moving around with the seasons and surviving in the desert valley close to the Santa Cruz River and Santa Catalina Mountains.

These people were called the Sobaipuris Indians. The hostile Apache Indians, an aggressive tribe, inhabited the nearby Santa Catalinas. The Santa Cruz Valley became the northern most point of this land the Spanish *conquistadores* called Pimería Alta [202] – the present day Southern Arizona.

When Jesuit Father Eusebio Kino made his first journey around the Santa Catalinas and through the Santa Cruz Valley in 1697, the natives outnumbered the Spanish settlers, miners, clergy, and military.

The following year, he made a more infamous expedition. This particular event developed into legendary status when several historians brought up the topic and linked it to minerals in the Santa Catalinas.

The most widely accepted historical documentation about this event comes from Herbert Eugene Bolton, the authoritative historian on Kino's life. In 1919, Bolton published translations from Kino's diaries and other letters about the expedition called "Kino's

---

[202] It was also referred to a New Galicia and Upper Sonora.

100

Historical Memoir of Pimería Alta." [203] Bolton (in 1919) and historian Sylvester Mowry (in 1857) relied on similar Spanish documents to compile their accounts.

Even though the event did happen, there are several historical anachronisms in the legend. Some early Spanish sources have been overlooked. Many authors in the 20th Century embellished the facts to create a distorted account, and their version of the story became woven into the legend of the mountains [204]

According to this particular legend of Father Kino, in 1698 local Indians reported to the Spaniards that they found gold in the Santa Catalina Mountains (some versions use quicksilver, others say it was silver). The legend claims that the deposit was located and the Indians were eventually forced to mine it. [205]

However, the missionaries had different interests than their military escorts.

---

[203] Kino's Historical Memoir of Pimería Alta A Contemporary Account, Volume 2. From Spain in the West, A Series of Original Documents From Foreign Archives, Volume IV. Semi-centennial publication of the University of California, 1868-1918. Copyright by Herbert E. Bolton, 1919.

[204] Those documents are quoted and footnoted throughout this and other chapters. Every attempt was made to seek out the earliest source and trace the pathway the different facts took to become part of this legend.

[205] This source might have taken the story told by John D. Mitchell in 1933: "Father Escalante (a Jesuit assistant to Father Kino at the Mission San Xavier del Bac) was the first to work it." From Arizona: A Guide to the Grand Canyon State, published by the Federal Writers' Project, 1940. Page 296.

1686-1711: Kino's Mission To Convert The Natives

Historically, the major reason that Father Eusebio Francisco Kino went to the New World was to enforce an edict from the King of Spain: [206] [207] It forbade the enslavement of natives in the mines. [208]

Graphic of a horseman and a guide.

Local mining activities were already in operation by Spanish colonists before the Jesuit missionaries made their way into Pimería Alta, [209] and the native Indians were being badly mistreated and forced to work in the mines. [210] [211] Kino wanted to prevent further abuse.

---

[206] "To the Very Catholic Majesty of Our Sovereign, Philip V," letter from Father Kino explaining his desire to attend to the new conversions. From Spain in the West, Volume 3, page 85. Also, page 107.

[207] "I (Kino) set out on December 16, having obtained from the Royal Audiencia the royal provision and the inserted royal cédula…" From "Kino's Historical Memoir of Pimería Alta," by Herbert Eugene Bolton. Volume 1, page 107.

[208] "Misionero nombrado para la reduccion de gentiles, y conversion a nuestra Sancta fe de los Seris, Huaymas, y Pimas en la provinzia de Sonora, Reyno de la nueua Vizcaya." Petition asking prohibition of taking Indians with seal to work in mines from his prospective missions. Guadalajara, Dec. 16, 1686. A.G.I. 67-1-36. Transcript in Bancroft Library." From Kino's Historical Memoir of Pimería Alta, Vol. 2, page 290.

[209] Mineral Appraisal of Coronado National Forest, Part 5. Department of the Interior, Bureau of Mines, MLA 25-94, 1994. Page 24. Based on Edgar Heylmun, 1981. Page 11.

[210] "They suffered them in the mines and farms to be guilty of the most abominable excesses, which the fathers took care to restrain their habitation." From A Natural and Civil History of California, published in 1759. Volume 1, Page 296. Translated from Noticia de la California, published in 1757. Tomo Segundo. Page 89-90 (see next footnote).

[211] "Fuera de las violencias se acudia, para extraerlos de las Missiones al diabolico medio de permitirles en las Minas, y Haciendas los vicio, y defordenes, que les impedian, y refrenaban los Padres en sus

Charles II, the King of Spain issued his Royal Cédula in 1686. It promised the natives that they would not be forced to work in the mines for a period of five years– then prolonged to 20 years– if they converted to Christianity. [212] [213]

The King made his decree:

> *"...promising in my name to all new converts that during the first twenty years of their reduction they will not be required to give tribute or to serve on estates or in mines, since this is one of the reasons why they refuse to be converted..."*

> Done at Buen Retiro, Royal Provision and Royal Cédula Which Favors The New Conversions, May 14, 1686. I, the King." [214]

Kino arrived in Sonora in February, 1687, with expectations that this "Catholic seal might well, and should, astonish and edify the whole world." [215]

---

reducciones." From the manuscript written in 1739 and published in "Noticia de la California Y De Su Cnquista," in 1757. Tomo Segundo. Page 90.

[212] "que no pudiessen ser compelidos a trabajar en Minas, y Haciendas los Indos recien conversion." From "Noticia de la California," 1757. Tomo Segundo. Page 89. See translation in next footnote.

[213] "...that the new converts among the Indians, should not, during the first five years of their conversion, be obliged to work on the lands or in the mines." Translated in A Natural and Civil History of California, 1759. Volume 1, Page 296.

[214] "Royal Provision and Royal Cédula Which Favors The New Conversions." This is the petition of Eusebio Francisco Kino, "missionary named for the reduction and conversion to our Holy Faith of the Seris, Huaymas, and Pimas in the province of Sonora, Kingdom of Nueva Vizcaya," regarding taking Indians under seal to work in mines, undated, but passed on by the Audiencia December 16, 1686; and petition of Father Azcarasso, undated, but considered May 2, 1687. From Spain in the West, by Herbert Eugene Bolton. Vol. 3, Chapter 2. Page 109.

[215] Ibid. Page 109.

1697: Kino Establishes Missions—
The Military Hunts For Minerals

Kino made several journeys from his base at Mission Nuestra Señora de los Delores and headed north into the Pimería Alta. Each time a military escort accompanied him. One of those soldiers was named Escalante. This may have been how the Escalante name became linked with Kino in the legend.

During Father Kino's first expedition in the autumn of 1697, he traveled past the Santa Catalina Mountains and along the San Pedro and Santa Cruz Rivers. Kino established several missions along the way. He named the rivers, mountains, and villages that were encountered. [216] [217] [218] [219] [220] It was during this journey he reportedly named the Santa Catalina Mountains.

Kino left Dolores in Sonora, Mexico, on November 2nd under the escort of Lieutenant Cristobal Martin Bernal, Alférez Francisco Acuña, Sergeant Juan Bautista de Escalante, and twenty soldiers from the Compañia Volante ("Flying Company") the mobile military unit that roamed the Pimería Alta to protect the settlers, mines, and missionaries. Their military objective was to determine the nature of the natives and to hunt for a cache of stolen goods. [221]

---

[216] November 21, 1697, Kino made the trip accompanied by Lt. Manje, Capt. Bernal and 22 soldiers. Spain in the West, Kino's Historical Memoir of Pimería Alta, Volume 1. Page 56.

[217] Annals of the Spanish Northwest: North Mexican States, |1531-1800| (1884) by Henry L. Oak. Page 264-265.

[218] The Papago County, Arizona, by Kirk Bryan Dept of Interior, 1925.

[219] Kino's Historical Memoir of Pimería Alta, Vol. 1, p. 186. By Herbert Eugene Bolton, Ph.D.

[220] Antigua California: Mission and Colony on the Peninsular Frontier, 1697-1768, by Harry Crosby. University of New Mexico Press, 1994. Page 440, Notes on pages 53-55.

[221] Oak uses the date of November 5th. Marched by the order of General Jironza, Sgt. Escalante's name is included in the list. From Annals of the Spanish Northwest: North Mexican States, |1531-1800| (1884). Pages 264-265.
http://archive.org/stream/annalsofspanishn01oakhrich/annalsofspanishn01oakhrich_djvu.txt

Carrying gifts for the Sobaipuri Indians, Kino's group met up with Capt. Juan Mateo Manje and ten Indians. As the entourage traveled up the east range of the Santa Catalinas along the San Pedro River ("Rio de Quiburi"), they met many friendly Sobaipuri Indians and made "numerous finds of artifacts." [222]

Kino brought along lots of livestock. At each Indian village he named, he left twenty to thirty of his "mission horses." [223] Some of those cattle and wild horses roaming Southern Arizona today are descended from Kino's initial herds. [224]

The group traveled farther north to the Gila River and saw the "Casas Grandes" (the Casa Grande ruins). [225] Sgt. Escalante wrote how he marveled at the structure. From there they went south along the Santa Cruz and passed several villages until they arrived at "San Xavier del Baac of the Rio de Santa Maria (Santa Cruz River)." [226]

The inhabited villages in the Santa Cruz Valley were named La Rancheria de San Cosmé de Tucson, San Agustin del Oyaut, San Clemente, and Santa Catalina de Cuitoabagum. [227] Kino named San Xavier del Baac after his patron, the apostle of the Indies in the New Galicia. [228] During that journey Kino rode about seven hundred and eighty miles in thirty days. [229]

---

[222] "Father Kino's 1697 Entrada to the Casa Grande Ruin in Arizona A Reconstruction," by Ronald L. Ives, reprinted from *Arizona and the West*, Vol. 15, No. 4, Winter 1973. Pages 345-370. Ives reconstructs Bolton's account of Kino's journey.

[223] The Critically Endangered Colonial Spanish Mission Horse, by Deb Wolfe.

[224] Ibid.. Kino Heritage Society. Endurance Rider: The Padre on Horseback. First Arizona Breeder of Horses. http://padrekino.com/kino-legacy/horseman/

[225] The Casa Grande ruins are located approximately halfway between Tucson and Phoenix. These are the same ruins reported by Coronado.

[226] The Works of Hubert Bancroft, Vol. XV, History of the North Mexican States, Vol. I, 1531-1800, A.L. Bancroft Publishers, 1884. The return route from Casa Grande on the 21st was along the Santa Cruz River past "S. Andres, Sta. Catalina, S. Agustin, S. Javier del Bac or Batosda, S. Cayetano Tumacacori, Guevavi, Cocospera, Remedios and Dolores." Footnote, Page 265.

[227] Spain in the West, Kino's Historical Memoir of Pimería Alta, Volume 1. Page 186.

[228] Arizona: The Jesuits in Pimería Alta, From American Journeys Collection, Report and Relation of the Near Conversions, diary notes from Father Eusebio Kino. Page 435.

[229] Ibid, Page 58.

Captain Bernal's account of that trip gave rise to the early legend about the report of minerals shown to the Spaniards.

Both history and the legend are correct. Father Kino was on an expedition when, somewhere along the trip, they heard reports from the Sobaipuri natives about rich minerals in the nearby mountains.

> *"El año 1697 el capitan Don Mateo Manje, pasando con el Padre Francisco Eusebio Kino por la rancheria de San Javier del Bac, cuarenta leguas disante de dicho rio gila, le dieron los indios una piedra de metal del poniente que parecia rico metal de plata."*

> Lt. Cristobal Martin Bernal [230] ("In the year 1697, the Captain Don Mateo Mange (Manje), went with Father Francisco Eusebio Kino to the ranch of San Xavier del Bac, distance of forty leagues of the Gila River, the Indians gave rock of rich metal setting that looked like silver metal.")

Manje, or someone else on that same trip, also wrote about the report of minerals as they traveled from Casa Grande towards San Xavier del Bac. [231]

> *"Many rancherias were visited by detachments wandering in different directions, and **reports were received of quicksilver mines,** and of white men bearing fire-arms and swords who sometimes came to the Colorado."*

This is where history and the legend merge. While the events are recorded, there is no mention of where the reported discovery originated. If the group left the Casa Grande ruins and headed south to San Xavier, they would have passed the Santa Catalina Mountains on their left. Along that route was the Santa Catalina visita.

Legend writer John D. Mitchell had been told this mine was discovered in 1698 by Indians who were hunting deer in the Catalinas on the "western slopes of the mountains and not far from the Ventaña, a hole in the rocks resembling a window." The mine could be seen from the light shining through the Ventaña in a "southeasterly direction from where they stood." [232] This may have been the unwritten portion of that find. The legend names the Catalinas.

---

[230] Materiales para la historia de Sonora, by Miguel Angel Paz Frayre, UNAM, 2007. A compilation of documents of the Archivo General de la Nación in Mexico City. Page 603.

[231] Possibly written by Manje or someone else on that trip. From Annals of the Spanish Northwest: North Mexican States (1531-1800), by Henry Lebbeus Oak, 1884. Volume 1. Page 265. The Spanish text is not provided, so the actual mineral is not known.

[232] Ibid.

1698: Kino's Expeditions & The Search For Minerals

"Discover the quicksilver mine reported among the Sobaipuris." [233]

For the next expedition in September, 1698, the military was given specific instructions to locate these alleged minerals and report back to the Crown. [234] [235] Capt. Diego Carrasco [236] is ordered to assist Kino on another missionary trip.

---

[233] Kino's Historical Memoir of Pimería Alta, by Herbert Eugene Bolton. 1919. Volume 1. Footnote, page 185. From Archivo General de Indias 67-3-28, originals housed in Seville, Spain, copies stored in the Bancroft Library.

[234] Expediente concerning Carrasco's expedition to the Gila River with Kino in 1698. May, 1698-Oct. 1699. A.G.I. 67-3-28.

[235] Kino's Historical Memoir of Pimería Alta, by Herbert Bolton. Volume 1, 1919. Footnote, page 184-185. Footnote 230. http://archive.org/stream/kinoshistoricalm00kino/kinoshistoricalm00kin0_djvu

Quoted from Bolton's footnote: "The editor has recently secured a diary of the expedition kept together with Jironza's instructions to Carrasco and his report to the viceroy. These new materials constitute an *expediente* in the Archivo de Indias (67-3-28). They comprise (a) a report by Jironza to the viceroy on May 16, 1698, recounting the Pima victory of March 30; (b) Jironza's instructions to Captain Diego Carrasco, September 15, 1698 **(he was expressly instructed to hunt for a quicksilver mine** reported to be in the sobaipuris **nation, to give staves of office to the chiefs, and not to leave Kino till he should be restored to his mission)**; (c) Carrasco's official diary, called Diario fecho, etc., a close copy or paraphrase (sic) of Kino's diary; (d) a report by Carrasco to Jironza, dated at Dolores, October 1, and giving a brief account of the expedition; (e) a report by Jironza to the viceroy, recounting the expedition, San Juan Baptista, March 8, 1699; (f) a dictamen fiscal concerning the matter by Lie. Baltazar de Tobar, Mexico, October 19, 1699.

Luz de Tierra Incognita (Unknown Arizona and Sonora 1693-1701), by Juan Mateo Manje translated by Harry J. Karns. Published by Arizona Silhouettes, Tucson, 1954.

Portions quoted in The Papago County, Arizona, by Kirk Bryan, U.S. Dept of Interior, 1925 http://pubs.usgs.gov/wsp/0499/report.pdf

[236] "Kino says Captain Diego Carrasco is the present lieutenant of this Pimería."

Carrasco, acting head of the Compañia Volante (Flying Company), is explicitly instructed to "keep a diary, give Saints' names to the Indian villages, count the inhabitants, make note of water supply and distances, appoint and give bastones of office to governcy of the villages, **"and especially" to do his best to discover the quicksilver mine reported among the Sobaipuris."** [237]

Father Kino and Capt. Carrasco left Dolores, Mexico and proceeded to the San Xavier del Bac mission and up the Santa Cruz River [238] to Gila River west of Casa Grande. A final report of the expedition was filed in March 1699. [239] Several more trips were made with Father Kino and different Spanish military escorts, including with Sgt. Escalante.

Apparently, they were unsuccessful locating the deposit.

Kino never made any mention of this hunt in his journals since this was a military matter, but he did write about a stop at the Santa Catalina visita.

Besides the report from Capt. Diego Carrasco, who accompanied Kino on his journeys, this is the only other story that ties the year 1698 with Kino and the Santa Catalina Mountains.

Sgt. Escalante was, in reality, a military officer and not a missionary as the legends claim. He became complicit in the legends– even if only by name association. But if any minerals were discovered at that time, Escalante would have known.

In Father Kino's journal about his spring 1699 expedition north, his military escort Sr. Lt. Juan Mateo Manje was instructed to go where the quicksilver mines were reported. It was on this trip that Kino was given some "curious and beautiful blue shells" he believed came from the western coast of California. This gave him the idea that there must be a land passage to California. [240]

---

[237] Kino's Historical Memoir of Pimería Alta, by Herbert Eugene Bolton. 1919. Volume 1. Footnote, page 185. From Archivo General de Indias 67-3-28, originals housed in Seville, Spain, copies stored in the Bancroft Library.

[238] The Santa Cruz River flows north.

[239] Expediente concerning Carrasco's expedition to the Gila River with Kino in 1698. A.G.I. 67-3-28. Transcript in the Bancroft Library.

[240] Ibid. Page 193-197. Kino gives a description of their excursion.

Soldiers were sent out in 1701, again with Kino to "see if certain mineral veins shown to them by the Indians was of gold or quicksilver." But it was delayed because of a change in military command. [241] History is not clear exactly where the minerals were located.

Another writer in 1940, probably repeating Mitchell's story, said "the usual story is that it was discovered by Indians hunting deer in the Santa Catalina Mountains in 1698. Father Escalante (a Jesuit assistant to Father Kino at the Mission San Xavier del Bac) was the first to work it." The Indians mined the gold, ground it with arrastras, and hid the bars in a secret strong room dug in the mountainside. Then it was sealed with an iron door. The Apache Indians eventually attacked and wiped out the mining camp, according to this version. [242]

According to one obscure story, two Indians named Big Deer and Raindrop went into the Catalinas to "where the god who rules the ranges lives." To find the place, one needs to peer through the "Hole-in-the-Rock" where the dwelling can be seen. As they camped, a "queer greenish light" awakened Big Deer. The light irradiated some symbols that Raindrop, a medicine man, had made on the ground during a ceremony before they went to sleep. Scared, he ran into the canyon and fell asleep. A green ball of light awoke him and he went running off again until he was too tired.

The next morning the first thing he saw were rocks that were similar to the kind that interested the Padres. He brought back a sample. The Padres were excited over his find, and they wanted to be shown the spot he found the yellowish rocks. After the spot was located, the Padres established a small village in the canyon, built a church, and cast golden bells from the mined minerals. This was the story relating how the Mine With The Iron Door was found. [243]

---

[241] Spain in the West, Vol. 1 by Herbert Bolton. Page 305.

[242] Arizona: A Guide to the Grand Canyon State, compiled by the WPA in Southern Arizona, edited by Joseph Miller, Arizona State Teachers College at Flagstaff, 1940. Pages 296-297.

[243] The Mine With The Iron Door, by Sazon. September 30, 1929. Source for newspaper article unknown. From the Mine and Mineral Resources – Lost Mines – Arizona – Mine With The Iron Door. Arizona Historical Society, Tucson, Arizona.

The Quicksilver Messenger

It is likely the legend about Kino and Escalante originated from the actual events that occurred in 1698. There was a Kino, an Escalante and the search for a mineral– all the elements of the legend.

The confusion with the military commander Escalante and a Father Escalante was possibly due to the story written by John D. Mitchell in 1933 titled "Lost Escalante Mine," [244] and a short article published in the 1940 edition of the WPA Guide. [245] Both stories implicated a 'Father Escalante' who they claimed was an assistant of Father Kino. Since then Escalante has been tied to the legend of The Mine With The Iron Door.

The Spaniards were interested in quicksilver since it was used for the amalgamation of gold. Quicksilver is another name for mercury. Cinnabar is the common ore of mercury, giving a pink, or bright red, color to the rock. In his translation of Kino's journals, Bolton uses "quicksilver," [246] while storytellers inserted "gold" as the sought after mineral. [247] Captain Bernal, who was in charge of the expedition, indicated the mineral was silver. [248]

There are several occurrences of mercury in Southern Arizona, including about nine miles east of Apache Junction in the Superstition Mountains, north of the Catalinas, and the Silverbell Cinnabar Mine about 45 miles north of Oracle. [249] There are an abundance of locations throughout the Santa Catalina Mountains proven to contain gold and silver deposits.

---

[244] Lost Escalante Mine, by John D. Mitchell. From The Lost Mines of the Great Southwest, 1933. Pages 43-45. Mitchell's story is the earliest reference to tie a Father Escalante mine with the discovery of gold in 1698. Also, The Mine with the Iron Door, by Jesse Rascoe, 1969. From Old Arizona Treasures, by Jesse Rascoe, 1969. Pages 107-113; also The Lost Escalante, by Eugene L. Conrotto. From "Lost Gold & Silver Mines of the Southwest, 1963, 1991. Pages 116-118.

[245] Arizona: A Guide to the Grand Canyon State, by the WPA," by Joseph Miller, 1940. Page 296.

[246] Kino's Historical Memoir of Pimería Alta, by Herbert Bolton. Pages 185, 186, 193, 199 and 305.

[247] Lost Escalante Mine, by John D. Mitchell and Arizona: A Guide to the Grand Canyon State, compiled by Workers of the Writer's Program of the WPA," by Joseph Miller, 1940. Page 296.

[248] Materiales para la historia de Sonora, by Miguel Angel Paz Frayre, UNAM, 2007. A compilation of documents of the Archivo General de la Nación in Mexico City. Page 603.

[249] Mercury Potential of the United States, by Bureau of Mines Staff, Chapter 4: Mercury on Arizona, by Robert T. Beckman and William H. Kerns page 60-63 and "East of Apache Junction, Superstition Mtns, Pinal Co., Arizona, USA," from mindat.org mineral directory.

1700: Kino's Mysterious "Blue Shells"

A curiosity of Father Eusebio Kino became a mystery during his lifetime. Some Indians showed Kino unique blue seashells (*las conchas azules*) [250] that seemed to be common among the natives.

Intrigued by this find, Kino spent seven days in conference with Indians from the Papago desert country–the San Pedro valley, Santa Catalina, and as far north as San Andres on the Gila River. The local natives gathered to meet with Kino at San Xavier del Bac Mission on April 25, 1700 to discuss the origin of the mysterious "blue shells" shown to him. [251]

Former Sergeant, now Captain, Juan Bautista de Escalante accompanied Kino's party to this conference.

This meeting was pivotal in Kino's decision to travel to California and establish whether it is an island or part of the mainland. He pondered that the blue shells possessed by the desert natives were not natural to the desert, so there might be some connection. This conclusion caused Kino to drop his plans to go to the Sea of California and make passage overland to California instead. [252]

These particular shells were originally found on the shores of the Pacific Ocean and not the Sea of California (Baja California), as everyone believed.

Excavations at the Romero Ruin near the Cañada del Oro in the 1980s uncovered 21 shell pieces, mainly Laevicardium and Glycymeris fragments. These pieces were found in a spot that could be considered used for manufacturing artifacts. [253]

---

[250] Las Conchas Azules (The Blue Shells): Father, abalones, and the Island of California, by Hans Bertsch. Deartamento de Ingrnieria en Pesquerias Universidad Autonoma de Baja California Sur. 2012. Pafe 189.

[251] The blue shells of the common abalone, Haliotis Linnaeus. The Quest of the Blue Shells, by Ronald L. Ives, Kino Heritage Society.

[252] Spain in the West, Volume III. Kino's Historical Memoir of Pimería Alta, by Herbert Bolton, 1919. Pages 55, 196.

[253] Archaeological Survey in Catalina State Park With A Focus on the Romero Ruin, by Mark D. Elson and William H. Doelle. Institute for American Research, Technical report No. 87-4, 1987. Pages 20, 30.

No suggestion to their origin is offered, but seashells are not common, or native, on the desert floor.

The Laevicardium shell is often called an "egg cockle" because its oval shape is a saltwater clam or cockle [254] and is found along Southern California and down through the Pacific coast of Mexico. [255]

The Glycymeris is also a saltwater clam that was used to make jewelry and traded among the Hohokam Indians. [256]

Three days after the conference, on April 28, 1700, Kino laid the foundation of a large church and house at San Xavier de Bac. [257]

---

[254] A Field Guide to Shells: Atlantic and Gulf Coasts and the West Indies, by R.T. Abbott and P.A. Morris. New York: Houghton Mifflin, 1995. 58-59.

[255] Seashells of Tropical West America, second edition 1971, by Myra Keen. Stanford UP. Page 160.

[256] Ibid.

[257] Kino's Historical Memoir of Pimería Alta, pages 235-237.

1702: Rich Mines Near San Xavier

W hile the missionaries may not have been directly involved in the mining operations, the legends always connected the early Spanish mines with the local missions.

Since the Jesuits were forbidden by their Order to do any mining anywhere in New Spain, they may have only preached to the natives with some supervisory roles. As the only educated people in the region, they may have taught the Indians how to mine. [258]

Father Kino was aware of great riches being mined in the area. Kino was very impressed with the new land and its potential mineral wealth. He mentioned it several times in his journals. In his diary on April 30, 1702, he wrote about mines near his San Xavier mission:

> *"...certain news of the treasure and rich mines which have just been discovered near here at Quisuani, Aygame, San Cosmé, etc., and very near to the new conversion or mission of San Francisco Xavier of the Pimas Cocomacaque of Pimería Baxa."*

> Eusebio Francisco Kino, April 8, 1702. [259]

In one entry, he talked about the closeness of the mines to the missions:

> *"In these new nations and new lands there are many good veins and mineral lands bearing gold and silver; and in the neighborhood and even in sight of these new missions and new conversions some very good mining camps of very rich silver ore are now being established."*

> Eusebio Francisco Kino, February 2, 1710. [260]

---

[258] The Mine With The Iron Door, by Edgar B. Heylmun, Ph.D., Mines and Mineral Resources- lost mines – Arizona – Mine With The Iron Door, Arizona Historical Society, Tucson.

[259] Spain in the West, a series of original documents from foreign archives, volume III; Kino's Historical Memoir of Pimería Alta, 1683-1711, by Herbert Eugene Bolton, Ph.D., published 1919, The Arthur H. Clark Company. Vol. 1, page 362. Signed April 8, 1702.
http://ia700409.us.archive.org/2/items/kinoshistoricalm00kino/kinoshistoricalm00kino.pdf more versions of this document: http://www.archive.org/details/kinoshistoricalm00kino

Mining In The Santa Ritas & Tumacacori

"Without a doubt the first and earliest mining in these regions was done by the Jesuits who founded a chain of missions in the Valley of the Santa Cruz and farther south in Mexico."

Fra. Ortega, "La Historia del Noayarit," about 1754 [261]

This statement– made in 1754– coupled with other reports published in the mid 1850s, forever entangled the Jesuits with early mining activities.

The Salero (Salaro) Mine, in the nearby Santa Rita Mountains west of Tucson, was mainly a copper mine with some gold, silver, and lead, that dates back to Jesuit times. [262] It reportedly was one of several mines "known to have been operated by the friars, and in places vestiges of their workings are found yet today (1916)," reports an early mining journal that unravels a story of early Spanish mining in the New World. [263] Of course, the friars didn't operate the mine, but they may have been on site. The Tyndall District was the "seat of some of the earliest mining of which there is any record on the Pacific Slope of the United States." The area covers forty or more groups of mines. Other mines named were the Alto and the Motosa. According to one report, near the Tumacacori mission south of Tucson, the friars discovered "rich silver mines." [264] That report, issued by the University of Arizona, bases its explanation on "this history of that time, and the records of the mission (Tumacacori)" preserved in Mexico and Spain.

---

[260] Arizona: The Jesuits in Pimería Alta, From American Journeys Collection, Report and Relation of the Near Conversions, by Eusebio Francisco Kino, 1710." Document No. AJ-020. Wisconsin Historical Society, 2003. Page 458.

[261] Ibid. Page 1. The author opens his article basing his statements according to La Historia del Noayarit, and Account of the labors of the Society of Jesus in Sempitronial America, written by Fra. Ortega, about 1754.

[262] "The Salero Mine," USGS Bulletin 582. Arizona Department of Mineral Resources. Tyndall Mining District, Sec. NE ¼ 25, T 21S, R 14E. Lead and silver principle metals. (From E&MJ, Vol. 166, No. 8, August 1965, p. 132).

[263] "Resources of Santa Cruz County," by Allen T. Bird, University of Arizona Bulletin Bureau of Mines 29, September 26, 1916. Page 5. This document details the Tumacacori mines operated by the Jesuits and their subsequent history through the end of the 19th Century.

[264] Ibid. Page 2.

The Military's Nefarious Role

There is some indication in the Spanish military's involvement in the legends of the Catalinas. Almost all of the complicity has been laid on the missionaries since writings seemed to suggest some knowledge of its existence and their records are more publicly available.

The military unit of the Flying Company– the *Compañia Volante*– had the duty to protect the new settlers and the missionaries from hostile Indians. But they had their own controversies that indicated their hands were not so clean.

Testimony by Captain Juan Mateo Manje on January 20, 1704, discussed the use of the "*Compañia Volante* for purposes other than strictly military." Father Kino also heard this testimony. [265] Other complaints about the military's performance in quelling rebellions were filed that year. [266] Juan de Escalante was named in the report among others. He was not necessarily accused. He was a *vecino* (neighbor) of Nacosari at the time and was not in the service, but he had to submit testimony in the investigation. The incidents did not happen specifically in the Santa Cruz Valley; but they occurred throughout Sonora.

Escalante would often correspond with Kino about activities in the Pimería Alta while Kino was away. In one instance, Kino asks for Escalante's assistance to rescue an Indian prisoner who was sentenced to death by soldiers. [267]

Capt. Manje was one of the officers who accompanied Father Kino on nine expeditions through the Pimería Alta and kept his own journals. [268] Manje founded the town of

---

[265] "Captain Juan Mateo Mange. Hablando de la compania Volante," January 20, 1704, 7p. UAiR, University of Arizona. Serial #100-01262.

[266] "Gobernador de Nueva Viscaya Juan Fernandez de Cordova," June 3, 1704. UAiR, University of Arizona. Serial #100-1265.

[267] Memoir of Pimería Alta, Volume I, by Bolton. Page 239-240.

[268] See "Libro Segundo Luz de Tierra hicognita en la America septentrional de todos los viajes de tierras, rios y naciones, by Capt. Juan Matheo Manje. 1693-1701." UAiR, University of Arizona Libraries, Serial Number 040-00312.

Motepori (Motepore), southwest of Arizpe. He was the mayor (*alcalde*) of Sonora from 1701-1703. [269]

Capt. Manje fell out of favor with the missionaries because he was critical of their work in Sonora. In 1707, after he submitted a list of grievances from the settlers to access farmland among the Indians and farmers, the missionaries threatened to leave. This upset the governor of Sonora who ordered Manje's arrest. His estate was impounded, and he was sent to jail. [270] Kino might have had some influence on his release, but Manje was arrested again after he confronted the governor who felt threatened. [271] Kino died in 1711.

An Order from the Viceroy on the abuse in Sonora of Indians by landowners, miners, and government officials was filed in 1716. The Order re-stated the regulations on Indian labor and wages. It also reprimanded local officials for taking matters into their own hands first. [272] Juan de Escalante's name appears in this report, as well.

New missionaries arrived in 1720 and found the churches built by Father Kino in ruins and the farmlands neglected. The Indians now went by the name of Papago (reason unknown by the missionaries). In San Xavier del Bac "the depravation was still greater, their having been twenty years without missionaries." Although funds were granted by 1739 to build two more missions and rebuild the remaining seven missions, it wasn't until after 1749 that they were finally disbursed. [273]

But, the lingering legendary – or historical– reference to a man called Escalante still remains.

---

[269] The Presidio and Militia on the Northern Frontier of New Spain, Part 1, edited by Thomas H. Naylor. University of Arizona Press, 1997. Page 281, footnote 8.

[270] "Juan Fernandez de Cordoba and capitan Francisco Pacheco Zevallos. Administrativo, expediente sobre la prision del capitan don Juan Matteo Manje acusado por los Jesuitas." December 29, 1707. UAiR, University of Arizona. Serial Number 100-01292.

[271] Chapter 12: Manje Writes A Report, 1705. Kino Heritage Society.

[272] "Despacho del virrey a los oficiales de Sonora sobre la tratamiento de los indio," May 16, 1716. Documentation May 16, 1715-September 5, 1715. 66 pages. UAiR, University of Arizona. Serial #100-01380.

[273] A Natural and Civil History of California, 1759. Page 176-177. Original Spanish in "Noticia de la California," 1757. Page 524.

How Did Escalante Get Implicated
With The Iron Door Mine?

**The Legend: Fathers Escalante & Kino worked the mines.
The History: An Escalante did work with Kino.**

"...the fabulous Escalante mine, more popularly known as the Iron Door, at last is believed to have been found."

Prescott Evening Courier, December 5, 1932. [274]

"The Lost Escalante Mine and its great store of gold bars is one of the celebrated traditions of the west."

"Lost Escalante Mine," John D. Mitchell, 1933. [275]

"The supposed site of the Escalante is in an area with a long history of placer gold mining. It is the Cañada del Oro, the pathway of gold between the Santa Catalina and the Tortolita Mountains north of Tucson."

, "Somewhere Out There Arizona," by Kearny Egerton 1974

The Iron Door Mine had been used in the newspapers as early as 1880. However, the link between that mythical mine and the Escalante name didn't become a public record until a reporter made the connection in a 1932 news story about a couple of prospectors who made an amazing discovery and an author who sensationalized the name a year later.

---

[274] "Iron Door Mine Reported Found," *Prescott Evening Courier*, Prescott, Arizona, December 5, 1932.

[275] The Lost Mines of the Great Southwest, by John D. Mitchell. 1933. Page 43.

C.W. McKee, one of prospectors, said an "old Indian" showed him and his brother two mining dumps in December 1932. C.W. thought that it might be the "famous Escalante mine," also called the Iron Door Mine. [276] Even though he said his claim was taken out of context, the discovery of the lost mine quickly brought nationwide attention to the Santa Catalina Mountains.

But, famed treasure hunter and author John D. Mitchell's 1933 story about the "Lost Escalante Mine," claimed that an old Indian guide told *him* the old mine was called the Escalante. [277]

Both McKee and Mitchell's story involved similar circumstances within a few months apart. McKee never said where he heard about the Escalante name, but he made the first connection of Escalante to the Iron Door Mine name.

Even though the Escalante legend may have been much older, it took these two statements to make a public connection. This is where history becomes muddled with more legendary tales and historical anachronisms.

---

[276] "Iron Door Mine Reportedly Found," from Prescott Evening Courier, December 5, 1932. Page 2. "...convinced McKee he was near an abandoned mine, probably the famous Escalante."

[277] "Lost Escalante Mine," from Lost Mines of the Great South West, including stories of hidden treasures, by John D. Mitchell, 1933. Page 43. Mitchell claims an old Indian named Calistro told him about the "famous Escalante Mine worked by the Spanish in the sixteenth century."

The Lost Escalante Man

This new interpretation of the folklore brought another element to the lost Spanish mine legend. Now, the name 'Escalante' is injected into the legend. [278] While the name may have been associated with the mine earlier, it wasn't until it made print that it became common knowledge.

Mitchell said it was "Padre Escalante who first worked the mine." This padre was an assistant to Padre Kino, asserts Mitchell. He would travel throughout the Pimería Alta to "investigate the mines and collect the church's share of the gold and silver." [279]

Mitchell credits Calistro, an old Opata Indian who lived near the Tumacacori ruins, for the old mine stories. The Indian said his grandfather knew many stories about rich Spanish mines in the Catalinas. One evening he sat down near a pool of water by the Cañada del Oro, and his grandfather "pointed up to the Santa Catalina Mountain and said the Escalante gold mine is located in that mountain." [280]

This was the second time a name was given to the person who supposedly managed this clandestine mine.

The first mention of Escalante and the mine was published several months before Mitchell's book. In the December 1932 news article, C.W. McKee described the "fabulous Escalante Mine, more popularly known as the Iron Door..." [281] But it was Mitchell's version of the legend, and implication of Escalante, that became the template for all successive interpretations of the lost mine legend.

---

[278] "Lost Escalante Mine," from The Lost Mines of the Great Southwest, by John D. Mitchell. 1933. Pages 43-45.

[279] Ibid.

[280] Ibid. It's not clear if the Indian actually used the name Escalante or Mitchell inserted the name himself.

[281] "Iron Door Mine Reported Found," Prescott Evening Courier, Prescott, Arizona. December 5, 1932. Page 2.

Mitchell's story was again published with more details in a 1952 edition of *Desert Magazine*. [282] In this article Mitchell made the link between the Mine with the Iron Door (the Escalante mine) and the ruins at the "south bank of the Cañada del Oro" where an old camp and foundations of a chapel stand. He gave a first name to Father Silvestre Velez de Escalante, the Jesuit priest who was Kino's assistant. The mine, he said, operated until 1767 when Spanish King Charles III expelled the Jesuits from Spain and the new lands. It was again destroyed on San Juan's Day in June 1769 by an Apache attack.

Juan Bautista de Escalante did accompany Kino on several trips around the Santa Catalina Mountains. However, this Escalante was not in the clergy; he was a military man. Mitchell erroneously named Silvestre de Escalante who lived decades after Kino died.

In 1956 Historian Donald Page repeated much of Mitchell's rendition about the LOST JESUIT MINE WITH THE IRON DOOR. His version didn't name Escalante, but he told a similar story. Page also described the location of the mine and mission at the Cañada de Oro. [283]

Father Escalante's mine was again a topic in Jesse Rascoe's story in OLD ARIZONA TREASURES. His story virtually repeated Mitchell and Page with all of the pieces– Father Escalante, the mission, and the Canyon of Gold. [284]

"A certain" Padre Juan Bautista Escalante was named as the assistant to Kino who was responsible to find mineral wealth throughout New Spain, suggests one writer in 1992 in an article about the Iron Door Mine. His job was to increase the wealth of the Catholic Church by locating mines in the Pimería Alta. [285]

According to geologist Edgar B. Heylmun in his "Mine With the Iron Door" paper, [286] the Escalante Mine may have been named after Father Silvestre de Escalante sometime between 1750 and 1767 when the Jesuits were expelled. Heylmun believed that the Mine

---

[282] Lost Mine with the Iron Door, by John D. Mitchell. Desert Magazine, July 1952. Page 25.

[283] Lost Jesuit Mine with the Iron Door, by Donald Page. Desert Magazine, October 1956. Page 11.

[284] "The Mine With the Iron Door," from Old Arizona Treasures, by Jesse Rascoe, 1969. Pages 107-113.

[285] Chasing A Legend, by Philip Varney, Arizona Highways, October 1992. Page 16. ("With the Iron Door holds that an assistant to Padre Eusebio Kino, a certain Padre Juan Bautista Escalante, came to the mission San Xavier del Bac in the early 18th century.")

[286] Mine with the Iron Door, by Edgar B. Heylmun, Ph.D. Page 3. Arizona Historical Society: Mines and Mineral Resources- Lost Mines- Arizona – Mine with the Iron Door.

with the Iron Door could have been the Escalante Mine and may have been hidden by debris from the 1887 earthquake. Although his storyline follows the general legend, the Escalante he cites– Silvestre– was not in Tucson at that time and was not even alive during Kino's lifetime. Also, Kino was a Jesuit whereas Silvestre was a Franciscan. [287]

Even though Heylmun made this error, he has been extensively cited in numerous geological reports and his views on colonial Spanish mining in the Santa Catalinas is widely accepted in journals. [288]

In Heylmun's GUIDE TO THE SANTA CATALINA MOUNTAINS OF ARIZONA, published in 1979, he told the story of The Mine With the Iron Door and the La Esmeralda silver mine that were both developed by the Spaniards somewhere in the Catalinas. He suggested that Kino named the Santa Catalina Mountains after his sister, Catarina. [289]

In LOST GOLD AND SILVER MINES OF THE SOUTHWEST, Eugene L. Conrotto also connects the Lost Escalante Mine with the Iron Door Mine. His 1992 rendition tells about the Papago Indians who helped the Jesuits work the Escalante Mine in the Santa Catalina Mountains prior to their expulsion in 1767. [290] It is an identical story to Mitchell's early account.

These 20th Century published accounts are the foundation for the Kino-Escalante and Iron Door Mine connections. But, they name the wrong Escalante. Another person misplaced in an historical anachronism. If the lost mine in the Santa Catalinas was named after someone called Escalante, which Escalante was it?

---

[287] Jesuit Father Eusebio Kino died on March 15, 1711. Franciscan Friar Silvestre Vélez de Escalante was born in 1750.

[288] Mineral Appraisal of Coronado National Forest, Part 5, Santa Catalina-Rincon Mountains Unit. Mineral Land Assessment 1994. MLA-25-94. Pages, 12, 13, 16, 19, 24, 25, A41, A49; also "Santa Catalina Mountains, Arizona. California Mining Journal, vol. 69, No. 1, Pages 11-15; and "Mine with the Iron Door," by Edgar B. Heylmun, Ph.D. Page 3. Arizona Historical Society. Heylmun authored "Guide to the Santa Catalina Mountains of Arizona," 1979.

[289] Guide to the Santa Catalina Mountains of Arizona, by Edgar Heylmun, 1979. Page 4.

[290] Lost Gold and Silver Mines of the Southwest, by Eugene L. Conrotto

121

Mucho Escalantes: Who Owned The Lost Mine?

T he Escalante family name has been prominent in early Spanish and Sonoran history for centuries. The name also has been associated with the legend of the Lost Iron Door Mine– also called The Lost Escalante Mine.

From the 1690s through the mid-1800s Escalante men played roles in military and government in Sonora, which encompassed the Santa Catalina Mountains. The only one who served with Kino, and was alive during Kino's lifetime, was Juan Bautista de Escalante.

A generation later, a second Escalante– Francisco Xavier de Escalante– also served in the Sonoran military Flying Company mobile unit. Since 1751 this Escalante had spent over 30 years scouting the new land and had an interest in the Santa Catalina Mission.

The third Escalante, Silvestre Velez de Escalante, is often mistakenly referred to as Kino's assistant. He lived several generations after Kino died and had either a connection with mining nor a presence in the Santa Cruz Valley. His plan was to explore New Mexico and Colorado as part of the Dominguez-Escalante Expedition. Fray Silvestre was a Franciscan– not a Jesuit, He did not pass through Arizona until 1776-1777 and never went near San Xavier del Bac (even though his counterpart Fray Francisco Garces of San Xavier del Bac was also summoned for this journey). [291] Silvestre Escalante's trip was over sixty five years after Kino died, [292] and ten years after the King of Spain expelled the Jesuits from the new land in 1767. [293] Silvestre's name, however, continues to be erroneously used– another historic anachronism– out of historic sequence.

A closer look at these Escalante men who may have been connected with the Santa Catalina Mission might provide a clue as to who garnished the long, lost mine with the Escalante moniker.

---

[291] The Way of the Fray: A Pictorial Diary of the Escalante Expedition Through North Central New Mexico, 1776, by H. L. James, New Mexico State Highway Department, Santa Fe, New Mexico, 1974.

[292] Eusebio Kino died March 15, 1711 in Magdelena, Pimería Alta, New Spain. Source; Wikipedia, Eusebio Kino.

[293] January 29, 1767, the expulsion of the Society of Jesus.

1680s: Capt. Juan Bautista de Escalante, The Military Man

istory records that a Juan (Bauptisa) Baustita de Escalante [294] actually spent time with Father Eusebio Kino. He was a decorated military commander, not a Jesuit priest. While he was in the Spanish Army in 1700, Escalante founded the city of Hermosillo, Mexico. [295]

Juan Bautista is the only recorded Escalante who was alive during Father Kino's lifetime. This Escalante may have been the founder of the prominent Escalante family who lived in the northern frontier of Sonora from the 17th through the 19th Centuries. [296]

He worked closely with the missionaries to provide protection as the Spanish forged their way northward along the El Camino Real– the Royal Road– from Mexico, to Arizona, and eventually to California. He was a Teniente de Fronteras (Lieutenant of the Border) – [297] the roaming soldiers of the Compañia Volante (Flying Company) who would often accompany missionaries and settlers for protection from the Indians throughout the Pimería Alta. [298] The Flying Company was a mobile, on the go, contingency that roamed the Sonoran frontier for decades. Escalante served as commander for many years. [299]

---

[294] Mission 2000 Database, Record #25967. Tumacacori National Park.

[295] Hermosillo: About the Municipality, by Hands Across the Border Foundation. Hermosillo was named by its founder, lieutenant Juan Bautista de Escalante.

[296] Ibid.

[297] Mission 2000 Database, Record #25967. Tumacacori National Park. His residence is given as Nacosari and title as Teniente de Fronteras. Event date 4/17/1728.

[298] From Kino's notes from October 23, 1704, "Chapter VIII: A Letter from Captain Juan Bautista de Escalante," Spain in the West, Volume 4, Kino's Historical Memoir of Pimería Alta, by Herbert Bolton. Pages 108-109.

[299] Empire of Sand: The Seri Indians and the Struggle for Spanish Sonora, 1645-1803, edited by Thomas E. Sheridan. University of Arizona Press, 1999. Page 58. This book also contains the "Diary of Alférez Juan Bautista de Escalante." Pages 36-96.

Juan Bautista de Escalante escorted Father Kino and a group in 1697 around the Catalinas along the San Pedro River to the east of the Santa Catalina Mountains [300] and was in contact with Kino from January through May 1700, according to correspondences preserved from Father Kino. [301]

Escalante, along with Capt Diego Carrasco, also accompanied Kino on that journey around the Catalinas on November 5, 1698, expedition. Escalante led Kino and ten of his servants with a military escort of twenty soldiers of the Compañia Volante ("Flying Company") with explicit instructions to find the minerals reported "among the Sobaipuris." [302 303 304] It is this historic journey that links Kino and Escalante to the legend. It also ties them both to the lost Santa Catalina mission when it was located near Picacho Peak.

Escalante had interests in the area long before his trip with Kino. A letter written by Juan Bautista on May 11, 1689, to Generale Blas de Castillo, concerned the state of the Sonoran frontier, including the depopulation, illnesses among the remaining inhabitants, and the mines that are being abandoned because of Indian ambushes. [305] Castillo then wrote gobernador Juan Isidro de Pardinas Villar de Francos a letter concerning the *vecinos* ("neighbors") who were unable to work the mines and the fact that the province is falling into ruins like New Mexico. [306] Although there are no records of Capt. Juan de Escalante being involved with any mining ventures, he would have had knowledge of any mining activities in Sonora, the Pimería Alta.

---

[300] "Diary of Alférez Juan Bautista de Escalante, 1700," from Empire of Sand: The Seri Indians and the Struggle for the Spanish Sonora, 1645-1803, Thomas E. Sheridan, 1999. Page 36.

[301] Spain in the West, a Series of Original Documents from Foreign Archives Volume III, Page 109. Kino's Historical Memoir of Pimería Alta, A Contemporary Account of the Beginnings of California. Herbert Eugene Bolton, Ph.D., (1919)
http://ia600409.us.archive.org/2/items/kinoshistoricalm00kino/kinoshistoricalm00kino.pdf

[302] Kino's Historical Memoir of Pimería Alta, Vol. 1, p. 186. By Herbert Eugene Bolton, Ph.D.

[303] Antigua California: Mission and Colony on the Peninsular Frontier, 1697-1768, By Harry Crosby. Page 440. Notes to Pages 53-55. University of New Mexico Press, 1994.

[304] The Papago County, Arizona by Kirk Bryan Dept of Interior, 1925. Page 9.
http://pubs.usgs.gov/wsp/0499/report.pdf

[305] "Juan de Escalante to gen. Blas de Castillo letter concerning state Sonoran Frontier," Serial Number 041000751. University of Arizona Libraries, Institutional Repository, UAiR.

[306] "Blas de Castillo to gobernador Juan Isidro de Pardinas Villar de Francos letter concerning said state Sonoran frontier," Serial Number: 041-00754, June 12, 1689. University of Arizona Libraries, Institutional Repository, UAiR.

Juan Bautista de Escalante helped Kino route out rebellious Apaches who threatened the missions and settlers, according to Kino's letters and historical documents. Capt. Escalante often would capture Indians and turn them over to the priests or keep them as prisoners. [307]

In one instance, he helped Kino rescue an Indian prisoner from death. In his journal, Kino included a 1701 letter from Escalante about his attack against the Apaches:

> *"I went on the campaign which our beloved and loving Pimas made against the enemies of our holy faith, in which it has gone very well with us; for our friends, three hundred and thirty-two in number, set out with only the provisions which they could carry in their bags...after having marched some days we attacked a rancheria of Apaches, where seventeen of the enemy were killed.*
>
> *We captured sixteen persons, of whom the Pimas are taking twelve and have sold us four, because I told them that whatever was captured should belong to the captor, in order to rouse in them a stronger desire to display valor. And such was the case, for they, being many, captured fourteen, and we two."* [308]

Kino took advantage of that victory to appeal for ten or twelve new missionaries. This was the "purpose for which the Breve Relación was written." [309]

On January 20, 1704, however, Escalante was mentioned in a testimonial regarding the "use of the Compañia Volante for purposes other than strictly military." The charges

---

[307] "Juan Baptista de Escalante. Operations in the war, which is being waged against the rebellious Indians, January 29, 1700." 49p. Describes field notes of a military expedition taken in response to conflict between Seris and Tepocas. Good ethnographic info- battle techniques, poisoned arrows, reed boats, some population and baptismal statistics. Much documentation of conflicts between the Seris and Tepocas. Accounts of Spanish executions of murderers. Also, unsuccessful efforts to reduce Salineros. (folder also contains certifications by Bartiromo and Linse, as well as another set of field notes by Escalante dated 4/20/1700. Persons: Escalante, Juan Baptista de (Alferez), Kino, Eusebio Francisco (S.J.). http://uair.arizona.edu/item/219295

[308] Kino's Historical Memoir of Pimería Alta, page 295.

[309] Presidio of Corodeguachi, p. 183, April 13, 1701. Juan Bautista de Escalante kisses the hand of your Reverence." Spain in the West a Series of Original Documents from Foreign Archives Volume III. Page 176-177. Kino's Historical Memoir of Pimería Alta, A Contemporary Account of the Beginnings of California. Herbert Eugene Bolton, Ph.D., (1919) http://ia600409.us.archive.org/2/items/kinoshistoricalm00kino/kinoshistoricalm00kino.pdf

weren't specified. [310] Escalante went on to California to become Captain of the Presidio of Loredo in 1704, [311] but was removed a year later by Father Juan Maria Salvatierra for mismanagement and misconduct. He may have been a victim of someone else's power struggle within the Jesuit order. [312]

Through 1712, Juan Bautista de Escalante's name occasionally appears as padrino ("godfather") in baptismal records of the Baja missions. [313] After he retired in 1722 he served as teniente alcalde, or Mayor, of the mining town Motepori, south of Arizpe, where he retired. [314 315] While Mayor, he would reportedly take long absences and could be found in the mining town of Nacosari. [316]

This Captain Escalante is most likely the Escalante named as Kino's "assistant." But he was too busy chasing after Seri and Apache Indians and traveling to different posts to operate a clandestine mine in the Santa Catalina's at the same time. His friendliness to the missionaries could have confused legend spinners to label him as a Padre since he did accompany Kino on assignments that included the search for a mineral deposit.

There isn't any documentation connecting this Escalante with the Lost Escalante mine, but he would have known about any mining in the Santa Catalina Mountains. He may, however, have become the namesake for that mineral discovery in 1698.

Throughout Sonoran history, there were several other Escalantes who were also connected in some way to the Santa Catalinas and the mission. Any of them could have been aware of clandestine operations in the Catalinas.

---

[310] "Captain Juan Mateo Manje, Hablando de la Companu Volante," Serial Number: 100-01262. University of Arizona Libraries, Institutional Repository, UAiR.

[311] Las Mision Jesuita Su Arquitectura u Urbanismo, en American Española http://www.slideshare.net/utpl/arquitectura-y-urbanismo/v 1

[312] "Diary of Alférez Juan Bautista de Escalante, 1700," from Empire of Sand: The Seri Indians and the Struggle for the Spanish Sonora, 1645-1803, Thomas E. Sheridan, 1999. Page 36.

[313] Ibid, and Mission 2000 Database.

[314] "Escalante, Juan Bautista de," BID Number 19764. University of Arizona Institutional Repository, UAiR.

[315] "Diary of Alférez Juan Bautista de Escalante, 1700," from Empire of Sand, edited by Thomas E. Sheridan. Page 36.

[316] Ibid.

1752: Francisco Xavier de Escalante

Fifty years after Juan Bautista de Escalante left Father Kino's side, another Escalante was placed in history where reported Spanish mines operated. This Escalante was a soldier in the frontera of Sonora like Juan Bautista de Escalante was before him.

From 1720 [317] Francisco Xavier de Escalante [318] traversed the northern Piman frontier as a member of the Spanish military. He made numerous trips to the towns and rancherias of northern Pimería and knew the land well.

When Father Ignacio Keller traveled to baptize the local Indians, this Escalante may have accompanied him.

Francisco Escalante had also witnessed and reported on the Pima revolt of November 21, 1751. In one incident after the uprising in December, 1751, a trial was held for one of the Indian prisoners Pedro de la Cruz, who was accused of knowing– or being involved– in the uprising. He maintained his innocence. Lt. Escalante spoke in favor of "La Chihuahua," as Pedro was called. Escalante had seen Pedro around for many years and didn't feel he should die regardless of his involvement. Escalante later wrote that Pedro was executed "without first having received a superior order." [319] [320] Pedro, who was Luis of Saric's cousin, was involved in a confrontation with the padres in September when he was admonished for carrying a baton of the Pima nation, granted by the Governor without the Padres' knowledge. [321]

---

[317] Tubac Through Four Centuries: A Historical Resume and Analysis, by Henry F. Dobyns, Chapter VI. http://parentseyes.arizona.edu/tubac/cpt6-C.htm

[318] Mission 2000, Personal ID #4873. Francisco Xavier de Escalante, "Teniente, Viudo de Margarita Granilla; Mario de Maria Loreta Calderon."

[319] Ibid. Escalante was "involved in the apprehension and arrest of Pedro Chiguagua after the Pima uprising of 1751." See statement below about what Escalante had to say in the matter.

[320] From Pedro de la Cruz, alias "Chihuahua, Tumacacori National Historical Park: "Pedro de la Cruz was shot and his execution caused internal strife because it appeared that they should not have proceeded without first having received a superior order. Francisco Xavier de Escalante, San Miguel de Horcasitas, April 2, 1752." (AGI, Guadalajara 419, 3m-56, page 3.

[321] Ignacio Xavier Keller, Tumacacori National Historical Park. http://www.nps.gov/tuma/historyculture/ignacio-xavier-keller.htm

As part of a plan to refortify the Pima lands, in 1752 Lt. Francisco Xavier de Escalante of the Fronteras garrison and Father Sedelmayr advocated building two forts. One Spanish fort would be four or five leagues [322] north of San Francisco Xavier del Bac Mission at Tucson, or at Santa Catalina. [323]

At the time of the expulsion of the Jesuits, on October 1, 1767, Francisco X. Escalante was among 51 men listed as "Hermanos coadjutores que se han secularizado" (co-adjutor brothers who have secularized) in a report on the expulsion of the Jesuits and the dissolution of the Company of Jesus. [324] The connection of an Escalante being a Jesuit brother, may have contributed to the legend of a priest named Escalante. Jesuit "brothers," or "coadjutors," would work almost exclusively in the Jesuit community providing support services– as cooks, secretaries, etc. This group of brothers would perform the more "worldly jobs." [325]

As a Spanish military officer who roamed the frontier, Francisco X. Escalante would also have had knowledge of any mining activities conducted in the Santa Catalina Mountains. While there were reports of mineral discoveries in the region as early as 1702 [326] and 1736, [327] there is no documentation that associates this particular Escalante with the Escalante Mine.

In some versions of the legend of the Escalante Mine, another Escalante, Silvestre, is specifically named– but his participation is extremely dubious.

---

[322] Four to five leagues are between thirteen and seventeen miles.

[323] Tubac Through Four Centuries: A Historical Resume and Analysis, by Henry F. Dobyns, Chapter IV. It is not specified if he meant the visita or Santa Catalina Mountains.

[324] De la explusion de los jesuitas a la extinction de la Compañia de Jesus, Parte I: 1766-1770," by José A. Ferrer Benimeli. Page 195.

[325] "Jesuit Formation," wikipedia.

[326] Spain in the West, volume III,; Kino's Historical Memoir of Pimería Alta, Kino, 1683-1711. By Herbert Eugene Bolton, Ph.D., published 1919, The Arthur H. Clark Company. Vol. 1, page 364. http://ia700409.us.archive.org/2/items/kinoshistoricalm00kino/kinoshistoricalm00kino.pdf more versions of this document: http://www.archive.org/details/kinoshistoricalm00kino

[327] Pimería Alta After Kino's Time, by George Hammond 1929: 237-238 and Tubac through Four Centuries, by Henry Dobyns.

1776: Fray Silvestre de Escalante, The Franciscan

Fray Silvestre Vélez de Escalante, arrived on the scene decades after Capt. Juan de Escalante and Father Kino had died and after Francisco Xavier de Escalante had finished his commission.

Some legend-tellers have erroneously attributed this Escalante, Silvestre, as Kino's assistant.

The most well known version, first told by John D. Mitchell, says the Escalante mine was worked for many years by Father Silvestre Velez de Escalante. He called him a Jesuit priest and an assistant to Father Eusebio Kino at Mission San Xavier del Bac near Tucson. Mitchell said church records report the mine was operating in 1767 when the edict was issued to expel the Jesuits. [328]

Silvestre Velez de Escalante could not have been the Father Escalante named in the legends. He lived years after the Jesuits left San Xavier del Bac mission in 1767 and decades after Kino died in 1711. Father Silvestre Vélez de Escalante was not a Jesuit priest. He was a Franciscan missionary and explorer who helped lead a famous expedition throughout the West in 1776. [329]

Frey Silvestre Escalante may have passed through northern Arizona in 1776, but there are no records of his visit to the Tucson area or his involvement in any mining activities. Frey Francisco Garces, the Franciscan missionary at San Xavier del Bac at the time, was invited to join Escalante a year earlier to explore the West and prepare a report for a possible road to California. He never made the connection with Escalante who traveled north while Garces went west. [330]

[328] Lost Mines of the Great Southwest, Including Stories of Hidden Treasures, by John D. Mitchell; first published 1933; and "Lost Mine With the Iron Door," in Desert Magazine, July 1952.

[329] The Way of the Fray: A Pictorial Diary of the Escalante Expedition Through North-Central New Mexico 1776, by H. L. James, New Mexico State Highway Department, Santa Fe, New Mexico. New Mexico Geological Society Guidebook, 1974.

[330] Ibid. Page 1.

Mitchell might have mistakenly assumed that a 1778 letter written by Father Silvestre Velez de Escalante was the Escalante who was named by his Indian friend. That letter was in a collection of documents about Kino's 1698 expedition used by earlier historians.

These papers may have set the stage for the legends to come. The letter from Silvestre de Escalante found within the collection, however, may have wrongly implicated this Escalante in the legend.

Silvestre de Escalante may have been connected to the Escalante legend only because of the association of his last name and Mitchell's confusion with historic dates to create another historical anachronism.

If John Mitchell used that letter to give a first name to an Escalante co-conspirator, he was off by almost 100 years. The Escalante in Mitchell's version might have been one of the earlier military men who were actually familiar with the region. Mitchell's error could be just mistaken identity by name association.

Still, another prominent Escalante had some association with the region after the Spanish were shoo'ed out of Mexico.

1829: Manuel Escalante & The Missions

Manuel Escalante y Arvizu had a vested interest in the missions of all Pimería Alta when the Mexican government took control over the land.

Two years after the Spanish were expelled in 1827, a federal decree banned all priests who came from Spain. Jefe Politico Escalante y Arvisu became the Mexican commander of the Arizpe district, including Tucson. He visited all of the missions in the former Spanish territory. The missions were to be turned over to civil commissioners. He was shocked at the condition. Some of the authorities were accused of plundering the missions. The properties were so disintegrated and there wasn't enough money to cover the pay for even one civil position. The lack of money in the military also decimated what was left of the local economy. The Indians, who depended on the Franciscans and their missions, were not being fed, clothed, and housed. Escalante y Arvisu advocated the return of the missions back to the Franciscans. He was also ordered to confiscate thousands of pesos from people who owed debt to the missions. [331] [332] [333]

If that weren't enough, Apache aggressions made matters worse. Much of the population had abandoned Tucson in late 1828. Mexico separated the church from the state, and the missions lost their main funding. [334]

The Franciscans were allowed to return to the missions in 1830. Escalante y Arvizu became acting governor of the Mexican state of Sonora in 1831. [335] The Sonoran territory remained under control of Mexico until the land was sold to the United States as part of the Gadsden Purchase in 1854. [336]

---

[331] Friars, Soldiers and Reformers, Hispanic Arizona and Sonora Mission Frontier, by John L. Kessell. University of Arizona. Chapter 11, 1828-56. National Park Service.

[332] A letter written by Escalante on January 13, 1830 from A Frontier Documentary: Sonora and Tucson, 1821-1848, by Kieran McCarty. University of Arizona Press, 1997. Chapter 8. Page 19-21. There were "missions at Tumacacori, San Xavier del Bac and Tucson's Pueblito." Later, it is explained that the satellite mission is ten miles north. There are two other villages nearby Santa Ana and Santa Rosa.

[333] On the Bloody Road to Jesus: Christianity and the Chiricahua Apaches, by H. Henrietta Sockel. UNM Press, 2004. Page 97.

[334] Tucson: Portrait of a Desert Pueblo, by John Bret Harte, Windsor Publications, 1980. Pages 20-25.

[335] Ibid.

[336] Gadsden Purchase, 1853-1854. Office of the Historian, U.S. Department of State.

Escalante y Arvisu could also possibly have some knowledge of mining activities, if it existed. But, he was busy with military and governmental duties. His arrival on the scene is also more than 100 years after the first Escalante, Juan Bautista.

To add to the Escalante surname confusion, there were even more Escalantes who served as Governors of Sonora over the years. [337]

> Leonardo Escalante y Mazon (1760-1844), gobernador de Sonora
> Tomas Escalante y Mazon (1764-1848), gobernador de Sonora
> José Escalante y Noreno (1809-1870), gobernador de Sonora
> Manuel Escalante y Arvizu (b. 1794 born), gobernador de Sonora

There was also several Escalante's who served as bishop (Obispo) in Sonora:
> Juan Francisco de Escalante, obispo (1782-1792) [338]
> José Antonio Subirá y Escalante, (23rd Bishop)
> vigésimo tercer obispo, (1791-1862) [339]

Pasquel Escalante had been a Presidio soldier in 1778 and his several children carried the Escalante surname, [340] including the aforementioned Governor Manuel Escalante. [341]

---

[337] "Arizpe," Encyclopedia de los Municipios y Deligaciones de Mexico, Estado de Sonora.

[338] Ibid. From Mission 2000: "Citizen Bachiller Juan Francisco de Escalante, Interim Priest Supli" in the Holy Church Parochial Pitic, May 16, 1826. Pitic (Petic) is near Hermosillo, founded by Juan de Escalante in 1700.

[339] Ibid. Arizpe, Sonora.

[340] Pioneer Families of the Presidio San Augustin Tucson. Page 94; and Friars, Soldiers and Reformers, by John Kessell, chapter 11.

[341] Ibid, page 118.

Naming The Lost Escalante

So, which Escalante accompanied Kino in a search for minerals and operated a clandestine mine in the Catalinas, later called the Escalante Mine?

Even though Juan Bautista de Escalante was busy chasing after Indians, he is most likely the one linked to the legend since he was in that 1698 entourage that sought after reported minerals in the mountains. That has all of the elements of the legends.

But, who spent more than three decades on the open frontier and must have known the area even better? That would have been Francisco Xavier– more than a decade later.

Although Juan Bautista de Escalante can be credited with participating in the discovery of minerals with Kino, his predecessor, Francisco Xavier de Escalante had more idle time on his hands and spent decades roaming the frontier.

History won't tell which Escalante for whom the lost mine was actually named. Most likely any of the Escalante's who had knowledge of mining operations conducted in the Santa Catalinas during the 1700s could have been involved, or at least aware of any activities.

No other records are readily available, nor other legends known how the Escalante mine was named other than the stories told here. Perhaps the storytellers were partially right.

The legends and history only confound the search for what really had happened to a mine called the Escalante.

The Lost Mission
Of Santa Catalina

The Legend: There is a lost mission in the Santa Catalinas.

The History: There was a mission called Santa Catalina.
It may have been in the Santa Catalinas at one time.

The legend of the lost mission is another one of the mysteries hidden in the backdrop of the lost mine legends. This mission has a lot of history and legend of its own.

While some ruins and early mining activities are found in the Santa Catalina Mountains, proving this mission's existence is more elusive. However, numerous records from the 1700s document its existence.

A Jesuit mission in the Santa Catalinas is one of the main threads in the legends of the Catalinas.

The Lost Mission of the Santa Catalinas legend is rooted in some truth. Historically there was a missionary outpost named Santa Catalina (or Santa Catarina). [342] It existed for nearly seventy years and then disappeared.

During his first expedition in 1697 into the northern reaches of Pimería Alta, Father Kino named one Indian village as Santa Catalina del Cuytoabagum. [343]

---

[342] There are several spellings used in handwritten manuscripts, journals, reports and maps: Catalina, Catarina, Catharina and Catherine. (Editors note: Depending on the author cited, either spelling is used. The default choice is the current spelling of Catalina.)

[343] Guide to Catholic-Related Records in the West about Native Americans, Marquette University. 2006. States that Santa Catarina operated from 1699-1767 (closed). Santa Catarina del Cuytoabagum Visita (Pima) [Rio Santa Cruz] http://www.marquette.edu/library/archives/NativeGuide/AZ/W-113.pdf

In the late 1690s, the Jesuits established at least four missions and *visitas* [344] in the Santa Cruz Valley: [345] [346]

1692-present	San Xavier del Bac - Mission [347]
1692- before 1767	San Cosmé de Tucson - *Visita*
before 1767-1850s	San Agustin de Tucson – Mission
1699- before 1767	Santa Catarina del Cuytoabagum– *Visita* [348]

In Father Kino's 1699 account of an exploration into Pimería Alta he took with the Spanish military, he wrote the name of the nearby missionary outpost as "*Santa Catalina*"– using an *l* instead of *r*. [349] Different authors use with the *l* or the *r* in their manuscripts. Their use is preserved in each of their accounts.

The original location of Santa Catalina was at least thirty miles west of the Santa Catalina Mountains, near Picacho Peak, and about forty five miles northwest of the San Xavier del Bac Mission.

One translation says "La Mision de Santa Catarina, sobre el Santa Cruz" was a rancheria of Santa Catarina de Cuituabagu and its fields at Akohin. [350] Cuituabagu means the "well

---

[344] A *visita* is a village where the missionaries would visit to conduct baptisms and other services.

[345] This list is from "Guide to Catholic-Related Records outside the U.S. about Native Americans," Marquette University, 2006. Archdiocese of Durango, Mexico. "The Jesuits established their missions Nueva España (also known as the Mexicana Province) in Mexico in 1571 and were expelled in 1767. Their province established and administered the following missions in the United States."

[346] Mission Architecture as Exemplified in San Xavier del Bac, including a complete list of the Missions in the Southwest, 1919, By Prent Duell, A.M., published by the Arizona Archaeological and Historical Society, Tucson, Arizona. Page 129. Santa Catarina is opposite Picacho Peak.

[347] "San Xavier del Bac- belonged to the Rectorate of Nuestra Soñora de los Delores and was the cabeccera of the visitas of San Cosmé de Tucson and Santa Catarina del Cuytoabagum," from Empire of Sand: The Seri Indians and the Struggle for Spanish Sonora, 1645-1803, edited by Thomas E. Sheridan. Page 153.

[348] "Guide to Catholic-Related Records in the West about Native Americans," Marquette University. 2006.

[349] Kino writes: "Sa Catalina," from Kino's Report on Exploration, 1699, page. 7. Holographic copies at the University of Arizona Libraries Digital Collection. Online example of handwritten notes: http://universityofarizona.worldcat.org.ezproxy2.library.arizona.edu/title/report-of-an-exploration-written-at-mission-dolores-Pimería-alta-1699/oclc/31688441&referer=brief_results

[350] "Commentary by Father Bonaventure Oblasser," on article in Arizona and the West, Vol. II, No. 2, Summer 1960 entitled: "The Unlucky Jesuit Mission of Bac," by J. Augustine Donohue, S.J. Note (9)

where people gather mesquite beans." [351] The village was also called Cuitoakbagum (Kuitoakbagum), [352] Coytoabagum, [353] and Cutcia vaaki, [354] depending on the author and time period. [355]

The San Xavier del Bac, south of Tucson, is the only mission that remains standing and active. The location of San Cosmé and San Agustin [356] are documented near downtown Tucson, but the placement of the Santa Catalina has been reported in several areas. At one time, it may have been located along the Cañada del Oro, according to early Spanish documents.

Although the Santa Catalina mission faded from history, it may have played a part in the legends of the Santa Catalina Mountains. Whether this was the long, lost mission of the legend it is not fully authenticated. However, the similarity in name– and proximity– is worth consideration.

The following is the first full account of the forgotten Spanish Mission of Santa Catalina.

From a collection of notes and manuscripts of Frank Pinkley, Kino Pimería Alta Missions, Tumacacori National Park, United States Department of the Interior. Page 343. This author uses the spelling of Catarina in some spots and Catalina in others. Akohin is also called Actun, Agtun and Aquituni by different authors.

[351] Tucson: The Life and Times of an American City, by C.L. Sonnichsen, page 11-12.

[352] Spelling used in Spanish Colonial Tucson, Continued Jesuit Proselytizing, 1756-1767, Southwest Library, University of Arizona. Page 18. http://southwest.library.arizona.edu/spct/body.1_div.3.html

[353] Carrasco used Coytoabagum. The Pima name used by Manje was Cuitaubagu. The Franciscan name was Aktciny, from Hispanic Acculturation of the Gila River Pimas, American Anthropological Association, Vol. 63, No. 5, Part 2, October 1961, Memoir 90). Page 334.

[354] "Another cluster of mounds in the neighborhood of Picacho," from "Aquituno Ruin (Akutchiny)," Smithsonian Miscellaneous Collections, 1910. Vol. 52. Pages 418-419.

[355] Santa Catarina de Caytuabaga (1699, Mange 92); Santa Catarina del Cuytoabagum (1699, 15 leagues from San Cosmé de Tucson; Kino, in Bolton 1948, 1:206); Santa Catarina de Cuituabagu (1774, village of 200 in 40 houses SE of the Picacho, near the Oiuar mentioned by Anza, in Bolton 1960, 376). "Place Names of Southern Arizona and Northern Sonora," by Alan H. Hartley, Logotheras.

[356] "San Agustin: The Original Tucson," Archaeology in Tucson, Vol. 1, No. 3, Spring 1987. Newsletter of the Institute for American Research. Page 1.

Locating The Lost Santa Catalina Mission

There are several preserved early Spanish maps with the location of the Santa Catalina visita. But, there are discrepancies as to exactly where it was located.

During Father Kino's lifetime, the mission was originally near Picacho Peak. [357] It may have been moved somewhere near the Cañada del Oro after Kino's death. [358] [359] [360]

The early map drawn by Kino in 1701, places 'Santa Catalina' on the west side of the Santa Cruz River, [361] near Picacho Peak Pass (about 40 miles northwest of Tucson). On Kino's map, the Sobaipuri nation includes the Santa Catalina Mountains. All maps drawn over the next century were based on Kino's original map. Copies were duplicated in Europe, usually London or France. The French maps used the name St. Catherine or St. Catharina. Kino wrote in his diary the name of the nearby missionary outpost as "Santa Catalina" using an *l*. [362]

Maps drawn as late as 1757 [363] also place the "S. Catalina" on the west bank of the Santa Cruz River. An Amsterdam drawn map in 1765 also marks 'S. Catarina' on the west

---

[357] Picacho Peak State Park is located nearly fifty miles north of Tucson and thirty miles south of Casa Grande, Arizona.

[358] See the upcoming section in the year of 1732: "seven leagues to the east" of San Agustin.

[359] Tucson, The Life And Times of An American City, by C.L. Sonnichsen. Page 11.

[360] Donald Page report (upcoming). Page calls a site at the Cañada del Oro the Mission of Ciru in the Pueblo Viejo ("old town").

[361] "Navigation Methods of Kino," by Ronald L. Ives, from Arizona and the West, map insert after page 215.

[362] Kino writes: "Sa Catalina," from Kino's Report on Exploration, 1699. Page. 7. Holographic copies at the University of Arizona Libraries Digital Collection. Online example of handwritten notes: http://universityofarizona.worldcat.org.ezproxy2.library.arizona.edu/title/report-of-an-exploration-written-at-mission-dolores-Pimería-alta-1699/oclc/31688441&referer=brief_results

[363] Named as Ste. Catalina. "Carte de la Californie, Levee par la Societe des Jesuites," map drawn by Padre Miguel Venegas, London. 1757.

bank. [364] The map Herbert E. Bolton used in his book on Kino also placed the site on the west riverbank of the Santa Cruz and called it 'St. Catherine.' [365]

Picacho Peak, north of Tucson and west of the Santa Catalina Mountains. This is near the first location of the Santa Catalina (or Catarina) del Cuytoabagum visita, described in Father Kino's diaries.

---

[364] 1765, Isaac Tirion, Kaart van het Westelyk Gedeelte Nieuwe, Amsterdam.

[365] Inside front page, written as St. Catherine, from Earliest print of Kino's Map of Pimería Alta, 1705. Published in Kino's Historical Memoir of Pimería Alta, Vol. 1. Spain in the West, Vol. III, by Herbert Eugene Bolton, 1919.

On a map that covers the period between 1727-1741 about life after Kino's time, 'S. Catharina' is placed on the *east* side of the river and closer to the Santa Catalina Mountains. This map legend marks the spot with an image of a church, the same icon used for S. Agustin and San Xavier del Bac. [366]

This conflicts with other maps of the era that just copied the original with no modifications. But, the new location is backed up by a document signed by several prominent Jesuits at the time. In the years after Kino's death, Santa Catharina was described in a document as being "seven (leagues) to the east (of San Agustin mission)." [367] Seven leagues is about 24 miles. [368]

If it was *east* of the Santa Cruz River, this location points to the Cañada del Oro at the Santa Catalina Mountains, not *north* to Picacho Peak.

There are no ruins or indication exactly where this mission and nearby village stood when it was located by Picacho Peak. There are ruins near the Cañada del Oro. Those ruins are still shrouded in mystery.

---

[366] Inside cover of Pimería Alta: Life After Kino's Time, by George P. Hammond, Prof. History, University of Southern California, Los Angeles. Reprint from New Mexico Historical Review, 1929. Map is dated 1727-1741.

[367] "Oficiales varios al rey Conquista y conversion de la Pimería alta California y Nuevo Mexico, 1737," submitted by several missionaries, including Ignacio Javier Keller. Also see Pimería Alta After Kino's Time, by George Hammond, 1929. Page 229.

[368] One league, unit of distance, equals about three miles or so. The actual measurement varies depending on who makes the measurement. It is based on the distance a person, or horse, can walk in about an hour. The Spanish legua is close to 2.6 miles or 4.2 kilometers. From How Many? A Dictionary of Units of Measurement, by Russ Rowlett and the University of North Carolina at Chapel Hill.

1697-1711: The Story Of Padre Kino's Santa Catalina

"…and in the neighborhood and even in sight of these new missions and new conversions some very good mining camps of very rich silver ore are now being established."

Eusebio Francisco Kino, February 2, 1710. [369]

W hen (Padre) Father Kino first met the inhabitants of the *visita* Santa Catalina, there were enough families to establish a missionary outpost. [370] Kino gave its Christian name when their entourage passed through on November 23, 1697. [371]

It was at Santa Catalina where Capt. Juan Mateo Manje said they were received with "festival lights and three crosses." Manje counted 200 people living in 40 homes. They preached, baptized four children, and received, and gave, some small gifts. [372] The following year Captain Diego Carrasco "received their oaths of obedience." [373]

---

[369] "Arizona: The Jesuits in Pimería Alta," from American Journeys Collection, by Eusebio Francisco Kino, 1710. Document No. AJ-020. Wisconsin Historical Society, 2003. Page 458.

[370] Father Kino's 1697 Entrada to the Casa Grande Ruin in Arizona A Reconstruction, by Ronald L. Ives, reprinted from Arizona and the West, Vol. 15, No. 4, Winter 1973. Pages 345-370. Ives reconstructs Bolton's account of Kino's journey in great detail.

[371] "Commentary by Father Bonaventure Oblasser, on article in Arizona and the West, Vol. II, No. 2, Summer 1960: "The Unlucky Jesuit Mission of Bac," by J. Augustine Donohue, S.J. Note (9) From a collection of notes and manuscripts of Frank Pinkley, Kino Pimería Alta Missions, Tumacacori National Park, United States Department of the Interior. Page 343.

[372] Ibid. Page 367. Ives says that Santa Catarina (he uses the *r* version) was southwest of Red Rock and a few hundred feet southwest of the present crossing of the Santa Cruz River at Sasco Road. Archaeological evidence shows it was a long-occupied settlement. The riverbed was dry in 1697, and drinking water was obtained at El Aljibe (Montezuma's Tank) about a three-mile radius of Lat. 32.52 N Long 111.34.30 W. This is about three miles WSW of La Palma, Pinal County. El Aljibe has not been uncovered.

[373] Ibid. This was recorded on September 28, 1698.

After Kino's 1698 journey through the Pimería Alta, he wrote that he saw "its fertile land, with its industrious and loyal Indians...with its many natural minerals." [374] He described Santa Catalina as being 'fifteen leagues' from San Xavier del Bac. [375]

Cristobal Martin Bernal, who led the expedition, wrote its location from San Agustin as:

> *"Dista esta ranchería de la Santa Catalina diez leguas. Prosegui marchando hasta llegar a la ranchería de San Agustin, distante de la orta seis leaguas."*
>
> Cristóbal Martin Bernal, 1697. [376] ("Distance to the rancheria of the Santa Catalina ten leagues. I continued marching up to the rancheria of San Agustin, distant from the other six leagues.") [377]

According to his diaries, military journals and preserved letters Father Kino visited Santa Catalina several times over the years as he journeyed with his military escort. [378]

---

[374] Octubre 25 de 1698, Eusebio Francisco Kino, from Materiales para la historia de Sonora, by Miguel Angel Paz Prayre, UNAM, 2007. "y desengañese los poco afectos a esta Pimería, pues ella, con la divina misericordia, con sus fertiles tierra, con sus indio laborioso y leales, con su temple tan ameno, con sus muchos minerales y sus numerosos naturals" Page 532-533.

[375] Spain in the West, Volume III; Kino's Historical Memoir of Pimería Alta, by Herbert Eugene Bolton. Volume I. Page 206. From San Xavier del Bac... "Meantime, on the second of November, the Señor lieutenant and Antonio Ortis Corest and I went on to Santa Catarina del Cuytoabagum, a journey of fifteen leagues."

[376] Materiales para la Historia de Sonora, by Miguel Angel Paz Frayre, UNAM, 2007. Page 522.

[377] Ibid. He said it was in the *valle de correa*.

[378] Kino's Historical Memoir of Pimería Alta, 1683-1711. Volume II Pages 186, footnote 235, also refers to it as Cuituabagum [Cuitoabagum], (ranchería in Santa Cruz Valley): see Santa Catalina del Cuitoabagum (Sobaipuri village on Santa Cruz): Kino at, I, 206, 235, 236 Index. Also as Santa Catalina del Caitoabagum (page 186) http://www.archive.org/stream/kinoshistorical02kinogoog/

1711-1732: Missionary Visits To Santa Catalina After Kino

After Kino's death in 1711, the Santa Catalina de Cuytoabagum missionary outpost was still operating. Services and several baptisms were recorded at Cuituaboc (Cuituavo), a village close to Santa Catarina, from 1724-1728. [379] [380]

A baptism record from March 8, 1724, mentions the village of Cuituaboca. Padre José Agustin de Campos traveled 160 leagues from his base at San Ignacio to the territory of Sobaipuri. During one visit he stopped in Cuituaboca "because of the sicknesses that was ravaging them and the smallpox that already hit." He baptized over 60 souls there. [381] He returned to Santa Catarina on April 25, 1726. [382]

On April 29th, Campos went to Cuituavo to baptize over two-dozen nearby residents, and "on one side of Cuituaboc (he) baptized Lorenza." [383]

On July 20, 1728, Father Gallardi baptized arrivals from "Cuituaboc on the Gila Road (Santa Catarina)." [384]

During this time, all indications are that the Santa Catalina was located north of San Xavier mission– until a priest wrote out a different direction.

---

[379] "Commentary by Father Bonaventure Oblasser, on article in Arizona and the West, Vol. II, No. 2, Summer 1960. Tumacacori National Park, U.S. Dept of Interior; Father Kino, collection of Frank Pinkely. Page 336.

[380] Mission 2000 (National Park Service database): March 8, 1724 at Cuitaboca (#2162 and #2164, page 46); April 20, 1726 at Cuituaboc (Cuituavo) (#2402, page 61); April 29, 1726 also at Cuituaboc (Cuituavo) (#7861, pages 61 and 62). The spelling of Catarina is used in the document.

[381] Mission 2000: March 8, 1724 at Cuitaboca (#2162) San Ignacio-B book, page 46.

[382] "Commentary by Father Bonaventure Oblasser," by J. Augustine Donahue, on an article in Arizona and the West, Vo. II, No. 2, Summer 1960, Page 336. This spelling uses an *r*.

[383] Mission 2000: Event ID 7861, San Ignacio-B book, pages 61, 62.

[384] Ibid.

1732: Santa Catharina "7 leagues to the *east*"

"...Santa Catharina al Oriente siete..."

Decades after Kino's death, the Santa Catalina missionary outpost may have been moved near the "Cañada del Oro eight or ten miles north of Black Mountain and close to the Catalina foothills, thereby gaining its saint's name." [385]

Almost all references to the visita of Santa Catalina refer to its location near Picacho Peak, as first reported by Father Kino. But one mention of this missionary outpost several decades after his death points it *"east"* towards the Santa Catalina Mountains instead of *northwest* from San Xavier del Bac.

On May 3, 1732, three German priests accompanied Capt. Juan Bautista de Anza to the Santa Cruz and San Pedro Rivers. One of the Jesuits, Father Filipe Segesser, took on the task of converting the Indians in rancherías of Bac, San Agustín and "Santa Catharina." [386] Their assignment was to manage a third of the trifecta of new missions just established throughout the region. The area that Father Igancio Keller covered was:

> *"Third: San Francisco Xavier del Bac; and its visitas, San Agustin, five leagues toward the north-west, Santa Catharina, seven leagues to the east, Casa Grande, twenty to the northeast; with other small rancherias to the north as far as the Gila river, in which there must be over 1,300 souls."* [387]

---

[385] Tucson, The Life and Times of an American City, by C.L. Sonnichsen, page 11. Although it was already named as Santa Catalina more than a decade before Kino died. Note: One league is about three to three and a half miles. Seven leagues measure about twenty four miles. This position, northeast of San Xavier del Bac falls between Cañada del Oro and La Ventaña in the Santa Catalina Mountains. The Actun location identified by Father Kino (at Picacho Peak) is north by northwest of San Xavier del Bac.

[386] Chronology of Tumacacori National Monument, Field Division of Education, National Forest Service. The spelling of Catharina is used for Catalina.

[387] Pimería Alta After Kino's Time, by George Hammond. Page 229. Hammond translates from the Spanish document, "Conquista y Conversion de la Pimería Alta." The spelling of Catharina was used in Hammond's translation of the original 1757 manuscript, "Conquista y Conversion de la Pimería Alta." (See Spanish text in next section)

This statement was in a letter co-signed on July 31, 1732 [388] by Fathers Keller, Segesser, Capt. Juan Bautista de Anza, and several other priests in a report of their experience in founding the new missions. [389]

Whether this is an overlooked historical reference or a three hundred year old transcription error, that statement puts Santa Catharina outpost in a different location– *east* instead of *northwest*.

George Hammond first used the English translation, of the following statement, in his 1929 article about that historic event. It matches the Spanish text used in a 1757 manuscript from a collection of documents about the events between 1732 and 1737 called "Conquista y Conversion de la Pimería Alta (Conquest and Conversion of Pimería Alta)."

> *"Almas: Tercera, S. Francisco Xavier de el Bac, u sis Visitas, S. Augustin, entre Norte, y Poniente cinco leguas, <u>Santa Catharina al Oriente siete</u>, la Cas grande, veinte al Nordeste con otras pequeñas Rancherias al Norte hasta el Rio Jila..."* [390]

"7 leagues to the east" of San Agustin instead of 15 leagues northwest as Kino described it, is one clue of a secondary location. [391]

If the original Spanish statement is correct– Santa *Catharina* (Santa Catalina) did exist east of Tucson (San Agustin de Tucson). That would place it somewhere in the vicinity of the ruins at the Cañada del Oro in the Catalina Mountains. [392]

---

[388] Pimería Alta After Kino's Time, by George Hammond (Reprinted in the New Mexico Historical Review, 1929). Pages 229-235.

[389] Ibid, page 235. Letter signed July 31, 1732 by "Father Visitor Cristobal de Cañas, Father Rector Luis Maria Gallardi, Father Phelipe Segeeser, Father Juan Baptista Grazhofer, Father Ignacio Xavier Keller and Juan Baptista de Anza, Captain of Sonora."

[390] Underlined words are the author's emphasis. Conquista y Conversion de la Pimería Alta (nacion de indios gentiles vecina de los Apaches) California y Nuevo Mexico, Santa Rosa de Corodeguache, 1727-1737. Page 5. Offset copy of document located at Newberry Library, Chicago, Illinois. Ayer 657.6 c7. Catharina is used in the original Spanish.

[391] As written in Conquista y Conversion de la Pimería Alta (nacion de indios gentiles vecina de los Apaches) California y Nuevo Mexico, Santa Rosa de Corodeguache, 1727-1737. Page 5.

144

Kino originally described it as being "fifteen leagues" further from San Xavier del Bac. [393] (another author uses San Agustin de Oaiur as the start point). [394]

Between 1732 and 1737 mission records show several entries of Keller's visits to 'Agtun' (at Picacho). [395] However, there are no records of Santa Catharina at this location until it was written up in that report to the bishop in 1737. [396]

There is no actual proof yet that explicitly connects the Romero Ruin site, or any other spot in the Santa Catalina Mountains with the lost mission of Santa Catalina. However, the "7 leagues to the east" direction towards the Catalinas may reinforce a link.

If at any time in history, there had been a Spanish mission at the Cañada del Oro, it would have probably been in operation during this period. This was a time when peace with the natives enabled mass baptisms, according to missionary records. [397] There was also reported mining activity in the area at the time.

For the Spaniards who were settling in the area and the missionaries who were converting natives by the handful, things seemed calm on the northern front. But, underneath the peaceful relations between the natives and their encroaching neighbors, there was resentment building up once again.

---

[392] C.L. Sonnichsen suggested in Tucson, The Life and Times of an American City, that "Later, it seems to have been pulled back to a location in the Cañada del Oro eight or ten miles north of Black Mountain and close to the Santa Catalina foothills, thereby gaining its saints name." Page 11.

[393] Spain in the West, Volume III, Kino's Historical Memoir of Pimería Alta, by Herbert Eugene Bolton, Volume I. Page 206. From San Xavier del Bac... "Meantime, on the second of November, the Señor lieutenant and Antonio Ortis Corest and I went on to Santa Catarina del Cuytoabagum, a journey of fifteen leagues."

[394] Kino's Eighth Arizona Entrada,1699, from On the Trail of a Spanish Pioneer the Diary and Itinerary of Francisco Garces, by Elliott Coues. Volume II. Page 546. Spelling used: "Santa Catarina de Caituagaba."

Bolton makes reference to its location relative to San Xavier del Bac, while Coues uses San Agustin (which is said to be about 5 leagues north of San Xavier).

[395] Mission 2000 database: Keller's visits Santa Catalina de Agtun on December 20-21, 23, 1736 and on August 13, 1737 (ID 6118) at.

[396] Visitor inspection to the Bishop of Durango, December 19, 1737, presented by Keller. Mision 2000, Event ID #6118.

[397] Search church records by person, year or place at Mission 2000 Searchable Spanish Mission Records, Tumacacori National Historical Park. http://home.nps.gov/applications/tuma/search.cfm

1734-1736: Indians Revolt, Minerals Discovered

Local Indians revolted against the settlers and missionaries on July 31, 1734, at San Xavier del Bac and Geuvavi. [398] That day, as Fathers Keller, Gaspar Stiger, and Filipe Segesser prepared for the feast day of Saint Ignatius, they noticed the natives had run into the nearby hills. Some stole cattle, and others broke into Father Stiger's house and took everything, including six adorned vestments. [399]

Captain Juan Buatista de Anza I [400] rushed to the region to protect the three vulnerable missions since there was no presidio nearby. It was a rocky period for Keller who was involved in a personal altercation years later that caused another tragic rebellion among the local natives. After peace was established, new discoveries led to a resurgence of mining activity.

When it was safer to return two years after the revolt, recoverable minerals on a grand scale were found in northern Pima County. [401] Padre Jacobo Sedelmayr wrote that various mines had been discovered near the missions of San Xavier del Bac, Santa Maria, Soanca, and Guevavi." [402] [403]

---

[398] "Filipe Segesser," by Ginny Sphar, Tumacacori National Historical Park. Cited from Bolton and Treutlein. http://www.nps.gov/tuma/historyculture/felipe-segesser.htm Also, "Gaspar Stiger," by Ginny Sphar.

[399] Ibid.

[400] Juan Bautista de Anza I spelled his name as Anssa. His son had the same name, but spelled his last name as Anza. From Tumacacori, National Park Service. History and Culture.

[401] Pimería Alta After Kino's Time, by George Hammond 1929: 237-238 and "Tubac through the Centuries," by Henry Dobyns.

[402] Misc. notes Arizona Historical Society file: Missions -- Arizona – Guevavi.

[403] Capt. De Anza wrote in a letter to Bishop Benito Crespo: "Toward the end of last October (1736), between the Guevavi Mission and the ranchería called Arizona, some balls and slabs of silver were discovered, one of which weighed more than one hundred arrobas (2,500 pounds), a sample of which I am sending to you, Most Illustrious Lord." This was the earliest known record of a place named Arizona.

"hace el proposito lo que sucedio el ano de 1736, pues pcos anos despues que la catolica majestad de nuestro rey (que Dio guarde), funo las tres nuevas misions en la Pimería, es a saber, se decubrieron cerca de ellas varias minas y distante de Guebavi como ocho leguas, el famoso cerro de las bolas en que se hallaron barretas de plata virgen ("

Jacobo Sedelmair, Marzo 20 de 1747. [404] ("what happened the year of 1736, for a few years after the Catholic majesty of our King three new Missions in Pimería, to wit, they uncovered several mines near and distant Guebavi as eight leagues of the famous hill of the balls that virgin silver barrettes were found, and many pounds of metal."

While making his visits to San Xavier del Bac, Padre Keller held services and conducted baptisms at Agtun (another reference to Santa Catalina) on December 20-23, 1736. [405] [406] Keller also returned to Santa Catalina de Agtun [407] on August 13 and 14, 1737 [408] to neighboring Cuitaboc (Cuituavo) where he baptized fifty two people. [409] [410] A Visitor Inspection report presented to Bishop Martin de Elizacoechea by Keller on December 19, 1737, provided lists of baptisms, marriages, and burials of the natives of villages, including 'Santa Catharina.' [411] The last mention of Cuituaboc was in baptism records for 1743. [412] Through 1748, missionaries were still baptizing children and adults from Agtun, the latest rendition of the *visita* of Santa Catalina and the nearby village of Cuituaboc. [413]

---

[404] "Materiales para la historia de Sonora," by Miguel Angel Paz Frayre, UNAM, 2007. Page 603.

[405] Mission 2000 Database, National Park Service, December 20, 1736, #6111; December 23, 1736, Event ID #5964, #5965, and #5966. Suamca Book, pages 19-20.

[406] "Commentary by Father Bonaventure Oblasser," by J. Augustine Donahue, page 337. ("en Agtun" on December 20th and on 23rd 1736.)

[407] Spelled as Actun in "Commentary by Father Bonaventure Oblasser," page 338 ("En S. Catalina de Actun en 13 de Agosto. En Cuituavo en 14 de Agosto. En San Xavier del Baac en 19 de Agosto.").

[408] Mission 2000: August 13, 1737, Santa Catalina de Agtun, Suamca book. Pgs 25-26. Event #6118

[409] Mission 2000 Database, August 13, 1737, Suamca Book, page 25 and August 14, 1737, #6119, Suamca book page 26. Event ID #6116.

[410] Mission 2000: August 14, 1737, at Cuituaboc (Cuituavo), Suamca book page 26. Event ID #6119

[411] Mission 2000: December 19, 1737, Visitor inspection, Suamca book, page 27. Event ID #4125. Also, "Juan Bautista de Anza, Basque Explorer in the New World 1693-1740," by Donald T. Garate, University of Nevada Press, 2005. Page 202. Garate also lists Quitoabo.

[412] Mission 2000: August 9, 1743, Suamca book, page 107. Event ID #6480.

[413] "Aquituni," New Mexico Historic Review, University of New Mexico, Vol. XXXVIII, (April) 1963. Page 174. The name Aquituni was mentioned by Anza when he stopped there in 1775.

1751: The Fatal Pima Indian Revolt

A deadly Indian uprising, the Pima Indian Revolt occurred on November 21, 1751. [414] It was another downfall of the missionary efforts in the Pimería Alta.

This tragic event is blamed on Father Keller's argument with native Luis Oacpicagigua (Luis of Saric), [415] but other issues among the natives were brewing. Luis was the leader of the Pima Indians. He encouraged the Pimas and the Papagos to drive the Spanish settlers from their land, and he started the uprising at his hometown in Saric.

The last straw was when Father Keller had commented that Luis was a "Chichimec dog, whose proper attire was a coyote skin and a loin cloth and whose proper pastime was chasing rabbits and rodents in the hills." [416] This insult offended Luis; he decided it was time to take his revenge.

Everyone was taken by surprise on that fateful Thursday when Luis tricked a group of Spaniards and Indian servants to take refuge in his home by suggesting an impending Apache attack. Instead his Pima Indians attacked the house and burned it down; twenty died.

Simultaneously throughout the area, Pimans attacked settlers throughout the region. Those who didn't escape were slaughtered in ambushes. [417]

During the attack Father's Tomas Tello of Caborca and Enrique Ruben of Sonoyta were killed. [418] The revolt decimated all of the missions of the Pimería Alta, and they were again abandoned; that included Santa Catalina.

---

[414] The last recorded baptism at Guevavi on the same day as the uprising. Page 95. "On this day (November 21, 1751) this Pima nation rose up and rebelled. For this cause it has been without a minister until the year 1753, in which year they re-established their village and humbled themselves in peace. For this truth I sign - Francisco Pauer, Minister of Doctrine for His Majesty." Mission 2000: Event ID #2411, Guevavi.

[415] Tubac Through Four Centuries, by Henry Dobyns. Chapter V, The Pima Revolt of 1751. http://parentseyes.arizona.edu/tubac/cpt5-A.htm

[416] "Ignacio Xavier Keller," Tumacacori National Historical Park. http://www.nps.gov/tuma/historyculture/ignacio-xavier-keller.htm

[417] Ibid. See Mission 2000: Event ID #2411– the last recorded baptism, possibly conducted during the start of the uprising.

When a Spanish scouting party passed through the Picacho site on December 27, 1751, they wrote that the Santa Catalina village was not occupied. The natives may have left and become absorbed into other settlements after the revolt. [419]

The result of the incident between Keller and Luis of Saric laid the groundwork for a second military expansion into the Pimería Alta the following year.

A graphic of an uprising.

---

[418] "The Pima Outbreak," New Mexico Historical Review, University of New Mexico. Page 343.

[419] "Aquituni," New Mexico Historic Review, Vol. XXXVIII, (April) 1963. Page 174.

1752: A fort At Santa Catalina?

A year after the Indian Revolt, as part of a plan to refortify the area, Lt. Francisco Xavier de Escalante [420] of the Fronteras garrison advocated building two military forts enclosed with adobe walls. One would be at Tubac and one at another location in northern Piman frontier (now Pima County).

From 1720 through 1752, Lt. Escalante spent more than 30 years in the northern frontier. [421] This Escalante would also have been aware of any mission or mining activity, in the Santa Catalina Mountains. [422] He had influence with the Spanish military and the missionaries and had a strong interest in the activities of the locals.

Father Visitor Jacob Sedelmayr advocated for the dual fort concept. He suggested that one could be fixed "four or five leagues north of San Xavier del Bac Mission at Tucson or Santa Catarina, and the other somewhere in the valley extending from Saric and Tubutama to Caborca. [423] [424]

> *"Pero si se han de erigir dos presidios, en tal case es mi parecer que uno se plante como cuatro o cinco leguas más allá de San Xavier en Santa Catarina o en Tucusona, y Tubutama."*

---

[420] Francisco Xavier de Escalante is not Juan Bautista de Escalante who accompanied Kino on his journeys through Santa Catalina visita and mountains decades earlier. He had already died. Francisco Xavier de Escalante was involved in the apprehension and arrest of Pedro Chiguagua after the 1751 Pima uprising (Mission 2000, Database National Park Service, #4873).

[421] Tubac Through Four Centuries, by Henry Dobyns. Escalante, April 22, 1752: 90v.

[422] Mission 2000 database sponsored by Tumacacori National Historic Park, National Park Service, U.S. Department of Interior. There are 63 records with the surname Escalante. http://www.nps.gov/applications/tuma/

[423] The Presidio and Militia on the Northern Frontier of Sonora, edited by Thomas H. Naylor, Charles W. Polzer. Page 420. May 10, 1752.

[424] Cathalina is the spelling used in Tubac Through Four Centuries, An Historical Resume and Analysis, By Henry Dobyns. Chapter VI: The Royal Fort of St. Ignatius at Tubac. Locating the Post. (Cited from Sedelmayr, May 10, 1752: 102v).

> Jacobo Sedelmayr, Mayo 10 de 1752 años. [425] ("But if you have to build two presidios, in which case it is my opinion that one is planted four or five leagues beyond San Xavier in Santa Catarina or Tucusona and Tubutama.")

Father Rector Gaspar Stiger suggested if one fort were established, Tucson was the proper place. If two were founded, they should be four or five leagues north of San Xavier at Santa Catalina [426] or Tucson (Tucusona) and one at Ocuca.

> *"y tengo por más cómodo y acertado el paraje del Arizona, y si acaso pusiensen dos, me conformo, la misma manera que el Segundo se ponga en Santa Catalina o Tucuson."*

> Padre Gasper Stiger, 1752. [427] ("And I'm more comfortable and successful the site of Arizona, and whether to put the two, I'm content, the same way that the second is set in Santa Catalina or Tucuson.")

Father Visitor Filipe Segesser also suggested one of the two forts be placed at Tucson or Santa Catalina, and a second one near Saric. [428] Twenty years before, Segesser had spent time at both *visitas* of Tucson and Santa Catalina.

> *"el que los dos presidios que vuestra señoria ha de situar en ella, el que el uno se ponga en el paraje de Santa Catalina o en inmediato nombrado Tucuson, por ser ambos abundantes de agua u pastos así (para) la poblacion, como para las caballadas y cría."*

> Padre Felipe Segesser, 1752 [429] ("which the two presidios that your ladyship has to be placed in it, the one place in the area of Santa Catalina or Tucuson

---

[425] The Presidio and Militia on the Northern Frontier of Sonora, edited by Thomas H. Naylor, Charles W. Polzer. Page 432.

[426] Ibid. Cited from Stiger 1752:103. The spelling used is Catharina in one reference and Catalina in The Presidio and Militia on the Northern Frontier of New Spain, page 432 (Spanish), 420 (English).

[427] The Presidio and Militia on the Northern Frontier of Sonora, edited by Thomas H. Naylor, Charles W. Polzer. Page 432.

[428] Tubac Through Four Centuries, An Historical Resume and Analysis, By Henry Dobyns. Cited from Felipe Segesser, May 25, 1752.

[429] The Presidio and Militia on the Northern Frontier of Sonora, edited by Thomas H. Naylor, Charles W. Polzer. Page 431.

immediately named, being both abundant water or pasture and (for) the population, and for caballadas and breeding.")

The Royal Fort of St. Ignacius was instead built at Tubac, about 50 miles south of Tucson. [430]

It took until 1754 to quell the Indians before the missionaries returned. For better protection, a new mission was established. Before that, the missionaries had to travel to the visitas of San Agustin de Oaiur (Tucson) and Santa Catalina from their base at the San Xavier del Bac mission to get to locations such as Santa Catarina. [431] [432]

---

[430] Ibid. Page 424; and Tubac Through Four Centuries, An Historical Resume and Analysis, By Henry Dobyns.

[431] Tumacacori's Yesterdays, By Earl Jackson. 1951. National Parks Service.

[432] An account was published in "Tumacacori Mission is Ancient Arizona Church," *The Bisbee Daily Review*, Bisbee, Arizona. June 23, 1913. Also printed in the *El Paso Herald*, El Paso, Texas. July 5, 1913.

1757: Middendorf's Mission In Tucson With '2 Pueblos'

An attempt to establish another mission in the Santa Cruz valley proved futile when German Father Gottfried Bernardo Middendorf tried to become the first priest to live north of San Xavier del Bac in 1757. [433]

His new mission would become one of the mission branches in "the Tucson with two pueblos." If successful, Middendorf would have been in charge of both "Oaiur and Santa Catalina Kuitoakgaum." [434] This may have been the reference made by Father Och about the new mission in Santa Catalina. [435]

Six years after the dual fort plan was proposed, Father Middendorf took ten soldiers for protection with orders to establish a mission near San Agustin on January 5, 1757. He carried gifts of dried meat and attracted about 70 local Indian families.

There was no church or building on the site, so Middendorf and the soldiers had to "sleep under the open sky" until he was able to erect a brush hut. He celebrated Mass under a ramada made of "four posts that supported a reed-and-rush roof."

By March, he was short of supplies, had no wine for Mass and suffered from nausea when he ate meat. Since he didn't learn the Northern Piman language before he arrived, he had to rely on an interpreter. [436]

---

[433] See the translated account from an article by Theodore E. Treutlien in the New Mexico Historical Review, October 1958, page 310.

[434] Spanish Colonial Tucson, 2. Continued Jesuit Proselytizing, 1756-1767. A Priest for Tucson, page 18. Rector Carlos de Rojas reported this to the provincial in mid-March of 1757 (Roxas Marzo, 15 de 1757).

[435] "Father Middendorf established a new mission among the Pápagos in Santa Catalina but the Indians were soon tired of it because they were barred from their vices, nightly dances and carousing. . . ." from Missionary in Sonora, The Travel Reports of Joseph Och, Treutlein, T. E., 1965. California Historical Society, S.J. San Francisco. Pages 43-44. and "Bernardo Middendorf," by Ginny Sphar, Tumacacori National Historic Park.

[436] "A Priest for Tucson," from Spanish Colonial Tucson, by Henry Dobyns. Page 18.

Despite Middendorf's efforts to appease the natives, underlying hostilities were brewing once again.

The Indians, who were forbidden "from their vices, nightly dancing, and carousing," were upset about the restrictions. They stole food from Middendorf, antagonizing him and his support team.

On a night in May, 1757, Indians attacked the village. The Padre and his ten soldiers hightailed it to San Xavier del Bac and barely made it alive. [437] Middendorf's attempt to proselytize the Papagos ended rather abruptly.

In 1764, Rector Manuel Aguirre advocated colonizing Santa Catalina and Buenavista (on the upper Santa Cruz) with Papagos as part of the plan to "to remove the Sobaiporis from the San Pedro River Valley."

---

[437] Described both in "A Priest for Tucson", from Spanish Colonial Tucson and "Bernardo Middendorf," by Ginny Sphar, Tumacacori National Historic Park.

1767: Jesuits Expelled, Franciscans Acquire Missions

"Repair with an armed force to the houses of the Jesuits. Seize the persons of all of them and within twenty-four hours transport them as prisoners to the port of Vera Cruz... If after the embarkation there should be found one Jesuit in that district, even if ill or dying, you should suffer the penalty of death."

Translated letter from King Carlos III to Carlos Francisco de Croix, viceroy of New Spain, June 24, 1767. [438]

On February 27, 1767, the Jesuits were expelled from the New World, and their property was confiscated. [439] All of their plans ceased.

The Santa Catarina del Cuytoabagum Visita on the Rio Santa Cruz was eventually closed in 1767, according to church-related records. [440]

There may have been several reasons why King Charles III expelled the Jesuits from New Spain. There is no agreement about his actual motivation or an official explanation. The popular speculation was that he had been upset at the Jesuit Order because he wanted to marry outside his faith.

A more clandestine and controversial explanation was because the missionaries' failed to adequately pay the Spanish Crown its "Royal Fifth," ("*quinta*") the taxation on the gold and silver they were supposedly hoarding. When questioned by Clement XIII about his reasoning, the King replied:

> "*In order to keep from the world a great scandal. I shall conceal in my breast the abominable machination which has been the motive of this severity. Your Holiness must believe me on my word; the security and*

---

[438] Translation from Francisco Garces, by Spartacus Educational.

[439] The Pragmatic Sanction of 1767. Ibid. Also, Congressional Serial Set, 1895. Page 1349.

[440] Guide to Catholic-Related Records in the West about Native Americans, from Marquette University. History of the San Xavier del Bac Mission. The Jesuits and Franciscans attended Santa Catarina from 1699 through 1752 when it was closed along with San Cosmé y Damian de Tucson Visita.

repose of my existence require of me the most absolute silence on this subject." [441]

The sealed notices were delivered by the Spanish military in the early morning with the instructions that they should take possession of the "houses and colleges of the Jesuits" and not let any member escape.

The once powerful Jesuit "black robe" missionaries became prisoners. The soldiers escorted them to a place for later deportation. The Crown also acquired the Jesuit fathers "pious fund" which was a collection donated by private people to aid in the "conversion of the heathen" and was divided between the Franciscan and Dominican orders. [442]

Franciscan missionaries of the College of Queretaro were placed in charge of the Pimería Alta missions and gained control of San Xavier del Bac along with the other missions. When the Franciscans arrived at San Xavier and Tugson (Tucson) in the summer of 1767, they found Indians still inhabiting the Santa Cruz Valley. [443] The Jesuits left them abandoned and in disrepair. [444] The natives were assured they could continue to live in their land without as before being forced to move. Their acquisition was short-lived, however, when the Apaches attacked and left more desperation in April and July 1769. [445] [446]

---

[441] "The Removal of the Jesuits," from The University of California Chronicle, An Official Record, Volume XIII, 1911.Page 3.

The text of Charles III's February 27, 1767 decree of expulsion is printed in Spanish, Real Decreto, in "La expulsión de los Jesuitas de las Provincias de Sonora, Ostimuri y Sinaloa en 1767," disteration by Alberto Francisco Pradeau. Antigua Libria Robredo Mexico, 1959. Pages. 28-29.

[442] "Mexican Claims Commissions," from History and Digest of the International Arbitrations to the United States Has Been a Party, U.S. Government Printing Office, 1898. Page 1349. Also, "Congressional Serial Set, 1898", page 1349.

[443] Spanish Colonial Tucson, Chapter 3, page 30.

[444] The Real Pragmatica Sancion, issued by Charles III on 27 February 1767 expelled the Society (of Jesus) from the Spanish dominions. "Military Consequences of Sobaipuri Relocation" in Spanish Colonial Tucson. Chapter 2, page 23.

[445] Ibid.

[446] Tumacacori's Yesterdays (Tumacacori Gains Importance Under the Franciscans), by Earl Jackson, 1951 from Chapter 3. Tumacacori National Historic Park.
http://www.nps.gov/history/history/online_books/tuma/jackson/chap3.htm

1769: San Juan Day June Massacre

On San Juan Day, June 24, 1769, the Apaches raided the mining camp at Cañada del Oro and killed the Papago Indians and their families, according to treasure hunter John D. Mitchell's version of the legend. This was called the San Juan Day Massacre during which the settlement was destroyed and forgotten.

"The treasure vault was near the south bank of the Cañada del Oro...the ruins of an old camp and the foundations of the little chapel where the priests said mass may still be seen," Mitchell explains in his story about the Iron Door Mine. [447] No Apache attacks were noted on that day other than Mitchell's claim, but Franciscan records at Guevavi-Tumacacori from 1769 through 1825 record burials of people killed by Apaches each season, especially "a manos de los Apaches" (at the hands of Apaches) that July 1769. [448]

Two years after the Franciscans arrived on June 23, 1769, the King's visitor general José de Galvez issued a decree to distribute the mission lands among the Spaniards and the *castas*. It was hoped this would help "civilize" the Indians and bring them closer in contact with the Spaniards. Once the Indians were prepared for this transition, they were to pay a tribute to the Crown; [449] but no specific incidents were recorded.

San Juan Day, *el dia de San Juan*, marks the traditional start of the monsoon season. One legend tells that Francisco Vasquez de Coronado prayed for rain on June 24, 1540, and it rained just after he finished. The event used to be regularly celebrated on June 24th in Mexico and throughout the Southwest, including Tucson. June 24th is also the feast day of St. John the Baptist. [450] If anything happened that day, only Mitchell knows the source, but 1769 was not a quiet year for the Franciscans.

---

[447] Lost Mine With the Iron Door, By John D. Mitchell, Desert Magazine, June 1952, pages 25-26. http://dezertmagazine.com/mine/1952DM07/files/195207-desertmagazine-1952-july.pdf

[448] Friars, Soldiers and Reformers: Hispanic Arizona and the Sonoran Mission Frontier, 1767-1856, by John L. Kessell. University of Arizona Press. Chapter 3, Note 57. Fr. Francisco Moyano, Noticia de las misiones que ocupan los Religiosos del Colegio de la Santa Cruz de Querétaro, Oquitoa, Feb. 5, 1805, AGI, Mex., 2736. From National Park Service.

[449] Demographic and Social Change in Northwestern New Spain, by Robert Howard Jackson. Thesis submitted to the Faculty of the Department of History, University of Arizona. 1982. Page 148-149. The decree was issued from Alamos.

[450] "El Dia de San Juan" Pima County Public Library, Librarian files.

Aquituni– The Land Near Picacho

In early 1769, Fray Francisco Tomas Garcés Maestro wrote that there were two Pima villages between Tucson and the Gila River, but they were abandoned because of Apaches. [451]

He used the name Aquituni to describe the northernmost *visita* of Santa Catalina. In his letter to Padre Presidente Fray Mariano Buena y Alcalde he described a recent Apache attack on San Xavier del Bac where three hundred and fifty sheep were killed. He also complained about the terrible conditions in Tucson— the lack of water, supplies, and adequate defense. [452]

Garcés noted that the neighboring "Opa and Cocomaricops possess blue shells traded from some other seacoast than California because they are enemies with the Yumas" (the tribe between them and the ocean). [453] Garcés recommended that missionaries be sent to Tucson, San Marcelo de Sonoita, Ati, and Aquitum. [454] (Aquituni). His efforts helped to establish a fort at San Agustin de Tucson, the future home for the village of Tucson.

On his expedition to California, Juan Bautista de Anza stopped at a Papago village on October 29, 1775, where the "pasturage ends" and he called it "the flat of El Aquituni." [455] De Anza's camp was just east of Picacho Peak near the old Santa Catalina *visita*. On departure the next day, he mentioned in his diary about the lack of water, but complimented the endurance of the people who lived there.

---

[451] "To Governor Juan de Pineda, San Xavier del Bac, February 21, 1769," from Desert Documentary, The Spanish Years 1767-1821, by Kieran McCarty, Chapter 3: Apache Tactics. Arizona Historical Society, 1976.

[452] "Fray Francisco Garces al .m.r. padre presidente fray Mariano Bueno y Alcalde. Sobre los defensos contra el enemigo," February 20, 1771. Letter, 7 pg. San Xavier del Bac. University of Arizona UAiR.

[453] Ibid.

[454] Ibid.

[455] Anza's California Expedition, Anza's Diary, Herbert Eugene Bolton, 1930. Page 13. Also read Picacho Peak State Park and Expedition Camp #21, De Anza Trail Guide. Page 19. And, see: Anza Trail Guide. http://www.anzahistorictrail.org/visit/counties/pinal

Frey Pedro Font, who accompanied de Anza, wrote that the place was "a little beyond a picacho, or peak which the Indians called Tacca." [456] Today, the mountain hill is called Picacho Peak.

Aquituni has also been written as Bajio de Aquitano [457] [458] and Aquituno [459] (Equituni). [460] Font said it was near a laguna– the "sink of the Rio del Tuqison y San Xavier," the present-day Santa Cruz. [461] A nearby rancheria close to Aquituni may have been Quitoac [462] (Quitcac, [463] Cuitoa [464] or Cuytoa [465]).

On January 19, 1796, the Papago Indians in the valley, along with 134 Papagos from Aquituni, were moved closer to San Xavier del Bac or San Agustin de Tucson. Capt. José de Zuñiga helped in the move, and Father J. B. Llorens baptized some of the infants in the group. [466]

After 1796 there is no record of religious activities or events conducted at Aquituni or Santa Catalina, although some families may have continued to live in the area.

---

[456] "Picacho de Tacca," from Dia 30 of Fray Pedro Font: diario intimo y diario de Fray Tomas Eixarch, Plaza y Valdes, 2000. Page 67.

[457] The Franciscans in Arizona, by Fr. Zephyrin Engelhardt, O.F.M. Holy Childhood Indian School, Harbor Springs, Michigan, 1899. Page 98. Also, "On the Trail of a Spanish Pioneer: the diary and itinerary of Francisco Tomas Hermenegildo Garcés. Page 84.

[458] On the Trail of a Spanish Pioneer, the Diary of Francisco Garcés, In His travels Through Sonora, Arizona and California, 1775-1776. By Elliott Coues, 1900. Pages 27, 84, 87

[459] Ibid. Pages 27, 84, 87, 527.

[460] Ibid. Pages 65, 87.

[461] Ibid. Page 84.

[462] Ibid. Page 84.

[463] Ibid. Page 84.

[464] Ibid. Page 84. Spelling by Font.

[465] Ibid. Page 84. Spelling by Font.

[466] "Franciscans At Work: A Mixed Group of Converts," from Spanish Colonial Tucson, by Henry F. Dobyns. Page 45-46. Also, Sharing the Desert: The Tohono O'odham in History, Winston P. Erickson, University of Arizona, 2003. Page 55.

The Morman Battalion later traveled through Picacho Pass in 1846. [467]

It would be quiet for the next few decades until the Civil War broke out. When the Mexican army left the Tucson Presidio in 1856, they took all civil, church and military documents. Some records were recovered and are in collections at the Bancroft Library in Berkeley, California. They were found in a closet in Imuris in 1878 after Francisco Solano Leon said they were taken to the city and he had lost track of them. [468] Some of these may have been the documents that Sylvester Mowry used in his reports about the new Territory.

There are many church and civil records available in an online searchable database at Mission 2000. [469] Other records are still unavailable, possibly still buried in storage cabinets or boxes.

[467] "The Battle of Picacho Pass," The War Times Journal.

[468] Ibid.

[469] Mission 2000 is a searchable Spanish Missions Records database, sponsored by Tumacacori National Historic Park, National Park Service, U.S. Department of Interior. http://www.nps.gov/applications/tuma/

1862: The Civil War Battle At Picacho

The Battle of Picacho Pass, on April 15, 1862, was a fight between a roaming Union patrol from California and Confederate soldiers. Tucson was the farthest point west under the Confederate flag. By that time all traces of the Santa Catalina *visita* were gone.

In August, 1861, the entire New Mexico Territory, which included Arizona, was declared part of the Confederacy. Confederate Captain Sherrod Hunter was sent to Tucson with a garrison of seventy-five troops. The Union responded quickly with a force of one thousand four hundred troops dispatched from Fort Yuma under Brigadier General James H. Carlton. The Confederates pulled out of Tucson and headed north toward Picacho. [470]

The 1st California Volunteer Cavalry encountered Hunter's troops staked out on the slopes of Picacho Peak waiting in ambush. Only part of the Union troops entered the Pass; the other group came upon the flank of the skirmish line.

Three of Hunter's men were captured, and four were wounded and killed. The Confederates withdrew. This was the same year that Union soldiers were negotiating the "Cañada del Oro Treaty" about thirty miles east in the Santa Catalina Mountains.

Picacho Peak is now part of the 640-acre Picacho Peak State Park, officially opened in 1968. [471] Every year, re-enactments of the Arizona Civil War battle are held at the Park sponsored by the Arizona Parks Foundation. Visitors can camp and hike the park's 1,500 feet tall peak.

The story of the Santa Catalina Mission may have ended with the Pima Uprising of 1751, or when Tubac was chosen as the Presidio in 1752. It could have ended with the expulsion of the Jesuits in 1767, [472] or the final blow could have been on San Juan Day in 1769.

Either way, at one time, the lost mission did exist.

---

[470] Picacho Peak State Park web site: http://azstateparks.com/Parks/PIPE/index.html

[471] Picacho History: Arizona State Parks. Opened Memorial Day, May 30, 1968. Ibid.

[472] "Guide to Catholic-Related Records in the West about Native Americans," 2006, from Marquette University. The mission operated from 1699-1767 (closed).

History Time Shifts Into Legend: What Is Fact From The Legends?

"A mine is a hole in the ground with a liar standing next to it." [473]

So was there a mission located near a hidden mine or mines left by the Spaniards in the Santa Catalinas? Were the military and settlers complicit? There is and always will be speculation.

Any assertions, outside of accepted agreement and historical documentation, will always remain a part of the legends– even if they fill in history's gaps.

What is part of the historical record so far is that in the winter of 1698 Father Eusebio Kino, accompanied by Sgt. Juan Bautista de Escalante, traveled around the Santa Catalina Mountains, at least once together, with a directive to meet the natives, name locations, and locate a reported mineral deposit. This could have been gold, silver, or quicksilver.

There was a Spanish missionary outpost named for the Santa Catalina Mountains. It was recorded at one time to have been located somewhere near Picacho Peak and then another time somewhere near the Cañada del Oro– "seven leagues to the east of San Agustin." Another Escalante, Lt. Francisco X. Escalante was in the Fronteras military command that covered the region, including the Catalina mountains.

While evidence of early mining in the Santa Catalinas has been acknowledged with the presence of old mine shafts and arrastras, no records of taxes paid to the Crown for mining minerals in the Santa Catalinas or land records have yet been uncovered. If they exist, those documents may still be stored in the Archivo de Indias in Seville, Spain, along with other records still in Mexico. [474] Or perhaps they were never paid.

Nearly one hundred years later when Americans started to explore the Catalinas, they discovered the remains of mining activities and the tales connected with them.

---

[473] Quote credited to Samuel Langhorne Clemens (Mark Twain). But, it may not have originated with Clemens. See Kim A. McDonald, "Many of Mark Twain's Famed Humorous Sayings Are Found to Have Been Misattributed to Him," Chronicle of Higher Education (Sept. 4, 1991), A8.

[474] Archivo de Indias records are stored in the State Archives of the Ministry of Education, Culture and Sport, Spain.

Lost Mines Of The Santa Catalinas

The Mine With The Iron Door

Old Spanish Mines Of Sonora

Goldberg's Lost Ledge

Lots Of Old Mines In The Mountains

"The Santa Catalina range, one of the grandest and most sublime of the great upheavals in southern Arizona is the home of the lost mine... The lost mines are as ubiquitous as the lost tribes of Israel. They exist in story and song, they are ignus fatuous of the gold seeker..."

"The Fallacy of Lost Mines," June 15, 1885. [475]

Discoveries of old, abandoned mines scattered around the Santa Catalinas became more frequent as American scoured the nearby mountains in the 1800s.

The legends of lost Spanish mines in Southern Arizona were well known at the time. According to local Mexican residents, Spanish colonists with forced Indian labor worked the mines. They were abandoned when they were attacked by Apaches or after the expulsion of the religious groups in charge of the New World.

In the 1870s the U.S. military advancement by General Crook into the "Land of the Apaches" made it safer for prospectors to explore the many tunnels and ruins. That allowed Mr. Breyfogle, a seasoned prospector, to search fruitlessly for the "lost mine" the southern portion of Arizona in 1871." [476] As early as 1875, Isaac Goldberg, one of those treasure hunters and a prominent Tucson businessman, reported finding an old mine and some ruins in the Catalina Mountains. [477]

In 1880 one lost mine in the Catalinas was given a name after two prospectors claimed to have found an old tunnel with an iron door. Since then the Iron Door Mine has become linked with the legend of lost mines and become the prize booty. It wasn't until the early 1930s when it got personal. The Escalante name became synonymous with the Iron Door Mine– the Lost Escalante Mine. Both terms could have been used much earlier than when reported in the newspapers, but it gave a name to one elusive treasure hunt.

---

[475] "The Fallacy of Lost Mines," Mohave County Miner, Kingman, Arizona. June 15, 1885. From the Tucson Citizen.

[476] "All the World for Arizona," from the Ely Record. Printed in The Weekly Arizona Miner, Prescott, Arizona. August 19, 1871. General Crook is credited with making the area safer.

[477] "Evidence of old towns..." The Arizona Weekly Citizen, Tucson, Arizona A.T., March 6, 1875.

Mine With The Iron Door Legends

"The Tombstone (town) has the threadbare story of the mine with the iron door, located in the Cananea mountains. When tradition fastened the iron door to the mine of fabulous riches, iron doors were more scare than rich mines."

Arizona Weekly Citizen, May 1, 1886

T he legend of the Mine with the Iron Door in the Santa Catalina Mountains did not start with Harold Bell Wright's book by the same name. The Iron Door Mine was already embedded in the local legend fifty years earlier [478] and could have been part of oral tradition for many generations.

The Mine with the Iron Door, called mina con a puerta de hierro in Spanish became romanticized nationwide by Wright's 1923 book of the same name, THE MINE WITH THE IRON DOOR. His story

---

[478] First account of "The Iron Door and the Nine Mile City of the Santa Catalinas" was published Arizona Weekly Star, March 4, 1880.

brought attention to the legend, although it was more about love and less about the treasure and its legend. Yet Wright did subtly reveal some of the Catalina's secrets.

The old Spanish mines were reportedly sealed with large doors, made of iron or wood, according custom. [479]

The Spaniards may have actually used a re-enforced wooden door, a "strong door."

When the white man arrived in the new Territory, the name became corrupted to the "Iron Door," according to one prospector who explored the Catalinas in the 1930s searching for the legendary lost Spanish mines. The legends are similar; they didn't leave behind records of their tunnels when they left, so it is anybody's guess.

The abundance of timber in the Catalinas provided the means to build a sturdy wooden door, but a tremendous amount of minerals would have had to be mined and smelted to make a door of solid iron. Perhaps the wooden door was just reinforced with iron or lead bars.

From the 1880s on, numerous prospectors– including prominent Tucson businessmen and lawmen– claimed to have found an iron door, or remnants of one, which sealed off a remote abandoned mine. Some reportedly found treasures inside or quartz veins still streaked with precious minerals like gold and silver. Occasionally, local newspaper reporters verified samples brought from the mountains.

This section follows the discoveries reported by early Tucson pioneers as they explored different parts of the Catalinas in pursuit of the local legend of the Iron Door Mine. Those expeditions led the way for an industry that extracted millions of dollars of wealth from the Catalinas.

The iron door image, however, still makes a nice story.

---

[479] From the San Bernardino County Sun, December 29, 1932.

Iron Door Mines In The United States

While there are hundreds of lost mines around the United States, there are only a few places called the Iron Door Mine. Other mines may share the name, but the most famous is the Mine with the Iron Door in the Santa Catalina Mountains.

An abandoned mine called Iron Door Mine is located in California in the Providence Mountain Range of San Bernardino County.[480] There is one in New Mexico,[481] Oklahoma, Oregon,[482] and Utah. In Arizona mines in Lake Havasu City,[483] Tombstone and Tumacacori also share the name of the Santa Catalina's legendary mine.[484]

The Lost Cave With the Iron Door in the Wichita Mountains near Lawton, Oklahoma reportedly contained eleven million dollars in Spanish gold ingots and doubloons. A heavy iron door closed off the entrance. The skeletons of seventeen Indians guarded the treasure. A strange twist to the story involved outlaw Jesse James. He was reported to have stored two thousand dollars of loot in the cave. Other stories suggest that Belle Starr also stored $500,000 in the cave.[485] [486]

---

[480] "Iron Door Mine," Sierra County, California, USA, "Commodities (Major) Gold," mindat.org.

[481] "Lost Mines of Arizona and Sonora," Arizona Silver Belt, December 3, 1892.

[482] Iron Door Mine, Rye Valley District (Morman Basin District), Oregon. Main commodity was gold. USGS Mineral Resource Data System. Also, Shorty's Not So Lost Mines and Treasures of Southern Oregon: Mines and Treasures, by Steve "Shorty" Owen. 2009. Pages 32-33.

[483] "Iron Door Mine," from Lake Havasu Hikes, by Lake Havasu, Arizona City Convention and Visitors Bureau. Located near Bison Falls.

[484] "Lost Mines of Arizona and Sonora," Arizona Silver Belt, December 3, 1892.

[485] Interview with Roy Roush, treasure hunter author, from his treasure files. 2014.

[486] "Lost Cave With the Iron Door," from Classic American Ghost Stories: 200 Years of Ghost Lore from the Great Plains, New England, the South and the Pacific Northwest, edited by Deborah L. Downer, August House, 1990. Page 85.

The rumors drove so many prospectors to those mineral hills in 1897 that soldiers from nearby Fort Sill had to eject them. Even though the mountains were heavily guarded by Indians, "some day some one will strike it rich." [487]

The Utah Iron Door Mine is in the Rock Creek-Cabin Creek region. This mine was located by a fisherman/doctor named Rhodes in 1925. No story of this mine is known. [488]

Tombstone, the "Town too Tough to Die," had its own Iron Door Mine story in the nearby Cananea Mountains. "When tradition fastened the iron door to the mine of fabulous riches," stated a newspaper story in 1886, "iron doors were more scarce than rich mines." [489]

A large iron door prevented a Tucsonan from entering a mine near the Tumacacori mission in 1884. He said he found an old rusty antique key, but could not find the lock to insert it. The last word was that he went back to Tucson to look for investors to finance his search. [490]

Today, the Iron Door Mine adventure ride at Old Tucson Film Studios and the Iron Door Restaurant on top of Mt. Lemmon give tribute to the glory of the legend.

---

[487] "Ejecting Prospectors," The Guthrie Daily Leader, Guthrie, Oklahoma. February 28, 1897.

[488] Following the Legends: A GPS Guide to Utah's Lost Mines and Hidden Treasures, By Dale R. Bascom. 2007. Page 153.

[489] The Arizona Weekly Citizen, May 1, 1886.

[490] "Arizona Stories, Mysterious Iron Door," (Tucson Star), published in the Daily Alta California, San Francisco. December 13, 1884.

1880: The Mine With The Iron Door & The Nine Mile City

According to legends there was an old Spanish mine in the Santa Catalina Mountains that supposedly held multi-millions in treasure and it was buried somewhere in the canyons.

The earliest published account of the Mine With The Iron Door in the Catalinas was in an 1880 article in the *Arizona Weekly Star*. Two prospectors told how they acquired an old map, found the lost iron door mine, and a lost city, deep in the Santa Catalinas. [491] [492] Finally one of the lost mines acquired a name– the Iron Door Mine.

This article was the first mention in print of a door actually made of iron that sealed off an old, abandoned mine. According to the reporter, the tale of the lost mine began about a hundred years before when the Jesuits where the dominate force in the region.

During the late 19th Century it was commonly believed that a hundred years earlier the Jesuits had "large fields under cultivation and many men employed delving in the earth after precious metals and turquoise stones." The nearby town was called the Nine Mile City, *"Nueva Mia Ciudad,"* probably because it was located nine miles from some specified location. [493]

"At that time the principle gold mines were situated in these mountains and there was a place called Nueva Mia Ciudad, having a monster church with a number of golden bells that were used to summon the laborers from the fields and mines, and a short distance from the city which was situated

---

[491] "The Iron Door and the Nine Mile City of the Santa Catalinas," Arizona Weekly Star, March 4, 1880.

[492] The Arizona Historical Society in Tucson has a typewritten copy of that article in its archives, "The Mine with the Iron Door & the Nine Mile City of the Santa Catalinas' (Arizona Weekly Star, Mar. 4, 1880) COPY: by Mrs. Geo. F. Kitt, Sec'y, Arizona Pioneer's Historical Society." Mrs. Kitt, secretary of the society "would not vouch for the authenticity of the story but does assert that the story was given credence locally to the extent of publication in a Tucson weekly." From "Mine With the Iron Door Still Lures Adventurous; "Lost City' Once Visited?" Tucson Citizen, August 7, 1927. A recount of the prospectors 1880 venture was published in the August 7, 1927 edition.

[493] "Mine with the Iron Door and the Nine Mile City of the Santa Catalina Mountains," The Arizona Weekly Star, March 4, 1880.

on a plateau, was a mountain that had a mine of such fabulous richness that the miner used to cut the gold out with a 'hacheta." [494]

The early Spanish, however, did not use miles as a measurement. They counted distance by leagues, leguas. One league is about 3.45 miles. Nine leagues are about 31 miles — the distance from one of the early Tucson settlements to this old city. Perhaps it should have been called Nueva Legua Ciudad (Nine League City).

In that case the lost city would be roughly 30 miles from Tucson's town center. That direction, towards the northeast, leads to the Cañada del Oro (*about 7 leagues east of San Agustin*).

According to this story when the Jesuits were expelled in 1767, this city became destitute. They supposedly left behind their riches buried in the mine, and the secret of its location was lost. It was called the Iron Door Mine because the bars of gold were secured behind an "iron door." There were only two entrances to the lost city and both were "obliterated" to conceal its location. [495]

Those prospectors in 1880 told the reporter they became interested in the Iron Door Mine when they stopped at the Mexican town of Caborca. They were shown a handwritten diary about the events of those days, including directions how to find the mine with the iron door. The Mexican said the book belonged to his grandfather and would not part with it, so they made a copy.

The two men headed for the Cañada del Oro from Martin and Albert Weldon's Mining Camp near Oracle in January 1880 and went up the canyon to find the place "where water would exist the year round." After days of hiking and camping, they found a canyon that was walled on the three sides and discovered a stairway cut in the rock. A vaulted chamber that closed into a narrow passage was eventually discovered. In one place, was an inscription engraved on the wall in Latin - "Dominus vobiscum" – "go with God."

They traveled farther on and found a tract of land covered with pines and oaks. As they walked in an easterly direction to the Nueva Mia Ciudad, they came to a stream of water glittering with "shining particles" and alive with trout.

> *"The next day, we moved on for another mile where we came into ruins, which, as we proceeded grew larger and could be seen for two miles in*

---

[494] "The Iron Door and the Nine Mile City of the Santa Catalinas," Arizona Weekly Star, March 4, 1880.

[495] Ibid.

width. To think, probably, that we had walked four miles when we came upon a stone building (granite and marble) that was in a fair state of preservation excepting the roof, which had fallen in; the structure was something after the style of the Old Cocospari church in Sonora, and we decided that this must have been the place of worship of the people of this once populous city. Here we spent some time in looking over this edifice searching for gold and silver which was buried in the church, but having no tools, we could do nothing. [496]

They spent three days searching until they found the "mine with the iron door." According to one of the prospectors, "The old door was eaten off by rust and the iron bars that secured it lying down at the mouth of the tunnel." After they entered the tunnel, they saw a vein about ten inches wide. They followed the tunnel for about four hundred feet until they came upon an iron object that resembled a pick. They struck it against the mineral vein and "the gold rolled down in nuggets on the floor." The newspaper reporter witnessed one hundred pounds of silver and gold that the miners displayed. [497]

The two prospectors who claimed they found a city of ruins and an old mine with an iron door in the Santa Catarinas stopped off at the Oracle mining camp and told Solomon Allis, the U.S. Deputy Mineral Surveyor and Civil Engineer, about their adventure. [498] "I tell you these gold nuggets gave us a good deal of faith; and further. I am one of the oldest prospectors in these mountains, and I never known anyone to go up these canyons," concludes the newspaper reporter signed ,"Respectfully, Redoubtable." [499]

Allis claimed he saw a "hundred pounds of nuggets in their back packs." [500] They described in detail to him about the days-long hike far into the canyon and their ultimate discovery. It was the first time Allis heard of anyone exploring that deep into the Catalinas. Nothing further was heard from the two men or if they actually filed their claims. When word hit Tucson of the miner's discovery, prospectors rushed to locate those claims in the Catalinas, but no one succeeded.

---

[496] Ibid.

[497] Ibid.

[498] The background of the story is based on an account given by Donald Page, "Lost Jesuit Mine with the Iron Door," Desert Magazine of the Southwest, October 1956. He names Allis as the person who wrote the article and met with the prospectors.

[499] "The Iron Door and the Nine Mile City of the Santa Catalinas," Arizona Weekly Star, March 4, 1880.

[500] "Mine with the Iron Door and the Nine Mile City of the Santa Catalina Mountains," The Arizona Weekly Star, March 4, 1880.

The week before the two prospectors told their story to the Mineral Surveyor, C.D. Hays and C. R. Norman told a reporter that they found "rich diggings and plenty of water" in the Catalina placer formations. [501] It is unknown if these were the two prospectors and what happened to their claim. Allis indicated that he was going to find the valley and cave with some partners but there has been no further word on his success or failure.

The week after the prospectors find, a small article was published about Tucson dentist Dr. Theron S. Hitchcock's "rich and rare specimen of gold ore" that came from the "Iron Door" mine. The rock had gold, silver and galena. [502]

Dr. Hitchcock was a collector of rare artifacts and displayed many of them in his office. The next week's newspaper edition carried a brief article about Dr. Hitchcock's stone-ax that was found by some Mexicans in the Santa Catarina Mountains. The seven-inch blade was highly polished and quite sharp. [503] The next week, a reporter was shown an Old Spanish buckle plowed up near the Mission (possibly San Xavier del Bac). It was silver and had a knight in full armor and was thought to be a relic from the Spanish conquistadores. [504]

Those two prospectors, whoever they were, may have stumbled onto something. By following their route from the entrance of the Cañada del Oro, through the inner canyon, they could have discovered the stone remnants of the fabled Lost City, near Mt. Lemmon where stone ruins still stand. Those prospectors did not, however, come upon the remains at the Romero Ruin on the west side of the Catalinas. That area was well known at the time and exposed to travelers along the Cañada del Oro road to Oracle.

This newspaper article spurred the legends about the connection between the Lost City and Lost Mine, and this became the popular version of the iron door mine legend today.

For the first time in print, it explained the familiar local legend of the Spanish mines, Kino and the expulsion of the padres that led to the lost mine or Mine with the Iron Door. Tales of rich prospects in Arizona and the "fabulous richness of the mines under the Spanish regime" [505] continued to blend the legends into Arizona's early history.

---

[501] The Arizona Weekly Citizen, Tucson, A.T., February 14, 1880.

[502] The Arizona Weekly Star, Tucson, A.T., March 11, 1880.

[503] "An Ancient Battle-Ax," The Arizona Weekly Citizen, Tucson, A.T., March 27, 1880.

[504] "An Ancient Relic," The Arizona Weekly Citizen, Tucson, A.T., April 3, 1880.

[505] Arizona Weekly Citizen, July 10, 1886.

1883-93: Lost Spanish Mines South Of Tucson

The area around Tubac and Tumacacori, south of Tucson, was also well known for rumored buried Spanish treasures and its own "iron door" mine.

In 1883 a gentleman from Tucson reported finding the much sought lost Tumacacori mine, south of Tucson, but he said he was prevented from entering it because of a large "iron door." A year later, Tio (uncle) Nasario, an old Mexican who knew all of the local legends, was near the west side of the Old Tumacacori Mission where he found an old rusty iron key. He tried to find some investors to raise five hundred dollars to hunt for the lock to the key, believed to be from the iron door of the lost mine. [506]

Another story exists of a wealthy miner who went to search for a "lost mine" near Arivaca in October 1891. He had previously discovered ruby quartz in a mining dump supposedly left by the Spaniards a century before. The miner, James B. Cusenberry, left Missouri for Tucson to meet with United States Judge Barnes who told him the story of an old mine that had been worked by the Spaniards a century or two before. According to the legend that Cusenberry followed, charts showing its location were found years ago among some church papers in Spain. A Jesuit priest brought them to this country in 1887, and he supposedly found a large amount of bullion but could not find the actual mine. [507]

Treasure hunters Ron Quinn, [508] his brother Chuck, and friends Walter Fisher and Roy Purdie spent two years exploring and hunting for buried Spanish treasures around Tumacacori in the 1950s. They returned in 1983 and again in 1985. At an outcropping of rock on a summit, their metal detector received a strong reading. They dug less than two feet and uncovered bars of shining yellow gold, and two-by-two inch gold squares, totaling eighty seven pounds. They sold it for $410,000. Their find was reported in the 1986 edition of Treasure Magazine. [509] Quinn described their discovery and other attempts to find treasure in the Tumacacori mountains in his book *"Searching for Arizona's Buried Treasures."*

---

[506] Daily Alta California, San Francisco, December 13, 1884. California Digital Newspaper Collection.

[507] "Barnes' Imagination," Tombstone Epitaph, September 20, 1887.
http://chroniclingamerica.loc.gov/lccn/sn95060905/1891-09-20/ed-1/seq-2/

[508] Searching for Arizona's Buried Treasures, by Ron Quinn, 2013. Pages 221-225.

[509] Treasure Magazine, Vol. 17, No. 8, August 1986, Pages 56-59, 61.

1891: An "Iron Door" Found

While hiking into a box canyon in February 1891, an unnamed editor said he found a "worn iron door leading to an ancient Jesuit mine." The iron door "has been found to be another opening to this treasure vault" which was located just below the "old pueblo" he found a few years before.

The editor said he made a discovery earlier in the decade where, in a "rugged and precipitous defile" of the Santa Catalinas, he found ruins of an old pueblo near numerous old shafts. He found a flight of stone steps that lad to a "veritable cryptogram of workings" that had ruby and local silver and sparkled with gold. He had to abruptly stop his search when confronted by numerous bears. His find stirred some political heat.

> *"There is trouble and discontent, here, however, over the fact that this discovery is so close to the Pinal line that the county may claim it, and it is proposed to introduce a bill in the Legislature that shall cut off a liberal slice of Pinal and insure this new discovery to good old Pima and her sanitarium."* [510]

The county line that separates Pima County (to the south) and Pinal County (to the north) cuts the Santa Catalina Mountains in half. The mine could be located closer to the southern portion of the Catalinas. Today, the borderline between Pima and Pinal County currently lies parallel to the southern edge of the retirement community of Saddlebrooke.

This spot could be near Oracle Ridge where foundations of stone structures still remain. There is a box canyon within the Catalina Mountains close by the Reef of Rock where the Cañada del Oro begins. The box canyon and iron door description is similar to the story told by the two prospectors who said they discovered the Iron Door Mine eleven years earlier. [511] These two reports were not about the Cañada del Oro ruins. That site was well known as Romero's Ranch at the time.

---

[510] Published in the Tombstone Prospector, Tombstone, Arizona, AT, February 17, 1891. The article was also published in the Tombstone Epitaph on February 22, 1891.

[511] "Mine with the Iron Door and the Nine Mile City of the Santa Catalina Mountains," Arizona Weekly Star, March 4, 1880.

1894: Bullock's "Lost Mine"

Another lost mine discovery in the Santa Catalina Mountains was reported in May 1894. Local rancher Thomas Bullock and an Indian supposedly found an abandoned gold mine there.

According to local tradition, the mine once belonged to a soldier from Ft. Lowell who originally located the claim. After his discharge he stayed out at the claim. His prospect gained a reputation as being rich. When the soldier died, its whereabouts became unknown.

Bullock and the Indian sought the location for over a year. They made several attempts into the mountains from time to time without any luck. On one trip, the Indian recovered a crowbar that supposedly belonged to the soldier. But, they were unable to locate his lost mine.

Later the Indian went into Tucson with news that they finally found the long, lost soldier's mine and they had staked a claim. A "prominent local mining man" furnished him with a burro outfit. [512] No further report on their find was made.

---

[512] "A Lost Mine Probably Found," Mohave County Miner, May 12, 1894.

175

1895-1896: More Old Mines Discovered

In May 1895, Mr. Gibson, a local rancher, accidentally discovered an old mine tunnel in the Catalina mountains. The mine was "worked by the Jesuit priests, mention of which is made in old church records," the Arizona Daily Star (daily Tucson newspaper) said. One tunnel was eleven feet wide and nine feet tall with traces where "rich pockets have been." [513]

Another find that summer was the "fabulously rich Barn Door" mine discovered in the Catalina Mountains. That mine was described as either a natural rift in the bluff or a man-made opening. What they agreed upon was recoverable minerals were found. The writer said there was evidence of a former town with scattered ruins and arrastras throughout the Santa Catalina Mountains "where the Aztec or Jesuit slaves once crushed his ore." [514]

The next month, an article reprinted in several Arizona newspapers in June, 1895, downplayed any significance to the lost mine legends in Arizona and California; then it exalted some significant finds. Several Mexicans reportedly discovered a thirty-foot tunnel in the Santa Catalina Mountains, according to an 1896 account. They believed it was an entrance to an old mine. Nearby, they found "several assayer's cupels and some ore carrying gold." The article mentioned "Nobody knows of any mines that have been worked in recent years in that vicinity." [515]

Tucsonan Sam Hughes had remarked to a reporter that year about a "town four miles north of Tucson to Santa Catalina" that had disappeared from the map and was also a "large town eighteen miles northwest" of Tucson. [516]

In 1898, a report of an Indian cave and a copper deposit was discovered on the hill north of Redondo's Canyon in the Catalinas. Nothing of historical interest was found, except it provided evidence of having been occupied "at no distant time by the Apaches." [517]

---

[513] "Referring to the old mine..." The Tombstone Epitaph, May 26, 1895. Reprinted from the Arizona Star.

[514] Ibid. Also, see next footnote.

[515] Graham Guardian, Safford, Arizona, March 27, 1896.

[516] Arizona Weekly Citizen, February 22, 1896.

[517] Tombstone Epitaph, June 3, 1989.

1899: Charley Brown & The Iron Door Mine

Finding the legendary "gold mine of the early Indians" was a longtime quest for Tucson businessman Charles O. Brown. Charley was a staunch believer in the legends the lost mine in the Santa Catalinas.

Charley Brown believed that the Indians had operated the mine and at the mouth of this mine there was an iron door. When the invading Spaniards came, they "caved in the entrance and left." [518]

As owner of the Congress Hall [519] saloon, Charley was well known for his prospecting in the Catalinas. He spent many years, and $60,000 in mining expenditures during his quest of the mountain's unique stones and fabled lost mine. [520] Charley kept a large mineral cabinet on display at his saloon with some of his rare collections. [521]

Charley and his son Billy headed for the Catalina Mountains in July, 1899, after a recent discovery demonstrated to their satisfaction that they had finally found an old mine. The top rock of the mountain showed a "high grade of copper with gold predominating."

The ledge was four feet deep and five feet wide according to Charley. The newspaper that reported Charley's find also said his friends "wished him better success than his former experiences, where he spent thousands of dollars without receiving a lota compensation." [522]

---

[518] "Think Long Lost Gold Mine Is Found, Days of Romance Have Not Entirely Passed," Weekly Journal Miner, November 25, 1908. Page 6 (From Saturday's Daily).

[519] "Roar of the Tiger," Arizona Weekly Citizen, September 3, 1892. Also, "Helldorado: Bringing the law to the Mesquite," By William M. Breakenridge. U of Nebraska Press, 1992. Page 115. Born in New York, Charles O. Brown was Tucson's leading saloonkeeper. He built Congress Hall in 1867-68. It was the place where the first territory legislature met.

[520] Arizona Weekly Citizen, August 13, 1892.

[521] "A Magnificent Cabinet," Arizona Weekly Citizen, October 1, 1892.

[522] Arizona Republican, July 8, 1899.

In mid-November, some Mexican woodchoppers discovered a small hole that appeared in a half-filled excavation. They dug through the dirt to discover the entrance to a shaft inside of a cave. They covered it up and related the find to their friends in Tucson. [523]

A few days later, a group of six or seven Mexicans set out to the Catalinas loaded with a wagon of tools and provisions. No further word was heard from them. Since the discovery was near the place Charles "Charley" Brown had insisted was the legendary iron door mine, there was some hope that they were in the right area. But Charley died in August, 1908, at age seventy nine, without locating his cache. [524]

After that, the search for the iron door mine became a forgotten pastime for several decades. While curious prospectors filtered through the Cañada del Oro and hiked the precipices of the Catalinas, there was very little news about the Iron Door Mine until Howard Bell Wright published his book and shook the country, and Oracle at the time.

---

[523] Ibid.

[524] Charles Owen Brown, born October 27, 1829 and died August 13, 1908. He arrived in Tucson in 1864 or 1865. Find A Grave, findagrave.com, #11925254.

1923: Howard Bell Wright's "Mine With The Iron Door"

"And yet– those who look for it still find "color" in the Cañada del Oro. Romance and adventure still lives in the Cañon of Gold. The treasures of life are not all hidden in a lost mine behind an iron door."

Harold Bell Wright, THE MINE WITH THE IRON DOOR [525]

Author Harold Bell Wright popularized the story of mine with the Iron Door in 1923. His top-selling novel, THE MINE WITH THE IRON DOOR, became the basis for a series of movies and several treasure stories.

In 1915 an ailing Wright came to Tucson to relieve his tuberculosis. For a while, he stayed at Rancho Linda Vista, located near the bend of the Cañada del Oro. He lived in a remote cabin built in the center of the Santa Catalinas at the Coronado Camp, just over the Samaniego Ridge to the east of Saddlebrooke. [526] [527]

Wright learned about the legends of the mountains and the whereabouts of the lost mine. This desolate spot, deep in the mountains, is where Wright composed his book, THE MINE WITH THE IRON DOOR, in 1923.

Other than the Bible, Wright's was the first book to ever sell over one million copies. [528] [529] He also wrote the "Shepard of the Hills" – the first movie that John Wayne had starred. [530]

---

[525] The Mine With The Iron Door, by Harold Bell Wright, 1923. Pages 4-5.

[526] Tucson: The Life and Times of an American City, by C.L. Sonnichsen. Pages 151-153.

[527] Harold Bell Wright Estates Historic District, National Register of Historic Places Registration Form. May 31, 2012.

[528] The Shepard of the Hills, by Howard Bell Wright published in 1907, became the second most popular book sold in America, after the Hoy Bible. Harold Bell Wright Museum, World's Largest Toy Museum.

Wright's story is a romantic fiction set in the Cañada del Oro. His characters and story came from the likes of local residents in Oracle and their tales about the lost mine. In Wright's version the mystic guardian Indian watched over the mine. In the end he gave the hero burro loads of gold from the fabulously rich mine.

As with most of Wright's novels much of the story was a moral fight with right and wrong, greed and noble aspirations. Finding both love and gold, the couple rode off into the sunset to live happily ever after.

Shortly after Wright made camp in the Catalinas, just before Christmas in 1915, he caught a bad cold and had to go to Saint Mary's Hospital. He was so pleased with his treatment that he wanted to repay the kindness. [531] He staged a series of performances of his two novels, "The Shepard of the Hills," and "Salt of the Earth" the following year. He donated the proceeds minister Oliver E. Comstock's Adams Street Mission, established in 1909, for tuberculosis patients. [532]

A neighborhood on Tucson's eastside, near Speedway Boulevard and Wilmot Road, honors Wright who had a home among 35 acres of land in the 166-acre subdivision. Streets within the Harold Bell Wright Estates are named after his books and some of its characters, [533] among whom is Natachee, the Indian guide. [534]

The guide character is similar to Alexander McKay's guide in 1878 as well as Charles McKee's 1932 story of an Indian who showed them where minerals were located in the Catalinas.

"He's right though about some Indian like Natachee holding the secret," remarked William "Curly" Neal, the owner of the distinguished Mountain View Hotel in Oracle, "I

---

[529] Harold Bell Wright Papers, 1890-1946. MS 360. University of Arizona Libraries, Special Collections. While in Tucson, Wright composed several novels.

[530] John Wayne's son, Norman, went on to help write Bambi, Fantasia and the Wonderful World of Disney in true wild western fashion.

[531] Tucson: The Life and Times of an American City, by C.L. Sonnichsen. University of Oklahoma Press, 1987. Page 151.

[532] Breathing Space: How Allergies Shape Our Lives and Landscapes, by Gregg Mitman. Yale University Press, 2008. Page 110.

[533] A Guide to Tucson's Historic Neighborhoods, by City of Tucson.

[534] Harold Bell Wright Estates Historic District, City of Tucson. Blenman-Elm Neighborhood Association.

know of a case where a white man at Fort Lowell came home with a tomato can full of gold nuggets– virgin gold. It's there somewhere. No doubt of it. Mr. Wright don't know where or he wouldn't be wouldn't be writing books about it." [535]

"However, the only living person who has received any treasure from the Mine With the Iron Door is Harold Bell Wright who used that name for the title of one of his books." [536]

While that statement may have been meant to discourage any credibility of the Iron Door Mine, it didn't stop even more risk takers from seeking the Catalina's hidden treasures.

---

[535] "Buffalo Bill Believed in "Lost Mine" In Catalinas And Organized Company; William Neal Thinks It really Exists," undated. Arizona Historical Society.

[536] Arizona: A State Guide, from North American Book Dist LLC, January 1, 1940. Page 297.

1924: "Mine With The Iron Door" Movies

The original Mine with the Iron Door film, based on Harold Bell Wright's book of the same name, was released in 1924 as a silent film. The theme was recreated in several other full-length motion pictures.

Wright's novel, THE MINE WITH THE IRON DOOR, was published in 1923. The next year THE MINE WITH THE IRON DOOR was the first Western movie that was filmed in Southern Arizona. The film was shot on location at the local Linda Vista Ranch, Oracle at the entrance to the Canyon of Gold– the Cañada del Oro. The movie was directed by Sam Wood and starred Dorothy MacKail with Pat O'Malley, Raymond Hatton, Charles Murray, and Bob Fraser. [537]

The original THE MINE WITH THE IRON DOOR premiered in 1924 at the Rialto Theatre in Downtown Tucson. A print was rediscovered ninety years later and presented in the same theatre during an October 2010 screening. [538]

In 1936, the film of THE MINE WITH THE IRON DOOR was re-shot in Hollywood but in this version the search is for the buried treasure of San Capello. Richard Arlen played the lead role of Bob Harvey, and David Howard directed this movie. [539]

In 1956, The Secret of Treasure Mountain [540] was pieced together from parts of the 1949 film Lust for Gold. The hunt for a Spanish treasure and an Apache curse kept Valerie French and Raymond Burr on their defenses. [541]

---

[537] The Mine with the Iron Door, October 24, 1924. IMDB.com at http://www.imdb.com/title/tt0015140/

[538] Screened at the Tucson Rillito Theatre on Friday, October 8 and 10, 2010. Tucson-born New York-based composer and pianist Brian Holman composed the score performed during the 2010 screening. The Rialto's 90th Birthday Bash, featuring a screening of Harold Bell Wright's THE MINE WITH THE IRON DOOR.

[539] The Mine with the Iron Door, film released on May 6, 1936, from IMDB.com.

[540] Secret of Treasure Mountain, June 25, 1956. Columbia Pictures Corporation. Directed by Seymour Friedman, from IMBD.com

[541] The Secret of Treasure Mountain, from MSN Entertainment.

'MacKenna's Gold' In The Canyon del Oro

"A thousand years ago in the Southwest, there was an Apache legend told about a hidden canyon guarded by the Apache Gods, and rich with gold. As long as the Apaches kept the canyon a secret and never touched the gold, they would be strong– powerful. That was the legend. When the Spanish Conquistadores came, they searched for that canyon. They called it Canyon del Oro, meaning Canyon of Gold. But, they never found it. Three hundred years later, the Americans came. They heard about the legend. But, they called it the Lost Adams. That was because a man named Adams claimed he had seen it. But, whether he did or not– He never saw anything again, because the Apaches burned out his eyes. Everybody knew about it– that legend. And, a lot of people believed it. The Canyon del Oro– the Lost Adams. Then, for awhile back there in 1874. They called it MacKenna's Gold."

Edward G. Robinson narrating MacKenna's Gold. [542]

Another movie that carried on the lost treasure theme and mentioned both Canyon del Oro and the Apaches, the two elements that thread through both the history and legends of the Catalinas Mountains was MacKenna's Gold.

The movie was filmed in Canyon de Chey in Northern Arizona, but it invoked the concept of the tradition.

The motion picture, released in 1969, told the story about Sheriff MacKenna (Gregory Peck) who discovered an old map that led to "Canyon del Oro." MacKenna overcame various obstacles including the greed among his group and the ever-impending attacks from Apache Indians as he followed the map that led to a rich gold vein in the mountains. The film also starred Omar Sharif, Telly Savalas, Eli Wallach, and Edward G. Robinson, as Adams.

---

[542] MacKenna's Gold. Released May 10, 1969. Quoted from Lost Cities and Ancient Mysteries of the Southwest, by David Hatcher Childress. 2011.

There was an actual Los Adams Mine– actually several across the U.S. One was found in 1906 near Holbrook, Arizona. An old Indian, John Daisy, told Ed Owens about the long, lost mine. [543] Another Lost Adams Mine reportedly contained a treasure trove, but it was located near Gallup, New Mexico. [544] [545]

A take-off of Secret of Treasure Mountain remade in 2003 as The Buttercream Gang in Secret of Treasure Mountain [546] strayed from the theme, but contained some of the Spanish treasure elements.

In 2010 Little Big Horn Productions released a film called Buffalo Bill, Beyond the Legend." [547] The film had a special appearance by William Carter, who claims to have found the Iron Door Mine. Carter defended Cody's reputation earned by his expended finances in search of the fabled mine.

Although the original Iron Door movie and its spin offs did much to romanticize the lost mine theme, those two prospectors from 1880 had actually pioneered the American-version of the legend.

---

[543] "Lost Adams Mine Found at Last," Holbrook Argus. August 18, 1906.

[544] Mr. L. S. Goroon of Wingate, New Mexico reported the find in 1888. "A Rich Find. A New Mexico Man in Kansas City Who Tells of the Lost Adams Mine. It Is Believed Gold Nuggets Are Lying in Wait for the Picking Up- Endeavoring to Organize a Company," Ft. Worth Daily Gazette, Ft. Worth, Texas. May 10, 1890.

[545] Captain John Samuel Jones spent a large sum of money over ten years– since 1906– in his search for $300,000 in gold. From, "Lost Adams Mine," St. John's Herald and Apache News, St. Johns, Arizona. July 13, 1916.

[546] The Buttercream Gang in Secret of Treasure Mountain, Feature Films for Families. 2003.

[547] Buffalo Bill, Beyond the Legend, by Jack Hubbell, Little Big Horn Productions

1929-1933: Men Work 'Ancient Mine'

Three miners reported in 1929 that they had discovered an ancient mine once operated by the Spanish padres 160 years before. The mine was located two miles away from the Pueblo Viejo ruins just off the Oracle Highway near the old steam pump.

The miners easily saw the old road from the ruins to the mine although it was mostly obscured by brush. The area described is similar to the spot near the Romero Ruin today.

The three men who found the mine C.V. Rinehart, Ed Druizman, and J.F. Gill reported they had found the mine and ruins on a "bluff overlooking the Canyon del Oro wash" in 1929.

The largest building was fifteen by thirty five feet and built from boulders set in adobe. They observed a wall enclosing a patio about one hundred and fifty by one hundred and fifty feet. To the south was a shallow indentation like an oval pit surrounded with some boulder walls. Traces of an old irrigation ditch led from the Romero Canyon. [548]

They cleared a blocked mine that opened into a twenty five foot tunnel when they were stopped by water. Old mesquite timbers had been removed to expose an old shaft. They decided to wait until the water could be taken out with more equipment. Reinhart told a reporter "the vein matter is ten feet from the front wall to hanging wall." [549] No follow up to their venture was reported.

The ruins they discovered were the current Romero Ruin and Hohokam Village. Francisco Romero long abandoned the ranch home that he built on top of the old Indian ruins in the 1880s. The three prospectors must have stumbled upon those remains.

At this same time in 1932, prospectors Charles "Will" McKee and his brother Harry started their hunt for the Iron Door Mine's buried treasures. [550]

---

[548] "Men Now Work Ancient Mine," The Arizona Daily Star, January 25, 1929. Read more about their mining discovery later on.

[549] "Men Now Working Ancient Mine," The Arizona Daily Star, Tucson, Arizona. January 25, 1929.

[550] See section on the McKee's hunt for the Iron Door Mine.

McKee Stakes Out The
"Fabulous Escalante Mine– The Iron Door Mine"

In the fall of 1932, a group of prospectors, including Charles "Will" McKee and his brother Harry armed with old Mexican documents, headed into the wilderness near Oracle, Arizona ,in search of the "fabulous Escalante mine or more popularly known as the Iron Door Mine." [551]

Will spent the last fifteen years of his life in his search for the elusive mine.

This became one of several attempts to strike it rich in the Catalina Mountains by the McKee brothers. It is also one of the earliest published mentions of the Escalante mine and the first connection with it to the Iron Door Mine. The McKees' account made newspapers around the country with their discovery.

After spending the previous ten years and thousands of miles roaming the desert, Will filed a location claim for the Golden Dream mining site on September 7, 1932. The claim was a half-mile from the "Buffalo Bill Mill (west) & Bound on East end by Patented property." [552] The brothers built a cabin west of Campo Bonito, six miles from Oracle. [553]

Unknown to the McKee's at the time, they would soon make an amazing discovery.

It was on Friday, December 2, 1932, [554] when an old Indian paid a surprise visit to the brothers and took them on a long hike. They walked from their cabin to a "muck" dump

---

[551] "Iron Door Mine Reportedly Found," Prescott Evening Courier, December 5, 1932. Page 2.

[552] Notice of Location, mining claim filed September 12, 1932. Witness: M.C. Harden. Also, published in Casa Grande Dispatch, September 23, 1932.

[553] McKee's first site near Campo Bonito was last worked in 1990 when Linda and Charles Taraldson filed a dozen claims. Source: Bureau of Land Management, Mining Claim Index Report, 1980-1991. M14 T0100S R0160E, Sec 18, SW, SE. The Taraldson claim is noted as a former underground gold prospect that included an adit that partly caved and flooded in 1994. A three-meter 'arrastre' was found in front of the adit. Source: U.S. Bureau of Land Management Unpatented Mining Claim #94830. Mindat.org Taraldson claim.

[554] "Romantic Story of Mine With Iron Door Began With Conquistadors and Indians," by Sherry Bowen. Part 1 of 6, The Arizona Daily Star, Tucson, Arizona. December 21, 1932. Part 1 of 1.

186

on the Apache Trail "about three miles south of Oracle." [555] The Indian took them up into the hills to a rocky area where the Cañon del Oro empties into the Tucson desert. They arrived at a nearly inaccessible spot in the mountains, not far from Sombero Peak. [556] This was the fabled Canyon of Gold where quartz veins along the canyon walls were said to contain gold. The Indian guide then brought them to a small gorge and waved his hand in a half circle around the gorge. [557]

The McKee's were convinced there was an abandoned mine nearby. It was possibly the infamous Iron Door Mine. They found a large pile of small, loose stones packed against the hill. It was recognized as a mining dump, but no mine entrance could be found. They did find two old shafts farther up the gorge. [558]

Charles, Harry, and associate Paul E. Perkinson went back out the next day. They walked along the old Indian trail to the head of the Cañon del Oro that lies on the opposite side of the ridge from the muck dump. They found two holes that could have been vertical shafts. Farther down the canyon they found a pile of muck packed against a hillside. [559]

A tunnel was revealed when the blockage was cleared away. They followed the tunnel but were stopped by a cave-in. They figured the course of the tunnel would emerge on the other side of the hill between those two dumps they found on the other side. Some high-grade ore and some large pieces of free gold they had found on the dumps were brought back to Tucson. Harry had found a small chunk of a gold nugget assayed at $16,000 a ton from the same area several years earlier. A few years before, according to Perkinson, a burro's skeleton was found up the Cañon del Oro with a bull skin filled with enough gold ore to earn the finder $19,000. [560]

Perkinson believed that the Spaniards "located the Escalante mine and forced the Indians to help them work it. Finally the Indians turned on their oppressors, killed them all and dumped huge quantities of gold ore, which had been loaded on burros for removal from the mine, onto the floor of the tunnel and then sealed up the entrance of the mine with

---

[555] Ibid and "Iron Door Mine Reportedly Found," Prescott Evening Courier, December 5, 1932. Page 2.

[556] "Iron Door Mine Reported Found," Spokane Daily Chronicle, Spokane, Washington. December 5, 1932.

[557] "Romantic Story of Mine With Iron Door Began With Conquistadors and Indians," by Sherry Bowen. Part 1 of 6, The Arizona Daily Star, Tucson, Arizona. December 21, 1932. Part 1 of 1.

[558] Ibid.

[559] "Iron Door Mine Reported Found," Prescott Evening Courier, Prescott, Arizona, December 5, 1932.

[560] Ibid.

187

dirt, rocks and worthless ore." [561] [562] This was the first time the name of Escalante was linked to the famous mine.

Perkinson believed that the burro's skeleton with the ore was one of the animals that escaped during the rebellion. He said that a trail from the mine leads to the "old Dakota Mission" where about four hundred men worked the mine for eight years. After the ore was removed, it was transported by ox train through Altar, Mexico, to the Gulf of California and then shipped to Spain. [563]

Will and the Indian traced the trail from the mines to the "ruined mission at the mouth of the Cañon del Oro." He found similar trails throughout the mountains, some worn five feet deep through the rock by burros as they carried bags of gold. Mules carried gold to the mission, however, an old Mexican Mayo Indian told McKee that there it was loaded on two-wheeled carts and driven to the Gulf of California and loaded on ships destined for the Isthmus of Panama or Nicaragua to be taken to Spain, according to Will's version of the legend. [564]

Before they returned to Oracle, word of their discovery was already known. One man heard them say they found the Mine with the Iron Door. Will tried to reassure him that they only discovered an old tunnel and not the actual, long sought Iron Door Mine. Kirk T. Moore, a Tucson attorney, overheard the conversation. [565]

He told the editor of the local Tucson newspaper, Arizona Daily Star. The story was sent over the Associated Press wires that Sunday, December 4th. After McKee got home in Phoenix, the discovery of the "Mine with the Iron Door" hit the major newspapers the next day.

The morning Tucson newspaper, Arizona Daily Star, ran the headline "Mine With Iron Door Found" and related the story based on the overheard conversation. The article

---

[561] Ibid.

[562] "Say Lost Mine Is Found," Pittsburgh Post-Gazette, Pittsburgh, Pennsylvania. December 7, 1932.

[563] Ibid.

[564] "Mayo Indians Gave Aid to Seekers for Iron Door Mine," by Sherry Bowen. The Arizona Daily Star, Tucson, Arizona. December 24, 1932. The Mayo Indians had connection with the Mayas, according to the article. Part 4 of 6.

[565] Newt Well's Manzanita corner store on the way to Phoenix, according to "Mine With the Iron Door Found," The Arizona Daily Star, December 5, 1932. This article spells McKee as McGee and names Perkinson as Peters. The newspaper made a correction a few weeks later when it published series of articles about the McKee discovery.

misspelled McKee's name as McGee. [566] The *Prescott Evening Courier* in Northern Arizona picked up the story out of Phoenix on December 5th. [567] It was republished in newspapers across the country and often with embellished facts. [568] [569] [570] [571] The local Tucson newspaper published a six-part series about the Mine With Iron Door during the last week in December. [572] The first day began with the romantic story of the "Mine With Iron Door." A correction was published in the next day's installment; McKee did not find the actual Iron Door Mine. [573]

But it was too late. The story had actually been in print weeks before. It was "written and rewritten until many papers carried stories which contained statements without the slightest foundation in fact," a frustrated McKee complained. [574]

The newspaper articles made it sound as though McKee actually had found the old Iron Door Mine. He emphasized in later articles that he only found some old mining dumps, but the story spun out of hand.

---

[566] "Mine With Iron Door Found Again in Oracle Hills, Phoenix Man Makes Claim To Re-Discovery Of Fabled Ore Body In Region Described By Tucson Novelist Harold Bell Wright, In His Book," The Arizona Daily Star, December 5, 1932.

[567] "Iron Door Mine Reported Found," Prescott Evening Courier, Prescott, Arizona, December 5, 1932.

[568] "Say Lost Mine Is Found," Pittsburgh Post-Gazette, Pittsburgh, Pennsylvania. December 7, 1932. "Hidden in the fastness of the Santa Catalina Mountains of Southern Arizona for more than two centuries, the famous Escalante Mine, more popularly known as the mine with the iron door, is believed to have been located" by "Charles and Harry McKee and Paul E. Perkinson, all of Phoenix."

[569] "Report Finding of Gold Mine With Rich Ore, Prospectors Believe They Have Uncovered Vein Lost For Two Centuries," The Evening Independent. St. Petersburg, Florida. December 6, 1932.

[570] "Mine With Iron Door Is Found, Arizona Man Claim to Have Solved 200-Year Old Spanish Secret, Gold is Fabulous. One Chuck of Ore Is Said To Have Assayed $160,000 to Ton." The Spokesman-Review. Spokane, Washington. December 6, 1932.

[571] "Iron Door Mine Reported Found," Spokane Daily Chronicle, Spokane, Washington. December 5, 1932.

[572] "Romantic Story of Mine With Iron Door Began With Conquistadors and Indians," by Sherry Bowen. The Arizona Daily Star, Tucson, Arizona. December 21, 1932. Part 1 of 1.

[573] "Mine But No Iron Door, Is McKee Story of Old Spanish Mine With Strong Door Hidden in Fastness of Canada del Oro," By Sherry Bowen, The Arizona Daily Star, December 22, 1932. Part 2 of 6.

[574] Ibid. December 22, 1932. Part 2 of 6.

"These stories are making a liar out of me and I should like to have the real facts known," McKee tersely remarked. So far as he knew, "there is not and never has been any iron door." Instead the Indians called the old mine "strong door– a heavy wooden door," but when the white man came, it was corrupted to "Iron Door." The new discovery of the tunnel may have been the other end of the mine that the McKees had discovered seven years before. Since 1925, they found only small samples of gold. It was a long process because they had little money for supplies. [575] [576]

McKee made an agreement with the local Indians. If he found the treasures, it would be given to the tribe. McKee would then get back all of the money he had spent searching for the mine and would "get a good living for the rest of his life." The rest would go to the entire tribe. [577]

Moore, the man who brought the story of McKee's discovery to the newspaper, also told about a man named Crawford who came from Sonora a few months before the McKee find. While Crawford was prospecting the Catalinas, he said he kept finding caches of low-grade ore "dumped on the ground as if it has been hastily unloaded from burros, perhaps at the approach of Apaches."

It was this story that prompted the McKees to start their search for the treasure. There was also the story of a site called San Ysidro at the bottom of the Cañada del Oro, not far from the Pusch steam pump. Many people believed this town was connected to the famed Escalante mine. [578]

After locating the main source, McKee hired W.A. Bondurant of Phoenix and a group of workers to develop the property over the next year. By summer 1933, a tunnel had been extended forty feet into the rock and revealed four veins that averaged forty dollars to the ton in gold, according to Bondurant. The tunnel, hopefully, would cross the old shafts they believed to be there. [579]

---

[575] Ibid. December 22, 1932. Part 2 of 6.

[576] From the San Bernardino County Sun, December 29, 1932.

[577] "Indians Will Get Benefits If Iron Door Mine Is Real," by Sherry Bowen. The Arizona Daily Star, Tucson, Arizona. December 26, 1932. Part 6 of 6.

[578] "Mine With Iron Door Found Again in Oracle Hills, Phoenix Man Makes Claim To Re-Discovery Of Fabled Ore Body In Region Described By Tucson Novelist Harold Bell Wright, In His Book," The Arizona Daily Star, December 5, 1932. The article misspelled McKee as McGee.

[579] "Hunt is Continued for Historic Mine, Famous Iron Door's Tunnels Are Sought In Oracle Hills," The Tucson Citizen, July 11, 1933.

In 1934 mining was a big business in the state. Arizona mines extracted over $22.7 million of gold, silver, copper, lead, and zinc. The amount had doubled the value over the previous year. [580] To recover his findings, the following year Charley took out a classified advertisement to solicit financial help.

> *"Have small developed gold producing property. Twelve thousand dollars development. Want three more to cut larger ledges. Interest given. Big producing gold. Silver, lead property. Shipper. Smelter tests. $2,500.00 down, pay balance out of mine. C.W. McKee, 702 North Seventh Ave., Phoenix, Arizona."*
>
> "Capital Wanted," "The Mining Journal," United States Bureau of Mines, April 15, 1935 [581]

Yet it would still take McKee several years more before he was able to intensify his search.

---

[580] "Metal Production Figures for 1934," The Mining Journal, United States Bureau of Mines. January 30, 1935. Page 3.

[581] "Capital Wanted," The Mining Journal, United States Bureau of Mines, April 15, 1935. Page 28.

1937: McKee Seeks Iron Door Mine, Again

"The famous Escalante mine, hidden in the fastness of the Santa Catalina mountains of southern Arizona for more than two centuries, is reported to have been relocated by three Phoenix prospectors. This rich gold mine is more popularly known as "the mine with the iron door."

Massena Observer, New York, March 5, 1937 [582]

Another treasure seeker and friend of Charles "Will" McKee was determined to find the elusive Mine with the Iron Door in the Santa Catalina Mountains.

Nathan Sturdy of Pittsburgh was a mining engineer and a member of the Smithsonian Institute. A firm believer in the lost mine legend, he owned a quarter of the land shared by McKee and the Apache Indian reservation. [583] Sturdy said this Escalante Mine interest was inspired by Harold Bell Wright's novel, THE MINE WITH THE IRON DOOR. [584 585 586 587 588 589 590] However, Wright never mentioned Escalante by name in his novel. This may have been the first public mention of the infamous Escalante Mine.

---

[582] "Discover Famed Mine," Massena Observer, Massena, New York, March 5, 1937.

[583] "Pittsburgh Engineer to Seek Legendary "Mine With the Iron Door" Near Tucson," Prescott Evening Courier, Prescott, Arizona. September 15, 1937.

[584] "Hunt for Mine Full of Gold To Be Resumed, Engineer Now Believes He Will Be Able To Find Vast Sum," The Evening Independent, St. Petersberg, Florida. September 15, 1937.

[585] From The Winnipeg Tribune. Winnipeg, Canada. September 15, 1937.

[586] "To Seek $90,000,000 in 'Mine With Iron Door,'" Ottawa Citizen, Ottawa, Canada. September 15, 1937.

[587] "Will Search for the 'Mine with the iron door'," Clovis News-Journal. Clovis, New Mexico. September 15, 1937.

[588] "Hope to Find 90 Millions In Gold In Hidden Mine," The Norwalk Hour. Norwalk, Connecticut. September 16, 1937.

[589] "To Seek Historic Mine's Iron Door, Legend Says Gold Hoard There Worth About $90,000,000," Ludington Daily News, Ludington, Michigan, September 26, 1937. Page 2.

[590] Lost Gold and Silver Mines of the Southwest, by Eugene Conrotto, 2012. Conrotto repeats the story told to the newspapers in 1937.

Sturdy teamed up with McKee to help provide some technical knowledge. Sturdy hoped not only to find the location of the mine, but also more than ninety million dollars million in gold said to be stored within the mountains four centuries earlier. Sturdy told a newspaper reporter about the legend of the Spanish missionaries who accumulated great hordes of gold from the local Indians in the 16th Century. The gold was to be shipped to Spain from the California coast. The priests hid the gold until pack mule could transport it out.

But according to Sturdy, the last of the priests, Francist, had been recalled before he could ship his load out. The tradition is that he stored the gold behind the "iron door of the Escalante mine." When he finally left, Francist took maps of the Mogul Fault area where the treasure was hidden. The Mogul fault cuts through the Santa Catalina Mountains near the town of present day Oracle. According to Sturdy, Francist wrote on the map that there was two and a half million ounces. At 1937 prices it would be worth ninety million dollars. [591]

In September Sturdy received a letter from his friend, Charles "Will" McKee who "found the old mission and the dump of the mine. I haven't yet found the door, but we will. I am certain." [592] [593] Again, the story of The Mine with the Iron Door was romanticized in newspapers around the country. Wright's book and the movie release the previous decade, under the same name, just added fuel to the legend frenzy.

McKee, William Peterson, and Dix Henecke went back in the hills that same year digging for more treasures after their great find five years earlier. McKee had been hunting for the mine since 1923. They were also in search of that buried two and a half million ounces of gold.

To get to the spot, McKee said, "take that second fork of the Skeleton Gulch trail, turn left there where old Alkall Ike shot down them four stagecoach bandits, bear gradually up the slope above Rattlesnake Arroyo and cut across the valley on the lower part of the Lazy J range. You cain't miss it." [594]

---

[591] "To Seek Historic Mine's Iron Door, Legend Says Gold Hoard There Worth About $90,000,000," Ludington Daily News, Ludington, Michigan, September 26, 1937. Page 2.

[592] "Mine with Iron Door and Wealth, Object of Hunt," The Knickerbocker News. Albany, New York, September 15, 1937.

[593] "Hope to Find 90 Millions In Gold In Hidden Mine," The Norwalk Hour. Norwalk, Connecticut. September 16, 1937.

[594] "Found the Fabulous Mine With the Iron Door," by Oren Arnold. The Denison Press, Denison, Texas, December 11, 1937. From The Portal to Texas History, University of North Texas Libraries.

McKee always believed there was an abandoned mine in the area, although the Iron Door name was not emphasized until Wright's book was published a few years earlier. McKee said he used about forty old maps and markers he gathered over the years to locate the mine. The spot was not in an area were other workings were known. Finding an ancient shaft further fueled McKee's determination that "the story was dependable."

McKee said he heard archaeologists working in the area had been finding things identical to those taken out of King Tut's tomb." He was told this area was as old as Egypt. [595]

According to McKee's version of the legend, the Spaniards came through the Southwest in 1539 [596] and established a mission near the present site of Oracle. It was known as the Spanish City. The Spaniards oppressed the local natives, and about 1680 the Indians decided to rid the Spaniards from their land. They killed the drivers and soldiers guarding a long train of burros packed with gold to be shipped to Spain. The priests in the nearby Spanish City stored the remaining gold underground until it was safe to recover. A room was sealed off 80 feet back from the mineshaft and filled with sold rock and mud to hide its treasures. The location was known only to a few padres and recorded on some maps. Eventually, the rebellious Indians destroyed the Spanish City.

Historically, in 1539 Franciscan friar Marcos de Niza set out from Culican to find the fabled Seven Cities of Cibola. They not locate any gold, nor did they establish any mission at the time. When Coronado passed through a few years later, he didn't stop for long. It wasn't until Father Eusebio Kino's expedition in the late 1690s that the Spanish started any settlements in the area. Also according to McKee in an interview, fifty years earlier than McKee's attempt, a great-great nephew of Francist arrived from Spain with some of the maps McKee possessed. The nephew hired a prospector named Old Pearson to search for the treasure. After months of searching they were unsuccessful. A Frenchman, named Charleux (also spelled Chareleux), [597] searched forty years using the maps but could not locate the iron doors. McKee knew a local resident who told that his great-great grandfather worked for Francist. Accordingly, one of the rooms of the Escalante tunnel had a "ledge of solid gold, six to eight inches thick." The property where McKee claimed the mine is located is half owned by the nearby Apache Indians. McKee owned the other half and sold half of that interest to Sturdy for his assistance. [598]

---

[595] "Indians Will Get Benefits If Iron Door Mine Is Real," by Sherry Bowen, The Arizona Daily Star, December 26, 1932.

[596] He is referring to Franciscan friar Fray Marcos de Niza and his journey in the search of the cities of gold.

[597] "Mine with Iron Door," Knickerbocker News, Albany, New York, September 15, 1937.

[598] "Search Launched for Legendary Gold Mine in Arizona," The Victoria Advocate, September 30, 1937.

"However, in spite of the chances I have taken," continued Sturdy, "I do not consider the mine a bad investment. I know there are two old veins of gold in the mine which can be opened up. Should we lose on the Francist treasure, we expect to ship sufficient gold from these veins to get the money out." [599]

C.W. was the most persistent of the group to find the lost treasure. He spent the last fourteen years of his life in its search. He believed that he would be the one to find the legendary Mine With The Iron Door. A few days before he died he told friends, "The mine is near Oracle. I'm going to be a rich man." [600] The hunt for the Iron Door Mine was halted with the death of C.W. McKee on May 25, 1938. [601] [602]

If McKee had among his forty maps some plat survey maps of the Cañada del Oro, he wouldn't have needed an Indian guide to point out the shafts and tunnels. He would have known that those spots were claimed and patented decades earlier. McKee may have actually rediscovered the 1880 Bonanza claim, [603] or the remnants of 1901 claims owned by Edwin Scott, [604] or the sixty six acres of the Arizona Copper Hill Mining Co.'s 1901 claims for the Copper Hill, Rattlesnake, and Gold Hill. [605] The land was surveyed again in 1921, 1923, and 1925 before McKee trekked the Canyon. [606]

---

[599] Ibid.

[600] Ibid. Also appears in "Desert Mining Briefs: Phoenix, Arizona..." Desert Magazine, August 1938. Page 27.

[601] "McKee, C.W., Arizona Republic, 5/27/38, Phoenix, Bio, Death Halts Hunt for Iron Door Mine," Arizona State Library Archives and Public Records. November 13, 1937.

[602] "Legendary Mine Character Taken By Death; Sought Iron Door Riches," Nevada Mining Journal, Reno, Nevada. May 30, 1938. McKee died of a heart ailment.

[603] July 16, 1880. Plat Survey No. 189, Lot No. 37. U.S. Survey General's Office. Located 769 ½ feet west of Mount Ivenah, U.S.M.M. No. 1. Claim by Frank Schultz, C.P. Watson and B.C. Parker. Surveyed by L.D. Chillson.

[604] August 27, 1901 Plat survey No. 1546. Claim of Edwin Scott

[605] August 27, 1901. Plat Survey No. 1547, Lot No. 37. U.S. Survey General's Office. The Gold Hill claim was located April 2, 1887 and Copper Hill on July 15, 1897.

[606] Surveys of T10S, R14E: May 23, 1921, Survey of 5,200 acres, includes locations of houses, shafts and dumps. April 28, 1925 Plat of claim of J.H. Aikins and P.R. Moulton, known as the Virginia, Francis and Martha Belle lodes. The Virginia adjoins the Gold Hill to the West. August 25, 1928, resurvey and retracement.

1946: Prospector Dies Seeking The Lost Mine

While on the hunt for the lost Spanish gold mine in the Catalinas, Albert ("Rabbit") Johnson disappeared and was believed to be dead, according to Pima County Sheriff E. W. Roach.

The Sheriff conducted a wide but futile search over the rugged areas where temperatures sometime "exceed 150 degrees."

Johnson confided to a friend that he previously found one of the lost mines. According to one story the friend was told, a prospector found a cave during a sandstorm. While he waited out the storm, he was digging around and discovered some rich ore. He stuffed his pockets and made a note of the hill of gold. [607]

It's possible "Rabbit" got access to those notes and got lost trying to find the hole.

---

[607] "Mine Secret May Die With 'Rabbit,'" by Murray Sinclair, Tucson Daily Citizen, Tucson Arizona. July 22, 1946. Page 7. Also published: "Prospector Finds Lost Mine in Arizona, The Disappears," by the Associated Press, Iowa City Press Citizen. June 22, 1946. Page 4; "The Location of a "lost" Spanish gold mine may be locked forever," The Bee, Danville, Virginia. July 22, 1946.

1966-1988: Mayor Hunts For Treasure

The Mayor of Kearny, Arizona, Ernest McCallister, claimed to have "found the treasure vault of the Escalante mine." He said he discovered a forty foot tunnel in the side of a mesa in 1966 while using a divining rod. At the time the landowner would not give him permission to dig.

In 1982 McCallister applied for a land-use permit from the Arizona Land Department but was told that "Rancho Romeno (sic)" was sold and the parks department leases the land. The parks department denied his request. McCallister said all the artifacts he found would be turned over to the state Arizona Historical Society. The property became part of the Catalina State Park. [608]

Despite all these efforts, there is no definitive source that confirms the discovery of the one lost mine that everyone was searching to find. However, when the rush started in the 1800s, it did generate a new business for Tucson.

---

[608] "Board denies bid to hunt gold cache in state park," Arizona Republic, August 14, 1982.

A sample nugget from the Cañada del Oro– also called Cañon del Oro or the Canyon of Gold. Photo courtesy of William Carter.

The Tucson Arizona Gold Rush

Pioneer American Prospectors
Lucrative Mining Ventures
Gold • Silver • Copper

The Canyon Of Gold In The
Cañon del Oro

Old Hat Mining & The Town Of Oracle

Marble Peak & Oracle Ridge

& 'Buffalo Bill' Cody Mines

Gold Discoveries In The Santa Catalinas

"...silver runs in ledges and gold is where you find it." [609]

The search for gold in the Santa Catalina Mountains, north of Tucson, has generated stories of hidden riches embedded in the mountains, early Spanish mines, a lost city, and a lost mission possibly near the Canyon of Gold.

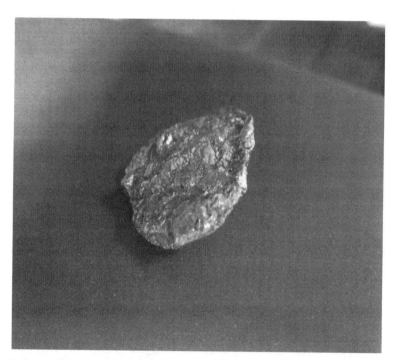

As time passed, the whereabouts of the Spanish mining operations faded from memory, except through the few who heard the stories from their parents and grandparents.

Then, came the Tucson Gold Rush in the 1870s and everything changed.

Chalcopyrite with copper and gold nugget found in the Cañada del Oro canyon. Photo courtesy of William Carter.

---

[609] South Pass, 1868: James Chisholm's Journal of the Wyoming Gold Rush, by James Chisholm. University of Nebraska Press, 1960. Page 151.

The reports of ledges of quartz embedded with gold, copper and silver in the Santa Catalina Mountains have been documented since settlers first arrived. While prospectors scoured the valleys and canyons searching for lost mines, other enterprising individuals saw the potential and established large mining operations.

Gold typically occurs in quartz veins. Gold embedded quartz, often streamed with silver, was found in abundance along the Cañada del Oro in the 1870s. [610]

According to a mineral report from the U.S. Department of Mines, some possible sources of gold bearing quartz are found near the Southern Belle. Heylmun (1989, p. 15) reports visible free gold in the Valerie May vein and "good gold values." He also notes there are "a number of gold bearing quartz lenses and pockets in igneous and metamorphic rocks on the rugged south and west flanks of the Catalina Mountains, much of it being in areas withdrawn from mineral entry." [611]

Extracting gold or silver from these hard quartz veins was historically referred to as quartz reef mining. After all of the visible ledges were scraped, the early American mining companies had to sink very deep shafts to get to the gold laden quartz deep underground. The gold was brought to the surface as small particles embedded in lumps of quartz. The quartz was then crushed into a fine dust by stamping batteries in a stamping mill. [612]

The earlier gold discoveries focused on random findings of nuggets in the creek or in slabs or ledges of quartz rock streamed with gold or silver. It took money to turn it into a business.

---

[610] Mineral Appraisal of Coronado National Forest, Part 5. U.S. Department of the Interior, Bureau of Mines, MLA 25-94, 1994. Page 24.

[611] Ibid.

[612] Quartz reef mining, http://en.wikipedia.org/wiki/Quartz_reef_mining

1850-1890: Gold-Quartz Jewelry Popularized

G old-in-quartz became fashionable as jewelry in the mid 1850-1890s. Clear or cloudy quartz stone etched with veins of gold and/or silver was a highly prized commodity.

Tiffany & Company gemologist George F. Kunz, who published a book popularizing gold quartz in the 1890s, explained that miners would often grind up the stone to extract the gold. Gemologists would instead prefer to form jewelry made of quartz in gold. [613]

A twenty-carat drop earring with yellow quartz in eighteen carat gold currently sells by Tiffany & Company for $1,500. A pendant of smoky quartz in eighteen carat gold sells for $7,000. [614] Today, similar stones are mined from the Santa Catalina Mountains and marketed as Cody Stone. [615]

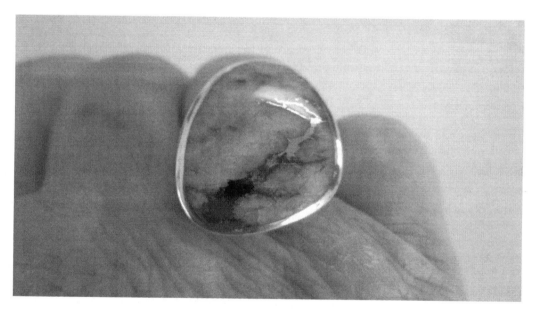

Jewelry made from silver and gold embedded in quartz from the Santa Catalina Mountains. Fabricated Cody Stone jewelry by Orlando Jewelers, England. Photo courtesy of William Carter.

---

[613] "Gems and Precious Stones of North America" by George Frederick Kunz, 1890. (Dover Books, 1892). Pages 118-119.

[614] Tiffany & Co. web site http://www.tiffany.com

[615] Cody Stone is a trademark named by William Carter.

The Rush For Tucson Gold

"Thar's gold in them thar hills." [616]

One hundred years after the Spanish conquerors left, much of their presence became lost in history. A few lingering legends and newspaper articles kept the story alive. Those stories of gold in the Santa Catalina Mountains brought new frontiersmen to the dusty streets of Tucson.

Some of the pioneers who visited Tucson in the 1850s remarked that the Santa Cruz River was a laguna "covered with rushes and cat tails." [617] At the time, the San Xavier del Bac mission was a ruin. [618]

As prospectors began to scour the Santa Catalinas in the 1870s for minerals, they also went looking for the legendary lost mine. They heard the stories back home and from old time local residents who repeated the traditions their elders told them.

---

[616] Mark Twain did not actually use the phrase "Thar's gold in them thar hills" in his any of his books. It has been attributed to Twain's (Samuel Clemens) fictional character Mulberry Sellers in American Claimant, (1892) who actually said the line, "Colonel, if the half of this is true, there's millions in it–millions." Page 36. Twain also used the phrase in Glided Age, as "millions upon millions on it!" Page 57. Twain apparently heard the phrase from miners who came to California from Georgia.

Apparently, in 1849, Georgia state geologist Dr. Matthew Stephenson pleaded with Georgian miners to stay in Georgia instead of leaving for the California Gold Rush. He uttered the original phrase "there's millions in it" and it became corrupted to "there's (thars) gold in them thar hills" by miners. Source: Where There Are Mountains: An Environmental History of the Southern Appalachians, by Donald Davis. University of Georgia Press, 2011. Page 156. Also, Auraria, The Story of A Georgia Gold-Mining Town, by E. Merton Coulter. University of Georgia Press, 1956. Page 1.

[617] "Ancient Irrigation, Traces of It to be Seen in the Vicinity of Tucson- The old Ditches – Ruins of a Dam – Pueblo Viejo," Arizona Weekly Citizen, September 7, 1889.

[618] Arizona Weekly Citizen, April 18, 1878.

In early 1858, gold was discovered between Tucson and the San Pedro River. One report said that they were able to prospect forty cents to the pan. The gold was taken from a shaft that had "evidently been opened by Mexicans, long ago, and hastily abandoned." The shaft was filled with stones and rubbish. [619]

After the California Gold Rush ended in 1859, some of the disillusioned, the well financed and the adventurous eventually migrated to Southern Arizona in search of gold. Prospectors dug all around the Santa Catalina Mountains. At the time, the national gold standard was a steady $18.93 per troy ounce.

The white man's Tucson Gold Rush first started in the Cañada del Oro after several chance discoveries of the precious ore.

The land around the Cañada del Oro was being homestead by Mexican rancher Francisco Romero in the mid-1850s, followed by other settlers, including Pedro Charouleau [620] and Mariano G. Samaniego.

The period between 1860 and 1870 brought Tucson an increase of more than three times the population, from 915 residents to 3,224. The Tucson population more than doubled to 7,007 by 1880. By 1890, the number of residents dropped to 5,120 and increased back to 7,531 by 1900. [621]

---

[619] *Sacramento Daily Union*, Sacramento, California. April 14, 1858.

[620] Also spelled as Charaleau.

[621] "Tucson Census," Education and Outreach, Arizona History Society.

American's Mining Gold From The Canyon Of Gold

The Catalina Mountains had a reported production of 1,000 ounces of gold from 1904 to 1949. Today it would be valued at over $1.3 million. [622] One nugget weighed over six ounces. [623]

In 1982, a reported two hundred and thirty ounces of gold was recovered in a resource assessment test on "placer gravels allegedly near two hundred year old placer sites of the Spaniards." [624] At today's prices, it would be worth over $300,000.

From the 1880s into the mid-1900s, Americans extensively mined copper, silver, and gold in the Santa Catalina Mountains. Some of Tucson's pioneer community leaders like Mariano Samaniego, E.O. Stratton and Sheriff Bob Leatherwood were prominent prospectors who lived and worked around the Catalina Mountains. Even William "Buffalo Bill" Cody heavily invested and explored the hills in search of precious minerals, and for the Mine With The Iron Door with his friend William Neal. Gold mining the Catalina Mountains still has some lucrative prospects according to a mining assessment report published by the U.S. Bureau of Mines in 1994. [625] While American mining ventures have taken out as much of the gold and copper as it could from the Catalina mountains, there are still some spots that haven't been explored in a long time.

Today the Oracle Ridge Mine near Mt. Lemmon and the Mammoth Mines near Oracle have both resumed operations. The Little Hills Mine near Oracle has been running for decades. Only one prospector [626] still holds an active mining claim to a remote spot in the Santa Catalina Mountains. On most weekends amateur prospectors still roam the mountains for that precious mineral. While most of the substantial gold bearing quartz

---

[622] Based on $1,340 value of gold in 2013. Gold values remained a constant $18.93 starting in 1993 a troy ounce through 1871 when it had increased a penny and continued to fluctuate a few pennies each year throughout most of the 1880-1890s. Source: Prices from 1883-1994, World Gold Council, from Timothy Green's Historical Gold Price Table.

[623] Mineral Appraisal of Coronado National Forest, Part 5, 1994. Page 25. The Spanish placer sites were suggested by Edgar Heylmun, 1989, Santa Catalina Mountains, Arizona: California Mining Journal, vol. 69, No. 1, p. 11-15.

[624] Ibid, page 25.

[625] Ibid, pages 12-14.

[626] William T. Carter has the only current, individual mining claim in the Santa Catalina Mountains.

ore has been hauled away from the mountains, fortunate prospectors can still find quartz bearing gold and silver in select areas of the mountains.

> *"Prior to 1932, this county, which ranks sixth among the gold-producing counties of Arizona, yielded approximately $5,474,000 worth of gold of which about $3,120,000 worth came from lode gold mines. The Mammoth district made most of this production, in the Quartz is an abundant mineral in the Santa Catalina Mountains, north of Tucson. Gold trapped in quartz is a valuable commodity that helped spur the Arizona Gold Rush of the 1880s."* [627]

The Cañada del Oro, or Canyon of Gold, flowing south out of the Santa Catalina Mountains. The name came from the gold that prospectors found as they settled the mountains. According to the legends, the Spanish knew this area as a source of gold.

---

[627] Mineral Appraisal of Coronado National Forest, Part 5. Page 25. Reprinted 1983. U.S. Department of the Interior, Bureau of Mines, MLA 25-94, 1994.

A view of Rancho Solaño where the Cañada del Oro runs along the fence to separate private land from the national forest. The land became home for Tucson pioneer Mariano G. Samaniego in the mid-1880s. Samaniego, who is the namesake for Samaniego Peak, staked numerous mining claims with dozens of other prospectors along the Cañada del Oro. The CDO became a short cut stagecoach passage from Tucson to the newly developing mining community of Oracle and nearby Fort Grant.

The Cañada del Oro has been a consistent source of gold and mineral ore. [628] The Spanish name– Cañon de Oro– means the "Canyon of Gold." This golden gulch sparked the Tucson gold rush in the mid-1850s. At different times the creek was also called Canyon del Oro and Gold Canyon Creek. [629]

---

[628] Mining claims in the Cañada del Oro date back into the 1870s, but prospecting had been conducted for centuries.

Arizona Bureau of Mines Bulletin, No. 132 (1932), Arizona Gold Placers and Placering, by G.M. Butler. Pages 59-61; Arizona Bureau of Mines Bulletin, No. 142 (1937); Arizona Gold Placers and Placering, pages 74-77; Gold Placers and Placering in Arizona, by E.D. Wilson, page 61. 1978; and the Arizona Department of Mineral Resources Gold Channel placer, #1T036 file. Cañada del Oro Mine (Old Hat placers; Gold Canyon placers; Gold Channel Placer #1-3), in the Cañada del Oro Wash, Oracle District (Control District; Old Hat District; Santa Catalina District), Santa Catalina Mts, Pinal and Pima Counties, Arizona, USA (mindat.org).

[629] Gold Canyon Creek is cited in the Official Map of the Territory of Arizona, compiled from Surveys, Reconnaissance's and other sources, by E.A. Eckhoff and P. Riecker, Civil Engineers, 1880. From the David Ramsey Collection, Cartography Associates. Publisher, The Graphic Co., Photo-Lith. NY.

The view east into the Santa Catalina Mountains where the Cañada del Oro flows out of the mountains and runs along the western slope. In the late 1880s and early 1900s, a wagon trail led into this canyon as a short cut to the mining town of Oracle. This is the fabled "Canyon of Gold."

Discovering the Gold Canyon

The Tucson Gold Rush started in the Cañada del Oro. After the explorers left, the prospectors arrived. Then the businessmen came and extracted millions of dollars of gold from this river of gold.

The Cañada del Oro as it flows south towards Tucson. Besides a source of placer gold, this area is immersed in history and legend.

> *"At the present time (1858) Tuscon (sic) is deserted for the cannon and with the exception of a few Mexican herders, most of the male population are at work in the mines."* [630]

---

[630] From Arizo, It's Resources and History. The Apache Indians. Correspondence for the N.Y. Times, Tucson, A.T., April 1, 1858. From New York Daily Tribune, New York City, New York. May 24, 1858.

American prospectors came to the Santa Catalina Mountains after the end of the California Gold Rush in the 1850s. These miners and cavalry troops regularly discovered gold nuggets in the "Canyon of Gold" where gold literally flowed out of the Santa Catalina Mountains.

It wasn't always easy to recover the gold because for centuries the canyon and the Catalinas were controlled by the Apache Indians.

Once the hostile Apaches had been cleared from the mountains in the late 1800s, this deep canyon became a major passage from Tucson to Camp Grant for stagecoach travelers and the U.S. Cavalry. It was a quicker route to haul supplies to Oracle and the Old Hat mining district and bring back ore to Tucson. It also opened the gateway into the Catalina Mountains for mining ventures and settlers.

Prospectors immediately laid claims to extract gold from the mouth of the Canyon of Gold. Homesteaders, like Mariano G. Samaniego and Francisco Romero, settled along the riverbanks in the mid and late 1800s.

Early newspaper articles and authors used either "Cañon de Oro" or "Canyon del Oro" through the end of the 1890s. The Canyon spelling appeared in print in 1870, while the Cañon use was much earlier. The more popular name, "Cañada del Oro," became more common in the early 1900s.

The Cañada del Oro valley is a stark contrast between the flowing waters coming from the Catalinas and the desolate nearby hills of brush and cactus.

One of the earliest diaries to report on an expedition against the Apache Indians was written in September, 1793. Captain Don Pedro de Allande was ordered to leave Tucson and enter the land of Apachería. They traveled to the Cañada del Oro, went through the "pass of Molola (north end of Santa Catalina mountains), and made their way to the Cañada de San Simón (Camp Grant Wash) towards Oracle." [631]

---

[631] Campaign from Tucson through the Arivaipa Canyon, September 9-10, 1793 from Expedition into the Apacheria, Arizona Historical Review, Pages 5, 7. The diaries notes were translated in Forgotten Frontier, by Alfred B. Thomas. Oklahoma University Press, 1932. Pages 247 and 254. They went from the mesa of the Cañada del Oro on September 10th at 6:00AM and arrived at the Agua de la Cañada del Carmen by 10:00AM.

1843: First 'Recorded' Discovery Of Gold In The Cañon del Oro

The first 'recorded' discovery of gold in the Cañon del Oro [632] was in 1843 by Spanish Colonel Antonio Pascual Narbona, who made his find as he commanded a military expedition against the Apache Indians in the area. [633] [634]

According to this version of history by historian Donald Page, on June 29, 1843, Narbona and his troops camped at a water hole by the north end of the lower canyon where they washed out some placer gold nuggets from the creek.

This often-repeated story has some fact. In 1843, a Commander Narbona did chase some Apaches around the Santa Catalina Mountains on that date. [635]

There was a Spanish army officer named Antonio Pascual Narbona. He was the acting commander, or Alférez, of the Tucson Presidio in 1794. [636] [637] [638] [639] But, after he served

---

[632] Cañon del Oro was the common spelling used in newspapers and books at the time.

[633] Lost Jesuit Mine with the Iron Door, by Donald Page, Desert Magazine, October 1956, pages 12 ("there his troopers washed out a little gold.").

[634] Lost Gold and Silver Mines of the Southwest, Eugene L. Conrotto, 1996, page 116 ("camped here and found placer nuggets"). Conrotto repeats a similar story told by Page. He probably got his sources from Page.

[635] Ibid.

[636] Narbona, Antonio (1773-1830, March 20), UAiR BID # 19876, University of Arizona.

[637] Military Awards of 1817, noted from March 7, 1808 in 1 1817 letter referencing "Antonio Narbona, acting commandant of the Tucson presidio."
http://www.library.arizona.edu/exhibits/desertdoc/military.htm

[638] "When the first fighting of the Mexican independence movement began in the fall of 1810, the Tucson presidio was commanded by Captain Antonio Narbona," from Hispanic Arizona, 1536-1856, by James E. Officer, 1989. Page 89. Antonio Narbona Sr. was born in Mobile, Alabama in 1773 when the city was part of Spanish Louisiana. He died in Arizpe in 1830. Page 362.

[639] Spanish Colonial Tucson, Peacetime Presidio 1792-1821. University of Arizona. Page 107.

as governor of New Mexico, he died in 1830. [640] [641] This Narbona does fit the title and location, but he died thirteen years before the reported find.

Col. Narbona, however, did have a son also named Antonio Narbona who fought Apache Indians and lived during that time period. Senior Col. Narbona's son is the likely person named in this legend.

But, outside of Donald Page's claim, there is no report of Narbona's gold discovery. Noted historians James Officer [642] and Hubert Howe Bancroft [643] both mention Narbona's expedition against the Apaches on that day. But, they leave out any reference to gold.

According to historical accounts of the event, Junior Antonio Narbona, the military commander of the Santa Cruz territory, assembled a force of two hundred and forty one soldiers and Indian allies in Tucson to fight against the Apaches on that June 29th.

The troops set out from the Tucson Presidio that afternoon and rode east toward the San Pedro River, probably along the south end of Rincon Peak. Several times, threatening Apaches yelled out insults to the passing troops. When a small contingent was sent into the Catalinas to challenge them, the Indians vanished.

The Apaches attacked Narbona's camp on July 3rd in a frontal assault, but fifteen Apaches were isolated and "wiped out." Narbona headed back to Tucson with some victory the following day. [644]

There is no other account of anyone in the group finding gold nuggets on their way out of Tucson on the date that Page attributes to Narbona's discovery. But, they were gone for four days before they returned.

---

[640] Narbona, Antonio, UAiR BID # 19876, University of Arizona. Born 1773 in Mobile Louisiana and died March 20, 1830 in Arizpe, Sonora. Narbona was the New Mexico governor from 1825 to 1827.

[641] Encyclopedia of Frontier Biography: G-O, by Dan L. Thrapp. Pages 1041-1042. Also, above 198.

[642] Hispanic Arizona, 1536-1856, by James E. Officer. Pages 169-170. Officer calls him Francisco Narbona on one page and then Antonio Narbona on the next page. Other sources refer to him as Antonio Narbona.

[643] Ibid and Arizona and New Mexico, 1888, by Hubert Howe Bancroft, page 405.

[644] Ibid.

It would have been impractical to find gold on June 29, the day they left. They would have departed from Tucson that afternoon, found gold nuggets at the Cañon del Oro on the northwest side of the mountains, and then, headed to the southern range of the mountains and then east towards the San Pedro before they camped by Rincon Peak, all within one day. That is nearly one hundred miles of travel on horseback which is highly improbable.

Somewhere in this area of the Cañon del Oro (Cañada del Oro), Narbona's troops reportedly stopped and found gold nuggets.

The distance from Tucson to the Cañon del Oro passage was about thirty miles, alone, enough for a single day's travel. A horse would take nearly eight hours at a four mile-per-hour gait. If they did make a stop at the Cañon del Oro, they most likely camped overnight at the river's bend on their return to Tucson a few days later. This is more probable.

Since Donald Page did not cite his source, that rumor cannot be confirmed. Perhaps Narbona, [645] or one of his men, did find some gold nuggets in the CDO and it was never written down– just one of those stories told among friends. History won't tell, and probably they didn't want it known. Some loose lips might have started the legend.

If he did find gold, this would have occurred almost five years before gold was discovered in California. [646] Such news should have brought a flood of hungry prospectors to the Cañon del Oro; however the constant threat of Apache Indians, and the extreme remoteness of Tucson could have kept any discovery a back yard secret for a long time. It was over a decade later when people started to search for this free flowing gold in the CDO.

Gold nuggets actually were found in the Cañon del Oro not long after. Once the word got out, the Santa Catalinas were never the same.

Maybe the rumor was true…

---

[645] Narbona Jr. was killed by the Chiricahua Indians, on the threshold of his home on December 23, 1848, from "Antonio Narbona," Wikipedia. His son attained the rank of Colonel. Another source says he died in 1849, from Encyclopedia of Frontier Biography: G-O, by Dan L. Thrapp. Page 1042.

[646] January 24, 1848 Gold discovered at Sutter's Creek. From This Day in History, History.com

1846-1848: Roadblocks To Gold Recovery

The Mexican-American War in December 1846 brought three hundred and thirty citizen soldiers from the U.S. Mormon Battalion to attack the Mexican Army in Tucson. The Mexicans withdrew without fighting, but returned after the Mormons left. [647] At the time two hundred to three hundred people lived near the Tucson Presidio. [648]

After the war with Mexico ended in 1848, the Mexican government sold most of the land in the Southwest. The Mexican military, however, remained in Tucson until 1856. As the Mexican territory shifted farther south, more Americans began to make a stop in Tucson along the way to California.

Over that next decade more Americans started to settle around Tucson. The more adventurous prospectors camped near the dangerous Santa Catalina Mountains on the rumors of gold in the hills.

---

[647] Political Intrigue at Tucson: The Mexican Garrison and the Mormon Battalion, by Clark V. Johnson, Professor of Church History and Doctrine at Brigham Young University.

[648] Tucson Chronology, Southwest Library, University of Arizona.

1850s: Americans Discover Tucson

When it was safe to settle, word started to spread that there was gold in the Southwest. But migrating Americans who often came from the east and the west coast in the mid-1850s did not favorably describe Tucson. They were very dismayed by the drab environment.

A visiting New Yorker in 1852 described Tucson as a "miserable place" made up of mostly Apache Mensos (civil red Apaches). The San Xavier del Bac mission, however, was the "most highly finished and elaborately ornamented church" ever visited by the writer. [649]

The Gadsden Purchase of 1854 opened up the Arizona territory to a wave of American settlers and prospectors. Up until then the land called Sonora belonged to Mexico. Tucson, as part of the province of Sonora, was in a mineral district where silver and gold could be found, according to one of the earliest printed reports about Tucson and gold in 1854. [650]

Adventurous Americans sometimes experienced the wrath of the Apaches as they tried to settle around Tucson. On August 21, 1854, a group of twenty Americans were eating dinner when a band of fifteen Indians ambushed them and took seven horses. Not a shot was fired even though the Americans were well armed. About the same time a group of Texans were attacked a few miles on the other side of Tucson. One American was killed, and twenty seven horses were taken. Another report claimed twenty five Americans had died because of lack of water. [651]

It was these kinds of stories, read in comfortable homes in the Midwest and the East that continued to paint the desperate image of the Wild, Wild West.

---

[649] "Mexican Boundary Commission: San Xavier del Bac," New York Daily Tribune, March 23, 1852.

[650] "Capabilities and Resources of Sonora," Daily Evening Star, Washington D.C., February 24, 1854, "to Tucson on the north, will very nearly include sections in which silver and gold is found."

[651] "Terrible Massacre by Indians," the Burlington Free Press, November 3, 1854 and from The Raftman's Journal, Clearfield, PA, November 8, 1854.

1855: Gold Found Near The Catalinas

I n 1855 reports of numerous gold placers were found near the headwaters of the San Pedro and Gila Rivers, on the east and north side of the Santa Catalina Mountains. But they were abandoned because of the "hostility of the Indians and difficulty of procuring supplies." [652]

Newcomers were surprised to find iron in abundance around Tucson, and "beyond a doubt, that gold does exist in the headwaters of the San Pedro and Gila." The whole area in the Gadsden Purchase was "as rich in gold depositories as California." [653]

The menacing Apache Indians still made it difficult to get near the Santa Catalina Mountains. The troops had to protect the residents of Tucson who lived near the walls of the Presidio and ranchers who were frequent targets. Mexican rancher Francisco Romero, who made his home near the Cañon del Oro about this time, was constantly fighting off the Apaches.

At the end of 1857, a newspaper article that appeared in the San Francisco Daily Alta California [654] laid the foundation for the legend of the lost mine and the Jesuits' involvement. It re-enforced Sylvester Mowry's claim of "the reports of the immense mineral wealth of the new country, made by the Jesuits." The article described the early Spaniards search for gold and silver and their travels through the Santa Cruz and San Pedro Valleys.

It was stories like these that fueled the beginning of a new immigrant wave– the American prospector.

---

[652] "The Gadsden Purchase," Edgefield Advertiser, Edgefield, S.C., April 18, 1855. On August 21, 1854, 50 emigrants from Texas were killed by Indians near Tucson, according to Burlington Free Press, Burlington, VT, November 3, 1854

[653] The Athens Post, Athens, Tenn., April 20, 1855.

[654] Daily Alta California, San Francisco, California, November 27, 1857. Also printed in the Mining Magazine, 1860.

1858: The Tucson Gold Rush Begins

Reports of gold and silver in the West, printed in East Coast and Mid-West newspapers, encouraged a new breed of adventurers to explore the territory that was acquired from Mexico called Arrizonia [655] with the village of Tucson as its aspiring capital. After the Butterfield Stage first came through Tucson on October 2, 1858, [656] [657] Tucson finally started to become recognized as a viable community.

A pamphlet published in 1858 by Capt. T.S. Cram of the United States Army Corp of Topographical Engineers described how to bring the lead, copper, silver, and gold of Arizona into the world markets. [658]

Even an outbreak of influenza in Tucson in 1858 that killed many Indians, Mexicans, and some Americans didn't stop the excitement about the "old Cañada de Oro placer mines, where rich diggings are said to have been found." [659]

A visitor wrote during his travels through the "Purchase" in February, 1858, that he saw "pieces of natural iron laying in the plaza at Tucson that weigh over a ton each taken from the surface of a neighboring mountain." [660]

---

[655] "Another New Territory," The M'arthur Democrat, McArthur, Vinton County, Ohio, December 4, 1856. Reported from the Nashville Union.

[656] The Memphis Daily Appeal, Memphis, Tenn, July 3, 1858.

[657] "Ring's Reflections: Stagecoaches set stage for Tucson's growth," The Arizona Daily Star, June 28, 2012.

[658] "Correspondence of the Daily Pennsylvanian, The Territory of Arizona, Washington, February 25, 1858. Daily Pennsylvanian, March 11, 1858.

[659] Letter from the Gadsden Purchase, extracted from a private letter printed in The Alta California from Tubac, March 15, 1858: "There is some excitement in the Purchase about the old Cañada del Oro placer mines, where rich diggings are said to have been found lately." New York Daily Tribune, April 28, 1858.

[660] Extracted from a letter "received by a distinguished Senator from a gentleman (Henry Pl. Sweetland), who has just completed a trip through Arizona." New York Daily Tribune, February 12, 1858.

Reports of gold in Arizona continued to lure the adventurous. But, the presence of the Apache Indians still kept most prospecting hopes at bay until a party of Tucson residents left for the gold canyon in February 19, 1858. After four days they returned with some gold specimens that yielded ten cents to forty three cents to the pan.

The prospectors were familiar with the story about the old mines and the Jesuits who were forced to leave the country in 1780 and again when the revolution occurred in 1815. According to the legends, they "closed all the mines and carefully erased all signs by which they might be recognized." The records of those mines are in Mexico City, according to author Charles Hall. [661]

As the excitement spread, picks and spades were sold at a premium. Tucson "is deserted for the Cañon, and with the exception of a few Mexican herders, most of the male population are at work in the mines." [662]

In April 1858, another group traveling in Leach's wagon between Tucson and Rio San Pedro discovered gold that "got a prospect of forty cents to the pan. It had been taken from a shaft, probably abandoned by Mexicans a long time ago, filled with rubbish and stones." [663]

Placers were being worked on at the nearby Santa Rita copper mine. The entire region was considered "gold bearing," even though there were an "immense number of silver mines around Tucson and Tubac." [664] Some prospectors tried to work around the Cañada del Oro area but left because of the Apaches. In the fall of 1858, a band of Apaches entered the village of Tucson and murdered an elderly Mexican man within four hundred yards of the town plaza. [665]

The 1860s and 1870s were a difficult time. As settlers and prospectors came to Tucson, they were still met with deplorable living conditions and constant threats from the Apache Indians.

---

[661] "From Arizo (sic), Its Resources and History, The Apache Indians," New York Daily Tribune, May 24, 1858.

[662] Ibid.

[663] Sacramento Daily Union, April 14, 1858. California Digital Newspaper Collection.

[664] "Gold Mines on the Gila," Dallas Herald, December 29, 1858.

[665] "By the Overland Mail," Glasgow Weekly Times, December 9, 1858.

It eventually took an American military intervention to make peace. After a treaty was negotiated at the Cañada del Oro, there was a pause to the ambushes.

It was just enough for some Tucson pioneers to discover a wealth of quartz bearing gold along with the legends and even more treasures hidden in the Santa Catalinas.

The view near Mariano G. Samaniego's Ranch, by the mouth of the Cañon del Oro. It may have been near this area where the U.S. military made a temporary peace with the Indians and camped from 1861-1866.

1859-1870: Civilizing The 'Cañon del Oro'

"Cañon del Oro is situated about thirty miles to the Northeast of Tucson, and is noted as having been the locality of a gold washing operation, about a year since. It is a fact that gold exists there, and several experienced California miners believe it would pay a small company to "sluice" the little valley at the upper end of the Cañon, as there is an abundance of good water at most seasons of the year. The party who once attempted to work the Cañon, being annoyed by the Indians, withdrew, and since that time few white men have visited the spot."

From the Weekly Arizonian, March 31, 1859. [666]

The Apache Indians continued to make it impossible for early American settlers to live, mine or travel in the Tucson valley or anywhere near the Santa Catalina Mountains.

An attempt to make "peace" with the hostile Pinal Apaches was offered in the spring of 1859 at the mouth of the Cañon del Oro, as the Cañada del Oro was called at the time. [667]

A flag of truce was arranged in early March when two chiefs went to Fort Buchanan with a promise to behave better and not plunder Americans any longer if the white man would not invade. The other Indian tribes considered the Pinal Apaches to be among the "most crafty, treacherous, and unreliable, besides being rapacious and cruel."

Capt. Robert Stoddart Ewell had been scheduled to conduct an extensive campaign against the Apaches a month before, but it was delayed by Lieut. Col. Reeves. [668]

Captain Ewell agreed to meet the tribe at Cañon del Oro on March 20, 1859, and hold a "talk" with them. [669] This was the first, friendly meeting between the Pinal Apaches and

---

[666] "The Late Indian Treaty," The Weekly Arizonian, Tubac, A.T. March 31, 1859. This article describes in detail the meeting between the troops and Apaches.

[667] Glasgow Weekly Times, December 9, 1858 and the Congressional Serial Set, U.S. Printing Office, 1860. No. 170, Santa Fé, New Mexico, August 12, 1859. Page 715.

[668] "The Pinal Apaches," The Weekly Arizonian, Tubac, A.T. March 3, 1859.

Numerous gold placer deposits have been found along the Cañada del Oro that flows between the Sahuaro cacti in the hills and the row of trees and cottonwoods. This may be the area where the U.S. Cavalry made a peace treaty with the Indians and Narbona reportedly found gold in the wash. It was also the place where, at least, two Tucsonans would pay with their lives.

the Americans and probably was the first time the Indians ever stood face-to-face with the white man.

The meeting was delayed another two days until the twenty second after two Pinal chiefs wanted to meet about fifty to sixty miles from the Cañon del Oro at Arivypa Canyon. The

Captain demanded they all meet at the original designated place. The Indians agreed, and all of the people in the Arivypa traveled to the Cañon.

A year before in this same spot, gold washing operations were conducted, but were abandoned by the threat of Indians. [670]

The troops, along with local citizens hoping to trade with the Indians, camped at the upper end of the Cañon between the mountains and a stream lined with cottonwood trees and a steep bluff on the east side. By two o'clock in the afternoon, three Pinal Indians wandered into the camp. After one departed small groups were seen on the distant hilltops. They cautiously descended and joined the camp. Both sides remained suspicious and guarded.

Ten chiefs, two hundred and eighty eight Pinal Apaches, twenty five Tonto Apache warriors and about six hundred women, children, and old men were present and faced the one hundred American dragoons.

---

[670] "The Pinal Apaches," The Weekly Arizonian, Tubac, A.T. March 31, 1859.

"Altogether, they were a dangerous, thievish, wolfish-looking set, as we ever happened to meet– of the cayote [671] type in all their action and characteristics, as near as it is possible for savage humanity to resemble a wild beast!" exclaimed the newspaper correspondent who attended the event. During the meeting the Indians sold the troops some gold brought from the Gila River. [672]

Doctor Steck, the Apache agent, arrived late to the meeting. Finally a treaty was made. The Apaches agreed "not to molest Americans in their persons or property," and the U.S. government agreed to distribute goods and provisions to them if they kept their promise. [673] This became known as The Cañon del Oro Treaty.

A month later the Pimo Indians, complained about the Pinal Indians who stole property from them and about the more hostile Apaches who were given beef, corn, and blankets while they (the Pimos) did not get any supplies. The government said it didn't consider them poor enough to need the goods. Their tribe received farming tools instead, to raise their own provisions. That seemed to console the Pimos, and they agreed not to take revenge on the Pinals. [674]

---

[671] "The Pinal Coyeteros occupy the country watered by the Salinas and other tributaries of the Gila." They number about "three thousand souls, of which seven hundred are warriors. This band lives directly north of Tucson and Tubac, and formerly committed many depredations upon the property of the unprotected citizens of that frontier." California Farmer and Journal of Useful Sciences, Vol. 19, No. 15, June 5, 1863.

[672] "The Late Indian Treaty," The Weekly Arizonian, Tubac, A.T. March 31, 1859.

[673] "The Pinal Apaches," The Weekly Arizonian, Tubac, A.T. March 17, 1859.

[674] "The Pimo Indians," The Weekly Arizonian, Tubac, A.T. April 28, 1859.

1861: The Ambush Of Page & Scott

T he road from Tucson to Fort Grant and Fort Breckenridge follows north along the Cañon del Oro [675] and abruptly turns to the right as it goes into the Santa Catalina Mountains. It was still a dangerous route in 1861 even though it was the fastest way to get to the Fort.

Travelers constantly complained about the many Indian "depredations" [676] along this rugged road. A noted Indian ambush on February 20, 1861, killed John Page [677] and Alf Scott near the bend of the creek. [678] [679] This was close to the same area where the Apaches and Americans had agreed to a peace treaty two years earlier.

With a wagonload of provisions for Fort Breckenridge, Page and his partners Scott and Jim Cotton were on the Cañon del Oro road with three Mexican men and a Mexican woman who rode the Wadsworth wagon.

After they passed the point later known as Samaniego's Ranch [680] where the gorge winds southward, Cotton thought he spotted Indians on the hill above them. Page dismissed his claims as imagination, and the group stopped for water.

---

[675] Cañon del Oro was the accepted name at the time for the Cañada del Oro.

[676] "Depredate," to lay waste; to engage in plunder. Merriam-Webster Dictionary.

[677] John Hemptsead Page married Larcena Pennington in December 1858. In 1860, at age 23, she was kidnapped by Apaches and thought dead, but was found barely alive. From "The Penningtons: Pioneers of Early Tucson," Historical Sketch by Robert H. Forbes, published by Arizona Archaeological and Historical Society, 1919. The story of her survival is on pages 12-22. The story is also retold in Larcena Pennington Page Survives Capture By Apaches, by Jan Cleere, "Chronicle of the Old West," Vol. 2, No. 4, March 2002.

[678] Pioneering in Arizona. The Reminiscences of Emerson Oliver Stratton and Edith Stratton Kitt, edited by John Alexander Carroll. Arizona Pioneers' Historical Society, Tucson, Arizona, 1964. Page 132.

[679] An account of this ambush is detailed in the Sacramento Daily Union, Vol. 20, No. 3108, March 14, 1861. California Digital Newspaper Collection.

[680] Mariano Samaniego moved to Tucson in 1869, from Tucson Volunteer Fire Department Mariano Samaniego.

As they went out of the wash, Cotton again thought he saw Indians. The group decided to camp for the night anyway. But as it turned dark Page and Scott were wounded in an ambush. Cotton, who was nearby fired at the Indians and they dispersed. Some of the group fled on foot back to Tucson leaving Page and Scott behind. While in town, they learned other attacks had occurred the day before.

Tucson businessman William S. Oury gathered a few men to retrieve the bodies the next day. It was night by the time they arrived at the Cañon and they were unable to find any remains.

The next morning they searched the area and found the overturned wagon at the head of the ravine and Page's body nearby. They concluded that Page and Scott had tried to elude the Indians for a while. Page might not have died until one or two days after the attack. Most likely Scott stayed near him for a while.

As they dug a grave for Page, they debated if he could have survived had they reached him sooner. An "impromptu autopsy" at the scene conducted by Tucson's Congress Hall Saloon owner Charles "Charley" Brown concluded Page might have survived with timely aid. Scott's body was found nearby a few days later in the Cañon del Oro. [681]

A year earlier Page suffered an indignation when the Apaches abducted his wife, Larcena Pennington Page. [682] On March 16, 1860, five Tonto Apaches kidnapped Larcena and ten year old Mercedes Sais Quiroz. Larcena was told they had killed John Page and his partner, William Randall.

Actually, it was almost exactly a year later when Page and his partner Scott were ambushed and murdered. Larcena's ordeal lasted two weeks before she was found wandering bloodied through the desert. The Pages were married in 1859, a year before her abduction.

---

[681] The story of the attack and autopsy in "With Their Own Blood: A Saga of Southwestern Pioneers," By Virginia Roberts, 2013. The Sacramento Daily Union on March 14, 1861 reported, "John Page leaves a wife to lament his untimely loss." Also, read Mrs. Page's story in the New York Daily Tribune, April 21, 1860, page 3.

[682] Larcena Pennington Page (1837-1913). See http://www.gvrhc.org/Library/PenningtonSaga.pdf Pennington Street in downtown Tucson is named after Larcena's father, Elias.

1862-1870: Treaty Broken Again; Cavalry Protects CDO Travelers

The peace treaty was broken, so the United States Army stationed Company A, B, D and E of the 1st Cavalry Regiments at the Cañon del Oro in order to protect travelers from the hostile Apaches from 1862 through 1866. [683] [684]

The route from Tucson to Camp Grant was about forty miles northeast and paralleled the river. Travelers had to cross through the river and pass through the mountains to get to Camp Grant.

There was another interruption in prospecting when the Confederacy established the Arizona Territory in February, 1862. The nearby Battle of Picacho Peak was held in April 15, 1862. [685]

On May 20, 1862, the Union forces of the 1st California Volunteer Cavalry entered the Tucson, Arizona Territory from the north and east via the Cañon Del Oro Road. [686]

From June to November, 1862, U.S. Cavalry operations were held around Cañon del Oro near Tucson and then at Revanton [687] from June to November, 1862. [688] The detachment of Company

CAVALRY

[683] "Inventory of the Military Department, Civil War Volunteers Records, 1861-1867," OAC, Online Archive of California.

[684] "U.S. Army Headquarters, Tucson, Arizona, 1862," Military History Online.

[685] The skirmish was the largest Civil War conflict to take place in Arizona on April 15, 1862. The site is near the rancheria of Aquituni, the former Santa Catalina Mission.

[686] "The Civil War in the Southwest, U.S. Army Headquarters, Tucson, Arizona, 1862," Military History Online.

[687] Revanton was about 40 miles south of Tucson and was settled shortly after the Gadsden Purchase. "Revanton is (Kitchen's Ranch) also known as El Potero, "Arizona Place Names," by Will C. Barnes, page 361. Also repeated in "The Civil War in Arizona: The Story of the California Volunteers, 1861-1865," by Andrew E. Maisch, 2012. Page 219. Maisch uses the spelling as "Revention" [Reventon].

[688] "The Apache Campaign," Weekly Arizona Miner, Fort Whipple, Arizona, July 20, 1864. Order dated May 1, 1864 "inaugurating the grand campaign against the Apaches of Arizona, will be preserved as of historic interest in connection with the Territory."

B, 2nd Cavalry was stationed at the Cañon del Oro in July. It may have been during this period when the camp or the Fort Cañada del Oro was operative. [689]

A soldier stationed in Tucson wrote in June, 1862, that his party went out prospecting in the Cañon del Oro with tin pans and buckets, and for several hours all got "color." They concluded from their rich diggings "the national debt could be paid out of the Cañon del Oro." [690] The soldier said the one or two years before "gold fever existed in the Territory, by gold being found" lying on the surface. [691]

In 1863 prominent Territorial pioneer and miner Sylvester Mowry published a book about the resources of Arizona and included a map of Sonora, Arizona. "Canada del Oro Gold Placers" is marked on the map although the site is not mentioned by name in his account. Mowry's book brought the link between the Jesuits and the mines to public discourse. [692] [693] This is the earliest known map marking the site of the Cañada del Oro.

This news might have been the impetus to spark the gold rush to the Santa Catalina Mountains.

---

[689] "Fort Cañada del Oro, (1862), Oro Valley. Located about 13 miles north of Tucson." From North American Forts, 1526-1956, American Forts Network. Also cited as Fort Cañada del Oro in The CDO: A Hairpin Curve Back to History, by Bill Norman, Desert Leaf. November 2011, Page 44.

[690] "Letter from the Volunteer Column from California," Daily Alta California, Vol. XIV, No. 4526, July 10, 1862, from the California Digital Newspaper Collection (CDNC). Quoted from "To Recapture Tucson," from "The Army of the Pacific: Its Operations in California, Texas, Arizona, New Mexico, Utah, Nevada, Oregon, Washington, Plains Region, Mexico, Etc, 1860-1866" By Aurora Hunt, 2004. Page 109. Also repeated in "Dispatches from the California Volunteers, 1862-65" from "The Civil War in Arizona: The Story of the California Volunteers, 1861-1865," by Andrew E. Maisch, 2012. Page 204.

[691] Dated June 16, 1862 from Tucson, Arizona A.T., "Letter from the Volunteer Column from California," Daily Alta California, Vol. XIV, No. 4526, July 10, 1862, from the California Digital Newspaper Collection (CDNC).

[692] The Geography and Resources of Arizona and Sonora, by Sylvester Mowry, A. Roman & Co., 1863, page 1 inside of cover.

[693] This map is published in The Geography and Resources of Arizona and Sonora, by Sylvester Mowry, A. Roman & Co., 1863, page 1 inside of cover. Printed in handwriting at the bottom of the map: Outline Map of Sonora, Arizona, including the Sierra Madre. Compiled from Authentic Sources and personal Observation for the Geography and Resources of 'Arizona and Sonora' by Sylvester Mowry of Arizona, 1863.

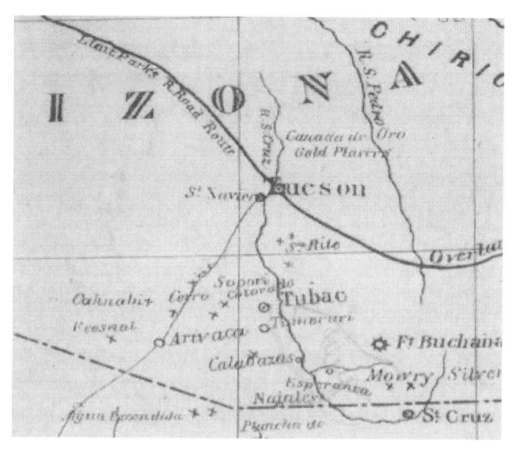

Mowry's 1863 map of Tucson indicating the "Cañada del Oro Placers." [694] This is one of the earliest maps labeling the Cañada del Oro, and, especially indicating gold placers.

[694] Outline Map of Sonora Arizona, by Sylvester Lowry, 1863. Published in The Geography and Resources of Arizona and Sonora, by Sylvester Mowry. An Address Before the American Geographical and Statistical Society, in New York, February 9, 1859. A New Edition With An Appendix, A. Roman & Co., 1863. Public domain document.

1863-1864: The Great Gold Exploration Is On!

The Grand Campaign against the Apaches

A "great influx of gold from the Arizona mines into Sonora" warranted a stagecoach line between Hermosillo, Sonora and Tucson in 1863. A mail route between Los Angeles and Tucson was opened, and a stage line to Los Angeles was being established. It was expected that Governor Goodwin would declare Tucson as the capital of Arizona [695] after the Territory of Arizona Act was approved on February 24, 1863.

Sylvester Mowry, a prominent American, published numerous reports in 1863 where he described a land once filled with silver and gold mines. His information came from a map drawn in 1757 and notes provided by Capt. Charles Stone and others. Since the Mexican government certified that those notes were accurate, it was accepted as common knowledge and fact. [696]

In March, 1864, Mr. Greeley wrote about his exploration of the Cañada del Oro with Abraham Lyons, the famous explorer, thirteen others. With picks, spades, pans, rifles, and revolvers they headed to the mountains in search of gold and wary of stalking Apaches. They found surface diggings by previous parties, including a twelve-foot hole and several abandoned tunnels, filled with rubbish. As they prospected the creek, they found one to two bits of gold to the pan. [697]

Ever since the Territory was occupied by the new Anglo arrivals, the Apaches had become more hostile. Finally on May 1, 1864, General Order #12 was issued to begin the "grand campaign against the Apaches." Col. Edwin A. Rigg, commander of the 1st Infantry California Volunteers, with a detachment of fivehundred soldiers went through the Cañada del Oro and the San Pedro below the Aravaypa (Aravaipa). A post was to be established on the Gila River called Fort Goodwin. This was supposed to put an end to

---

[695] "Additional From Sonora and Arizona," Daily Alta California, Los Angeles, October 15, 1863. The California Digital Newspaper Collection.

[696] Geography and Resources of Arizona and Sonora, by Sylvester Mowry, 1863.

[697] "Mr. Greeley's Letter from the Arizona Trail, Tucson, Arizona T., February 25, 1864," Daily Alta California, San Francisco, California, Vol. 16, No. 5230, March 17, 1864. California Digital Newspaper Collection.

the marauding Apaches. Peace did not last long. An Order was issued to kill whatever Apaches are encountered unless they gave themselves up as prisoners to "ensure a lasting peace and a security of life to all who go to that country in search of precious metals." Women and children were not to be harmed, only taken as prisoners. [698]

1867: Army Sets Up Camp Again In The CDO

T he ranchers and prospectors in the Cañon del Oro had had enough. They repeatedly asked for protection from the menacing Apaches. Something had to be done before anyone else was killed. The Army took action again.

This time troops from Camp Grant who were recovering from malaria were sent to a temporary convalescent camp set up in the Cañon in 1867. It was hoped the presence of the troops, even though they were convalescing, would scare off the Indians. [699]

An attack in the Cañon de Oro was thwarted in April, 1869, when six cavalry went on the road to Tucson to recover a wagon train owned by local merchant Ochoa , later found burned out at the Cañon de Oro. When they went to check out the scene the next day, Indians confronted several of the men, but they weren't caught. [700]

---

[698] "United States Military Posts on the Mexico Border (1856 to Present)," http://www.cdarc.org/pdf/scvnha/chapter04_j.pdf and reported in the Weekly Arizona Miner, "The Apache Campaign," July 20, 1864.

[699] United States Military Posts On Mexican Border, (1856 to Present), Interpretive Themes and Related Resources. Page 143.

[700] The Weekly Arizonian, May 15, 1869.

At the mouth of the Cañon de Oro is near the site where the U.S. Calvary stationed a convalescence camp for soldiers recovering from illnesses and provided an outpost to monitor murdering Apaches.

1867: Goldberg's "Lost Ledge"

"Gold is where I ain't" [701]

One of Tucson's early Jewish pioneers, Isaac Goldberg [702] heard from a local Indian that the summit of the Canyon del Oro [703] contained an abundance of gold.

When Goldberg arrived in Tucson in 1865, he saw a "some-time deserted city with buildings mostly in ruins." Despite that observation, he opened a business in Tucson with partner Philip Drachman because he saw it as a profitable investment.

In 1867 he organized a group of prospectors, including P.W. Dooner, General Sigel, Jack Shubling, and eight Mexicans to explore the area. [704]

They planned to discover "fabulous gold mines that were supposed to exist somewhere among the summit peaks of that rocky and almost inaccessible range" of the Santa Catalina mountains. [705]

The group entered through the north side of the range and wandered through the canyon for several days. They expected to find "pocketfuls of nuggets," but after they reached their destination, they were disappointed to find only large "chunks of 'ising-glass.' " [706]

---

[701] This phrase is attributed as a miner's saying. From Apaches and the Mining Menace; Indian-White Conflicts in Southwestern New Mexico, 1800-1886, by Hana Samek Norton, New Mexico Geological Society Guidebook, La Cruces, New Mexico, 1998. Page 55.

[702] Goldberg formed a merchandising and mail contracting business with his partner, and in-law, Philip Drachman. It closed because of losses from Indian depredations. Goldberg was born in 1836 and died in 1902 at age 66. From Bio of Isaac Goldberg, Arizona State University.

[703] Canyon del Oro is the spelling used at this time.

[704] An Old Timers Experiences in Arizona. A Story of the Pioneer Days of Isaac Goldberg, by Isaac Goldberg. Arizona Historical Review. Written for the Society of Arizona Pioneers, June 1894.

[705] The Goldberg Brothers: Arizona Pioneers, by Floyd S. Fierman, American Jewish Archives, Vol. XVIII, No. 1, April 1966, pages 13-15. Read about the life of Isaac and his brother Hyman Goldberg, Tucson Jewish pioneers and a description of his explorations. Pages 88-94.

On the dangerous return trip, they "found a mine, the rock from which assayed richly, but the contents yet remain undisturbed, owing to its uncommon inaccessibility." A huge ledge of "very fine copper ore" was discovered, but they didn't take careful note of its location when they left the mountains.

Goldberg made four or five futile attempts to search its location. It would take him more than a decade to again locate his very own, lost mine. [707]

Goldberg was pleased, however, to have the distinction of being the first American group to explore the "terribly precipitous heights known as the Santa Catalina Mountains."

Depredations by marauding Indians were reported at Canyon del Oro on May 11, 1869. A claim for $7,225 was filed along with several others around Tucson. [708] Some accounts state three hundred Indians attacked and five men were killed, mules were stolen, and the wagons were burned. A painting, titled "May 10," by Edward Zinn depicts the ambush. [709]

Goldberg decided to wait until the situation was calmer before approaching the deadly Canyon of Gold. In 1878 he left with his family to San Francisco "to have certain Jewish rites performed for his children." [710]

It wasn't until 1881 when Goldberg and his prospecting partners felt safe enough to venture back into the Santa Catalina's in search of his misplaced ledge of gold and the famous Lost Mine.

In the meantime, the Apaches continued to defend their territory from the invading Americans.

---

[706] Ibid. Page 93. Isinglass, thin sheets of mica, particularly of muscovite. Source: Encyclopedia Britannica. Mica is common in the Santa Catalina Mountains.

[707] Ibid. Page 93.

[708] Cases Decided in the Court of Claims of the United States, by W.H. & O. H. Morrison, 1879. Page 3. This date, 1869, has been confused with an incident in 1872 in the same location, by the same shipping company, Tully & Ochoa.

[709] This Day in History, May 10, from Arizona Memory Project, Arizona Historical Society, Tucson. The description is similar to an incident on May 10, 1872 - the mention of the 300 Indians and 5 deaths. See painting at http://azmemory.azlibrary.gov/cdm/singleitem/collection/ahsdinazh/id/460/rec/16

[710] Arizona Weekly Citizen, Tucson, A.T., October 19, 1878. The article didn't specify the "rites" – ranging from circumcision for newborn males to a bar or bat mitzvah for a child reaching age 13.

1870s: The Kennedy-Israel Massacre

On either May 28 or June 6, 1870, [711] [712] Apache Indians captured a wagon train and killed two Tucson citizens on the road between Tucson and Camp Grant near the deep canyon of the Cañon del Oro. The ambush was known as the Kennedy-Israel Massacre. There is a conflict about the actual date, a historical anachronism error. [713]

Hugh Kennedy and Newton Israel both owned a ranch on the San Pedro River, a mile below Camp Grant on the east side of the then called Santa Catarina Mountains. They went to Tucson to obtain laborers for their ranch. [714]

---

[711] This date may be in dispute. The earliest source, The Weekly Arizonian, says that on "Saturday, the 28th (May), the Indians attacked and killed Israel and Kennedy. But, the first paragraph starts with "On Thursday evening, the 6th ult., two teams belonging to Messrs. Kennedy and Israel left this town on their way to Camp Grant." All subsequent historical references use June 6th as the ambush date. June 6th would be acceptable, but the first account of the ambush was published on June 4th – two days before the event occurred! Also, 6th ult. (preceding month, of May) fell on a Friday. The event might have occurred on Saturday, May 28, 1870.

[712] "The Latest Horror. Twenty-one Unarmed Men and Two Women Attacked by Indians – Two Men Killed and Three Escape – Sixteen Men and Two Women Missing." The *Weekly Arizonian*, Tucson, A.T., June 4, 1870.

[713] The Weekly Arizona Miner, on both September 10, 1870 and March 3, 1871 editions, in a report of recent Indian attacks, lists June 6, 1870 as the date "Two hundred Indians attacked the wagons of Messrs. Kennedy and Israel, near Cañada del Oro, killed both men, captured the teams and goods and burned the wagons." A July 9, 1870 article by the same newspaper says "on the afternoon of the 4th ult., the savages were discovered." The Daily Alta California, San Francisco, California, October 28, 1871 uses the June 6th date.

A reference at History of Arizona," page 115 states, "On the 29th of May, Lieutenant Cushing" pursued the Indians after the wagon attack," from Books of the Southwest, History of Arizona, VIII, Chapter VI. The Military. Page 100-101. Southwest Library, University of Arizona.

This author contends that who ever wrote the first article at the Weekly Arizonian on June 4, 1870 used both dates in the first paragraph. And, who ever compiled the annual lists of Indian attacks at the Weekly Arizona Miner did not fully verify the date. That assumption became a recorded historical mistake for over a hundred years.

[714] Books of the Southwest, History of Arizona, VIII, Chapter VI. The Military. Page 100-101. Southwest Library, University of Arizona.

A group of twenty one men and two women left Tucson with a provision of liquor and dry goods. That Saturday afternoon, about twenty miles from Camp Grant, a large band of Indians "came out on the plain, surrounded their wagons, and at first volley from their bows and muskets killed Israel and mortally wounded Kennedy." The Indians "took possession of the guns of their victims." According to the news account, one of the Americans secured a remaining gun and headed northeast to Camp Grant with two other men. The fifteen Mexicans, including the two women and Tucsonan Samuel Hughes, eventually fled back to Tucson. Hughes swore that on "June 1870, he with twenty five others were attacked. Life and property are unsafe on the public roads." [715]

Eskiminzin, a notorious Aravaipa Apache chief who lived in the San Pedro Valley, reportedly lay in wait and wounded both Kennedy and Israel about five miles beyond Cañon del Oro. Israel was found tied to the wheels of the wagon and had been burned alive. [716]

Just after the incident mail driver George Cox was coming from Camp Grant to Tucson with a mail load where he saw the three men stumbling towards Camp Grant and reported the situation to the commanding officer. A company of cavalry was dispatched to the scene, taking a wagon of water and necessities for the wounded, if needed.

While the cavalry was being organized, Cox returned to the site. He found Kennedy on the roadside, "still alive, but with an arrow protruding from his breast, the point of which rested in his lungs." He tried his best to comfort the dying man and then continued to the scene of the ambush a mile away. He found the "iron work of the wagons lying in a pile of ashes." Nearby he saw Israel's mutilated remains. Israel's "feet were resting in the fire." He was "scalped and stripped of his clothing." One report added that his heart had been ripped out. The other party escaped to Tucson unharmed. They said the Indians addressed them in Spanish saying their intention was not to kill them, just to take their possessions. Israel's body and the injured Kennedy were taken away by cart. Kennedy died a few hours after they reached the hospital at Camp Grant. [717]

Newton Israel, a single man, was a former officer of the Fourth California Volunteers. Hugh Kennedy left a wife and several children. One journalist chided those – especially

---

[715] Memorial and affidavits, Showing the Outrages Perpetuated by the Indians in the Territory of Arizona During the Years 1869 and 1870, from Arizona Legislative Assembly, 1871. Page C8.

[716] A few days later, the same group killed Henry Long and Samuel Brown on the San Pedro River near Tres Alamos. "Eskiminzin," from Arizona: The Nation's Youngest Commonwealth Within A Land of Ancient Culture, by James H. McClintock, 1916. Vol. 1, Chapt. XV, page 199.

[717] Ibid. Also read the account published in Letters from Camp Verde, Particulars of the Recent Indian Raid, The Weekly Arizona Miner, Prescott, A.T. June 18, 1870

one Vincent Collyer and his clique - who sympathized with those "poor, persecuted Indians." [718] Cox was an ex-partner of the Camp Grant Store with Israel. They bitterly had dissolved their business relationship the year before. [719] Cox went on to become the first postmaster of the Camp Grant Post Office. [720] A month before the ambush the two fought it out in public, and the "Dr's bill will amount to $50 or $60." [721]

On May 29th, thirty four men under command of Lieutenants Howard B. Cushing and Smith of the 3rd Cavalry joined with forty more men to pursue a band of Indians for about one hundred miles. They discovered their camp on the afternoon of June 4th. Cushing directed the surprise offense the next morning. Lt. Smith and his party met the Indians as they ran down a canyon. Thirty Indians were killed, two escaped, and two were captured. [722] [723] [724] The group included Pinal, Apache, and some Aravaipa Indians under the command of Capitán Chiquito. [725]

The Indians had ingested a box of patent medicine, thinking it was whiskey. One account said that they followed the trail caused by the Indians as they "staggered along, running against the trees, bushes and cacti." The prisoners taken were mostly squaws. [726]

---

[718] "From Camp McDowell, a P.S. with a follow up on the attack and the comment from Editor of the Miner, Mr. McDowell. The Weekly Arizona Miner, Prescott, A.T. June 18, 1870.

[719] "NOTICE! The partnership heretofore existing between Newton Israel and George Cox has been dissolved..." Dec. 30, 1869. Published in The Weekly Arizonian, Prescott, A.T., January 22, 1870.

[720] "Blood Along the Cañon del Oro," Copper Area News. The Post Office was established August 19, 1869. The partnership started in October 1868 and ended September 1, 1869.

[721] The Weekly Arizona Miner, May 7, 1870.

[722] "From Southern Arizona. Brilliant Victory Over Apaches. Rumored Murder of Whites," The Weekly Arizona Miner, Prescott, A.T. July 9, 1870.

[723] "Account of Successful Operations Against The Apaches," The Weekly Arizona Miner, Prescott, A.T. August 8, 1870.

[724] "Accounts of Successful Operations Against The Apaches," The Weekly Arizona Miner, Prescott, A.T. August 2, 1970.

[725] Aravaipa: Apache Peoplehood, by Ian Wilson Record. 2004. American Indian Studies, University of Arizona. Footnote, page 524.

[726] Books of the Southwest, History of Arizona, VIII, Chapter VI. The Military. Page 100. University of Arizona, Southwest Library.

More Indian Depredations In The CDO

The 1870s started out rough for Tucsonans determined to prospect the Santa Catalinas. Apaches continued to prey upon white men seeking riches in the mountains.

In early May, 1870, the Apaches killed some Tucsonans, men and boys, who were panning for gold at the Cañon del Oro. [727]

Later that fall, on September 28, 1870, there was a Pinal Apache Indian ambush near the northern spur of the Catalinas by the mouth of the Cañon del Oro. The ambush was near the site of the recent Tully & Ochoa attack. [728] Angel Ortiz, who was in charge of a stagecoach train that belonged to Goldberg & Co., was shot and killed. Army paymaster Major Robert Morrow and eight troops were on their way from Tucson to Camp Grant when they heard the gunfire and rushed to the rescue. Morrow and his party "charged on the savages, killed two and wounded several." [729]

The load carried $7,150 in supplies, including coffee, sugar, bacon, tobacco, guns, mining equipment, and ten thousand pounds of barley. All of the items, plus twelve yoke, were lost in the Indian attack. Owner Isaac Goldberg, of the gold ledge fame, filed a claim of robbery for the property taken by the Apaches. But his records were incomplete, and he told the government he misplaced his accounting books. He did not receive any recovery for his depredation, [730] [731] another lost opportunity for Goldberg.

---

[727] Lost Jesuit Mine with the Iron Door, by Donald Page, page 12. Desert Magazine, October 1956.

[728] Tully, Ochoa & Company was one of the largest freighting companies in the United States. In 1875, it was the second largest business in Tucson. It also ran one of the largest mercantile stores in Tucson and retailed through company stores in such settlements as Camp Grant and Fort Bowie. From "Peacock in the Parlor," by Thomas E. Sheridan, "The Journal of Arizona History," Vol. 25, No. 3, Autumn 1984. Page 248.

[729] Indians---Military," The Weekly Arizona Miner Prescott, A.T. October 29, 1870.

[730] Bio of Isaac Goldberg, Arizona State University.
http://www.asu.edu/lib/archives/azbio/bios/GLDBRGI.PDF

[731] Goldberg filed his claim June 8, 1888. "In the Court of Claims: Isaac Goldberg, Surviving Partner of Isaac Goldberg and Philip Drachman, Deceased, *v*. The United States and the Apache Indians (Indian Depredations No. 6846), from The Drachmans of Arizona, by Floyd S. Fierman. Page 143. American Jewish Archives.

Subsequent attacks by Indians on October 8th near Tucson and Camp Crittenden prompted Lt. Cushing and his command to follow a trail of the Indians northwards toward the Pinal Mountains. Two of his men were wounded. Cushing's troops then went after the Indians and "distinguished themselves by killing Apaches." [732]

The famous 1871 Camp Grant Massacre, where local Tucsonans banded together to slaughter a group of menacing Indians, involved the passageway through the Cañon del Oro.

A military order was issued to "stop any and all persons going toward Camp Grant," until seven in the evening on April 30 to prevent people from knowing about the upcoming raid on the Indians. In the interim the massacre group took a side route to surprise the Camp Grant Apaches northwest of the Catalinas near Aravaipa Canyon.

The gang of avenging Tucsonans was spearheaded by prominent Tucsonans William S. Oury, his friend Jesus Maria Elías, Sidney R. DeLong, Hiram Stevens, Brevet Major General George Stoneman, Lt. Royal Witman, James Lee, and many others. It was bankrolled by William Zeckendorf, and [733] Samuel Hughes provided the guns and ammunition. Eight men and one hundred and ten Indian women and children were slaughtered within thirty minutes. The one hundred and four posse members were found not guilty in a December trial. [734] [735]

---

[732] "Indians---Military," The Weekly Arizona Miner, Prescott, A.T. October 29, 1870.

[733] Pages 343-345.

[734] "Camp Grant Massacre," by Howard Sheldon from DesertUSA.

[735] The United States vs. Sidney R. DeLong et al.

1872: Mining Law Encourages Prospecting

The federal Mining Law of 1872 authorized prospecting and mining for minerals such as gold and silver on public lands. [736]

The year before the citizens of the Village of Tucson had organized a village government. The town site of Tucson was established in 1872 after $1,600 was paid to the government for a United States patent for two sections of land. [737]

As more people began to settle in Tucson, the constant violence by Apache Indians still made travel outside of the village dangerous. The persistent Apaches did not stop harassing people who wandered too far away from the protection of Tucson.

There is some doubt about one story of an attack on May 10, 1872, when three hundred Indians ambushed the Tully, Ochoa, and DeLong freight wagon train in the Canyon del Oro. [738] Five men were killed, mules were stolen, and their wagons were burned, according to the account. This occurred about the same area where Kennedy and Israel were killed two years before, but the details are too similar. This mistaken date may actually have occurred in 1869. [739]

---

[736] Mining Claim Information, Bureau of Land Management (May 19, 1872). http://www.blm.gov/az/st/en/prog/mining/requirements.html

[737] Old Tucson, A Hop, Skip and Jump History from 1539, by Estelle M. Buehman, Tucson, Arizona, 1911. Chapter 6.

[738] Today in Arizona History, Tues, May 10, 1872, *USA Today*. May 6, 2011. Also, "May 10, Today in Arizona History," Arizona Daily Star. May 10, 2013. Referred Canyon del Oro.

[739] The actual date of 1869 is in dispute. See the footnotes on the Israel-Kennedy massacre. "The Latest Horror. Twenty-one Unarmed Men and Two Women Attacked by Indians – Two Men Killed and Three Escape – Sixteen Men and Two Women Missing." The Weekly Arizonian, Tucson, A.T., June 4, 1870. This disputed date is also based on a painting dated as May 10, 1869, when the "Tully and Ochoa wagon was attacked in Canyon del Oro by 300 Indians." From "Wagon trains; Apache Indian Wars," Arizona Memory Project, Arizona Historical Society. The AMP uses the May 10, 1869 date. From painting by Edward Zinn depicting the scene.

The Tully, Ochoa & DeLong company dropped the DeLong partner from its firm name. At the time, it was "one of the heaviest, as it is one of the most reliable firms in Arizona." The Arizona Weekly Citizen, Tucson, A.T., January 13, 1872. Image 3. There is no newspaper article about such an attack in the Arizona Weekly Citizen about that date.

Sixteen upper San Pedro citizens got so fed up with the Apaches on August 13, 1872 they pursued a group of them into the Santa Catarinas and killed "three healthy warriors" without harming any of the citizens. [740] Captain Sumner's troops that chased Apaches into the Santa Catarinas on August 24, 1872, after they stole mules from a rancher near San Xavier del Bac. [741]

In March 1873, Isaac Goldberg went back into the mountains in search of gold and his "lost ledge." On his return he showed a newspaper reporter gold dust, said to be worth several dollars. He said he bought the gold from some miners "down the creek half way between Tucson and Camp Grant." [742]

The lack of water in the creek, though, made it difficult to do much mining. Goldberg still was unable to locate his find. [743]

Goldberg's bad luck was also felt in his business life. The next month a Sheriff's Sale was held to auction off properties owned by bankrupt Goldberg and the estate of Philip Drachman. [744]

[740] "Three Good Indians," The Arizona Weekly Citizen, Tucson, A.T. August 17, 1872.

[741] Arizona Weekly Citizen, Tucson, A.T. August 31, 1872.

[742] The Arizona Sentinel, March 22, 1873. Condensed from the Citizen.

[743] "Apaches Near Tucson," The Arizona Weekly Citizen, Tucson, A.T. March 15, 1873 and March 22, 1873.

[744] "Sheriff's Sale," The Arizona Weekly Citizen, Tucson, A.T. April 5, 1873.

1874: Apaches Keep People Out Of The CDO

"Gold does not breed cooperation." [745]

Apache Indian attacks continued in the north and northwest of Tucson with fresh trails leading from the scenes of atrocities. [746] Prospectors approached the Catarinas [747] with caution.

In mid-March, 1874, Apache Indians committed several 'outrages' around the Tucson valley. A command led by Lieutenant Ward was on the Apache Trail at Cañada del Oro [748] when they encountered eight Apaches driving three head of cattle stolen from S. Heran's ranch.

A few days before that a hunting party of Papago Indians returned from the Cañada del Oro with some of the stolen animals – a half dozen cattle. The Papagos were temporarily under suspicion for the theft, but since the cattle were returned, they were forgiven. [749]

Then in May near the northwest point of the Santa Catarina Mountains, Indians attacked miner James Lee's camp and killed a man. Lee said Indians had been hanging around for several days, and when one of his employees went out hunting, he was killed. The daily newspaper warned travelers that they should "look well to themselves." [750]

---

[745] Anonymous quote from The Savvy Dictionary: A Vein of Witty Definitions, by Heck Tate. Abbott Press, 2013. Page 47.

[746] "Local Matters," Arizona Weekly Citizen, Tucson, A.T. March 3, 1874

[747] Santa Catarina. This is the spelling used at the time.

[748] Cañada del Oro. This is the spelling used at the time.

[749] "Apache Theft and Murder" and "Local Matters," Arizona Weekly Citizen, Tucson, A.T. March 14, 1874. The spelling of Cañada del Oro is used.

[750] Arizona Weekly Citizen, Tucson, A.T. May 9, 1874.

Lee withdrew his team and ceased work on his claim. A few weeks later Major Randell of the 23rd Infantry sent an expedition into the Santa Catarina's to drive out the hostile Apaches. [751]

Capt. Hamilton of H Company, 5th Cavalry, returned with the news of the old Camp Grant massacre by the Apaches. On his return he came through the Santa Catarinas and discovered some deserted wikiups and two dead Apaches. One was headless. It may have been the head of Chuntz of the San Carlos Apaches. If so, it meant the war with the San Carlos Apaches had ended. [752]

Even with the threat of the Apaches, by summer the first professional mining company organized with some of the Territory's prominent leaders to begin corporate placer mining in the Canyon.

---

[751] "Apaches," The Arizona Weekly Citizen, May 16, 1874. The Apaches also attacked Leopoldo Carrillo's ranch, beyond Camp Lowell, killing a horse and wounding another. The day before that raid, a scout went out to find the Apaches who killed the man at James Lee's camp the week before.

[752] Ibid.

1874: First Mining Company In The Cañon del Oro

"The placer mines at the mouth of the Cañada del Oro, if in California, would be sources of wealth, and in time, will be here."

"Letter from Col. Hodge. *Arizona Weekly Citizen.* April 17, 1875. [753]

"There is a large body of ground in the Cañon which contains gold in every panful."

The Arizona Weekly Citizen, September 5, 1874. [754]

With word of gold in the Cañon del Oro [755] and a fragile peace with the Apaches, a small, unincorporated placer mining company was created along the creek. The Santa Catalina gold rush was officially on– simple prospecting turned into a big business.

It was known for many years that gold existed in the Cañon del Oro, but menacing Indians wouldn't allow anyone in the area.

Tucson businessman Isaac Goldberg had been persistently exploring the Catalinas to relocate that misplaced ledge of gold quartz he discovered in 1867. When a group, including Isaac Goldberg and John A. Meredith went out in the summer of 1874 to explore for water, they found gold instead.

Goldberg reported that water could easily be taken to the mining location that had rich placer diggings. They struck a four-foot vein of gold bearing quartz. A venture was formed to conduct placer mining for gold in the canyon. [756]

---

[753] "Letter from Col. Hodge. His Impressions After a Very Detailed Examination of Much of the Territory," Arizona Weekly Citizen. April 17, 1875.

[754] "Local Mining Company," The Arizona Weekly Citizen, Tucson, A.T., September 5, 1874.

[755] Both Cañon del Oro and Cañada del Oro are the spellings used in this story by the various sources mentioned.

[756] "Local Matters," The Arizona Weekly Citizen, Tucson, AT. August 22, 1874

They spent one thousand dollars to test the ground, and in August, 1874, the new mining company was organized with Col. David Taylor, Arizona's Governor A. P. K. Safford, Thomas Ewing, C.E. Curtiss, John A. Meredith, M.W. Stewart, P. Lazarus, and Isaac Goldberg. [757] Anson P. K. Safford, who served as president of the mining group, was the third governor of the Arizona Territory. Col. Taylor was an active army paymaster in the Arizona Territory.[758]

Near the Old Camp Grant Road a small crew completed a ditch, dam, and sluices in September. They didn't have enough water from the creek and had to wait until after the winter rains to resume work. Gold reportedly lay in large quantities in the bed of the creek. [759]

By October three men at work were reportedly making $5-6 a day of gold. [760] That month Lazarus sent specimens of some of the copper and silver ore to San Francisco for analysis. [761] The next month Goldberg wired back a telegram with the results, "Ore assays thirty two percent. Copper and two ounces silver." Earlier in the month Capt. Meredith and three others went to the Cañon del Oro to restart their work on placer diggings. [762]

Prospecting finally became a business.

---

[757] "Local Mining Company," The Arizona Weekly Citizen, Tucson, A.T. September 5, 1874.

[758] Sacramento Daily Union, Sacramento, California, August 28, 1874. California Digital Newspaper Collection.

[759] The Arizona Weekly Citizen, Tucson, AT, September 12, 1874.

[760] "Local Mining Work," The Arizona Weekly Citizen, Tucson, AT. October 3, 1874.

[761] "Local Mining Matters," The Arizona Weekly Citizen, Tucson, AT. October 31, 1874.

[762] "Local Mining Matters," The Arizona Weekly Citizen, Tucson, AT. November 21, 1874.

1874: First Steam Pump Installed

A long the Oracle Road south of the Cañon del Oro crossing, partners John Zellweger and George Pusch pulled their resources together in 1874 to buy a piece of land to install the first steam pump in the territory at the Steam Pump Ranch. [763] [764]

The ranch became the stopping point where ranchers could water down their cattle before shipment back east. Pusch was a member of the Constitutional Convention to help Arizona attain Statehood. [765] Pusch and Zellweger also opened the Palace Butcher Shop on Meyer Street in Tucson on September 30, 1876. [766]

The Steam Pump Ranch also became a popular waypoint for travelers as they took the road from Tucson to the "summit region called Oracle." By 1891 there were 1,500 gallons of water being pumped into tanks every hour for ten hours a day, and "vast herds of thirsty brutes have worn paths from every direction leading to the troughs for water." [767] Business was so good that by 1897 the Pusch & Zellweger company had shipped ten thousand head of cattle to Denver. [768]

Besides running a busy ranch and butcher shop from 1899 through 1915, Pusch had mining interests, mostly in Pinal and Pima counties. [769] One 1903 patent for a federal land exchange allowed Pusch to trade property in California for forty acres of land, what is now the intersection of North 1st Avenue and Oracle Road (I-77). [770] Pusch Ridge bears his name today.

---

[763] "Steam Pump Ranch," Pima County, Cultural and Historic Resource Acquisitions. Oro Valley.

[764] "The First Steam Pumps in Arizona Territory," Archaeology in Tucson Newsletter. Vol. 11, No. 4, Page 2.

[765] Ibid.

[766] Advertisement: "Palace Butcher Shop, Maish and Driscoll Building, Meyer Street, Tucson, Arizona...Call and Satisfy Yourself," Arizona Weekly Citizen, October 21, 1876.

[767] The Steam Pump Ranch was managed by C. Glassman. Arizona Weekly Citizen, July 25, 1891.

[768] "Cattle Shipping Notices," The Border Vidette, Nogales Arizona. May 15, 1897.

[769] 18 patents. George Pusch, Patents. Bureau of Land Management, General Land Office Records.

[770] Forest Exchange Patent. George Pusch, July 31, 1903. Accession FE-04560175, Document 2332. Bureau of Land Management, General Land Office Records. Pusch indicates the FE from his property at

1875: Goldberg Returns For Another Try

I n February, 1875, placer miners took several ounces of gold out of the Cañon del Oro.[771] At the time the national gold standard was valued at $18.93 an ounce. [772]

By April 1875, the Missouri Valley Life Company issued insurance policies for mining partners Thomas Ewing ($10,000), Col. David Taylor ($8,000), and Isaac Goldberg ($5,000). [773]

Goldberg's main job now was hauling freight, but he continued to be drawn to the Catalinas. [774] Goldberg and Mr. Scott, who had been prospecting the Catalina Mountains for a mine, reported evidence of ruins five miles to the northwest of Tucson. They found deep steps cut into natural stone walls, perhaps used to carry "ores or something else," or the place was a dwelling. [775] The ruins that Goldberg saw were not the Romero Ruin; Romero had lived on top of the ruins at the Cañada del Oro decades before Goldberg passed through.

Goldberg found more riches, however, in "white gold" – water. In 1876, he started to supply the growing Village of Tucson with water from the pristine springs around the Cañada del Oro. [776] "Uncle Isaac Goldberg," as he was called, boasted about an unlimited supply of water from the season's snow now available for sale. [777]

---

the San Jacinto Forest Reserve in San Bernardino County, California for 40 acres at T 012S, R 014E, Sec. 7, SW ¼ NE ¼ (as per Forest Lieu Selection-Non (30 Stat 11). BLM Serial No. AZAZAA 010991.

[771] Arizona Weekly Miner, February 12, 1875. Also, "By Telegraph," *The Weekly Arizona Miner*, February 12, 1875.

[772] Historic Gold Prices- 1833 to Present, Prices from 1883-1994, World Gold Council. Taken from Timothy Green's Historical Gold Price Table. London prices converted to U.S. Dollars. Per troy ounce. The $18.93 price of gold remained consistent from 1833 (at $18.93) through 1918 (at $18.99).

[773] The Arizona Weekly Citizen, April 10, 1875.

[774] "The Goldberg Brothers: Arizona Pioneers," American Jewish Archives, April 1966. Page 16.

[775] The Arizona Weekly Citizen, March 6, 1875.

[776] "The Goldberg Brothers: Arizona Pioneers," American Jewish Archives, page 15. From The Arizona Weekly Citizen, January 8, 1876.

[777] The Arizona Weekly Citizen, April 9, 1882.

Other Mining Ventures Around Tucson & The Santa Catalinas

During this time several other placer miners recovered gold worth $17 per ounce from the Cañada del Oro. [778]

Local ranchers, a pioneer settler Francisco Romero (named for the Romero Ruin) and a Tucson businessman William A. Zeckendorf, had discovered a three hundred yard long vein of gold and silver on the eastern slope of the Santa Catarinas about twelve miles from Tucson. They named their find the Florencia in February, 1875. [779]

In May John C. Clark and John Davis found the extension of the Florencia lode. This claim in the southwest extension of the mountains, and the ore "assayed very rich." [780] The gold was assayed at $227.15 and silver at $188.54 – at the rate of $415.73 a ton. The vein was at the surface. Two miles away were the ruins of a large town where the area was littered with ruins of pottery and relics. [781] [782]

In 1876 the Zeckendorf brothers, prominent merchandisers in Tucson, were still working on their mines on the northwest slope of the Catarina mountains. They discovered an old mine in the area and staked their claim. [783]

A gold strike at the end of October, 1877, by John B. Hart and Charles A. Franklin recovered enough ore specimens to assay as high as $5,000 to the ton. It was discovered in the Boulder district on the northwest slope of the mountains. The mineral belt runs 25-30 miles and is two miles wide, the prospectors reported. The ascent on the mountain was difficult since there were no roads or trails into the Catarinas. The mineral wealth was said to be boundless, being rich in silver, gold, copper, lead, and iron. [784]

---

[778] Arizona Weekly Miner, February 12, 1875.

[779] "Evidence of old towns..." The Arizona Weekly Citizen, Tucson, Arizona A.T., March 6, 1875

[780] "Mining Summary. Santa Catarina Mountains," Arizona Weekly Citizen, May 8, 1875.

[781] "Local Mining Matters," The Arizona Weekly Citizen, Tucson. May 6, 1875.

[782] The Arizona Weekly Citizen, Tucson. May 8, 1875.

[783] "Local Mining News," The Arizona Weekly Citizen, May 6, 1876.

[784] "New Strike Near Tucson," The Arizona Sentinel, December 8, 1877.

249

On the far north side of the mountains, newly arrived prospectors Alexander McKay, Albert Weldon, and James Lee were exploring the hills in 1878 in the area soon to become the town of Oracle.

Johnny Hart spent two months prospecting the northwest side of the Santa Catarina Mountains in the summer of 1878. His claim, The Pensacola, had gold assays at $502.23 and silver at $277.71. Tucsonans Tom Gates, Hardesty, Gable, and G.H. Oury made other claims in the mountains. [785]

In January, 1879, P.H. Loss presented the local newspaper with ore samples from the Canyon de Oro. He said there was a ledge three feet wide with both gold and silver. "Gold washes from the canyon sands in large amounts, so there must be some rich ledges nearby," he figured. [786] The next month Isaac Goldberg made another discovery in an unnamed location near Tucson (possibly the Cañon del Oro). [787]

There were favorable reports of chloride and black sulphurite mines in the Catarinas–assaying as high as $350 per ton in September that year. [788]

Peter Forbach said he "struck several good mines in the last month, some of which assayed at $3,000 per ton. Some are gold and silver." Some of the claims he offered for sale were in the Cañon del Oro and Owl Head Mountains in July, 1879. [789]

At the same time that prospectors were digging around the northwest side of the Catarinas along the Cañon del Oro, M. McKenna was working some gold claims in the Santa Rita Mountains to the southeast. [790] Lack of water made placering difficult, but Mexican laborers were retrieving "considerable gold by dry washing." A number of people, including Fred Hughes and G.H. Morse who both said they did very well were working claims scattered across twelve miles in the Santa Rita Mountains in 1876. Many others, however, were not as fortunate. The hostility of the Indians still made life hard in the desert. [791]

---

[785] The Arizona Sentinel, Yuma County, A.T., July 13, 1878.

[786] "Local Matters," The Arizona Weekly Citizen, January 18, 1879.

[787] The Arizona Sentinel, Yuma County, A.T. February 1, 1879.

[788] The Arizona Sentinel, County, A.T. September 27, 1879.

[789] "New Locations," The Arizona Weekly Citizen, Tucson, A.T., July 18, 1879.

[790] Ibid.

[791] "Local Mining Matters," Arizona Weekly Citizen, May 6, 1876.

South of the San Xavier mine near the San Xavier mission, other new stakes were being developed at the rate between $86-339 a ton. The Rusk and the France claims assayed up to $130 in silver and mainly contained lead.

After those attempts by Americans to prospect gold in the CDO and to cross through the area, the interest in gold mining would further develop into a major lure for prospectors in the decades to come.

To encourage new commerce, in 1897 a road was built to the summit of the Cañon del Oro and extended to Camp Grant so freighters could pass over it with their heavy teams.[792]

Repairs were to be made on the Cañon del Oro road and Rillito hills after a report was filed with the Globe Road Commissioners by Mariano G. Samaniego and Hylor Ott who were appointed to examine the work.[793] The road ran past Samaniego's ranch that sat along the Cañon del Oro where he had staked claims.

---

[792] The Arizona Weekly Citizen, October 11, 1879.

[793] "At a meeting of the Globe Road Commissioners," The Arizona Weekly Citizen, October 4, 1897.

1880s: Good News From Gold Canyon

In the 1880s copper became a more valuable commodity, and it became safer to hike into the interior of the Santa Catalina Mountains. Prospectors were becoming miners as more claims were being located.

The Bonanza lode, discovered in the Gold Cañon Creek [794] (the Cañada del Oro) in July 1880, was one of the earliest claims awarded. Frank Schultz, Dr. C.P. Watson, and B.C. Parker owned the claim. The United States Mineral Surveyor, Lorenzo D. Chillson, confirmed their large ore find during a patent survey of the area. [795]

While in the canyon Chillson established the United States mineral monument known as Mount Ivenah. He placed a marker at its location– near the current site of the patented Burney mines group five miles within the Cañon del Oro entrance. [796]

The Bonanza claim [797] consisted of an excavation of sixteen by twenty foot and ten feet deep and a one hundred and forty four foot long tunnel, located nearly eight hundred feet west of Mount Ivenah, in the Cañon del Oro. The Bonanza claim holders brought a large piece of ore for assay into Tucson. It was valued $3,172.87 in silver. The specimen came from croppings on the claim that was twenty-five feet by forty feet wide and a thirty feet thick vein of gold bearing quartz. The specimen was put on display at Charley Brown's saloon, the Congress Hall– the "favorite resort for miners." [798]

---

[794] Official Map of the Territory of Arizona Compiled from Surveys, Reconnaissance's and other sources, by E.A. Eckhoff and P. Riecker, Civil Engineers, 1880." From the David Ramsey Collection, Cartography Associates. Publisher, The Graphic Co. Photo-Lith, NY.

[795] "Good News from Gold Canyon," Arizona Weekly Citizen, July 10, 1880.

[796] "A Fine Prospect," Arizona Weekly Citizen, June 19, 1880.

[797] "Plat of the Bonanza Mining Claim," July 16, 1880. Lot No. 37, General Survey Number 189. U.S. Survey General's Office. Located 769 ½ feet west of Mount Ivenah, U.S.M.M. No. 1. Claim by Frank Schultz, C.P. Watson and B.C. Parker. Surveyed by L.D. Chillson. This spot is in the vicinity of the Burney Mines group several miles west of the mouth of the Cañada del Oro.

[798] "A Fine Prospect," Arizona Weekly Citizen, June 19, 1880. The Bonanza mine is about four miles above the old Government watering camp in the CDO. The ledge runs northeast and southwest across the canyon.

That summer Chillson staked his own claim as an extension of the Bonanza and called it the Braganza. [799] Shultz sold his interest to Benjamin Morgan for $1 the following January. [800] The San Bernard mine at the head of the Cañon del Oro was being worked at the same time.

On the other side of the mountain in the spring of 1880, the Old Hat mining district near Oracle was running assays between $49 and $550 per ton.

C.H. "Charlie" Laberee brought samples of silver and gold ore from his properties in the Canyon del Oro to Tucson in April, 1880. One of the rocks was an odd reddish color, similar in resemblance to "Leadville ores." [801]

By October, 1880, there was discussion to extend the Atchison, Topeka, and Santa Fe Railroad down to the Canyon del Oro and then to Tucson. The line would pass a continuous stretch of mining districts and coals fields of northeastern Arizona. [802]

With the lure of gold was also the lure of greed. Claim jumping– stealing someone else's mining claim spot– was a constant threat. The miners would often have to sleep out in the open to guard their precious finds. An example of taking their case to the media:

> *"**Notice of Caution** TO PETER MATTHEWS, E. L. SULLIVAN, Mr. Sweetman and all others claiming any interest in or intending to purchase, a claim called the "Quartzite No. 2," in the Canyon del Oro, Catarina Mountains, in Pima County. You are hereby notified that said claim conflicts with the "Alta" claim, and that said Alta claim has the prior right and best title to the premises, and that we are the owners of said Alta claim.*
>
> FRANK O'BRIEN, WELLS SPICER. Tucson, Sept. 21, 1880. [803]

---

[799] Ibid.

[800] "Mining Deeds. Frank Schultz to Benj Morgan, Bonanza mine, Canyon del Oro, January 3, 1882, $1." The Arizona Weekly Citizen, January 15, 1882.

[801] "More Good Prospects," The Arizona Weekly Citizen, April 3, 1880.

[802] "Another Version," The Arizona Weekly Citizen, October 2, 1880.

[803] "Notice of Caution," The Arizona Weekly Citizen, October 9, 1880.

In 1881 Tucson was a burgeoning community of ten thousand residents, mostly Mexican and English speaking. A large number of people "come in from the surrounding mountains periodically, and make this place their point of connection with civilization for a few weeks at a time." The telephone was introduced to Tucson that year, and the City of Tucson Water Works began construction. [804]

Throughout 1881 dozens of new claims sprung up. Wm. L. Lammon boasted to the local newspaper of good success where his partner, Sam Charles, and he prospected that January. [805]

Henry and A.C. Brown reported on new mines opening in the area, including one with very rich silver ore owned by Joseph Goldtree and Kiesler. [806] With so much activity in early 1881, a mill was planned for the Canyon del Oro. [807]

In March Charlie Laberee displayed some "very fine black sulphuret ore from the Maryland" mine, owned by Laberee & Co. The ore had an assay of $35 in silver. A thirty five foot tunnel on the claim revealed a three and a half foot ledge. The Maryland claim adjoined the recently struck Bonanza mine. [808]

Several claims were started in June to fully develop mining interests owned by Lorenzo D. Chillson (the U.S. Mineral Surveyor) and the Lot Bowen Mining Company. The Chillson and McC Elliott group had three mines operating on the Lot Bowen property. [809] [810]

It was difficult to get into the mountains with any type of mining equipment and provisions since the only way to reach the canyon was by mule. All supplies were hauled

---

[804] "Tucson of the Present," Page 13. "Events in 1881," Page 23-24. From the Tucson Directory, 1881. Tucson incorporated from a village to a city in 1877.

[805] "Fine Prospect," The Arizona Weekly Citizen, January 1, 1881.

[806] "Returned," The Arizona Weekly Citizen, Tucson, A.T., January 8, 1881.

[807] The Arizona Weekly Citizen, Tucson, AZ. February 27, 1881.

[808] "A Persevering Prospector," The Arizona Weekly Citizen, March 6, 1881.

[809] "Canyon del Oro," The Arizona Weekly Citizen, Tucson, AZ. November 6, 1881. Chillson has numerous mining interests throughout Arizona.

[810] Some other claims included: Rough Diamond and the Oakland, Feb 9, 1881 by Fred Frasier, W.L. Lammon, Samuel C. Childs, Samuel Beard. From "Mining Locations," The Arizona Weekly Citizen, Tucson, AZ. April 10, 1881.

to the mouth of the canyon near the Samaniego Ranch and packed by horse or burro five or six miles to the camp locations.

The miners planned to petition the Pima County Board of Supervisors in November, 1881, for a good county road from Tucson to get to their claims. The new road would cut ten or twelve miles off travel to Oracle, they argued.[811]

Gold fever did, of course, attract its share of characters. Towards the end of November, 1881, an oddly dressed man in a worn hat from Kansas stepped off the train in Tucson with a satchel in one hand and a shovel in the other. He pointed to the Catalina Mountains and called out to some bystanders, "Look here, strangers, are those hills all been blasted, shook and turned upside down?" They replied, "Why, certainly not." The Kansas prospector proclaimed that on the next day he "shall begin to plow and stir up that whole range and if mineral is lodged in those mountains I will unearth it if I have to use all the giant that's contained in this sack!" He walked down Congress Street and must have aroused suspicion. He ended up in jail. The next morning, when he realized where he was, he began to yell at the top of his lungs to attract a jailer's attention. Judge Myers fined him $10 and the "Kansas prospector" was last seen boarding a train for Kansas.[812]

[811] "Canyon del Oro," The Arizona Weekly Citizen, November 6, 1881.

[812] "Kansas Prospector," Arizona Weekly Citizen, November 20, 1881.

1882: Goldberg Returns; Claims Expand In CDO

Fifteen years after his first trip into the Santa Catalina Mountains, Isaac Goldberg returned with some friends to find that lost ledge of copper. After four of five attempts over the years, Goldberg's group finally rediscovered the ledge "a thousand feet from the mountain stream, which below the mountains is called Rillito Creek."

Although it was only fifteen miles in a straight line to Tucson, the trail was about eighty miles from the opposite side of the Catalinas. The specimens they brought back returned an assay over thirty percent copper. The ledge, located by Goldberg, James Lee, Andrew Cronley, and Samuel Hughes, was "enormously wide, with strong bold croppings." Old miners who had seen the ore, considered Goldberg's find as the area's most important discovery ever made in Tucson. [813] On January 2, 1882, Goldberg, Cronley, James Lee, and R.C. Brown filed location claims in an unidentified district in Pima County. [814] Later that month, Golderg sold one of his deeds for the Ironclad mine in the Santa Catalinas to F.H. and H.P. Burns for $10. [815] A new post office was established in the Santa Catarina Mountains on April 26, 1882. [816] Louis Goodman was appointed postmaster. [817] Despite the growing activity in the area, the Cañada del Oro post office in Pinal County was closed in October, 1882. [818] But Isaac Goldberg was still busy nearby; he set up a mill site on November 14, 1883, with A. Britcha and C.L. Hammond. [819]

---

[813] "A Lost Mine. Rediscovery by a Party of Prospectors – Immense Beds of Copper in the Santa Catalinas," Weekly Epitaph, Tombstone, Arizona, January 9, 1882. From "Fine Prospect," The Arizona Weekly Citizen, January 1, 1881. Also, see Daily Los Angeles Herald, January 15, 1882.

[814] "Location Notices: Goldberg, no district, Pima County, Jan. 2. Interests as follows: Jas Lee, 750 feet; I Goldberg 325 feet; A Cronley, 325 feet; R C Brown, 150 feet." The Arizona Weekly Citizen, Tucson, A.T., January 15, 1882.

[815] "Mining Deeds," The Arizona Weekly Citizen, January 22, 1882.

[816] Arizona Place Names, by Will C. Barnes. University of Arizona, 1935. Page 389. Cites both Santa Catarin (sic) and notes that some geographers, and the post office, spelled the name wrong. The Santa Catarina Post Office was established April 26, 1882.

[817] The Arizona Weekly Citizen, June 4, 1882.

[818] The Arizona Sentinel, October 21, 1882.

[819] "Official Records," The Arizona Weekly Citizen, Tucson, AZ. November 24, 1883.

1880s: Samaniego Stakes A Claim in Cañada del Oro

Near the site of a massacre only a dozen years earlier and the CDO Indian treaty two dozen years before that, Mariano Gil Samaniego [820] found the canyon peaceful enough to build a home and stagecoach line through the mountains in the 1880s.

One of the buildings on the former Samaniego Ranch property prior to its restoration by William Carter. This structure may be much older. Its stone foundation is similar to some of the other stone ruins built before Americans arrived in the mid 1880s.

M.G. Samaniego [821] arrived in Tucson from Las Cruces, New Mexico, in 1869 with his new bride, Dolores Aguirre. He operated a freighting business that extended to forts and

---

[820] Mariano G. Samaniego, or M.G. Samaniego, was born 1844 and died in 1907. Source: Arizona Memory Project, Arizona Historical Society.

[821] Mariano Samaniego had a cousin, also named Mariano, who was a well-known dentist in Durango, Mexico. Dr. Samaniego moved to Tucson in December 1878 where his brother Mariano Gil, or M.G., lived. Dr. Samaniego helped establish St. Mary's Hospital and left for El Paso a year later. Source: Tucson Citizen, by Paul Allen, January 22, 2003. Doctor Mariano Samaniego y Delgado lived from 1832-1905.

257

army posts as far east as the Mississippi River. He was wounded several times by Indians and became a legend in his role to rescue a kidnapped boy. [822] In 1868 he lost several wagons and men during frequent Indian attacks, including a financially devastating attack in Las Cruces, New Mexico. [823]

The same stone and adobe building on the Samaniego Ranch building after being restored by William Carter in 2014.

Mariano G. Samaniego was a prominent Tucson politician. He held more offices than any other Mexican and served nearly three decades in city, county, and state government, including ten years on the Pima County Board of Supervisors and Arizona State Legislature. [824] Samaniego served four terms in the Arizona Territorial Assembly, on the Pima County Board of Supervisors, and Tucson City Council. He was a Pima County Assessor, President of the Arizona Pioneer's Historical Society, and was one of the founders of the Hispanic American Alliance. [825] He was one of the first members of the board of regents of the

[822] M.G. Samaniego, by Richard G. Schaus, from Tucson Volunteer Fire Department Foundation. Mariano Samaniego (1844-1907) served as a volunteer fire fighter for many years. Page 14.

[823] From Tucson Daily Citizen, August 18, 1975, by Kerry Hibbs. Tucson Volunteer Fire Fighters Foundation.

[824] Ibid. Page 254.

[825] "Tucson Mexican Pioneers," Ring Brother's History.

University of Arizona. In 1876, he had a townhouse, now known as the Samaniego House, built in downtown Tucson.[826] The preservation of the building, at 222 South Church Street, was written into the land contract for La Placita.[827]

Some of the other jobs Samaniego held included volunteer fire fighter, running a saddle and harness shop in Tucson, and operating a stagecoach line that hauled people and loads.[828]

Samaniego's ranch property was used for a stagecoach stop.[829] Through this location he provided stagecoach service from Tucson to Arivaca and Oro Blanco from 1892-1908.

To get to the mining camps, the main road to Oracle went through the mouth of the Cañada del Oro past the front door of the Samaniego Ranch.[830] One line ran between Oracle, American Flag, and Mammoth, and the other line went to Tucson, Arivaca, Oro Blanco and Old Glory.[831]

Despite his accomplishments, Samaniego faced competition from the new railroad and a personal tragedy.

The Southern Pacific Railroad came to Tucson in 1880 and was able to deliver goods cheaper than stagecoach.[832] In October, 1881, his brother, Bartolo, was killed at Cedar Springs by an Indian ambush while he was freighting a load.[833] More than 100 men and

---

[826] "M.G. Samaniego," by Richard G. Schaus. Tucson Volunteer Fire Department Foundation.

[827] The original address was 24 Jackson Street, "Tucson City Directory," 1881. The building was damaged by fire, according to the Tucson Daily, February 10, 1914.

[828] "M.G. Samaniego," by Richard G. Schaus. Tucson Volunteer Fire Department Foundation.

[829] In August 1896, the fare between Tucson and Mammoth was increased to $4 each way and the fare to Oracle, along the same line, was $3 each way. The Arizona Weekly Citizen, Tucson, A.T. August 1, 1896.

[830] The History of Stagecoaches in Tucson, Arizona, by Bob Ring, page 10. 2012.

[831] Peacock in the Parlor: Frontier Tucson's Mexican Elite, by Thomas E. Sheridan, The Journal of Arizona History, Vol. 25, No. 3 (Autumn 1984). Page 254.

[832] "Mariano G. Samaniego," by Manuel G. Gonzalez, from the Journal of Arizona History, Summer 1990, Volume 31, #2.

[833] "Killed by the Indians, The Only Brother of Hon. M. Samaniego and Five Teamsters Killed at Cedar Springs by Indians," The Arizona Weekly Citizen, October 9, 1881. Telegram announcement dated October 3rd. According to Treasure Land, Arizona Advancement Company, Tucson, 1897, page 38. He was killed in Willow Springs, Graham County.

twelve wagons were lost. That next day a very upset Samaniego boarded a train to Wilcox to retrieve his brother's body. On the way through Dragon Pass, he fired several shots at some Indian Army scouts he mistook for hostiles, wounding one. He was arrested when he got to Wilcox, but was released due to a friend's influence. [834]

Samaniego became bitter over the experience and sold his freighting interests to establish the Cañada del Oro Ranch at the northwestern foothills of the Santa Catalinas for cattle grazing and mineral prospecting. He was reimbursed $11,000 from the U.S. government for his losses over the years. Samaniego also owned the Rillito Ranch on the southern slopes. [835]

Samaniego reported constant attacks on his Cañada del Oro ranch by Apache Indians. He complained in June 1882 that Apaches stole two of his horses, two mares with colts and two mules. His other ranch, farther towards the Tortolita Mountains to the west, was also attacked. Up to forty head of cattle were stolen there. [836]

Samaniego saw promise in the mineral opportunities in the Cañada del Oro and made several mining claims in the area. One mining claim was filed on his ranch property in September, 1883, designated as the Samaniego Placer Claim. The twenty acre claim was situated on the same land he used for a stagecoach station, ranch, and home. [837]

In 1885 Mariano G. Samaniego, and his friend Sheriff Robert Leatherwood assisted the U.S. military in their efforts to rid the area of hostile Apache Indians. General Crook had three thousand troops placed along the border from the Patagonia Mountains in Arizona to the Rio Grande in New Mexico to prevent raids into American territory and search for Geronimo his former "prisoner of war," and Nah-chee, the son of Cochise. In one hunt during April 1886, Samaniego and "Bob" Leatherwood led a company of citizens into the Catalinas, along with Lieutenant Clark and some troops. They rescued a nine-year old boy captured by the Indians. [838]

---

[834] From Tucson Daily Citizen, August 18, 1975, by Kerry Hibbs. Tucson Volunteer Fire Fighters Foundation.

[835] Ibid. In this area near the Cañada del Oro, Samaniego staked numerous mining claims.

[836] "Rumored Reports of Indians," The Arizona Weekly Citizen, Tucson, A.T. June 11, 1882.

[837] "Location Notice of Placer Claim," Mariano J. Samaniego, September 28, 1883. Arizona Historical Society, Samaniego Papers, Box 5, f. 78-85.

[838] "Geronimo (Concluded)," by John P. Clum, Arizona Historical Review, January 1921. Pages 8-16.

Across the valley in 1885, fifty men and nine carpenters were building a narrow gauge railroad to run north for seven miles until it crossed the Rillito creek and ended up at the Cañada del Oro. [839]

On the other side of the Catalina Mountains near Oracle in 1886, the Southern Belle mine had produced about $7,000 in gold bullion since it opened in January. [840] But the Apaches did not give up their vendetta. In 1887, Charabaus Vasquez was killed in the Cañon Del Oro. [841]

The area became safe enough by 1888 for Samaniego and his neighbor ranchers to hold a rodeo at the summit of "Canyon del Oro." [842] More rodeos were held between 1890 [843] [844] [845] [846] [847] [848] and 1896 [849] when ranchers Samaniego, George Pusch, Peter Charouleu, and Frank Romero got together to present the events on Samaniego's Ranch. The "Cañon de Oro Roundup" rodeos started at the Samaniego ranch and worked their way to the Steam Pump Ranch. [850] Romero's ranch was located at the present site of the Romero Ruin, south of Samaniego's and Charlouleu's ranches.

[839] The Arizona Sentinel, July 21, 1883.

[840] The Arizona Weekly Citizen, Tucson, A.T. February 26, 1886.

[841] "Killed by the Apaches," Evening Star, Washington, D.C. June 16, 1887.

[842] "Notice Rodeo," The Arizona Weekly Citizen. September 15, 1888. The rodeo was held September 10th.

[843] "Rodeo Notice," The Arizona Weekly Citizen. May 2, 1891. The rodeo was in progress working toward the Rillito from Samaniego's ranch.

[844] "Notice to Stockmen," The Arizona Weekly Citizen, March 17, 1890. Rodeo held March 15th.

[845] "Rodeo Notice," The Arizona Weekly Citizen. November 15, 1890. Rodeo was held November 24th.

[846] "Rodeo Notice," The Arizona Weekly Citizen, November 11, 1893. The rodeo was held November 6th.

[847] "Rodeo Notice" The Arizona Weekly Citizen, September 22, 1894. Rodeo was held September 18th.

[848] "Rodeo Notice," The Arizona Weekly Citizen. October 12, 1895. The rodeo was held October 25th.

[849] "Rodeo Notice" The Arizona Weekly Citizen, November 7, 1896. The rodeo was held November 10th.

[850] See above Rodeo Notices. "The Cañon del Oro round-up will begin Monday, Nov. 6 (1893), at the M.G. Samaniego ranch and will work to the Steam Pump ranch. M.G. Samaniego, Pedro Charouleu and George Pusch."

Samaniego's mining interests were recognized in 1898 when he was elected chairman of the Territorial Miners' convention. This event was a gathering of several hundred miners in Phoenix who represented miners in every Arizona county to organize a Miners' association. [851]

After Samaniego died on August 7, 1907, [852] his estate was assigned to his widow Dolores. It included his real estate holdings in Tucson and "a number of mining properties of considerable value." [853] The Aguirre family acquired the property along with the mineral and grazing rights. [854] Part of Samaniego's property is listed on the National Register of Historic Places. [855]

In 1911 George "Stone" Wilson acquired some of the land through back taxes. In 1933, Wilson acquired three hundred and twenty acres of surrounding land through the Homestead Act. Wilson's wife, Charlotta, named the dwelling Rancho Solaño. The land was incorporated into Wilson's cattle and guest ranch called Rancho Linda Vista. It was also known as Lower Linda Vista. [856]

Wilson's son, Tom, acquired Rancho Solaño after George's death and sold it to Lloyd Golder in 1960. Three years later Golder sold Rancho Solaño to Burton and Mary Alline Holly. [857]

---

[851] "Miners in Phoenix, A Permanent Organization to be Effected in March," Albuquerque Daily Citizen, Albuquerque, New Mexico. January 28, 1898.

[852] The Mohave County Miner, Mineral Park, A.T., August 17, 1907.

[853] "Samaniego Estate is valued at $25,000, Widow of Well Known Pioneer of Arizona Who Had Relatives in Albuquerque Appointed Administratrix of the Estate," Albuquerque Morning Journal, September 5, 1907.

[854] After Samaniego's death, his nephews Higinio and Epifanio Aguirre, bought the ranch for $10,000. The ranch included 300 head of steers. Schaus, "Samaniego," p. 44, "Portrait and Biographical Record," p. 578. Quoted from The Journal of Arizona History, Summer 1990, Vo. 31, #2, Mariano G. Samaniego.

[855] National Register of Historic Places, Notices of nomination. Rancho Solano, September 7, 1995. 34145 S. Golder Dam Road, Pinal County. Federal Register, Vol. 60, No. 162, August 22, 1995, #43612. Note: Samaniego "in 1899 purchased Rancho Solano, which is stated on his deed of purchase as having been built in 1897. At this time Mariano Samaniego called it Rancho Cañada del Oro as it was used as a stagecoach stop..."

[856] The registration form states both 1931 and 1933 as the year George Wilson purchased the Rancho Solaño property. National Register of Historic Places. Registration Form. July 31, 1995. Entered into the National Register, September 7, 1995.

[857] Ibid.

When Holly owned the ranch it had an orchard of rare delights. There was a tree planted by Luther Burbank just for Rita Hayworth's martinis. This tree and an orange tree are all that survive today. [858]

Golder said at one time the inner Cañada del Oro area had saloons and hotels and was largely populated at the turn of the 20th Century. In the early 1970s there was a three hundred and fifty acre lake in the area with a much different development in mind. Holly said that after the "Mine with the Iron Door" film was made in 1924 and later the Depression was over, more than ten thousand people were making a meager living from the great Cañada del Oro– Canyon of Gold– stream. [859]

Samaniego Peak and Ridge, which flanks the west side of the Santa Catalinas, is named for rancher and politician Mariano Samaniego. The north end of the ridge ends at his ranch property at the mouth of the Cañada del Oro.

Rancho Solaño & The Linda Vista Ranch

The Rancho Solaño property was the first guest ranch in the state. It was called Rancho Linda Vista (Linda Vista Guest Ranch) during the early 1900s.

In the 1920s Tucson dentist Dr. Peter Lackner built a hunting lodge on top of the hill overlooking the now-community of Saddlebrooke. [860] Lackner used the gold and silver from the area in his dentistry practice.

Before Motorola's and the Biosphere 2's ownership, the area originally belonged to the Countess of Suffolk, [861] a concert pianist. It was called Casa del Oro, or House of Gold. Some people report that the ghost of the Countess roams the Biosphere 2 property and the

---

[858] As told to William Carter by Lloyd Golder.

[859] Ibid.

[860] "Cattle, Gold and Science: a Land History of Biosphere 2," from The Desert Leaf, Tucson, Arizona.

[861] Lady Margaret Howard, Suffolk, England purchased the property in 1957 and built a home she called Casa del Oro. Inside Tucson Business, June 8, 2007.

Old Suffolk House. [862] Ira Hays, of Iwo Jima fame, helped dig the countess' well with Buster Bailey who hired him to do the job. [863]

Noted geologist Edgar Heylmun, Ph.D., believed that Rancho Solaño was "apparently the site of an old mining camp." While Heylmun didn't believe in the Iron Door Legend, he spent many years prospecting the Cañada del Oro for gold, writing several letters, and publishing articles on the subject.

Heylmun believed that the Spaniards "using Indian labor, did have small mines in operation at various times near the base of the Catalina and Rincon Mountains." [864] He theorized that to store the collected gold, silver, and iron, a "door of wood strapped with iron might have been possible." [865]

Heylmun wrote that William "Flint" Carter, who had staked mining lode claims throughout the Catalinas possibly "found more than just an old vault." [866]

However, as much as he prospected the mountains, Heylmun complained he had not been as successful as others reported, except for a few coarse flakes and small gold nuggets found in the creek-bed of the Southern Belle Wash. [867] Heylmun even staked a claim in front of one of the Samaniego buildings, occupied by Carter at the time. Carter complained that Heylmun staked his Procrastinator claim with a stack of rocks "right out in front of the door." [868]

Today, much of the valley is subdivided with homes for over nine thousand people living in the retirement community of Saddlebrooke. [869]

---

[862] Biosphere 2 News, Volume 1-1, Fall 2008.

[863] As told to William Carter by Buster Bailey.

[864] Research Dept. Ariz. Historical Soc., Tucson, Arizona, by Edgar B. Heylmun, Ph.D, September 25, 1981; and Re: "The Mine With The Iron Door,", April 17, 1990. Reference Room, Arizona Historical Society, Tucson, Arizona.

[865] Re: The Mine With The Iron Door, Heylmun, April 17, 1990.

[866] Research Dept. Ariz. Historical Society, Heylmun, September 25, 1981.

[867] Placer Gold Near Oracle, by Edgar B. Heylmun from California Mining Journal, January 1984. Pages 66.

[868] As told by William Carter.

[869] 2010 U.S. Census report for Saddlebrooke, Arizona.

Samaniego & The Victorio Treasure

There is a connection between the Samaniego family and another famous Spanish treasure at Victorio Peak [870] in New Mexico.

The Victorio name seems to figure prominently in the Samaniego family.

One connection was with Indian chief Victorio. In 1880, a relative of Mariano G. Samaniego, Dr. Mariano Samaniego of Bass del Norte, Mexico, told a newspaper reporter about a letter he received from his brother regarding the killing of Indian Chief Victorio and dozens of warriors, women, and children. Victorio and his group had murdered over 400 people during their rampages. [871]

In 1885 Mariano G. Samaniego had an interest in a Cañada del Oro gold mine, called Victorio, with a gentleman named Putnam. Samaniego put up a five stamp mill for a on third interest in the gold mine. [872]

Another story connects the Samaniego name to the treasures discovered more than a generation later at Victorio Peak in New Mexico.

In 1937 Dr. Milton "Doc" Noss, a foot doctor and treasure hunter, was hunting in the outcropping of Victorio Peak in the Hembrillo Basin in New Mexico. He discovered hidden inside a cavern sixteen thousand gold bars, a cache of Spanish artifacts, and treasures guarded by twenty-seven skeletons tied to wood posts. Noss told a relative of Mariano G., Bennie Samaniego, about his find. Since private ownership of gold was illegal at the time, Noss reportedly hid most of the bars in the desert. [873]

---

[870] This story is not written, or published, but has been circulated among locals for generations.

[871] From "Victorio Vanquished- The Boss Indian Killed and His Band No More," Salt Lake Daily Herald, Salt Lake City, Utah. October 21, 1880. The letter was received by Dr. Samaniego from his brother at Corriscoll.

[872] "From Arizona Daily Star," The Arizona Silver Belt, Globe City, A.T. September 19, 1885.

[873] Sources: "There could be gold in them thar hills, Doc's grandson leads mission to unearth Spanish treasure," Las Vegas Review-Journal, Nevada. August 31, 1993; "Gold Hunt May Resume Next Year," Albuquerque Morning Journal, Albuquerque, New Mexico. July 27, 1998; and "Was Doc's Treasure A Fortune or Hoax? Gold bugs family," Wall Street Journal, March 22, 1991.

Bennie Samaniego, a grocery clerk from Las Cruces, said in an interview with *Rolling Stone* magazine on December 18, 1973 that "I saw stacks of gold bars, skeletons, armor, old guns and statues. The skeletons were tied, kneeling to posts, as if they were prisoners left to die." In a local Las Cruces newspaper photo decades later, Bennie Samaniego displayed armor he said he found in another dry cave in the Caballo Mountains. [874] Benny Samaniego was supposedly a foreman at the 3C Ranch near Oracle at one time. [875]

Noss was murdered, and the location of the stash was never found. His wife, Babe, made a claim to the cave and its contents. But, she was not allowed to the site. The military made it part of the White Sands Missile Range and sealed off access in 1995. [876] There are several groups still trying to gain access to further explore the mountain. Tucson prospector William Carter was partners with Doc Noss's second wife's grandson, Jerry Cheatham, who came to the Catalinas in the late 1990s. He helped Carter open a covered tunnel where they found an old 1812 Mexican coin.

There has been speculation that Mariano G. Samaniego's Victorio claim in the Catalinas is somehow connected to Victorio Peak in New Mexico. There are many pieces in this particular story that are still missing, however.

Mariano Samaniego had visited New Mexico numerous times. [877] Mariano was born in Las Cruces and had many family members still living there. He had a freighting business that made transport, and concealment, of large loads very easy. The only way to transport heavy metal in those days was through freight lines.

While there is no direct connection between Mariano G.'s Victorio claim and Bennie Samaniego's Victorio Peak discovery, the coincidental use of the Victorio name alone could have spun this story out of hand.

---

[874] From Las Cruces Sun, Las Cruces, New Mexico. October 10, 1940.

[875] Reported to William Carter from Wilma Huggett, whose family owned the 3C Ranch at the time.

[876] "Victorio Peak," wikipedia.

[877] Arizona Weekly Citizen, May 1, 1881.

1887: Tucson Earthquake Rocks Discovery Of Gold

"Two large gold mines have been opened by the earthquakes in the Santa Catalina mountains. Some of these days an enterprising earthquake in Arizona will open a dry goods store or a barber shop." [878]

A major 7.2 magnitude earthquake rattled Mexico in 1887. It caused damage to buildings in Tucson, kicked up dust in the Santa Catalinas, and was felt for hundreds of miles– all the way up to Phoenix.

The Sonora, Mexico, Earthquake of May 3, 1887, was centered in Sonora, Mexico, about 40 miles east of Douglas, Arizona, by the international border. [879]

Tucson residents reported seeing large clouds of dust rising from the Catalina Mountains, probably as huge boulders rolled down the canyon walls into the valley. The earthquake may have also damaged the famous Castle Rock where "the old 'castle' and a portion of the familiar appearing landmark disappeared." [880]

On a trip into the mountains after the earthquake, several prospecting groups went to locate claims where the "whole side of the mountain slide down" and exposed two large veins of gold. [881]

Rancher and Oracle hotel owner William Neal believed that the earthquake buried the fabled Iron Door Mine and "tumbled" the hole in the mountain called The Window. The mine is "buried under all that rock," he said. [882]

---

[878] The Arizona Weekly Journal Miner, Prescott, Arizona, A.T., May 25, 1887.

[879] "The 1887 Sonoran Earthquake: It Wasn't Our Fault," Field notes, Vol. 17, No. 2, Arizona Bureau of Geology and Mineral Technology.

[880] The Arizona Weekly Journal Miner, Prescott Arizona, A.T., May 11, 1887.

[881] The Arizona Weekly Citizen, Tucson Arizona, A.T., May 14, 1887

1887: Drachman's "Chunks of Gold"

E ven prospectors had a sense of humor. In 1887 a group who returned from the Santa Catalina Mountains reported a huge gold find. They flashed specimens to convince the skeptics.

Their route from Pueblo Viejo (presumably the old Romero Ruin in Catalina State Park) took them through the Cañada del Oro and into the middle of the mountains. They wound through the canyon that opened into a large valley where,

> "…on one side of which they discovered, under the over hanging rock, a vein of reddish decomposed quartz, full of gold. Some pieces were as large as one's open hand, and every specimen found was inscribed on one side, "always buy your cigars at Sam Drachman's, Tucson." [883]

Samuel Drachman was the owner of Arizona's oldest local cigar store, opened in 1874 in downtown Tucson. [884]

---

[882] "Buffalo Bill Believed in "Lost Mine," undated newspaper article. Cody papers. Arizona Historical Society.

[883] Arizona Weekly Citizen, Tucson, A.T. March 12, 1887. Editor's Note: Sam Drachman was an early Tucson pioneer and merchant.

[884] "Drachman cigar store, oldest in state, was sold," The Arizona Daily Star. February 2, 1912.

1891: Gold Diggers In The Cañada del Oro

The Cañada del Oro Mines (limited) of London was the most active mining venture in Southern Arizona. Capt. J.D. Burgess, mine supervisor, reported glowing prospects. [885] The CDO mine had been operating almost twenty years since 1874.

Tucson pioneer Samuel Hughes, along with local postmaster Mr. Corbett, had been mining in the Catalinas in an undisclosed location, according to a June, 1891, newspaper story. Their find was hailed as an "important discovery" that could open up a new industry in Pima County. [886] Burgess said that by May, 1892, twenty-two men were at work on the road to the Cañada del Oro Mines in the interior of the Catalinas and eighteen men were at work on the Silver Belle road near Oracle for more business.

The new smelter at the CDO Mines, run by Fred Snyder, will process thirty five to forty tons of lead and silver ore every day. A ledge chunk of oxy-sulphide ores carried pure red oxide of copper and ran three to fifteen feet in width. The ledge at the shafts in the Silver Belle Mine contained sixty two percent copper, one of the richest deposits of copper ore uncovered in the Arizona territory. [887] In May workman Jose Jerez brought in some gold and silver samples from the Cañon del Oro that assayed into the hundreds of dollars. [888] The Cañada del Oro smelter was running day and night by fall 1892– producing three to four tons of bullion that had a value of $320 per ton in lead, gold, and silver. [889] By October the company gave indirect employment to two hundred men. [890] Mr. T.J. Morris, who returned to Los Angeles after visiting Camp No. 1 of the Cañada del Oro mines, said many mining districts in the past season were abandoned because of lack of water. Recent rains, however, will bring many workers back. [891]

---

[885] "Cañada del Oro; What the Company Operating Those Mines are Doing," The Arizona Weekly Citizen, May 21, 1892.

[886] Arizona Republic, June 3, 1891.

[887] "Cañada del Oro; What the Company Operating Those Mines are Doing," The Arizona Weekly Citizen, May 21, 1892.

[888] From the Tucson Citizen and St. John's Herald, St. John's, A.T. May 5, 1892.

[889] The St. John's Herald, October 20, 1892.

[890] "The Cañada del Oro," Arizona Weekly Citizen, October 22, 1892 and November 5th.

[891] "Reprinted from Tucson Star, November 12th" in the Los Angeles Herald, Vol. 39, No. 34, November 14, 1892.

1896: Gold Quartz Re-Discovery

A local Mexican who accidentally stumbled upon a trail in the Santa Catalina Mountains discovered some gold quartz in 1896. He followed the trail and found a thirty-foot tunnel.

There were old picks and shovels with moss covered handles at the entrance and a "quantity of gold bearing quartz." The find was reported to Tucsonan B. Brichta who grubstaked a party to explore the old mine. The exact location wasn't disclosed. [892]

A footnote to a reprint of an article a few weeks later said that the editor of the Argus prospected those hills in June, 1878. [893]

Elsewhere, twenty-five men were working on building a dam along two square miles of land of the Cañada del Oro in 1897. The claim, owned by Major H.C. Reno and Frank Newman, would be well stocked with water for their mining ventures. [894]

---

[892] "Local News," Arizona Weekly Citizen, Tucson, A.T., March 28, 1896.

[893] The Arizona Journal-Miner, April 15, 1896.

[894] Treasure Land: A Story, Volume 1, by John George Hilzinger, Arizona Advancement Company, 1897.

1897: Gold Hill In The Cañon del Oro

Mining fever continued to fuel as more prospectors became miners and staked claims on the north bend of the Cañada del Oro. The area would also become a major roadway to Oracle and its nearby mines on the north side of the Santa Catalinas.

These new claims cut between the Bachman Wash just north of the Cañada del Oro.

West of that were sixty six acres of the Arizona Copper Hill Mining Co.'s claims for the Copper Hill, the Rattlesnake, and the Gold Hill. The Copper Hill adjoined the Pittsburgh. The Gold Hill lode was located on April 2, 1897, followed by the Rattlesnake lode on June 18, and the Copper Hill lode on July 15.[895]

The Arizona Copper Hill Mining from Denver, was the first mine on the road from Tucson to the Cañon del Oro Mining District.[896] The land eventually became part of the Little Hills Mine group in the 1970s.

In February, 1898, a group of Tucsonans– Messrs. Sparks, Young, and Butler– reported to have gone to the "Canyon del Oro." When asked about their objective, they said it was "merely to get a little practical work in geology." But, the reporter believed they inferred that it was actually the legend of the Spanish mine that lured them to the area.[897]

---

[895] August 27, 1901. Plat Survey No. 1547, Lot No. 37. U.S. Survey General's Office. The Gold Hill claim was located April 2, 1887 and Copper Hill on July 15, 1897.

[896] Gold Hill located April 2, 1897; Rattlesnake located June 18, 1897; Copper Hill located July 15, 1897. Source: Plat of the claim of the Arizona Copper Hill Mining Company in the Cañon del Oro, August 27, 1901. Mineral Survey 1547.

[897] Arizona Republican, Phoenix, Arizona. February 21, 1898. Page 8.

1899: Ledge of Gold Found In The Cañon Del Oro

A half pound of ground ore, yielding about $5 in gold dust, was discovered by a Mexican in January, 1899. It came from a large gold quartz ledge somewhere in the Cañon del Oro mining district. [898]

Dr. N.H. Matas' foreman reported a new strike in May with a gold value of $500 per ton.[899]

Later that summer, Dr. Matas and Judge Purcell staked out about 50 claims along the Cañon del Oro after a two and a half foot ledge shimmering with gold was found near an abandoned shaft earlier that year.

The average assay of the entire ledge went from $800 to $8,000 in gold and one hundred ounces in silver, according to certificates of assay made at the University of Arizona. A sample taken earlier gave an assay of $5 a ton value in gold and a little silver. [900]

[898] "Arizona," New York Sun, New York City, New York, January 30, 1899.

[899] "Arizona," New York Sun, New York City, New York, May 22, 1899.

[900] "Arizona," New York Sun, New York City, New York, August 14, 1899.

1900s: Rich Gold Strikes In The CDO

By 1900 several mines were operating across four hundred acres along the Cañada del Oro as it flowed through and out of the northwest edge of the Santa Catalina Mountains. This stretch of rich lode was called the Canyon of Gold. [901]

Over the next few years, the owners of the Arizona Copper Hill Mining spent $125,000 in improvements after purchasing the claims for $75,000, but closed down while a $2 million sale was pending. [902] The company was organized in 1900 with one million dollars in shares and covered two hundred and fifty acres with copper veins seventeen to seventy feet wide and over four thousand feet long. [903]

By 1901 just above the Copper Hill claim, Dr. Matas was working some rich gold claims. He reportedly accumulated quite a quantity of free gold found in a body of ore. [904] Judge Purcell "took out $2,000 of ore in six feet of work from his claims." L.G. Davis, brother of Judge Davis, and W.E. Murphy of the Surveyor-General's office also had claims in the district. The Cañada del Oro district was one of the "most promising in this part of Arizona." [905]

One set of claims, owned by Edwin Scott in 1901, spanned over eighty acres across the north bank and top of the Canyon as it made its way into the Santa Catalina Mountains. Those claims included the Pittsburgh, the Copper Cliff, Denver No. 1, and Denver No. 2. [906]

---

[901] Cochise Review, Bisbee, AZ., November 13, 1900.

[902] "Canãda del Oro: A Rich Mining District in the Catalina Mountains," The Arizona Republican, Phoenix, August 31, 1901. Page 3.

[903] "Arizona Copper Hill Mining Company," The Copper Handbook, Volume 2, 1902. Page 298. Edwin Scott, president; A.B. Bell, secretary and treasurer.

[904] "Canada del Oro: A Rich Mine in the Catalina Mountains," Arizona Republican, Phoenix, August 31, 1901, p 3.

[905] The Copper Era, Clifton, Arizona. December 5, 1901.

[906] August 27, 1901. Plat Survey No. 1546. U.S. Survey General's Office. Claim of Edwin Scott, known as the Pittsburgh, Copper Cliff, Denver No. 1 and Denver No. 2. 82.49 acres.

1901-1907: Bauer's Unfortunate Luck

Tucson Mayor Charles J. Schumacher and partner Charles Bauer [907] had been mining a two and a half foot ledge of gold ore near the mouth of Cañon del Oro in 1901 that "has the appearance of honeycombed rock having been filled with melted gold." [908]

Bauer dug out 100 pounds of the "precious rock" from the Ella claim that adjoined mines owned by Tucson Dr. Matas. An estimated "85,200 st (straight tons) of indicated resources of auriferous vein material" was found along the rich strike. [909]

In November, 1901, Mayor Schumacher sold half of his interest in the Cañada del Oro claim to Frank Olsen. One thousand dollars in gold was paid to seal the deal, and a balance, no less than $25,000, was paid in various sums over a year. Bauer owned, and kept, the other half interest. One of their claims had a two hundred foot tunnel to extract gold, silver, and copper. [910]

But, Bauer's luck didn't last – at least in his personal life. Just before Christmas 1901, Bauer killed an acquaintance who was harassing his wife, Augusta who complained that Charles Kinstler had "repeatedly entered their home and used violence toward her." Bauer purchased a pistol for protection. He was a bit suspicious of his wife, though. Bauer hid in a closest. During a confrontation with Kinstler, Bauer shot and killed him for assaulting his wife in his presence. Bauer surrendered to authorities, but he was exonerated after a jury gathered at his ranch to conduct an inquest. Mrs. Bauer, who was unaware of the verdict, implored the authorities not to take her husband away until

---

[907] Charles J. Schumacher served on the Tucson Council from January 4, 1892 through January 1897, and as Mayor from January 7, 1901 through January 1905. Mariano Samaniego, a local Cañada del Oro rancher, also served on the Council during the 1890s. Source: Tucson City Mayors and Council members 1871-2005, City of Tucson.

[908] "Canada del Oro: A Rich Mine in the Catalina Mountains," Arizona Republican, Phoenix, August 31, 1901, p 3

[909] "STRIKES IN PIMA COUNTY Glittering Yellow Metal Found at Canada Del Oro," The Arizona Republican, August 12, 1901.

[910] "Mines In Arizona: Canyon del Oro; Fred Olson Buys Seventeen Claims In That District," The Arizona Republican. November 19, 1901.

Christmas. When told her husband was free from blame, she was overcome with joy. "The scene was a touching one." [911]

Not long after the incident, Bauer charged his wife with insanity. She was tried, convicted, and sent to the territorial hospital for the insane. Bauer was granted a divorce from Augusta on grounds of infidelity three years later. Kinstler was named as co-respondent in the divorce. [912]

However, Bauer's luck turned fatal when he was shot on June 29, 1907, in cold blood by George H. Wells at the Park View Hotel in Tucson. The motive was "jealousy, inflamed by drink." [913] Mrs. Annie Wells, George's wife, used the "unwritten law" in defense of her husband. She confessed that while she was at work for Bauer at his camp near Tucson, she was "on too familiar terms with Bauer." Shortly after, Wells was released from the county jail, [914] but a few days later Wells was rearrested because someone who commits a murder cannot be released on bail. [915]

Wells was eventually declared "not guilty" in December after a jury believed Bauer was on "familiar terms with his (Well's) wife" and Wells was justified for killing him. [916] Bauer's widow moved to California and made claim to the remaining estate of about $700. It was contested because she did not reside in the territory any longer. [917] There is no further word on what became of Bauer's share of the claim.

---

[911] "Every Bullet a Message of Death; South Side Tragedy; Charles Kinstler Was Pumped Full of Lead by Charles Bauer, Husband of the Woman He Had Persecuted. Bauer Gave Himself Up, but Coroner's Jury Exonerated Him From Blame– Testimony Offered." The Arizona Republican, Phoenix, Arizona, December 23, 1901. At the time, Bauer lived at his ranch near Mesa, Arizona.

[912] "Bauer Is Free; Another Incident Following the Killing of Charles Kinstler," The Arizona Republican, January 7, 1904.

[913] "Woman Cause of Tucson Murder; Old Man Kills His Rival in Cold Blooded Manner– Was Under Influence of Liquor and Went to Sleep After Committing Crime," The Arizona Silver Belt, July 7, 1907.

[914] "To Play In Role Of Evelyn Thaw; Tucson Murderer Will Seek His liberty Through Unwritten Law Route and His Wife Will Make Revolting Confession on Witness Stand," The Arizona Silver Belt, Globe, Arizona, September 15, 1907.

[915] "Mistake to Bail Man Charged With Murder," Bisbee Daily Review, September 17, 1907.

[916] "Great Plan to Develop Land; Ohio Capitalists Promise Great Things for the Vicinity of Tucson; Bring 1,000 Persons," Bisbee Daily Review, February 17, 1912.

[917] "Legal Technicalities Are Involved," Tombstone Epitaph, May 3, 1908.

CDO Claims Continue To Abound

While several prominent Tucsonans were working their CDO claims in the summer of 1901, a group of six copper claims on the east side of the Cañada del Oro, "at the point where the Pima and Pinal county line crosses the canyon" were also worked on by Frank M. Pool, J.H. Pool, and J.L. Storry. The claims lay on the Pinal side of the county.

The Eureka Development Company was given a twelve month working bond to mine a vein that carried a small streak of 20 percent ore. The abundance of water and a "short ten miles up to the belt of heavy pine timber on Mount Lemon (sic)" will provide the supplies needed. A short road built down the canyon will connect to the wagon road graded up the canyon by Capt. Burgess a few years earlier. [918]

But in 1902 mining in the Catalinas was at a standstill– at Copper Hill, Camp Condon and Catalina camp. New strikes in the Rincon Mountain shifted attention. Anticipation of the Phoenix and Eastern railroad through the Catalinas provided some encouragement that the region would develop. [919]

The next year, the Copper Hill went forward on plans to install a leaching plant to process up to one hundred tons a day with a start up for January, 1903. About five hundred tons of five percent carbonate and silicate ore were already blocked out. A twenty four mile traction engine road to Red Rock was planned. [920]

By October, 1904, prospects weren't as promising for the fledgling Copper Hill Mining Co. with mines nearby on the west side of the Cañada del Oro. Despite an inspection by some of the Michigan investors and an unfavorable report about the progress, supervisor Captain N. F. Allen insisted that work wouldn't be abandoned and that they were pushing further in hopes to finding good pay ore. [921] Their claim may have started to tap out.

---

[918] "The Mining Field; Will Erect Plant," from The Arizona Blade September 14, 1901.

[919] Arizona Republication, June 21, 1902.

[920] Bisbee Daily Review, August 6 and 14, 1902.

[921] Arizona Republican, October 2, 3 and 4, 1904.

1907: Samaniego's Esperanza Mine

Near Mariano G. Samaniego's land in the Cañada del Oro, Samaniego and Tucson attorney Francis M. Hartman incorporated the Esperanza Copper Mining Company in 1907 and began work on a silver, carbonate, and sulphide-copper mining adventure. [922]

Samaniego served as president and Hartman was treasurer and manager. The mine had a capitalization of $600,000 and shares at $1 each. Six claims were held covering ninety acres of the Esperanza Group with a shaft of about one thousand feet of workings. In 1909, the mine shipped about two hundred tons of good grade ore. [923] Hartman was also the Tucson attorney for the Catalina Copper Mining Company, a Boston corporation with mining interests at the head of the Cañada del Oro. [924]

In May, 1907, Eastern capitalists paid one million dollars for seven gold, copper, and silver claims on the New South Mining and Arizona properties in the Cañada del Oro mining district. Considerable work had already been done on the mines. The copper ore ran $206.28 to the ton with gold and silver assays as high. The deal was one of the largest in mining properties negotiated in Los Angeles. [925]

---

[922] Bisbee Daily Review, February 24, 1907.

[923] "Mines Register: Successor for the Mines Handbook and Copper Handbook," Vol. 8-9, 1909. Samaniego died in 1907. Subsequent listing in the 1910 and 1911 editions listed the Esperanza Copper Co. request letter as returned unclaimed and presumably idle. Mariano Samaniego, president; Arturo M. Elias, vide-president; H.C. Young, secretary; Francis M. Hartman, treasurer; Capt. C.T. Roberts, manager; E.W. Pike, superintendent.

[924] "Mining News," The Oasis, Arizola, Arizona. September 14, 1901.

[925] Mohave County Miner, May 4, 1907.

1912: CDO Water Rights More Important Than Gold

Living in a desert was a constant reminder that water was a finite and precious resource, more valuable than the gold that flowed through it.

In 1912 when Arizona obtained Statehood, the Catalina Power Company of Tucson was sold under option to John E. Stelzer of Nogales. Stelzer planned to develop ten thousand acres of land in Cañada del Oro, mainly on the Antelope Plains, a few miles northwest of Oracle. Included in the option were four gold claims covering five hundred and sixty acres of placer ground. [926] His grandiose plans were to "colonize the country north of the Cañada del Oro" with one thousand residents. Stelzer secured an option on the water, surface and underflow of one hundred thousand acres by the stream. At the time, the CDO was one of the few rivers in Arizona to flow continuously throughout the year. Plans called for four reservoirs, a lake, a dam, and several acres of alfalfa. Besides the farmland, there were about five hundred and sixty acres of gold placer land that had been previously worked. [927] The project never materialized.

1922: "Rich Gold Strike" In The Catalinas

A gold pocket was discovered again in the Catalinas' Sierra Pellon district and on Willard White's state leased land in 1922.

Kendall Greathouse and Roy Rist showed several samples of their find. Assays made by Elizardo Jacobs and A.L. Pelligrin reported that it tested two hundred and fifty six ounces of silver and one thousand two hundred ounces gold, "approximately $26,000 to the ton." [928]

When Buster Bailey, a well known pioneer, prospector, and ranch hand came to Arizona at age sixteen in 1927, his parents built a house on the north side of the Canyon del Oro wash, by the old Steam Pump Ranch. He said that there were still a few people panning gold in the creek. [929]

---

[926] The Oasis, Arizola, Arizona, February 10, 1912.

[927] Bisbee Daily Review, February 17, 1912.

[928] "Rich Gold Strike Reported in Hills Near Old Pueblo," The Prospector, July 31, 1922.

[929] "Mines of the Catalinas," Old Mines, Lost Mines, Working Mines Spanish Mines, Mythical Mines," by Buster Bailey. Buster Bailey papers, 1927-1981. Arizona Historical Society.

1930s: Still Progress In Finding Gold

In the early 1930s thirty men conducted small scale rocking and panning on the northern flank of the Cañada del Oro creek with some success. The bed of dry gravel along the creek still contained the veins of gold bearing quartz.

From 1931-1932, the workers from the Gold Channel Placer Company spent the winter season in the lower Cañada del Oro with some success. At the same time in the upper Cañada near the crest of the Catalinas, several other men were working the higher gravel banks with sluices. They earned enough to make fair wages. [930]

By then, most of the available gold was in the red clay seams that acted as bedrock for the deposits. Pulverizing the material this way to extract the gold was called "dry washing." One $25 nugget and a few $5 nuggets were reported during their prospecting. At the time, gold was valued at about $35 an ounce.

Gold bearing quartz veins were found at the Copeland, Kerr, Matas, and other claims along the upper creek within the interior of the canyon. [931]

---

[930] Arizona Gold Placers and Placering, by G.M. Butler, Arizona Bureau of Mines, University of Arizona Bulletin 132, Mineral Technology Series No. 24, 1932, pages 59-61. PDF copy of the entire book: http://repository.azgs.az.gov/sites/default/files/dlio/files/nid1225/b-132_az_gold_placers_placering.pdf

Also see: Gold Placers and Placering in Arizona, Eldred D. Wilson, University of Arizona Bulletin 124, 1927, State of Arizona Bureau of Geology and Mineral Technology, Geological Survey Branch, p.2 61-6.

[931] Ibid. Page 60.

1933: Gold Outlawed, Prospecting & Mining Shifts To Copper

Prospecting gold came to a stop when President Franklin D. Roosevelt signed Executive Order 6102 into law on April 5, 1933. The order criminalized the "hoarding of gold coin, gold bullion, and gold certificates" within the United States. [932]

This new law put a clamp on gold mining and prospecting activities– or at least reported activities. Any new gold discoveries in the mountains remained secret, so it was dangerous to reveal any findings. Many gold discoveries went unreported during this period because of the law.

In September, 1933, the Civilian Conversation Corps (CCC) proposed to locate a camp of men and boys near the Cañada del Oro area because of the current drought and water supply shortage in the Oracle community. [933]

The CCC bulldozed the camp and Oracle's Ranger Station. [934] They also reclaimed the land from the residual toxins left by mining operations and human activity, along with the nearby Campo Bonito mining district. There are some foundation remnants on the spot, just southwest of Oracle near the wash.

[932] Franklin D. Roosevelt, Executive Order 6102 – Requiring Gold Coin, Gold Bullion and Gold Certificates to be Delivered to the Government, April 5, 1933. The American Presidency Project.

[933] "Letter from Horace W. Smith to Governor Moeur, September 13, 1933, re: feasibility of a Civilian Conservation Corps camp in Arizona," RG 1 Governor's Office Collection, SG 11 Benjamin Baker Moeur, sub-collection. Arizona Memory Project. http://azmemory.azlibrary.gov/cdm/ref/collection/archgov/id/307

[934] Oracle and the San Pedro River Valley, by Catherine H. Ellis. Arcadia Publishing, 2008. Page 58.

1982: 230 oz. Gold Near Spanish Placer Sites

A ground test recovered "230 oz. of gold" at a site in the Cañada del Oro. Dave McGee of the Little Hills Mine, Inc. conducted the test in 1982. [935]

The gold recovery was made on "placer gravels allegedly near two hundred year old placer sites of the Spaniards. These data suggested that some lucrative gold zones might be found in the Cañada del Oro District with additional prospecting." [936] This area also had a collection of mines called the Burney Mines. Robert Burney staked his claims in 1973. [937] Older tunnels from 1939 – possibly from the McKee brother's claim– ran fifty, twenty five, and ten feet long. [938]

William "Flint" Carter who had staked one hundred and seventy two claims in that area since the 1980s, [939] combined the Little Hills property and sold the claims for "five hundred million dollars." But the deal never went through, and there were various lawsuits for years. [940] Little Hill Mines continues to operate that claim group nearby the Cañada del Oro bend, northeast of the Biosphere 2, as Silica Mines with about seventeen employees producing mainly granite and decorative stone. [941]

While much of the gold has been hauled away from the mountains, fortunate prospectors can still find gold and quartz bearing gold and silver, in select areas of the mountains where the Cañada del Oro occasionally flows.

---

[935] From Mineral Appraisal of Coronado National Forest, Part 5, U.S. Department of the Interior, Bureau of Mines, MLA 25-94, 1994. Page 25.

[936] Ibid, page 25. Cited from "Santa Catalina Mountains, Arizona," California Mining Journal, Heylmun, E.B., 1989, Vol. 69, No. 1, page 11.

[937] Ibid, page 16. See also, "Little Hills Mines," mindat.org. A Cu-Mo-Pb-Ag-flagstone-silica mine located in the SW¼ sec. 5, T10S, R15E, (Oracle 15 minute topographical map), about 4¼ miles WSW of Oracle and about 1¼ miles NE of the Biosphere 2. Included the Copper Rose Mine, St. Anthony, Cañada del Oro, Birthday Mine, Lead Reef and Stove Lid tunnel. http://www.mindat.org/loc-62498.html

[938] "Little Hills Mine," mindat.org.

[939] Claims are filed with the United States Department of Interior, Bureau of Land Management, Mining Claim Geographic Report Index. Earliest claims beginning May 16, 1981 through present (2014).

[940] As told by William Carter.

[941] Ibid.

Mining Near La Ventaña

On the south side of the Santa Catalina Mountains, six miles north of Ft. Lowell ruins on Swan and Skyline Road, is the Pontatoc [942] and the Cargodera copper, silver, and gold mines at Finger Rock– a jutting extension of the Catalina Mountains.

The land is now surrounded by private homes, including Skyline Country Club Estates. At one time rancher George Wilson who had interests in the Cañada del Oro area had owned the mines. These nearby small mines are both one league from La Ventaña. The Cargodera is a mile or less from "a large 'town' on a mesa" that was a large Hohokam village dating to 1200AD. [943]

The Knagge family was prominent in both ranching and mining in the Catalinas. In the 1920s John Knagge built a cabin and mined near Kellogg Mountain by Mount Bigalow. The family took a pack train to the top of the mountain for early Mt. Lemmon residents. John's son Francis mined scheelite ore used to make tungsten near Finger Rock Canyon and Pontatoc Canyon. Grandson Pete knew of a spot near a diamond shaped rock in Finger Rock Canyon where his brother Sonny watched three men dig up a metal box, reportedly buried by "Father Escalante" when the Jesuits were expelled. [944]

Buster Bailey, a longtime resident and cowboy, remembered that farther east of Finger Rock Canyon, on the east side of the canyon, were obvious "old Spanish workings." The old Pontatoc mine was in that area. [945]

While mining activity was active around the Cañada del Oro, and south of the Catalinas, there was a growing community building up north of the mountains in a newly formed community of Oracle.

---

[942] USGS: Pontatoc Mine, a past producer of copper, gold and silver. MRDS M050656, Deposit ID 10234814. A more current spelling is Pontatoc.

[943] The Mine With The Iron Door, by Edgar B. Heylmun, Arizona Historical Society files.

[944] Ranches, Mines, Tracks and Trails: Pioneers of the Santa Catalina Mountains, by Connie Allen-Bacon, from Archaeology in Tucson newsletter of the Center for Desert Archaeology, Vol. II, No. 4, Fall 1997. Page 4.

[945] Mines of the Catalinas, Old Mines, Lost Mines, Working Mines, Spanish Mines, Mythical Mines, by Buster Bailey Undated. Buster Bailey papers. Arizona Historical Society.

Town Of Oracle - Old Hat District Mining

Oracle was founded in the late 1870s by prospecting miners and grew into a community hub for several mining districts– the Old Hat, American Flag, Campo Bonito, Apache Group, Mammoth, Oracle Ridge and others. Oracle is tucked away into the hills of the northern side of the Santa Catalina Mountains, about 40 miles northeast of Tucson. Today, several thousand people call Oracle home. In this photograph, the Oracle Inn Steak House (center) has been a popular diner and bar for decades.

A view of the north side of the Santa Catalina Mountains near Oracle, Arizona. The town of Oracle became home to several early American mining districts in the late 1870s.

Tucked into the hills of the northern range of the Santa Catalina Mountains is the town of Oracle. Originally, it started in the 1870s as an outpost for local prospectors and mining groups.

As more residents settled in Oracle, extensive mining operations were set up around the growing town to further explore and exploit the veins of minerals running through the mountains.

Some of the big producing mines in the Old Hat District near Oracle endured well into the 1900s. One of the Oracle deposits developed into the mining town of San Manuel. The San Manuel copper mine, northeast of Oracle, became the largest, underground producing copper and gold mine in the state. [246] One of the by-products of copper is gold. According to a U.S. report on the San

---

[246] According to David Ridinger, former president of the San Manuel Mine in 1985, it was "by far the largest underground mine in the state." From Going for Gold: The history of Newmont Mining Company, by Jack H. Morris. University of Alabama Press, 2010. Page 95.

Manuel Mine in 1988, thirty five thousand ounces of gold and silver were produced each year through a filtering process. [947]

A view of Oracle looking northwest towards American Avenue. The Oracle Inn restaurant sign is on the upper left. This photo is taken from the top of one of the summit peaks.

Like most small towns Oracle has had its own history and legends. Oracle was built for the miners who worked nearby during the late 1870s. New mineral discoveries brought many enterprising miners to the hills tucked into the northern edge of the Santa Catalina Mountains.

---

[947] "Site Visit Report: San Manuel Facility Magma Copper Company," U.S. Environmental Protection Agency, Office of Solid Waste. 1992. Page 3-52.

Christmas In The Desert
& The founding Of Oracle

Canadian prospector Albert Weldon made a trip around South America aboard his uncle's ship the Oracle to the deserts of southwestern United States [948] in 1877. [949]

His journey brought him to Tucson where he joined with James Lee, from Ireland, and Alexander McKay, from Scotland, to prospect for gold and silver on the north side of the Santa Catalina Mountains. They found that– and more.

Shortly after his arrival, Weldon staked a claim for the Oracle mine in 1877. He named it after the ship that brought him around Cape Horn to the U.S.

That next year Weldon told McKay how to get out to the mine and the natural spring just above it. [950] [951] [952] Eventually, Oracle would become the name of the new community north of Tucson.

In 1878 with two burros McKay ventured alone from Tucson into the northern slope

---

[948] "The ship Oracle, Captain Monison, from San Francisco, January 18th (1883), for Liverpool, was wrecked off Cape Horn and part of the crew drowned." Arizona Weekly Citizen, April 21, 1883. Also, the Oracle was built in Bath, Maine and launched on October 3, 1876, from http://www.florenceaz.org/visitor/pinal.htm

[949] Reminiscences of Alexander McKay as told to Mrs. George F. Kitt. Based on an interview with Alexander McKay and Mrs. Catherine Moss, March 14, 1936. Oracle Historical Society.

[950] Ibid.

[951] Description of Early History of Oracle, from the Town of Oracle. http://www.oracletown.com/history.html

[952] The History of The Lower San Pedro Valley in Arizona, by Bernard W. Muffley. Thesis. Department of History, University of Arizona, 1938. Page 37.

of the Catalina Mountains and encountered Indians. McKay said one Indian approached and called himself, "George, Eskiminzin's man." [953] Eskimizin was the notorious Apache chief. He warned McKay that Eskimizin and other men were coming. They did show up, with women and children, and asked for flour. They camped nearby a nervous McKay that night. [954] One story relates that it was an Indian who told McKay about minerals in the area.

In May, 1878, Lee and Charles Franklin made a discovery of free gold while Lee was building a road to the pine timber in the mountains. The ore is "full of free gold and is reported to be very plentiful– judged by the surface prospects." [955]

After some other prospecting that November, 1878, Albert Weldon sold two hundred feet of his claim, the Exchequer Mine, to C.H. Wheeler and A.J. Doran for $100. [956]

The next month Lee was still collecting "large quantities of decomposed quartz, gold predominating." Tucson pioneer Samuel Hughes staked the Esperanza Mine nearby after assays from the ore were into the "thousands." [957]

On Christmas Day 1878, Weldon and his partner McKay located some ore and made a claim to the Christmas gold mine. Then one week later, on New Year's Day 1879, they staked a claim for the New Years mine, just north of the Christmas. Both mines were located within the present day town of Oracle. [958]

Nearby, Weldon began a bush mining camp, called Weldon's Camp, [959] that had an abundant supply of timber and water available. A spring soon to be used as a grotto was included. [960] A tri-weekly stage brought mail from Tucson to the camp.

---

[953] This Eskiminzin was the notorious Aravaipa Apache chief born in 1828 and died in 1894. Eskiminzin, the Aravaipa Apache chief, reportedly laid in wait and had wounded both Kennedy and Israel in 1870, among other offenses.

[954] Reminiscences of Alexander McKay as told to Mrs. George F. Kitt, 1936.

[955] Arizona Weekly Citizen, May 17, 1878.

[956] "Real Estate Transfers," Arizona Weekly Citizen, November 23, 1877.

[957] The Arizona Weekly Citizen, December 14, 1878.

[958] The History of The Lower San Pedro Valley in Arizona. Page 37.

[959] From the Copper Corridor.

[960] "Old Hat District," Arizona Weekly Citizen, January 21, 1880.

A year later in November, 1879, Lee and others discovered a ledge of mineralized rock. An assay of part of the stone returned $80.43 in silver and $201.50 in gold. [961] Along with the new residents, came stories of even greater riches hidden in the mountains.

In 1879 McKay said he built the first house in Oracle. It was a one-room adobe for Weldon and himself. [962] [963] Another account credits James Lee with constructing the first permanent house. [964]

The Oracle mining property, now owned by Lee and Mayor Robert Leatherwood, was on the same ledge and south of the Christmas mine. It had a fifty foot shaft, but no work was being conducted. The purchasing parties forfeited their $40,000 bond. The nearby Christmas Mine, owned by McKay, Weldon & Co., had a sixty foot shaft in a four-foot vein of gold quartz.

One report said that James Lee had "grubstaked" one of Weldon's mines. Lee purchased the mines of Weldon & Co. in March, 1880. [965] Both Weldon and Lee together struck a rich load in the Lee Mine, on the ledge near the Summit House, a month earlier. [966]

The Christmas Mine, owned by McKay, Weldon & Co., held a four-foot vein of gold quartz, but they tapped into an underground stream and struck water at forty feet deep and flooded the shaft. They abandoned the dig. Instead McKay laid a four-and-a-half mile pipe down the mountainside, built a house on the mesa, and started a sheep ranch. [967]

An excavation into solid rock about twelve by twenty feet provided cold, clear water from the natural flowing spring at Weldon's Grotto. When U.S. Mineral Surveyor

---

[961] "New Discovery," Arizona Weekly Citizen, November 8, 1878.

[962] Reminiscences of Alexander McKay as told to Mrs. George F. Kitt, 1936.

[963] Tam Blake & Co., By Jim Hewitson. Page 90.

[964] The History of The Lower San Pedro Valley in Arizona. Page 37. It was located across the wash southwest of the present library building, according to Ms. Moss' account.

[965] "Embryo Bonanzas," The Arizona Weekly Citizen, March 27, 1880.

[966] "Old Hat District, Remarkably Good Prospects and Development in that Locality," Arizona Weekly Citizen, February 28, 1880.

[967] Tam Blake & Co., By Jim Hewitson. Page 90.

288

Solomon Allis and Mayor Leatherwood made a tour of the mines and camp, they noted seeing ruins on the southern summits of the Catarinas. [968]

Lee and Leatherwood owned the Oracle claim but in a possible misprint or confusion of spelling, the local newspaper reported that the 'Oricle' (sic) claim in the Santa Catarinas was sold in April, 1880, by James Lee and Mayor Leatherwood. The newspaper may have meant the Oracle claim. The buyers, unnamed eastern capitalists, reportedly paid $100,000. The croppings were ten to forty feet wide, and assays showed from $50 to $1,400 per ton. [969]

That summer a successful Wily Box sold his mine of the same name– an extension of the Oracle claim– for several thousands of dollars. [970]

In February, 1881, Peter Loss was appointed postmaster in Tucson and James Bronson was appointed postmaster in Oracle. [971] [972]

By the fall of 1881, at least eight operating mining claims were operating in the area– the Oracle, Christmas, Merrimac, Valleco, [973] Tiger, Fashion, Gypsy, and the Mexican. [974] The Richardson Mining Company of New York purchased the nearby American Flag mine, and the Oracle camp, in early 1881 for $100,000 and had forty men at work. [975] That year Frank Shultz first located the nearby Mammoth Mine. [976]

---

[968] "Old Hat District," Arizona Weekly Citizen, January 21, 1880.

[969] "Sold for $100,000," Arizona Weekly Citizen, April 5, 1880.

[970] Arizona Weekly Citizen, August 14, 1880.

[971] "Among the postal changes for weekend ending January 30th" Peter H. Loss, Postmaster at American Flag (Pima County) and James Bronson, postmaster at Oracle (Pima County); Stone Cabin (Pima County) John P. Zimmerman, postmaster. Arizona Weekly Citizen, February 6, 1881.

[972] It was closed July 16, 1890. "The Story of Oracle's Post Offices," Oracle Historical Society and Acadia Ranch Museum.

[973] Owned by Judge Robinson, W. A. Fowler and others. "A Fine Claim," Weekly Arizona Weekly Citizen, September 18, 1880.

[974] "Old Hat. A Citizen's Correspondent Visits the Santa Catarinas, and Relates Much That is Pleasant-Some Very Fine Claims and Their Owners, Weldon's Camp" Arizona Weekly Citizen, January 30, 1881.

[975] The History of the Lower San Pedro Valley in Arizona, page 25.

[976] Arizona Weekly Citizen, August 1, 1891.

Weldon eventually sold one-third of the Christmas mine and other Old Hat mines to McKay in May, 1881, for $2,000. [977] [978]

A second shaft in the Oracle was sunk in August and the prospects looked promising, according to Prof. Cooke, the Superintendent of the Oracle and American Flag Mines. [979] Another lucky strike in the Oracle was made in mid-October during the night shift. The soft chunky rock was estimated to contain $20 per ton in gold and silver. [980]

Besides the haul taken from the mines, smart miners bonded or sold their property while the values were still high.

[977] "County Recorder's Office, Deeds for Mines," The Citizen, May 1, 1881.

[978] "Deeds for Mines," Arizona Weekly Citizen, May 1, 1881.

[979] "Items from Old Hat," Arizona Weekly Citizen, August 7, 1881.

[980] "Strike in the Oracle," Arizona Weekly Citizen, October 16, 1881.

Peppersauce Canyon– A Spicy Mystery

Peppersauce Canyon is a popular public camping and hiking spot tucked away in the northern Santa Catalina Mountains, behind Oracle and the Old Hat Mining District. The canyon is known more for its name and beauty than as a site for mineral deposits.

The canyon was a comfortable retreat for the laborers from the nearby mines. There were several variations how Peppersauce Canyon acquired its name. According to one story in the 1880s, prospector Alex McKay stopped there for lunch and left behind his pepper sauce bottle. His friends reminded him about it, and he went back to retrieve it. His friends teased him by naming the canyon after the incident. [981]

In another story, McKay secretly stored his cache in the canyon nearby the mining camps. One day he discovered his prized bottle of hot sauce missing and he spent days searching for it in the canyon. The thief was never caught, but his friends perpetuated the name to remind him of his loss. [982] [983] [984] That bottle might still be out there.

During the 1930s local prospector and pioneer cowboy Buster Bailey, with his brother-in-law and several others, worked with a gold mill in the Peppersauce Canyon. When he was eighteen or nineteen years old, he hauled ore from the Southern Belle Mine to the mill in the Peppersauce Canyon. He spent hours feeding ore into a small crusher. It paid off, he said, but they eventually shut it down. Bailey said that "lots of gold (was) taken from this mining property. The old boys that did that work sure knew what they were doing." He remembered seeing an old money safe with its door blown off in the canyon not far from the Southern Belle mine. [985]

---

[981] "It's cool, shady in Peppersauce Canyon," by Bryan Lee, Tucson Citizen, July 16, 2007.

[982] "Peppersauce: A canyon with spice," Tucson Daily Citizen, January 28, 1972. Peppersauce Canyon is 11 southeast of Oracle.

[983] "Peppersauce Campground," Coronado National Forest.

[984] "The pepper sauce was stolen from their camp. So they called it for this incident," from "Pepper Sauce Wash," Letter from Frank C. Lockwood, Tucson, 1921. Source "Arizona Place Names," by Will C. Barnes. University of Arizona Bulletin No. 2, 1935. Page 325.

[985] "Mines of the Catalinas, Old Mines, Lost Mines, Working, Mines Spanish Mines, Mythical Mines," by Buster Bailey. Buster Bailey papers, Arizona Historical Society.

The Old Hat Mining District

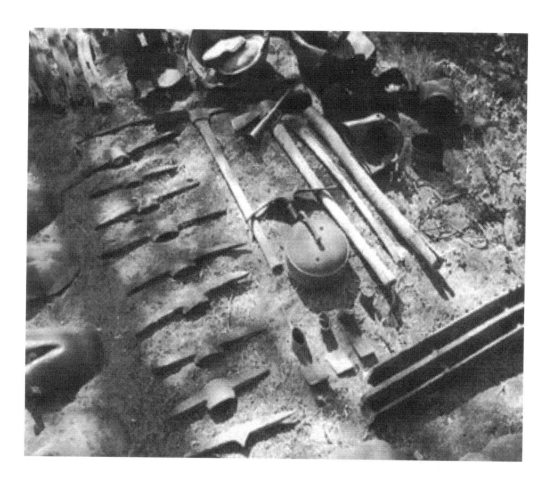

This is a collection of old mining equipment and parts of a Spanish arrastra found around the Santa Catalina Mountains. An arrastra is a primitive mill used for grinding or pulverizing gold and silver. Often, two or more flat-bottomed stones would be placed in a circular pit covered with flat stones. A center post would be connected to a long extension. Then, a horse or mule would drag the extended arm around the circle of stones to provide the grinding power to crush the ore. Phoenicians also used Arrastras. The Spaniards introduced arrastras to New Spain. Arrastras have been found throughout the Santa Catalinas, including the sites discussed. Gold ore was usually recovered by amalgamation with quicksilver after it was ground up with an arrastra. Photo courtesy of William Carter.

While Weldon, McKay and Lee were digging around the Oracle mine location, a few miles to the east during that summer of 1878, W. E. Guild, Louis DePuy (Depew or Dupuy), [986] and Mr. Ahern went to enjoy some time in the Catalinas and decided to do some prospecting. After nearly three weeks they returned to Florence with news of locating several ledges bearing gold and silver.

Isaac Laurin (his name has mistakenly been spelled as Lorrine or Lorraine) [987] located the American Flag [988] Mine in the area. Laurin and partner Bill Heneke struck silver and lead; that encouraged more prospectors. According to McKay it was Mrs. Laurin who broke off a piece of a big white ledge near the American Flag and found "free, coarse, heavy gold." [989]

A historical marker states that Laurin had built an adobe house near the mine about 1877, and it served as his residence and headquarters for nearby mining and ranching operations." [990] The home later became the first post office. The building still stands as a historic structure. [991] Laurin was also one of the founders of the Old Hat District. [992]

A meeting was held at the American Flag mill site on July 22, 1878, to form a mining district called The Old Hat Mining District. DePuy was appointed Chairman and Guild as

[986] Depew and Durpuy were used in the newspaper article references below.

[987] E.O. Stratton may have used the spelling as Lorrine. It is spelled as Laurin. He was born in Montreal, Canada and was a French Canadian. Other sources inaccurately claim he was a Frenchman from Martinique. From Isaac Laurin and the American Flag, by Catherine H. Ellis. Newsletter of the Oracle Historical Society. Volume 5 (2), Fall 2012.

[988] "American Flag Ranch and Acadia Ranch - The Story of Oracle's Post Offices," contributed by Oracle Historical Society, Arizona Memory Project, Arizona State Library, Archives and Public Records.

[989] Reminiscences of Alexander McKay as told to Mrs. George F. Kitt. 1936. Page 9.

[990] Historic marker, American Flag Post Office, Oracle, Arizona. This home was built before either McKay or Lee's claim to have built the first house in Oracle– see previous pages.

[991] American Flag Ranch Post Office #79000426, also known as American Flag Ranch; AR-03-05-05-01.

[992] Isaac Laurin and the American Flag, by Catherine H. Ellis. Page 3.

Secretary. [993] Depuy and Guild filed the first mining claims in the district that November. [994]

That same month Guild & Co. sold one of its claims and the Old Hat to M.A. Baldwin for $1,000 cash. [995] Ore that was assayed from the Old Hat, American Flag, Pioneer, and Bandit mines ranged from $75-1,200 per ton in gold and silver. [996]

Prospects looked so good that in December local capitalists and owners of the Arizona and Louisiana Mining Company incorporated the American Flag series of mines. The capital was $5 million with one hundred thousand shares of stock at fifty cents apiece. [997] M.A. Baldwin served as Superintendent, and Tucsonan Grantville H. Oury was attorney. [998]

---

[993] "New Mining Districts," The Arizona Weekly Citizen, August 2, 1878. The district is bound from the Old Camp Grant as the northwest point, down 25 miles along the San Pedro then across to the westerly side of the Santa Catarina mountains up along the summit of the mountains until it intersects the Old Camp Grant road from Tucson to Old Camp Grant (They sold part of their interest in the Old Hat in November for $1,000 – The Arizona Weekly Citizen, November 10, 1878).

[994] The History of the Lower San Pedro Valley in Arizona, by Bernard W. Muffley, 1938. University of Arizona, Pages 24-25.

[995] Arizona Weekly Citizen, November 30, 1878.

[996] "Florence Correspondence. The Mining Outlook as it Appears to Some of the Inhabitants of Pinal County- Miners in Owl Head and Santa Catarina Mountains," The Arizona Weekly Citizen, November 30, 1878.

[997] "From Florence. Mining Matters," Salt River Herald, Maricopa County, A.T., December 14, 1878. The trustees of the company are M.A. Baldwin, James Collingwood, Hon. Granville H. Oury, Hon, J.D. Walker, of Florence, and A.B. Seelye, of New Orleans, with the following named officers: Jos. Collingwood, president; Jos. Collingwood & Co., treasurers; John J. Devine, secretary; G.H. Oury, attorney; and M.A. Baldwin, superintendent.

[998] The Arizona Sentinel, December 7, 1878.

How The Old Hat May Have Acquired Its Name

There are several legends how the area acquired the name Old Hat. Traditionally, miners left their hats at the entrance of tunnels to alert others that someone was inside.

According to one tradition, an abandoned old hat was found on the property while it was first being prospected; thus it acquired the name.

A different story told of "tar heels" from North Carolina who settled in this area to prospect and farm. They all wore large broad-brimmed white hats that eventually became very old and "flopped."

Thus their neighborhood was called the old hat settlement. Later, the mining district became known as Old Hat." [999]

The Old Hat Mining District was located east of Oracle, on the northeast edge of the Santa Catalinas.

[999] "Nomenclature of Mines," Bisbee Daily Review, November 18, 1903, page 6.

Also see Mrs. Lalie C. Dodge, Letter to Dr. Frank Lockwood of Tucson, San Francisco, California, Sep. 23, 1919; Arizona Blade and the Florence Tribune, Florence, Arizona, Nov. 14, 1903.

1880: Prospectors Flood The Old Hat

Those two prospectors, the ones who told a newspaper reporter in 1880 about their recent discovery of the legendary mine with the iron door in the Catalinas, stayed at Martin & Weldon's Camp.

This newspaper account was the first published story to make reference to the Iron Door Mine name. [1000]

The legend of the Iron Door Mine and lost Nine Mile City (Nueva Mia Ciudad) was a familiar story to many Arizonans at the time. These stories were backed by embellished lore passed down from early Tucson residents. They brought treasure hunters and prospectors flocking to the Santa Catalina Mountains in search of the lost mine and the abundance of minerals just waiting to be extracted.

The sale of the American Flag to Robert Leatherwood and Mr. Haskell in July, 1880, was sealed for $11,800. Laurin, who was the original locator of the mine two years earlier, still maintained mining interests in the area. [1001] By August, 1880, the Patton mine, the Don Carlos, The Goldtree, the Valacio, the Lucky Mine, and the Emmery Mine were also operating in the Old Hat District. The Merrimac, owned by Wily Box and some partners, was on the same ledge as the Oracle. [1002] Wily sold his interest in the Wily Box mine, an extension of the Oracle, and the Tiger Mine, for several thousand dollars that same month. [1003] The Old Hat Mining District continued to grow. A large number of claims were being staked in the area. [1004] Over the next decades, the Oracle community would serve as a camp for miners working in the surrounding area– Campo Bonito, Apache, Oracle Ridge, and Mammoth Mining Districts.

[1000] "The Iron Door and the Nine Mile City of the Santa Catalinas," Arizona Weekly Star, March 4, 1880. Also, the Arizona Historical Society has a typewritten copy of that article in its archives, "The Mine with the Iron Door & the Nine Mile City of the Santa Catalinas' (Arizona Weekly Star, Mar. 4, 1880) COPY: by Mrs. Geo. F. Kitt, Sec'y, Arizona Pioneer Historical Society."

[1001] "Important Mining Sale," Arizona Weekly Citizen, July 10, 1880.

[1002] "Old Hat District," Arizona Weekly Citizen, August 7, 1880.

[1003] Arizona Weekly Citizen, August 14, 1880.

[1004] One group of mines was owned by Messrs. Heinikie, Laurina and Forbach. Another by Messrs. James and Abbott; and others by Mr. D. B. Rea. "Old Hat District," Arizona Weekly Citizen, January 21, 1880.

1881: Old Hat Expands, New Claims

There were enough men working at the mines by the end of January, 1881, that a post office opened at the American Flag. Peter Loss was appointed postmaster. James Bronson was appointed postmaster in Oracle. [1005] [1006]

Just southeast of the Christmas and New Year's mines, C.A. Wyatt and Pete Dumphrey started the Apache copper mine. In 1881 it became the Santa Catalina Copper Company of Boston when out of state investors bought the property. Emerson Oliver Stratton built a road from the mine to the San Pedro River. [1007]

Dr. Kane purchased the Apache, St. Nicholas, and Midas mines. "These are immense copper ledges; the detached float on the mountainsides alone is estimated at the very lowest calculation to be at least a thousand tons of high-grade copper ore. An assay made on Saturday from these mines showed eighty three percent copper, and $37.70 silver; total $103.76 per ton. These specimens were an average from the Santa Claus mine, taken from across the ledge fifteen feet in width." [1008]

Two years later, in 1883, the Apache ceased operations when it was determined there wasn't enough ore to be profitable. To recover $20,000 of ore, ten times that amount was spent. [1009]

The New Year's Mine, owned by McKay, was still considered one of the best in the Old Hat District during 1881. McKay's assessment work developed a five-foot vein of gold and silver ore. His Christmas Mine had a sixty-foot shaft with eight foot cross cuts, but with the overflow of water encountered in December, work was stopped until a pumping machine was acquired. Eight miles away from the Oracle, Weldon and Shultz were

---

[1005] "Among the postal changes for weekend ending January 30th" Peter H. Loss, Postmaster at American Flag (Pima County) and James Bronson, postmaster at Oracle (Pima County); Stone Cabin (Pima County) John P. Zimmerman, postmaster. Arizona Weekly Citizen, February 6, 1881.

[1006] It was closed July 16, 1890. "The Story of Oracle's Post Offices," Oracle Historical Society and Acadia Ranch Museum.

[1007] The History of The Lower San Pedro Valley in Arizona, page 25.

[1008] The Tombstone Epitaph, December 19, 1881.

[1009] The History of The Lower San Pedro Valley in Arizona, page 25.

starting work on a large ledge. In the Cañada del Oro the Captain Mine and others had men working on a "large body of high-grade ore." [1010]

The American Flag post office and saloon, outside of Oracle and located on the Old Mt. Lemmon Control Road, on the east side of the Santa Catalina Mountains. The building was originally Isaac Laurin's home. It still stands and is managed by the Oracle Historical Society.

[1010] "Old Hat District," The Citizen, December 4, 1881.

1882-1884: More Ore From The Old Hat; Railroad Planned

"Parties returning from the Santa Catalina mountains say there are a great many prospectors in the district and a large amount of ore are being put on the dumps. The Haskell prospects, in the Old Hat district, have at least $450,000 worth of ore in sight. The copper mines are developing most encouragingly." [1011]

By January, 1882, the Old Hat Mining District was steadily producing ore on the north side of the Santa Catalina Mountains. The Oracle Camp, also called Summit Springs, had seven or eight houses scattered around. [1012]

A five-foot ledge of silver bearing quartz was located at the Christmas Mine and was valued at $50-120 per ton. The nearby Imperial Mine had a four-foot ledge of gold bearing quartz carrying $20-40 per ton.

A few miles from the American Flag mine, the Southern Belle, Artic, Silver Prince, and Old Hat Group had active working claims. [1013]

[1011] Tombstone Epitaph, January 16, 1882, image 5.

[1012] "Old Hat District," Arizona Weekly Citizen, January 22, 1882.

Some of the homes belonged to Alexander McKay, James Branson (Oracle's first postmaster) and Edwin S. Dodge (built the Acadia Ranch between 1882 and 1885). Other ranchers in the area included J.C. Waterman and Henry Bockman (their properties became the Linda Vista Ranch). From National Register of Historic Places, Rancho Linda Vista, section 8, page 2.

[1013] "The Old Hat District," Arizona Weekly Citizen, Tucson, A.T., January 22, 1882. Reprinted from the 1881-1882 Congressional Edition, Vol. 2013, page 289 and in the 1882: Report of the Director of the Mint by the U.S. Bureau of the Mint.

Adventurous developers were building a road and planning a railroad to haul out the newly discovered gold and copper ore that January.

Dr. K. Kane, who was well know in Tucson for his ambitious projects, had spearheaded the movement to "build a three foot gauge road along the route now traveled by the Santa Catarina stagecoach line round the point of the mountains to the Oracle mine near where ex-Mayor R. N. Leatherwood, who is also actively furthering the project, has a large ranch." [1014]

The railroad, according to Kane's plan, would then run from Oracle Camp to the American Flag then lead to the camp of the Santa Catarina Copper Company by Marble Peak. It would join the road built by the SCCC to the San Pedro Valley. From there, it would lead down the valley to the Gila river, up to the mouth of Deer Creek, and to the coal fields nearby. It would continue until it "reaches the Atlantic & Pacific." This would open up one of the richest mineral sections in the territory. [1015] [1016]

[1014] "Another Railroad Company, to the Rich Mines of the Santa Catarinas, the Coal Fields and the Timber Lands of the North," from the Tucson Citizen, January 20 and reprinted in the Tombstone Epitaph, January 23, 1882.

[1015] Ibid.

[1016] Tombstone Epitaph, January 16, 1882.

New Road For Hundreds Of Workers

In February 1882, the Oracle district had forty six residents. [1017] A new road from the Santa Catalina Copper mines made it possible to haul freight to the mines.

E.O. Stratton, the contractor, hired Thom. H. Williams to build the road to shorten the distance from the Oracle to the American Flag by two miles. Two hundred men throughout the entire valley were dependant on the American Flag Post Office to get their mail. Many miners who worked and lived farther away complained because of the long distance. A store was established near the Comanche camp by William Zeckendorf's home. [1018]

By the end of 1883, local rancher Mariano Samaniego was operating a stagecoach line from Tucson to Oracle and the American Flag. [1019] [1020] Two years later, he began twice weekly mail delivery to Oracle, the American Flag, and Mammoth [1021] when the post office at Oracle was reopened in January 1885 having been closed for two years. [1022]

A dozen Old Hat mining claims owned by Nathaniel A. Boyton were sold to Louis LaFrance in January, 1884, to satisfy Boyton's creditors. The deal included the American Flag, Oracle, and Summit mines. [1023]

To protect his interests, McKay began surveying his land for a patent as average gold assays were going for $30-40 and had gone as high as $300. [1024] On April 18, 1884, the

---

[1017] "Pinal County Census," Arizona Weekly Citizen, Tucson, A.T., July 16, 1882.

[1018] "Old Hat District," Arizona Weekly Citizen, Tucson, A.T., January 23, 1882.

[1019] "Stage Line from Tucson to Oracle," Arizona Weekly Citizen, December 29, 1883.

[1020] "The Road to Santa Catalina Copper Mines," Arizona Weekly Citizen, February 19, 1882.

[1021] "Local News," Arizona Weekly Citizen, July 25, 1885.

[1022] "Re-established," Arizona Weekly Citizen, January 31, 1885.

[1023] "Deeds," Arizona Weekly Citizen, January 5, 1884.

[1024] "McKay's Mines," Arizona Weekly Citizen, March 15, 1884.

Christmas Mine, covering eighteen acres, was patented in the Old Hat Mining District. [1025]

Weldon and McKay were also two of the original locators of the famed Quijotoa mine in the Quijotoa mountains with partners W.C. Davis, George Teetsworth, Martin Meadley, and Mr. Roark. While the mine generated wealth, Weldon, Meadley, Roark, and Teetsworth ended up poor. McKay and Davis, however, were able to keep some of their earnings.

Weldon died penniless in February, 1895. He allegedly committed suicide as a bottle of strychnine poison was found near by. [1026]

Photograph of a former water tower converted into a residence in Oracle. This building may have been built near Weldon's grotto or camp.

[1025] "Application No. 368 for Patent for the Christmas Mining Claim, April 18, 1884," Arizona Weekly Citizen, June 21, 1884.

[1026] "Quijotoa Weldon Dead, Takes Strychnine at Phoenix– Died a Poor Man," Arizona Weekly Citizen, February 9, 1895.

1886: Chance Finding Of Gold Bearing Quartz

"A great gold belt will be opened, second only in size to the largest known gold lode in the world and first in productive capacity that will add many millions annually to the wealth of the country and give employment to quite an army of industrious people." [1027]

"Mr. Armstrong, who represents the syndicate bonding the property has ten men employed taking out such ore as will prove available for shipment and the recent outlook of the property is an extremely favorable one." [1028]

Gold bearing quartz in the Santa Catalina Mountains was reported in several newspaper articles during 1886. While more ventures popped up, others had their challenges.

With values like that by December, 1887, "work has again started upon the well-known American Flag mine and things are likely to boom in the Santa Catalina Mountains." [1029] There were several mines already in operation east of Oracle. The Mammoth Mine had a thirty stamp mill and a ten stamp mill was just completed at the Southern Belle mine. [1030] By February, 1886, the old Apache copper smelter had closed because of financial difficulties. The Southern Belle gold mine, which started up a few months earlier, had already shipped about $7,000 worth of gold. [1031] At $18.86 an ounce at the time, that would be over three hundred and seventy one ounces – more than twenty three pounds of gold. With today's prices, it would have been worth $4.82 million. [1032] Even all of that activity in the mountains did not detour Indian attacks. In June, 1887, Durand Daily, a stage driver for M.G. Samaniego, reported between Tucson and the Southern Belle that Indians killed one of Charlouleu's vaqueros in the Cañon del Oro. [1033]

[1027] Arizona Champion, Peach Springs, Mohave, A.T. Arizona, October 2, 1886, from the Tucson Citizen.

[1028] Arizona Weekly Citizen, September 18, 1886 and Mohave County Miner, December 24, 1887.

[1029] Mohave County Miner reporting on an article published in the Tucson Citizen, December 24, 1887.

[1030] Arizona Weekly Citizen, January 9, 1886.

[1031] Tombstone Daily Epitaph, February 20, 1886.

[1032] Gold value in 2013 is about $1,300 an ounce.

[1033] Arizona Weekly Citizen, June 18, 1887.

William "Curley" Neal Moves To Oracle

William "Curly" Neal, a former military scout, settled in the Oracle area in 1878. Neal was interested in the legendary Iron Door mine and encouraged his friend, Buffalo Bill Cody, to search with him. [1034]

Neal's father was of African-American descent and his mother was a Cherokee Indian. He was nicknamed "Curly" for his long black curls. He started a business in Tucson digging cellars and then opened a livery. He also delivered ore, wood, and water from the mines to the mills. [1035] In July, 1886, Neal began a stagecoach line and sublet for the mail delivery contracts. [1036] He held that job for forty-two years and delivered mail between the towns of Catalina, Oracle, American Flag, Southern Belle, Willow Springs, and Mammoth. [1037]

In 1894 two years after his marriage to Tucsonan Anna Magdalena Box, [1038] Neal lost the Mammoth mine mail contract to Mariano Samaniego, who had gained several other contracts, outbid Neal. [1039] Later that spring Neal built a two-story adobe home in Oracle, across the street from his soon-to-be built hotel. [1040]

Neal became the proprietor of one of the world's largest freighting outfits in connection with the mill at the Mammoth property. Three teams moved one hundred and forty five tons of ore three times a day. Each team had twenty horses with four wagons as big as boxcars. [1041]

[1034] Encyclopedia of Frontier Biography: G-O, By Dan L. Thrapp. 1991. University of Nebraska Press. Page 1045.

[1035] "Neal, William "Curly" (1849-1936)," BlackPast.org

[1036] "New Mail Contracts," Arizona Weekly Citizen, June 26, 1886.

[1037] "Neal, William "Curly" (1849-1936)," BlackPast.org

[1038] Ibid.

[1039] Arizona Weekly Citizen, January 6, 1984.

[1040] Arizona Weekly Citizen, May 19, 1894.

[1041] St. John's Herald, May 24, 1894.

Neal also supplied the smelter with oak wood from Oracle, but after objections from both residents and the federal government, he changed to mesquite trees from the San Pedro Valley. [1042]

By December of 1894, work was almost completed on Neal's new hotel, called the Mountain View, [1043] built on Neal's one hundred and sixty acre ranch. [1044] The two-story resort was opened with a housewarming party on Washington's Birthday, February 22, 1895 that lasted until five o'clock in the morning. [1045] There was some talk that the hotel was actually built with the support of his good friend and eventual mining investor, William Cody. [1046] While Neal may have provided the muscle, Cody, who was a hotelier as well as entertainer and miner, may have provided the financial means.

Neal was a big proponent of the Iron Door Mine legend and spent many years roaming the Catalinas to find it. He also encouraged his friend Cody to back him up in his search for the lost mine. [1047] Even though they never found it, Neal believed it was still somewhere in the mountains. He speculated that the great earthquake of 1878 buried the mine at the same time the hole in the mountain, "La Ventaña, was destroyed. [1048]

Neal's wife, Annie, said treasure hunters would visit the hotel on their way to find the Lost Escalante Mine. She hosted Harold Bell Wright at the hotel while he was working on his book, THE MINE WITH THE IRON DOOR. [1049]

[1042] "Oracle and the San Pedro River Valley," by Catherine H. Ellis, Arcadia Publishing, 2008. Page 24.

[1043] "Local News," Arizona Weekly Citizen, December 1, 1894.

[1044] Neal, William "Curly" (1849-1936) from BlackPast.org.

[1045] "Mountain View Hotel, A Charming Resort, and Finest Appointed Hotel In Arizona," Arizona Weekly Citizen, March 2, 1895.

[1046] Buffalo Bill and His Wild West, by Joseph G. Rosa and Robin May, University Press of Kansas. Page 195. This reference, from "The Lives and Legends of Buffalo Bill," by Don Russell who attributes the building of the hotel to Neal.

[1047] The Lives and Legends of Buffalo Bill, by Don Russell. Page 434.

[1048] "Buffalo Bill Believed in "Lost Mine" In Catalinas and Organized Company; William Neal Thinks It Really Exists," undated. Arizona Historical Society.

[1049] African American Women and the Old West, by Tricia Martineau Wagner. Globe Pequot, 2007. Page 74.

Neal died in a freak automobile accident in 1936 near his home at the Mountain View Hotel. He lived to age eighty seven. [1050]

The former Mountain View Hotel built by William Neal in 1895 is now the Mountain View Baptist Church. This photo is taken near the site of his home that was built across the street from the hotel on American Avenue in Oracle, Arizona.

[1050] Neal, William "Curly" (1849-1936) from BlackPast.org.

The 3N marker stone on William Neal's 3N Ranch's [1051] [1052] still sits at on top of the hill overlooking his Mountain View Hotel. Some theories are that it marks either a shaft or a property corner.

[1051] Neal, William "Curly" (1849-1936) from BlackPast.org.

[1052] "Annie Box Neal," from African American Women of the Old West, by Tricia Martineau Wagner. Page 75.

The Jail Tree And The Mountain View Hotel

irectly across the street from the Mountain View Hotel in mid-town Oracle is the infamous "Jail Tree" where most often miners were chained for showing up drunk. Inscribed on a plaque, placed in 1998 in front of the old oak tree:

> *"Local lore says this oak tree was once used as a tying post for outlaws until the Sheriff from the Town of Mammoth could come to take them to jail. The red brick building across the road was the Mountain View Hotel, one of the few remaining original historic building left in Oracle. This hotel, owned by William and Annie Neal, opened in 1895. Buffalo Bill Cody and stagecoach robber Pearl Hart were just two of its famous ledgers. Many exciting western tales are centered on this building."* [1053]

[1053] Plaque marker, 1998. Oracle, Arizona.

1900: Mining Becomes A Major Business in Arizona

Mining gained steam in February, 1900, when George F. Metz purchased a number of valuable mines in the Old Hat district for T. G. Condon. One group of twelve claims purchased from E. O. Stratton was valued at nearly $35,000. [1054]

Less than two months later, the Stratton-Condon deal was off. Metz entered into an agreement with someone else named Babcock for other claims instead. On his claims, Bob Leatherwood, the ex-sheriff of Pima County, recovered assays showing twenty seven percent copper and ten ounces in silver. [1055]

> *"The company engaged in developing the Geisman copper group in the Catalina Mountains east of Oracle, encountered a line body of ore, this week, at a depth of 69 feet. A crosscut, says our informant, proves the body of ore to be about forty feet wide and some of it very high-grade. The latter will make the average of the entire body high. It looks as if the Old Hat district, in which this group is situated, would yet fulfill its old time promise."* [1056]

Capt. J. D. Burgess, who was in charge of the Panama mine in the Old Hat district, sunk a shaft in September, 1900, and the ore has an "assay value of which is two hundred and thirteen ounces of silver, $1140 gold, eight ounces copper and thirty nine ounces lead. Burgess was "clearing and grading grounds for a large concentrating plant shortly to be erected, is also in progress." [1057]

> *In November 1900, "R. N. Leatherwood who has the Apache claim in the Old Hat district, Catalina mountains, reports that Geo. Metz, agent for Condon, New York, has located the hoisting plant on the Condon properties."* [1058]

[1054] "The Mining Field," Arizona Silver Belt, February 22, 1900.

[1055] The Arizona Daily Orb, Bisbee, Arizona, April 26, 1900.

[1056] Mohave County Miner, Mineral Park, A.T. Arizona, July 14, 1900.

[1057] Mohave County Miner, September 8, 1900.

[1058] Mohave County Miner, November 3, 1900.

The Santa Catalina Forest Reserve was created in July, 1902. Six years later the Santa Catalina and Santa Rita Forest Reserves became part of the Coronado National Forest.
[1059]

Miner's collection of pots, pans and other utensils that can still be found around the Catalina Mountains. Photo courtesy of William Carter.

[1059] History & Culture, Coronado National Forest, Forest Service, U.S. Dept. of Agriculture. Also listed in Township 11 South Range 16 E Historical Index Page (7/2/1908 Coronado NF entry. U.S. Forest Reserves entry 6/20/1900).

1901: A Rodent Leads To A Gold Discovery

In 1901, a prospector described the surprising discovery of quartz stones infused with gold he accidentally found while camping in the Santa Catalina Mountains.

N.H. Ingoldsby had been spending several months near Mammoth, east of Oracle, on the San Pedro River. He was there to "enjoy the hunting and make a collection of animals and minerals of the Southwest."

While camping, he often left his supplies lying around since he didn't expect any visitors.

But he started to notice odd disappearance of small articles. When something was missing, something else was left in its place– usually a bit of stone or wood. He discovered the culprit was a large rodent. Ingoldsby would often lie awake at night to watch for his nighttime visitor.

One morning a silver spoon was missing, but in its place he found a "piece of quartz carrying free gold." After several attempts, Ingoldsby followed the animal to its home where he found a large ledge of gold bearing quart nearby, the source of the rodent's gift.

Ingoldsby appropriately named the property the Rat Hole Mine. [1060]

[1060] This story was reported in at least three newspapers: "Rat Points Out Riches," The Arizona Republican, April 26, 1901. Also published in the Arizona Daily Journal Miner, April 27, 1901; The San Francisco Call, San Francisco, California, March 31, 1901; and The Copper Era, Clifton, Arizona, March 7, 1901 from the Mexican Herald.

1904: Rail Line Abandoned

The Southern Pacific Company abandoned plans for a railroad line expansion towards the Santa Catalinas in 1904 because of political pressure.

The Phoenix and Eastern Railroad had already arched at a point opposite the mouth of the San Pedro River. A line was planned to extend south along the east side of the San Pedro River to Benson. [1061] Despite that set back mining developments still continued.

Quartz outcrop near Campo Bonito mining district north of Tucson.

[1061] The History of the Lower San Pedro Valley in Arizona, by Bernard W. Muffley, 1938. A Thesis submitted to the faculty of the Department of History in partial fulfillment of the requirements for the degree of Master of Arts in the Graduate College University of Arizona, p. 72.

In January, 1903, Robert Leatherwood was enthusiastic over the future of the Apache mine, his property in the Old Hat district north of the city. [1062]

By 1908 the Apache Group was quite productive. There was a force of twenty-five workers constantly on the property. The group was being developed under the direction of Superintendent Cassett, and the Western Development Company held the option on the claims. The mine was very rich in copper with some silver and gold ore. A four hundred foot tunnel was driven through the property, and a shaft had been sunk to the one hundred and sixty foot level. Leatherwood was a "former sheriff of Pima County and during the World's Fair at St. Louis in 1904 was in charge of the exhibit from this territory." [1063]

Plans for the railroad were reinstituted in 1905:

> *"Chief Engineer Thompson of the Twin Buttes railroad is in the city from the grading camp which is located near the mines. The roadbed will be completed to the mines within a few days. It is expected that the rails and ties will be laid as fast as the material arrives."* [1064]

In 1909 it was announced that a "ledge six feet wide and running sixty percenter copper and $6 in gold" was uncovered from the Old Hat district in the Santa Catalina Mountains, on property owned by William Reid of Prescott. [1065]

[1062] Bisbee Daily Review, January 23, 1903.

[1063] "Apache Group Making Progress," Bisbee Daily Review, February 23, 1908.

[1064] Arizona Silver Belt, November 30, 1905, page 3.

[1065] Daily Arizona Silver Belt, November 23, 1909.

1911: Old Hat Gains New Owners– the Copper Queen

The Old Hat district, also called the Reid Mining District, had produced some excitement in 1911 "over recent strikes and the continued good showings of the more important properties being worked there." These prospects were several miles farther southeast of the American Flag.

> *"Immediately adjoining the Copper Queen property, the Copper Range Company in Arizona is busy at work. Attorney Francis M. Hartman being worked lies within 1,000 feet of the end of the Copper Queen tunnel, and the later company is working toward the Copper Range property.*
>
> *The camps are near together and present a busy scene, fifty or sixty men being employed. There are other properties, which are showing good prospects. But the Copper Queen and Copper Range companies are doing the chief developing and have the test prospects."* [1066]

In October, 1911, the Old Hat district gained new owners. An agreement with "F. Geessmaan (sic) was filed for record in the county recorder's office here yesterday." The agreement involved the Eagle, Copper Peak, York, Eagle No. 2, and Golden Peak No. 2 claims in the Old Hat district of the Catalina mountains. Thus far "$4,260 has been paid on the claims... and the balance of $59,750 will be paid on August 15, 1912." [1067]

The Copper Queen Company took an option on the Geeseman property at the same time as the Leatherwood, Lovell, and Reid claims. The Copper Queen Company, operating from the Apache camp, "has found the claims to be good ones, and will continue the development work steadily and rapidly. It is to this property that a movement has been started to have a highway constructed from this city, in order that the business of the camps, which now goes to the other side of the mountains, will come back here." [1068]

[1066] Bisbee Daily Review, Bisbee, Arizona, January 13, 1911, page 2. Also reprinted in Oasis, Arizola, Arizona, January 14, 1911.

[1067] Bisbee Daily Review, Bisbee Arizona, October 13, 1911, page 7.

[1068] Ibid.

The property again changed hands in the fall of 1912 when E.O. Stratton gave a bond on the claims to a group of Boston investors. This included the Chalcopyrite Peacock and Copper Matte claims which he owned south of the Giesman claims and north of the Leatherwood claims. The Copper Queen Consolidated Mining Company purchased those claims.

Prof C. F. Tolman, with the mining department of Standard University, "made a report on the Stratton group while he was still head of the department of mines at the University of Arizona and stated that the Stratton group deposits are similar in character to the neighboring ore bodies which deeper developments prove to have commercial value. He also stated that the Stratton property has as strong an outcrop as and a longer outcrop than any on which deeper work has been done." [1069]

[1069] "Stratton Has Given Bond on Claims," Mohave County Miner, Mineral Park, A.T., October 5, 1912.

1912: Arizona Statehood And Mining The Catalinas

By the time Arizona became a state in February 1912, mining in Southern Arizona had already gained a foothold. The Apache camp, located on the northern slope of the Santa Catalina range, continued to operate under bond by both the Giesman and Leatherwood properties.

Fifty men were at work at the Apache claims. At the nearby Daily claims there were fourteen men at work.

> *"The Foran group, under option to has been equipped with machinery capable of deep exploration. The Del Monte property, under the management of Donovan & Walker, of nine claims, the Simpkins and Martinez claims, are all located in this vicinity. The prevailing character of the ore of this district is a chalcopyrite, carrying gold and silver in addition to the copper values. Campo Bonito. To the north and west of Apache camp and at a lower altitude is the scene of the Cody-Dyer M. & M. company's operations. The company has thirty-six locations here and a forty-ton mill has been installed. There is a scheelite gold ore that yields to the milling and concentrating process. The Southern Belle, owned by the Cody-Dwyer Interests, is now under bond to Capt Jack Burgess."* [1070]

Both the Apache Camp and Campo Bonito are within the Old Hat Mining District and accessible to Tucson by wagon road through the Cañada del Oro. "The E.P. and S.W. railway has surveyed to the former camp and the course of line runs approximately near to all the important mining interests now known in that locality. Its construction is well within the realms of the possible." [1071]

[1070] "Santa Catalina Mountains and the Old Hat Mining Districts," Bisbee Daily Review, May 14, 1912, page 5.

[1071] Ibid.

1913: Leatherwood And The Copper Queen Old Hat Claims

In January, 1913, some of the claims in the Old Hat District changed hands again. Owners A. A. Trippel and others sold four claims to former Sheriff Robert Leatherwood for $20,000.

> *"It is a high-grade copper proposition," he asserted. "The poorest assays we secured were 10.10 percent copper, and the highest, 22 percent. The ore also carried gold and silver values."* [1072]

Thirteen more Old Hat claims at Apache camp also changed hands in May, 1913. The claims, owned by the Daily brothers and deeded to the Daily Arizona Copper Company, were between two properties purchased by the Copper Queen Consolidated Mining Company. [1073] Three months later the Copper Queen also became interested in E. O. Stratton's copper claims in the Old Hat District. [1074]

But by October, 1913, the Copper Queen was idle, even though there were still reserves of copper ore available– up to eight percent copper-sulfide. The planned extension of the E.P. & S.W. railroad from Tucson delayed operations. If built, the railroad would run around the west end of the Catalina Mountains and back through the San Pedro valley to Apache camp. The railroad was needed to get shipments to the Copper Queen smelter in Douglas.

> *"San Diego railroad authorities "profess to see in this move a step toward the long-discussed and often denied juncture between the E.P. & S.W. and the Spreckles, the San Diego and Arizona, at Yuma. Its construction is of the highest type corresponding to that of the E.P. & S.W. Ties and rails are heavy and all bridges and culverts are of concrete."* [1075]

[1072] "Sells four Claims Near Camp Apache, Group Is Reported as Disposed of and Consideration $20,000," Bisbee Daily Review, Bisbee, Arizona, January 21, 1913.

[1073] Mohave County Miner, Mineral Park, A.T. Arizona, May 24, 1913.

[1074] Tombstone Epitaph, August 31, 1913.

[1075] Bisbee Daily Review, October 3, 1913.

A few days later, an article titled "the Prospects for Early Railroad construction into the Old Hat causes immediate movement," revealed the plans for the railroad further.

> *"After spending several weeks here placing the stock of the Daily Arizona Copper Co. on the market, president W. H. Daily will leave tomorrow for his home in Tucson. He will spend a short time there with his family and then leave for Apache camp in the Old Hat district, where the properties are located, and commence development work. While in this city he interested over 75 people as stockholders in the company and late last week when the announcement was made that manager H. J. Simmons, of the E. P. & S. W., had made purchases of lumber in San Diego for the purpose of building a railroad through this district, Mr. Daily decided that he would not stay here any longer but go to the property and develop it so as to be ready to make shipments when the railroad is built to the district. The Copper Queen Mining Co. owns ranch property about the Daily-Arizona and have done considerable development work. The district is pronounced to be a very rich one, and old timers who are familiar say that it will be a second Bisbee camp in time to come."* [1076]

At the end of November 1913, the property in the Old Hat district was in acquisition by the Phelps Dodge Copper Company.

> *"The country rock consists mainly of limestone, quartzite, gneiss and porphyry, which have been fractured and faulted to a large extent. The majority of these faults are well mineralized carrying values in lead, silver and copper. Work to date has been confined to the mining of the oxidized ores and as a result sufficient depth has not been attained to determine the extent of the secondary enriched zone. Considerable ore has been shipped in the past to the El Paso smelter via Tucson."* [1077]

By April, 1915, the "Old Hat district covered an area of twenty five thousand acres, with an average thickness of one hundred and fifty feet. It has been very difficult to determine the value of this, owing to the fact that the gold is not equally distributed." [1078]

[1076] "To Develop the Daily Ground," Bisbee Daily Review, October 7, 1913, page 8

[1077] "Old Hat is being Entered," Mohave County Miner, November 29, 1913.

[1078] Mohave County Miner, April 24, 1915.

1915: The Castro's Discoveries In The Catalinas

The only reported discovery of several Jesuit treasure chests and jewels in the Catalinas happened in a cave near Apache Peak south of Old Hat District. This was done by local rancher Sistro Castro in 1915. [1079]

An Oracle couple also told a story about the father and the uncle of Ernesto Castro (Severiano) [1080] who discovered a large nugget of gold plus grains. They sold the nugget for $45,000. The senior Castro later returned to the spot to collect some smaller nuggets. When he planned on going to Tucson to sell them, his wife Lisa bought them instead. Gold was selling for less than $8 an ounce at the time. [1081]

In 1936 the Severiano Castro property held numerous gold-silver and copper claims located about two miles east of Apache Peak and southwest of Campo Bonito. [1082]

[1079] "The Business of Being Buffalo Bill," by Elizabeth Curl, back page map and legend of Campo Bonito.

[1080] Severiano Castro (1864-1943) was the son of Jesus Castro and Guadalupe. Ernesto Castro (1901-1983) was one of 10 children of Severiano (ref: Martinez-Krampel-Escalante-Doitch-Chance Family Tree, geneology.com.

[1081] "Couple Tells of Early Times in Oracle," by Annabelle Douglas, from the Oracle Historian, page 6.

[1082] Bureau of Land Management database, Severiano Castro, 7/17/1936; Golden Eagle Group (Severiano Castro property). Mindat.org.

The 3C Ranch "Mary West" Mine

Southeast of Oracle along the old Mt. Lemmon Highway is the 3C Ranch, one of the oldest ranches in Arizona. This ranch hosted celebrities of the 1900s, such as President Richard Nixon [1083] and Mae West. [1084]

Hidden on the property is a former underground mine, the Mary West. Sheriff and Tucson Mayor Robert Leatherwood originally owned it. The mine was also called the Three C Ranch Mine, a proven copper, silver, and gold quartz vein deposit between 3-4 feet wide. The mine had its first production in 1955. Mary West filed hundreds of mining claims in the area– from four hundred to eight hundred. [1085]

West was the daughter of the Texas cattleman who owned the old 3C Ranch. West bought the ranch in 1945 from the William Huggett Estate and sold it in 1959. [1086] Huggett was a famous photographer and tour guide. [1087] The property changed hands several times and is now owned by the Darimont family and operates as a guest ranch. It's unknown if Mae West and Mary West were related.

The ranch also features an active, natural spring that continuously flows from a network of underground water sources in the area.

[1083] In 1971, President Richard M. Nixon's Administration announced that the United States "would not freely convert dollars at their official exchange rate." From "Brief History of the Gold Standard in the United States," by Craig K. Elwell, Congressional Research Service, CRS Report for Congress, June 23, 2011. This Act repealed the limitation on gold ownership imposed by President Roosevelt in 1933.

[1084] "Welcome to the 3 C Ranch," website http://3cranchaz.com/

[1085] "Three C Ranch mine and mill file," Arizona Department of Mineral Resources. From Three C Ranch Mine (Mary West Mine), Peppersauce Wash, Apache Peak area, Oracle District, mindat.org.

[1086] "Oracle's Historic 3-C Ranch," by Elaine Raines. Arizona Daily Star, September 23, 2008.

[1087] William Huggett acquired the property in 1929 from Richard G. Brady; U.S. Department of Interior Bureau of Land Management.

Gold At Campo Bonito

All that remains of Campo Bonito mining camp is a crumbling fireplace and concrete slab– possibly the mess hall for the miners who toiled nearby.

When gold mining in the Cañada del Oro was in full swing by the late 1800s, prospectors looking for a quick path to riches were exploring a hidden valley on the north side of the Santa Catalina Mountains.

Mining in the Southern Arizona mountains became a big business at the turn of the century, especially for celebrities like William "Buffalo Bill" Cody.

The Camp Bonito site was one of the early mining camps formed in the Old Hat mining district just south of Oracle, Arizona in the Santa Catalina Mountains, not far from the YMCA Triangle Y Ranch.

At that time, the town of Oracle, north of Tucson, Arizona, was already settled with prospectors and homesteaders in the hills north of the Catalina Mountains. The Old Hat District was a proven producer of silver and gold.

The persistent legends of a lost city and a lost Spanish mine were overshadowed by recent discoveries of gold-embedded deposits that seemed to drip from the mountains and flow from the Cañada del Oro, according to newspaper accounts during the late 1880s. [1088]

The mineral list from the Campo Bonito mines [1089] included Calcite, Dolomite, Galena, Gold, Pyrite, Scheelite, Talc, and Wulfenite. [1090] Tungsten was also a main ore.

The Campo Bonito group consisted of several dozen mining claims spread through the valley on the northeast side of the Catalina Mountains to include the Apache Peak area (Juniper claim, Memory Lane group, the Pair O' Dice prospect, Red Dog claim, Southern Belle Mine (Southern Belle; Morning Star property/claims), and the Taraldson claim.

It also included the Maudina Mine claims/property, the High Jinks Mine and the Santa Rosa Mine (Cumaro claim). [1091] The land is now part of the Coronado National Forest and some private properties, including the privately owned High Jinks Ranch, the YMCA's Triangle Y Ranch, and numerous small ranches.

[1088] "The Iron Door Mine," Arizona Weekly Star, March 4, 1880. The story of the two miners discovery of the lost city and lost mine was widely known among Tucsonans, as described in this article.

[1089] USGS: Bonito mines is a past producer of Tungsten, Pure Gold, Morning Star M S 1836. Patented Claims M S 1836, Gold Bug, Campo Bonito. MRDS M050217, Deposit 10210244.

[1090] Pure Gold Mine, Campo Bonito Mines, Apache Peak area. Mindat.org Database.

[1091] Campo Bonito, Oracle District (Control District; Old Hat District; Santa Catalina District), Santa Catalina Mountains, Pinal County, Arizona. Mindat.org.

A drum and washbasin still remains at the Campo Bonito campsite, located off the Old Mount Lemmon Highway, just outside of Oracle, Arizona. The mining claims are 1 mile ENE of Apache Peak and about 2 miles SW of Campo Bonito. GPS coordinates: 32°33'29"N 110°44'8"W. [1092]

[1092] Locality Search, Campo Bonito. Mindat.org.

Jewelry grade silver embedded in quartz is still found in the Santa Catalinas. Samples, marketed as Cody Stone, are on display at several locations nationwide.

Displays are at the Gemological Institute of America (GIA) in Carlsbad, California; the Mineral & Fossil Hall at the House of Onyx in Greenville, KY; The Buffalo Bill Historical Center in Cody, WY; the Old West Museum at Fort Cody Trading Place and the Buffalo Bill Ranch in North Platte, NE; the Oklahoma Historical Society and the Buffalo Bill Museum and Grave in Golden, Colorado; and the Mining Hall of Fame, Leadville, Colorado. Cody Stone is named after Buffalo Bill Cody who owned several mines in the Oracle, Arizona, area. [1093] The market value suggested could be $5 a carat. [1094]

The University of Arizona analyzed one quartz-silver sample with a Scanning Electron Microscope (SEM) and a backscattered-electron detector. The stone was found to be primarily quartz– a common element– with traces of rare-earth elements. The most "abundant minerals other than quartz are lead sulfide (galena) and copper-iron sulfide (chalcopyrite). Silver was also present in the vein. [1095]

[1093] Provenance of the Cody Stone and mining ventures, by William Carter. 2014.

[1094] Stated by noted jeweler Michael Garcia, NaNa Ping. Aspen Mountain Studio, June 3, 1998. Also, stated by Larry Gray of The Mine Group, Boise, Idaho. August 21, 1997.

[1095] Analysis from Gary Chandler, Mineral Science and Engineering, University of Arizona, Tucson. September 25, 1998.

"Buffalo Bill" Cody's Mining Ventures In The Catalinas

"(To) J. Frank Cody:

Wait till I come, wonderful report from mines. Mill running on forty-dollar ore. Tucson Bank buying our concentrates as come from mill, get busy. Waldorf Hotel first November, telegraph there. High Jinks will be a winner too.

Love, W. F. Cody" [1096]

William F. "Buffalo Bill" Cody in front of a tent near Cody, Wyoming. November 1902. [1097]

[1096] From The Business of Being Buffalo Bill: selected letters of William F. Cody, 1879-1917, page 59. Night Letter, Columbia, SC 30-12. Note: High Jinks was a new tunnel in the Arizona Mine (near Campo Bonito). The High Jinks is also the name of the home built by Cody's foster son, Johnny Baker, near the High Jinks mine.

1902: Buffalo Bill Stakes His Claim At Campo Bonito

T he discovery of precious minerals near Tucson attracted the famous Western entertainer William "Buffalo Bill" Cody to Oracle in the early 1900s to invest in several mines in the Camp Bonito mining district.

Campo Bonito, located in a valley south of Oracle, held promising mineral wealth.

At age fifty six, "Buffalo Bill" Cody was the world's biggest icon of the 19th Century. He was one of the most popular entertainers in the world. Born as William Frederick Cody, he gained the nickname Buffalo Bill while in the Army. Cody later toured his Old West entertainment show, "Buffalo Bill's Wild West," around the country. He was invited to England in 1887 and gained international fame. [1098] He was also the first comic book super hero, thanks to Ned Buntline. [1099]

Cody first brought his Buffalo

[1097] William F. (Buffalo Bill) Cody in front of a tent on his TE Ranch, near Cody, Wyoming. Dated November 1902. Buffalo Bill Museum and Grave, Lookout Mountain, Golden, CO. ID# 74.0268. http://www.buffalobill.org/

[1098] The Buffalo Bill Museum and Grave. http://www.buffalobill.org/

[1099] In 1869, Cody met "Ned Buntline" an alias for Edward Zane Carroll Judson. From William Frederick Cody – Kansaspedia, Kansas Historical Society.

Bill's Rough Riders show to Tucson in September, 1902. [1100]

Another draw for Cody was the Santa Catalina Mountains and its mineral prospects. Cody was a friend of William Neal, an Oracle entrepreneur. They had known each other since the 1860s battle of Summit Springs [1101] in Colorado. Neal was also a former military scout and was Cody's good friend.

J. L. Clark and Fritz Ewe originally staked an independent-lode mining claim in the Old Hat Mining District on January 29, 1887. President Benjamin Harrison granted patent land rights to J.L. Clark and Fritz Ewe January 10, 1891. [1102] The land later became part of the Campo Bonito claims. Cody wrote about his new venture in a letter to friend George T. Beck on May 4, 1902: "The gold mine is a winner I guess beyond a doubt its being kept quiet just now as we want some property adjoining it and a water right from a stream nearby. We are getting out ore and the vein provides a true fissure." [1103]

Cody was encouraged by the gold samples produced by his partner, L.W. Getchell. A year later Cody wrote to his sister Julia on March 13, 1903, that the "long-sought vein of ore had been struck after seven months of night-and-day drilling, and predicted that the mine would begin to pay off within four months. As soon as the roads were passable, wagons would haul ore and their own mill would be built during the summer." [1104] This may have been in reference to the three searches for the Iron Door Mine made by William Neal and Cody. [1105] [1106]

[1100] "Buffalo Bill Rough Riders in Tucson," The Bisbee Daily Review, Bisbee, Arizona, October 3, 1902. Also, reference Buffalo Bill Museum and Grave.

[1101] The Battle of Summit Springs, July 11, 1869. Cody shot and killed Chief Tall Bull, the commander of the renegade Indians or "Dog Soldiers," as they were called. This event became an important scene reproduced in Cody's Wild West Show. From an account of "Battle of Summit Springs," The Arizona Republic, October 17, 1908.

[1102] Township 10S Range 16E Sections 16 and 17. The General Land Office Patent No. 17025.

[1103] William F. Cody Archive, letter from Cody to George T. Beck, May 4, 1902. Buffalo Bill Center of the West http://codyarchive.org/texts/wfc.css00543.html Source: University of Wyoming, American Heritage Center, Buffalo Bill: Letters to George T. Beck, 1895-1910 (Acc. #9972), ah031457-58. Cody was referring to Campo Bonito.

[1104] The Lives and Legends of Buffalo Bill, by Don Russell. Page 434.

[1105] Ibid. Page 434. Also, Neal mentions the search in "Buffalo Bill Believed in "Lost Mine" In Catalinas and Organized Company; William Neal Thinks It Really Exists," undated newspaper article, Arizona Historical Society.

In a display of his generosity in 1906, Cody sent thousands of dollars to the April 18th San Francisco earthquake [1107] and Mt. Vesuvius victims. [1108] Cody often supported many friends' ventures. There were even rumors in Washington of a possible Senator Cody from the new State of Arizona, but a reporter commented how out of place Cody would look in Congress with his long hair and Western wear. [1109]

Cody brought his Wild West Show and Congress of Rough Riders to Bisbee, a town southeast of Tucson, for the first time in October 1908. Five hundred fifty-cent tickets were sold for the first exhibition, and the second was sold out. It was a salute to a fading culture of the Old West that was becoming more civilized. Cody's Battle of Summit Springs was recreated with the splendor of the "sanguinary days of the old frontier." [1110]

[1106] In another motion picture in 2010, Buffalo Bill, Beyond the Legend, [1106] Tucson prospector William "Flint" Carter defends Cody's claim by Don Russell that he "hit the fabulously rich vein," which was in the region of the mine with iron door. From "Lives and Legends of Buffalo Bill, by Don Russell.

[1107] Cody cabled $1,000 contribution. From Complete Story of the San Francisco Earthquake and Other Great Disasters, by Marshall Everett. The Bible House, Chicago, 1906. Page 165.

[1108] Altoona Tribune, Altoona, Pennsylvania. April 17, 1906.

[1109] "There is a startling rumor that Co. W.F. Cody has designs upon the United States Senatorship from Arizona when that Territory is admitted as a State." From the National Tribune, Washington, D.C., March 23, 1911. Page 5.

[1110] "Buffalo Bill is in Bisbee Today," Bisbee Daily Review, Bisbee, Arizona. October 21, 1908. And, "Buffalo Bill Pleased Crowds," Bisbee Daily Review, Bisbee, Arizona. October 22, 1908

1908-09: Buffalo Bill Is Impressed With New Prospects

"I am very much impressed with the mineral law of the country, but of course, like all mining properties, it takes capital to produce the wealth. No doubt, there is a great future for Arizona and I believe it is on the eve of a boom."

W.F. Cody, *Bisbee Daily Review*, Bisbee, Arizona. January 23, 1909 [1111]

Williams "Buffalo Bill" Cody returned to Oracle in the winter of 1908-09 to inspect the Bonita mining properties with Captain John D. Burgess whom he had met years before. Burgess had encouraged Cody to invest in a new section of the mines. [1112]

Cody said he walked one hundred and fifty miles in four days and was impressed by the prospects. After his visit he went to New York to see his partners and generate capital to purchase some of the property at "Camp Bonita," as he called it. Cody suggested that Tucson should have a railroad to Mammoth, another mining community near Oracle, to tap into the potential wealth. [1113]

Cody returned the next winter of 1909-1910 to spend time with Burgess and the mining properties. [1114]

[1111] Quoted by William F. Cody. "Buffalo Bill Enjoys Life Near Tucson," Bisbee Daily Review, Bisbee, Arizona. January 23, 1909.

[1112] "Buffalo Bill May Become An Arizonan," Bisbee Daily Review, Bisbee, Arizona. February 20, 1909.

[1113] ibid.

[1114] "Territorial News," Graham Guardian, Safford, Arizona, September 24, 1909.

1910: Cody Expands His Mining Claims

B y 1910 Cody was fully involved in his mining venture near Oracle. Col. L. W. Getchell, Burgess, and Cody turned six claims at Campo Bonito into a $600,000 corporation under the name of the Campo Bonito Mining and Milling Company. [1115]

The nearby Southern Belle gold mine became property of the Cody mining enterprise in February 27, 1911. [1116] [1117] By June, they developed one hundred claims over two thousand acres. Burgess, a mining engineer, acquired many of the claims years ago and was convinced they contained valuable placer deposits. [1118]

That same winter, [1119] [1120] Cody encouraged Colonel Daniel Burns Dyer, a former Indian agent at Fort Reno, to join his mining venture to prospect tungsten, gold, silver, and lead in the northern range of the Santa Catalina Mountains near Tucson.

Both were friends socially until they invested in the mining venture. [1121] [1122] Dyer was the former president of the Augusta Railway in Georgia and a member of New York's Union League Club. [1123]

[1115] The Los Angeles Herald, June 26, 1910.

[1116] Capital stock certificate, Southern Belle Mines Company, February 27, 1911. 3,199 shares were issued at $100 per shared to William F. Cody. http://library.bbhc.org/cdm/ref/collection/BBOA/id/229

[1117] "Today In Arizona History," February 27, 1911. USA Today. Southern Belle Mines Company incorporated with Col. Cody as one of the incorporators. Capitalized at $1,000,000.

[1118] "Buffalo Bill Begins Mining in Arizona, Veteran Scout and Showman Takes Up New Life with Old Comrades" Los Angeles Herald, June 26, 1910.

[1119] "Buffalo Bill in Big Mining Deal, Heads Company That Has Taken Control of Campo Bonito Property," El Paso Herald, November 18, 1911.

[1120] 1911 is the officially published year of incorporation for the Cody-Dyer M&M. Other sources erroneously used the year 1902.

[1121] This source mistakenly says Cody-Dyer M&M was incorporated in 1902. The correct date is 1911. From The William F. Cody Archive, Buffalo Bill Center of the West, Cody, Wyoming. http://codyarchive.org/life/wfc.chronology.html

[1122] This source also mistakenly says Cody-Dyer M&M was incorporated in 1902. The Lives and Legends of Buffalo Bill, by Don Russell, p. 434.

The old Campo Bonito Mining Company was reorganized and formed the Cody-Dyer Arizona Mining & Milling Co., with the hope of discovering more precious minerals. The company started with a capitalization of $5,000,000. [1124] By November the "gold mines" of Cody-Dyer M&M were shipping a carload of tungsten ore to Germany. [1125]

The Cody-Dyer Company controlled forty five claims by February, 1911. Cody and a group of partners bought the Southern Belle gold mine in March, 1911, for $100,000. Capitalized at five million dollars, the articles of incorporation reserved the right to mine gold, copper, silver, lead, coal, and any other mineral found. Cody, Getchell, and R.G. Brady were among the incorporators. Dyer was not involved in the company, but he did help inspect the property. [1126]

The mines at Campo Bonito contained gold, silver, and tungsten that yielded about $30 a ton. Tungsten was an ore used in hardening of steel and making lamp filaments. With new light bulbs on the market the demand for tungsten began to increase. The plant had a capacity to process one hundred tons a day. "In one part of the estate the ores run to gold, copper and silver, in another to lead, silver and gold, and in another section to gold, lead and tungsten." That could be a profit of $2,000 a day, according to sources in the daily newspaper. Cody was known to carry around a pure gold nugget from Campo Bonito in his pocket. [1127] Worth $60 at the time, the 3.17-ounce nugget would be valued today at over $4,200. [1128]

Unfortunately for Cody there was a marked decrease in the overall production of tungsten in the United States in 1911. This was mainly because there was a lack of a market for tool steel for which tungsten was used. The price in 1911 ranged from $4.50 to $8.50 per unit depending on quality, quantity, and bargaining. However, the only deposit of scheelite in the state was at the Cody-Dyer mines. [1129]

[1123] This source also mistakenly says Cody-Dyer M&M was incorporated in 1902. Cody archives. http://codyarchive.org/texts/wfc.css00226.xml

[1124] "Buffalo Bill in Big Mining Deal, Heads Company That Has Taken Control of Campo Bonito Property," El Paso Herald, November 1911.

[1125] "Ships Tungsten from Mines At Tucson," Weekly Journal Miner, November 22, 1911. Page 2.

[1126] "Buffalo Bill's Company," Arizona Republican, Phoenix, Arizona, March 7, 1911.

[1127] Ibid.

[1128] Gold was valued at $18.93 an ounce in 1911.

[1129] "The Tungsten Industry," Engineering and Mining Journal, Vol. 93, January 6, 1912. Page 30.

Cody passed through Tucson again in the winter of 1911 to visit Campo Bonito, where a five-stamp Merrill's mill was working on scheelite ore and turning out high-grade tungsten concentrates, [1130] [1131] used in X-rays and light bulb filaments. [1132]

Getchell, Cody's general manager at Campo Bonito, encouraged Cody to invest in other prospects. A quartz mill was erected in October. [1133] In December, 1911, the Cody-Dyer syndicate took over the Cash group on mines in Yavapai county near Prescott. [1134] Cody also invested in an oil claim discovered in 1911 near Agua Caliente. Cody sent $6,500 worth of tools and machinery to drill for the oil. [1135]

Over the next few years Cody stayed in Oracle during the moderate desert winters so he could see how his investments in his mining ventures progressed. Cody often stayed at a little house at Campo Bonito with the miners for weeks at a time while his wife, Louisa, stayed at the comfortable Mountain View Hotel in Oracle, a few miles away.

On Christmas Day in 1911, "Buffalo Bill" Cody played Santa Claus to two hundred of the mineworkers' children in Oracle.

[1130] The Coconino Sun, February 10, 1911.

[1131] "News of the Territory," The Coconino Sun, February 10, 1911.

[1132] "Ships Tungsten from Tucson," Weekly Journal Miner, November 22, 1911.

[1133] Ibid.

[1134] "Buffalo Bill is Now Yavapai Operator," Weekly Journal Miner, December 13, 1911.

[1135] "Buffalo Bill's Oil Prospects," Arizona Republican, January 8, 1912.

This is one of the tunnels among the Campo Bonito mining claims. There are still several open tunnels, pits and gravel dumps in the area.

1911: Cody's Mines Supply Tungsten For Edison

When inventor Thomas Edison needed tungsten to make his light bulbs, he turned to William Cody and the Cody-Dyer Mine in Oracle, Arizona, for the precious metal.

By February 1911, after three years of operation, the Cody-Dyer mines had a five-stamp Merrill's Mill operating on scheelite ore and turning out high-grade tungsten concentrates.

By November besides Colorado, Tucson was considered one of the major shipping points for tungsten. A carload of tungsten ore was taken from the Cody-Dyer Mining & Milling Co., shipped to Hamburg, Germany, to be used "in commerce and the arts." [1136]

> *"As every man in it is already a millionaire in his own right, with an abundance of producing investments, and both the gold and tungsten properties have been developed to a surety and the owners are disposed to push development to the limit, there is little doubt as to that development."* [1137]

To accommodate the processing of the tungsten and gold ores, two forty ton mills were installed with another 100-ton mill planned at an expense of nearly $100,000.

Thomas Edison and Cody were friends, when Edison's company needed the tungsten ore to fuel his new inventions, he purchased it from Campo Bonito. [1138]

A few years earlier Edison had discovered the X-ray by "his application of a form of tungsten– Tungstate of calcium– and made it possible to look into a man's body and at his bones." Edison also created the tungsten lamp. [1139]

[1136] "Ships Tungsten from Mines at Tucson," Weekly Journal Miner, Prescott, page 2. Arizona, November 22, 1911.

[1137] Ibid.

[1138] "Cody-Dyer Arizona Mining and Milling Company Cash Sheet for Month ending 29, Feb, 1912. A. Edison $2651. Received from N.H. Getchell" from The Business of Being Buffalo Bill: Selected Letters of William F. Cody, By Sarah J. Blackstone, page 87.

[1139] "Ships Tungsten from Mines at Tucson." Weekly Journal Miner, Prescott, page 2. Arizona, November 22, 1911.

Cody was hopeful that after closing a contract with Edison, he, Edison, would build an "electrical reduction works" and purchase the entire output of the property. [1140] That never materialized.

Cody again visited his mines in the Catalinas the following February, 1912, along with L.W. Getchell [1141] when the territory of Arizona was finally admitted into the United States.

There was a rumor that Cody was interested in a Senatorship from Arizona when it became admitted as a State in February, 1912, but there was concern that Cody, with his rough style of dress and longhair, would not fit into the decorum of Washington, D.C. [1142] That rumor also never materialized.

The Cody-Dyer mine was steadily producing scheelite ore in thirty-six locations in 1912. At the time the nearby gold producing Southern Belle Mine was under bond to Capt. John Burgess.

But the prosperous venture had some hidden issues unknown to Cody at the time.

[1140] Denver Times, December 25, 1911.

[1141] Tombstone Epitaph, Tombstone, Arizona, February 25, 1912.

[1142] "Washington News," The National Tribune, Washington D.C., March 23, 1911. And, Arizona Republican, March 7, 1911.

1912: Ewing Shakes Up Campo Bonito

Edward J. (Ernest) Ewing, a mining engineer, joined the Cody-Dyer team at Campo Bonito in early 1912. He saw large outcrops of quartz on the Morning Star claim of the Southern Belle mine group which "rose some 25' or so above the surrounding limestone." He also observed some dire problems. [1143]

Out of concern for his mining property, Cody decided that he and his wife Louisa should pay a visit to the mine in Oracle February, 1912. L. W. Getchell, the Camp Bonito consulting manager, and Mike Russell, one of Cody's enterprise managers, accompanied Cody. Dyer turned to Ewing for advice on his investment and to look into its affairs. Ewing, the grandson of Col. Daniel Burns Dyer, was dispatched to Campo Bonito to assess its progress and deal with some "dubious practices." He expected to stay only a few weeks, but ended up spending decades on the claims.

Ewing arrived in February and met Cody and Capt. John D. Burgess at the Santa Rita Hotel in Tucson. Burgess, a well known mine promoter, had given the Bonito claims over to Cody through Getchell. Burgess held several other claims and had done some road building in the Cañada del Oro. He also operated the Pontatoc mine north of Tucson on the southern slope of the Catalinas. [1144] This was one of sites that are speculated to have pre-American ruins near Ventaña Canyon. [1145]

According to Burgess' description, floods from the Santa Catalinas apparently deposit the gold placers found in the Cañada del Oro in intervals. The gold is deposited throughout alternating stratas of deep red, clayey material nearly uniform in thickness of three to four inches and probably formed between floods. "All the gold is found in well-rounded nuggets ranging from fifty cents to five dollars in value." Apparently a sixteen pound nugget of gold with about forty percent quartz was reportedly found, but the discoverers were murdered in their camp sixteen miles northwest of Tucson. [1146]

[1143] The Business of Being Buffalo Bill: selected Letters of William F. Cody, 1879-1917, by Buffalo Bill, Sarah J. Blackstone.

[1144] Miscellaneous Notes Re: Campo Bonito, by E.J. Ewing, May 3, 1945. Pages 5-7. The Ewing Report was written decades after he first met Cody. Ewing eventually became one of the principles in the Maudina Tungsten Mine in the 1940s.

[1145] See chapter on the Stone Church in this edition.

[1146] Arizona Gold Placers and Placering, by G.M. Butler, Arizona Bureau of Mines, University of Arizona Bulletin 132, Mineral Technology Series No. 24, 1932, pages 60.

Besides the glowing prospects, there were several problems that Ewing found within days of his arrival. Ewing felt that the Bonito mill overall was in good operating shape, but he suspected mismanagement and believed the investment was more of a scheme. [1147]

He caught a worker spiking a load of scheelite to make it appear it had higher concentrates. Ewing also discovered that Cody was deceived in a sale transaction over the Bonito interests.

Ewing suspected that there were questionable dealings made between Getchell and some local prospectors. It was serious enough for Cody to threaten Getchell with arrest and prosecution. Cody didn't follow through after Getchell gave up his stock and some money. Ewing fired forty-five miners and scaled down the project. He concluded that the company had spent $70,000 but did not receive much value in return. [1148]

Cody tried to sell his interest to investors, including Thomas A. Edison who had been working on a patent that would reduce low-grade ores using the scheelite mined from the area. [1149] That didn't happen.

The Campo Bonito mine had closed on May 5, 1912 after Cody was said to have personally spent $100,000 on the property from the time he got involved with it. [1150] In July, with reorganization pending, a small group of men continued some development of the Campo Bonito mine. [1151]

At this point, Cody and his team directed their attention to gold. The Cody-Dyer Mining & Milling Co. purchased the nearby Southern Belle gold mine and the Maudina Mine that were under bond to 'Jack' Burgess. The company had thirty-six locations and had installed a forty-ton mill in 1912. "The ore is a scheelite gold ore that yields to the milling and concentrating process." [1152] The ore was also described as "disseminated sulphide carrying gold and silver values." [1153]

[1147] "Miscellaneous Notes Re: Campo Bonito," pages 7-10.

[1148] Ibid.

[1149] The Lives and Legends of Buffalo Bill, by Don Russell, 435-436.

[1150] "Cody's Mine Closed," Bisbee Daily Review, May 8, 1912.

[1151] "News of the State in Condensed Form," Tombstone Epitaph, July 14, 1912.

[1152] "Santa Catalinas And The Old Hat Mining Districts," Bisbee Daily Review, May 14, 1912.

[1153] "Santa Catalinas and the Old Hat Mining Districts," Bisbee Daily Review, Bisbee, Arizona, May 14, 1912. And, "Arizona's News of Interest," Tombstone Epitaph, May 5, 1912.

Cody also filed a claim for the High Jinks Gold Mine in 1912. Johnny Baker, Cody's foster son, left the Wild West Show to work the mine until Cody's death. Cody "loved to watch the view at High Jinks, pitch pennies, and drink booze. He played Santa Claus for the Oracle's children and rode in parades." [1154]

In August, 1913, at age seventy, Cody had to dispose the Buffalo Bill Wild West Show and the Far East shows property in a public sale to satisfy creditor claims. [1155]

Cody visited his mines again at Campo Bonito in December. "On the property are gigantic ledges outcropping of what was apparently country rock. A tramp assayer happened along and tested some of the rock and made a startling discovery that it was scheelite or tungsten." [1156]

A one thousand share stock certificate issued to W.F. Cody from the "Cody-Dyer Arizona Mining & Milling Company. Signed by W.F. Cody, President. March 24, 1913. [1157] The old stock certificates for collectors have brought up to $7,000 in value. Today, it is worth about $3,000.

[1154] High Jinks Ranch Historical Documents. http://www.highjinksranch.net/

[1155] "Buffalo Bill retires to a private life," Bismarck Daily Tribune, Bismarck, ND, August 22, 1913.

[1156] "El Paso Herald," El Paso, Texas, December 14, 1912.

[1157] Buffalo Bill Museum and Grave, Lookout Mountain, Golden, CO. ID# 74.0268.

Among some of Cody's papers and list of stockholders was a sheet of "codes" apparently used to disguise activities among the miners. Written on a Cody-Dyer Arizona Mining & Milling Co. undated letterhead was a list of twenty one names and eighty five mining claims with a coded reference. [1158] Col. Cody was called "Governor," Ewing was "Idaho," the Southern Belle Mine was called "Beauty," and the Pure Gold Mine was "Arkansas." Whether it was part of a game to idle away time in between work or a true coded system, no documents have been found yet that used the codes.

When the value of tungsten increased in the fall of 1915, Ewing advised Cody and Dyer to advance some operating funds and ramp up operations. Neither was able to make a move. Cody "was bled about white," and Dyer died shortly after a long sickness three days before Christmas in 1912. [1159]

Cody continued to perform [1160] until he died of kidney failure on January 17, 1917, [1161] in Denver, Colorado, after contracting a severe cold, possibly during his last visit in Oracle. That was the world's largest celebrity icon's last performance, when he entertained the orphan children of Oracle that winter.

"I remember it well," Mary Ewing, wife of Ernest Ewing, Cody's partner, reminisced. Cody went outside the schoolhouse and sat down on a rock. "He was perspiring and it was raining." She called out to him, "Mr. Cody, you're going to catch cold."

He replied, "No, Mrs. Ewing, I won't catch cold."

But, shortly afterwards he got a pain in his back. He was taken from Tucson and then to Wyoming. He wrote back to Mrs. Ewing that he felt better. Cody died the next month.

[1158] "Code," Cody-Dyer Arizona Mining and Milling Co., Oracle, Arizona.

[1159] Daniel Dyer died December 23, 1912. His estate was valued at $500,000. It was the "only venture wherein Dyer lost money." From "Col. Daniel Dyer Stricken in His Unique Home, Clarendon," *New York Sun*, December 23, 1912; and in The Business of Being Buffalo Bill: selected letters of William F. Cody, 1879-1917, by Buffalo Bill, Sarah J. Blackstone. Page 94-96.

[1160] Cody "appeared with the Sells Floto Circus in 1914 and 1915 as a headliner. He had made a couple of bad agreements with the Circus' owner Harry Tammen and had to appear with the Circus both to satisfy them and some other obligations. In 1916 he was able to leave the Sells Floto Circus and appeared with the 101 Ranch Real Wild West until the end of that season, when he caught a cold and then died of uremic poisoning in January." From Steve Friesen, Buffalo Bill Museum and Grave. BuffaloBill.org

[1161] "Buffalo Bill Cody Answers Last Duty Call," The Coconino Sun, Flagstaff, Arizona, January 19, 1917.

Mrs. Ewing, who had married Ernest the year before, eventually gained ownership of the mines. [1162]

W.F. Cody. By R. Zucker.

[1162] "Woman Recalls Buffalo Bill's Fatal Visit To Arizona in 1917," by Jack Hanna Sr., Arizona Republic, Phoenix, Arizona. August 16, 1917.

Ewing Takes Control Of Campo Bonito

After Cody's death Ewing secured a lease on his own and continued working the claims. Most of the debts of Cody-Dyer Mining & Milling Co. were paid off.

One debt to Cody's friend, Barney Link, was still due. Link died, and his estate secured title to the Campo Bonito property. Ewing managed the property in 1918 under an assessment contract and continued until September 1, 1943. [1163]

Link's heirs patented the claims, [1164] and Ewing along with his partner in the graphite business, Edward H. Molson, secured a bond and an option on the mines. After having success they later paid $20,000 for the property, plus a $20,000 loan repayment. They secured a patent in 1943 for twenty-eight of the twenty nine claims. The Cody claim on the south side of the group had been rejected because of insufficient work. [1165]

The claims by Molson and Ewing continued to be active through 1944 under the name of the Maudina Tungsten Mine. Molson acquired an interest in the property in 1943. Molson and Ewing also worked the nearby Pure Gold claim and extracted 1.51 percent tungsten from 7,825 tons of ore. A total of 15,000 short-ton units of WO3 were produced. [1166]

The Maudina mine was first worked for gold, then for tungsten. Two gold quartz veins cross the Campo Bonito property, and gold was found in the Cody tunnel, according to Molson. [1167] The Maudina Mine was named for Mrs. Maud Thomas of Tucson by her husband, a geology professor at the University of Arizona. Mrs. Thomas had cared for Cody and Burgess when they were in town.

Ewing kept working both the Maudina and the Morning Star, an extension of the Pure Gold claim, but felt the profits were too small. He shut down the mine and let the option

---

[1163] "Miscellaneous Notes Re: Campo Bonito," pages 8-10.

[1164] Mineral Survey No. 4250.

[1165] "Miscellaneous Notes Re: Campo Bonito," page 10-11.

[1166] "Tungsten Deposits of Yuma, Maricopa, Pinal and Graham Counties Arizona," by V.B. Dale, U.S. Dept. of Interior, Bureau of Mines, Report of Investigations #556. 1959. Page 52.

[1167] Ibid. Page 52 and 61.

to the Southern Belle lapse. Ewing later discovered a hand-size chunk of Wolframite in the area. [1168]

Even though Ewing all along had discounted the wealth and prospects of the mines, he continued to work on them for more than three decades. The Morning Star claim is now on property privately owned by the YMCA

Cody's impact on Oracle still remains with the Cody Trail, Cody Tunnel, and Cody Loop, all near the Campo Bonito properties.

Campo Bonito was much maligned for being a money pit. Perhaps its riches were embellished to gain Cody's investment. However, Cody did find success with his gold mining venture next door at the Southern Belle mine.

The burned out remains of a fireplace and foundation of the mess hall at Campo Bonito.

[1168] The Business of Being Buffalo Bill, pages 94-96.

Another tunnel at the Bonito Mine possibly used for storage of explosives and supplies.

"Throwing snowballs in front of Buffalo Bill's old mine near Oracle," January 1938, courtesy of Dwight and Christy Schannep, American Antique Mall, Tucson, Arizona.

The Southern Belle Mine

1881: Gold Extracted From Southern Belle

"The Southern Belle mine is one of the few in the Santa Catalina Mountains which has produced any significant quantity of auriferous ore." [1169]

The Southern Belle [1170] mine is one of the most well known gold mines in the Santa Catalina Mountains. It was also one of the holdings of "Buffalo Bill" Cody that returned a profit.

By the time Cody got involved, the Southern Belle had been a profitable gold producing mine.

"The gold is generally fine and free, any pyrites which formerly existed having been fully oxidized. The quartz is reported to be richer in gold where there is no galena." [1171] The report further stated "there are an estimated 85,200 straight tons of indicated resources of auriferous vein material along the full strike length." [1172] It suggested, however, that was not economically viable to leach out the remaining gold. That was when the mid-1994 price of gold was $387 an ounce.

The Southern Belle has been idle for decades and remained on private property. But its illustrious career as a major gold producing mine has endured in Arizona history.

[1169] Mineral Appraisal of Coronado National Forest, Part 5, Mineral Land Assessment, 1994. U.S. Department of the Interior, Bureau of Mines, Santa Catalina-Rincon District. UAiR.

[1170] USGS: Southern Belle is a past producer of gold and silica. Dolphin M S 1837 Patented; Apache Peak Cons, Mng.Co Property; Southern Belle M S 687, Patented; Careless M S 4090, Patented; Cross Town M S 2155-A, Patented; Apache Girl M S 1837, Patented; Morning Star Group. MRDS M241166, Deposit ID 10162340. From mindat.org: http://www.mindat.org/loc-63390.html

[1171] Ibid. Appendix A41.

[1172] Ibid. (A41)

'Struck It Rich' At The Southern Belle

The famous Southern Belle gold mine is located about one mile ENE of Apache Peak and two and a half miles south of the American Flag Hill. The gold mine was close to Campo Bonito, just over two miles southwest.

The original find was known for sometime among prospectors in the late 1870s, [1173] however, the ledge stood as high as one thousand four hundred feet and was impenetrable. C.G. Gillette and his partner, Capt. J.J. Young, were prospecting the claim in 1880 when that fall Mrs. Gillette, who had an interest in mining saw "no harm in trying," penetrated the cap rock and "struck it rich." She named the ledge the Southern Belle and gave half interest to her husband and his partner for prospecting the claim. The specimens that contained gold through the whole quartz assayed from $5,000 to $20,000. Visible gold could be found through the whole ledge. Among the other claims Mr. Gillette held was the nearby Morning Star, a visible four-foot silver ledge. Mrs. Gillette was lauded for her accomplishments by breaking sexual stereotypes among miners, but the sight of a feisty woman pounding out gold from the mountain probably seemed like a spectacle. [1174]

From 1881 to 1906, there were 18,666 st (tons) of auriferous quartz vein mined from the Southern Belle. Gold mineralization was a flat vein or "blanket" that dips twenty inches to thirty inches and about four feet of quartz below and two feet above a parting layer of red shale. [1175] E.W. Rice had bonded Isaac Lornine (correctly spelled as Laurin) several mining deeds to the Southern Belle in 1881. [1176] By the next year a four-foot vein of gold ore was yielding $20 to $40 per ton in gold. The claim was being developed; it showed to be very promising. [1177] Two years later Isaac bonded his claims to an eastern company that was taking out "ten tons of ore" for a mill test. The vein was reportedly five-foot

---

[1173] Mineral Appraisal of Coronado National Forest, Part 5. U.S. Department of the Interior, Bureau of Mines. MLA 25-94 1994. Page A40.

[1174] "Old Hat District– Rapidly Coming to the Front as a Great Mining Camp– Recent Important Sales of Claims– The Imperial, Southern Belle and Others," Santa Catarina was used in spelling. Arizona Weekly Citizen, September 4, 1880.

[1175] Mineral Appraisal of Coronado National Forest, Part 5. Page 12 and A40.

[1176] Arizona Weekly Citizen, May 22, 1881.

[1177] Arizona Weekly Citizen, January 22, 1882.

wide. [1178] A few months later a trail was made from the mine to the Ada mill and the new Southern Belle Mining company. With Col. J.R. James as superintendent, it is expected to pack out bullion from the rugged mountains soon. [1179] By August there were twenty tons of ore a day being turned out. [1180]

The Southern Belle mine was reached by a stagecoach that ran in 1884 from Tucson, passing "La Punta de la Sierra, Pueblo Viejo, up Canyon del Oro" and around the western foothills to Oracle. [1181]

Misfortune befell the Southern Belle in the summer of 1884 when in June Charles Hudson, manager of the Hudson & Co., was accused of carrying on mining business with bank money. Among the charges was a questionable overdraft of $18,147.57. [1182] The Southern Belle went into litigation with an assurance it would eventually resume to pay its dividends. [1183]

Despite the Southern Belle's legal troubles, as word of gold in the Santa Catalinas got out several other nearby strikes were made. S. E. Hall worked his Telfair mine about four miles south of the Southern Belle and averaged $56 in gold; the Cap mine assayed $60 in gold. Hall expanded his claims to the Tobe, Gold Hill, and Empire. The Telfair is a "mammoth ledge, the cropping along being over sixty feet wide." The "ore is a rusty yellowish quartz, light and honeycombed, assaying up to several hundred dollars." Hall reported he had a thousand tons of one hundred dollars of value in sight, but it was not the richest claim in the region. [1184]

By February, 1885, a ten stamp mill was proposed for the Southern Belle property. [1185] A survey on June 17, 1885, mapped out three-tunnels and a shop between them, plus a grade for the mill. [1186]

[1178] "Mining Matters," Arizona Weekly Citizen, March 25, 1883. From the Florence Enterprise.

[1179] Arizona Weekly Citizen, May 12, 1883.

[1180] Arizona Weekly Citizen. August 11, 1883.

[1181] Arizona Weekly Citizen , January 19, 1884.

[1182] Arizona Weekly Citizen, June 7, 1884.

[1183] Arizona Weekly Citizen, August 2, 1884.

[1184] Arizona Weekly Citizen, August 1, 1885.

[1185] Arizona Sentinel, Yuma, Arizona. February 21, 1885.

[1186] Survey 687. July 2, 1885.

Within a month after the mill started in December 31, 1885, [1187] twenty men were employed, [1188] and within two months $7,000 in gold already had been shipped. [1189] From 1885-1888, the Southern Belle reportedly produced "considerable quantities of gold." [1190] The camp had a post office and store operated by J. L. Clark. The Mammoth and the Mohawk mines were the only other two that produced any profitable quantity of gold bullion. [1191] At the time a bar of gold bullion– produced in ten days worth of effort– was valued at $9,000. [1192]

The Southern Belle gold mine had already shipped about $7,000 worth of gold by February, 1886. [1193] At $18.86 an ounce at the time, that would have been over three hundred and seventy one ounces – more than twenty three pounds of gold. With today's prices, it would have been worth $4.82 million. [1194]

By that summer Samaniego's stagecoach was running twice a week from Tucson to the Southern Belle. [1195] George B. Brajevich, who had the Cross Town claim adjoining the Southern Belle, came into Tucson one mid-August afternoon in 1886 to show off some large specimens of free gold, "although much of the rich ore does not carry an visible metal." He and his partner Mr. Johonnet believed several claims in the Catalinas, including the Southern Belle, had some promising prospects. [1196] The large ledge they dug from assayed about $40 per ton on average, and free gold was seen in "almost every piece of rock broken from the ledge." [1197]

[1187] Arizona Weekly Citizen, January 2, 1886.

[1188] Tombstone Epitaph, January 26, 1886.

[1189] Tombstone Epitaph, February 20, 1886.

[1190] "Mineral Appraisal of Coronado National Forest, Part 5." Page A40.

[1191] The History of the Lower San Pedro Valley in Arizona, by Bernard W. Muffley, 1938. Page 26, 69. UAiR.

[1192] Arizona Weekly Citizen, March 20, 1886.

[1193] Tombstone Epitaph, February 20, 1886.

[1194] Gold value in 2013 is about $1,300.

[1195] Arizona Weekly Citizen, September 11, 1886.

[1196] Arizona Weekly Citizen, September 18, 1886

[1197] Arizona Weekly Citizen, January 15, 1887

James W. Fellows, a wealthy New Yorker who had an interest in mining near Oracle, claimed 20 acres of land southeast of Campo Bonito in June, 1888. [1198] He received a Mineral Patent Lode for 10.4 acres for the Southern Belle section. [1199] Col. Lewis said the mill would start running in August, 1888, to crush ore furnished by the Messrs. Brajovich (sic) after having been idle for a while. [1200]

In the summer of 1893, Capt. J. D. Burgess threatened if the Cañada del Oro Company resumed the Silver Belle operations, he would stop the operations. He deeded the Silver Belle mine to the CDO Company for $25,000, which was still due to him, and another $21,000 in advanced stock. [1201] Fellows continued to work seven patented claims on the property until he died in 1897. A Sheriff's Sale was held in August, 1897, to satisfy a recovered judgment against Fellows who owed $275.85 plus interest. The title of the Southern Belle was auctioned off in front of the courthouse in Florence, Arizona, on September 20, 1897, [1202] after which then the property went into litigation over his estate.

After a long absence of activity, in 1905 Thomas Wilson, administrator of Fellows' estate, filed an application for a $45,00 bond to the Southern Belle group of gold mines. [1203] W. W. Ward became a principle interest in reopening the Southern Belle mine in early January, 1906. It was reported that the Southern Belle mining properties "produced considerable gold in the past, the ore having been run through a ten stamp mill located on the ground." [1204] To resume work, only the possibility of refurbishing of the mineshaft is needed. The stamp mill would be used, and some new machinery would be added. Two and a half miles of pipeline was finished by April. J. Knox Corbett and Roscoe Dale were named as interests in the property. [1205] About one hundred men were soon expected to work in the mine, a known gold producer. [1206]

[1198] Survey No. 687. Plat of the Southern Belle Mining Claim, Old Hat Mining District. Surveyed by George Roskruge, June 17-18, 1885. Plat dated: July 2, 1885. Lot No. 44. U.S.M.M. No. IV.

[1199] "Fellows, James W., Southern Belle," June 25, 1888. General Land Records, Document # 14165. U.S. Department of the Interior, Bureau of Land Management. T 10S, R 16E, Section 20.

[1200] Arizona Weekly Citizen, July 28, 1888.

[1201] Arizona Weekly Citizen, August 19, 1893.

[1202] Sheriff's Sale, Florence Tribune, October 2, 1897.

[1203] "The News of Tucson and of Pima County," Arizona Silver Belt, November 20, 1905.

[1204] Arizona Silver Belt, Globe City, AZ January 11, 1906, page 2.

[1205] Bisbee Daily Review, January 17, 1906, page 2.

[1206] Bisbee Daily Review, May 25, 1906, page 3.

1908-1910: Southern Belle Closed, Then Resumes

"This property is an old gold producer." [1207]

After producing over "one million dollars in gold," the Southern Belle was again temporarily closed down in 1908. [1208]

The national price of gold was $18.95 per ounce at the time [1209] – "one million dollars in gold" weighed nearly fifty three thousand ounces or almost thirty three hundred pounds. At today's value of around $1,200 an ounce, the load would have been worth $63,324,000.

The nearby Mammoth mine on the San Pedro had also produced "millions in gold" by 1908. Both mines were declared to still be in their infancy, but were closed because of accidents or mismanagement. [1210]

By the end of the year in 1909, the Southern Belle group resumed operations with a ten stamp mill. Through Tucson attorney John B. Wright who represented the Fellows Estate, William Taylor of San Francisco and his attorney H.J. McIsaacs secured a $45,000 bond on the Southern Belle. When alive, Fellows had refused $250,000 for his property. [1211]

[1207] Bisbee Daily Review, December 2, 1909, page 8.

[1208] "Pinal County Rich in Gold and Silver," Bisbee Daily Review, February 16, 1908.

[1209] Historic Gold Prices- 1833 to Present, Prices from 1883-1994, World Gold Council. Taken from Timothy Green's Historical Gold Price Table, London prices converted to U.S. Dollars. Per troy ounce. The $18.93 price of gold remained consistent from 1833 (at $18.93) through 1918 (at $18.99). 52,770 ounces or over 3,298 pounds

[1210] "Pinal County Rich in Gold and Silver," Bisbee Daily Review, February 16, 1908.

[1211] The Oasis, Arziola, Arizona. December 18, 1909.

A few days later the Southern Belle was "taken over by practical mining men of California and Nevada." The property, the newspaper noted, was closed fifteen years earlier after the former owner's death and had since been held in his estate. [1212]

In February, 1910, an article titled "Pinal County Rich in Gold and Silver" reported that this week the old Southern Belle mill began crushing ore after being idle for ten years. The paper credits Hugh J. McIsaacs and associates of San Francisco who had gained control of the property.

The hopeful owners believed that "the property produced a large amount of gold in the distant past and will duplicate that record in the future." [1213]

[1212] Daily Arizona Silver Belt, Globe, Arizona, December 5, 1909.

[1213] Bisbee Daily Review, Bisbee, Arizona, February 2, 1910, page 6.

1911: Cody Acquires The Southern Belle Gold Mine

William Cody, who already had the Campo Bonito mines, publicly confirmed his purchase of the old Southern Belle gold mine in April, 1911. His partner, Major L. W. Getchell, wanted to duplicate the mine's successful record as a gold producer. [1214]

Getchell spent the summer putting the property into shape while Cody went to join his Wild West Show back east. Cody considered returning in November and remaining permanently in Arizona. [1215]

By February, 1911, the Campo Bonito Mining Company went through reorganization as a new corporation called the Cody-Dyer Mining & Milling Company with Col. W. F. Cody as president. His partner, Daniel B. Dyer, served as the secretary and treasurer; Getchell was the consulting engineer.

They started with a $5,000,000 capitalization, but no stock was for sale, so that "every man in the company is already a millionaire in his own right." One of the assets of the purchase of the new company was the Southern Belle mine property. Together with the Campo Bonito property, they had 40 claims they could develop. A one hundred ton mill and new converters were to be installed at the Southern Belle. [1216]

For $14,000 Noble Getchell, son of L.W., negotiated the arrangements for the Southern Belle with R.G. Brady. Col. Dyer provided a note for the purchase. Brady had an agreement that Noble was to receive half of the purchase price as commission, but Brady left for Kansas City and sold the note, and never returned. When Cody learned about the deceit, he threatened the Getchells with prosecution. They both gave up their stock interest and some money. L.W. left the company, although there was no proof he was involved in the fraud. [1217]

[1214] "Col. Cody Confirms Report of Mine Purchase," El Paso Herald, El Paso Texas, April 5, 1911, Page 10.

[1215] Ibid. Also The Oasis, Arizola, Arizona, April 1, 1911.

[1216] "Buffalo Bill in Big Mining Deal, Heads Company That Has Taken Over Campo Bonito," El Paso Herald, El Paso, Texas, November 18, 1911.

[1217] "Mining Adventures of Buffalo Bill Cody," by Juanita Daniel Zachry. True West Magazine, April 1990. Page 40.

After the Southern Belle mine became the property of the Cody-Dyer M&M operations, the claim was passed on to Capt. Jack Burgess. The property was made up of nine mining patents and four unpatented claims. There was a ten stamp mill on the site. By then the Cody-Dyer M&M operation had thirty six locations throughout Campo Bonito with a forty-ton mill. [1218]

> *"Additional names which apply to this location: Southern Belle MS587 patented claim; Dolphin MS 1837 Patented claim; Cross Town MS 2155-A Patented claim; Careless MS 4090 Patented claim; Apache Girl MS 1837 Patented claim; Apache Peak Consolidated Mining Co. property; Ewing property; Careless; Gold Bug; General Hancock; Fortuna; Happy Thot. Mineralization is a tabular ore body hosted in Dripping Spring Quartzite and Bolsa Quartzite." By 1960, there were 12-patented mining claims. The mines produced scheelite, galena, pyrite, dolomite and calcite."* [1219]

Cody died in 1917, and the Southern Belle silently continued operation until all visible remaining lode was extracted.

[1218] "Santa Catalina Mountain's And The Old Hat Mining Districts," Bisbee Daily Review, Bisbee, Arizona, May 14, 1912, page 5.

[1219] Mindat.org mineral report on "Southern Belle Mine (Southern Belle Group; Morning Star property/claims), Apache Peak area, Campo Bonito, Oracle District (Control District; Old Hat District; Santa Catalina District), Santa Catalina Mts, Pinal Co., Arizona, USA."

1930-2010: Southern Belle Passes To New Owners

Between 1930 and 1932, leasing and development of the Southern Belle Mine continued by Molson & Co., a graphite company.

In 1931 Elizabeth L. Wood recorded a certificate of receipt for the Careless Mining lode claim. [1220] Mrs. Woods leased the properties while others worked the land. By 1934 the main portion of the Southern Belle was mined out and in 1945 the Campo Bonito Mines acquired the property along with several other neighboring sections. [1221]

In 1990 the Newmont Exploration Company, a Denver company, acquired options on fifteen of the mineral patents in the area of the Southern Belle Mine and also staked thirty eight new mining claims on the Coronado National Forest as far east as the eastern slope of Apache Peak. Their interest was in investigating deep gold targets with diamond drilling. [1222]

Pinal County public records show eighteen claims, and the BLM mining claims document a long string of claims and affidavits of labor from that time through 2010. Evidence of annual assessment work for mining claims/mining sites must be filed and recorded yearly to keep labor and mining claims current. Today the Southern Belle is an abandoned mine on private property. It is not necessary for a property owner to file a claim to mine.

The greatest gold mine in the Catalinas can end up in a backyard, but glory cannot.

There was also a Southern Belle mine near Tombstone, [1223] one in Yavapai [1224] and others throughout the country, but they were not connected with this Southern Belle in Campo Bonito.

[1220] U.S. Department of the Interior, Bureau of Land Management, General Land Office Records.

[1221] Ibid.

[1222] Mineral Appraisal of Coronado National Forest, Part 5, Mineral Land Assessment MLA-25-94, 1994. Page 14.

[1223] Arizona Weekly Citizen, April 3, 1880.

[1224] Weekly Phoenix Herald, December 1, 1882.

The rolling hills in the Campo Bonito Mining District, just south of Oracle on the north side of the Santa Catalina Mountains, covers hundreds of acres and had dozens of early American mining claims spread through the valley. William "Buffalo Bill" Cody said he walked one hundred and fifty miles in these hills when he owned mining claims at Campo Bonito.

An abandoned mining tunnel near Campo Bonito.

The Historic High Jinks Ranch

The historic High Jinks Ranch is on private property hidden in the northern mountain hills. While Buffalo Bill Cody never stayed there, his foster son constructed the ranch years later.

1933: High Jinks Ranch Built In Campo Bonito

On the north side of the Santa Catalina Mountains near Oracle, Arizona, the High Jinks Ranch stands as a monument to a long history of mining and perseverance.

The property once was owned by "Buffalo Bill" Cody as part of the Campo Bonito mining camp years before the ranch house was built.

The stonemason two-story home, called La Casa del High Jinks, was built by Buffalo Bill Cody's foster son Johnny Baker in 1933 and displayed Buffalo Bill's memorabilia until 1945.

Johnny Baker (Lewis H. Baker) was the founder of the Buffalo Bill Memorial Museum [1225] (The Buffalo Bill Museum and Grave) on Lookout Mountain, Colorado.

Six miles south of Oracle, Arizona, the privately owned, patented property called Campo Bonito District is surrounded by the Oracle State Park, next to the Coronado National Forest. The building complex is on the National Register of Historic Places in Arizona (1966).

Until his death in 2007, it had been the home of E. Dean Prichard who spent three decades preserving the property and helping open the Arizona Trail. Today, many hikers stop off near the High Jinks Ranch to rest along the Trail.

The historic property still contains deposits of black diorite, once used for statues and jewelry by ancient Egyptians, King David, Queen of Sheba, and others in the Middle East over three thousand years ago. The hardness and durability of the stone allows it to be carved into figurines and other artifacts. It is in this area the famed Cody Stone is found.

[1225] http://www.buffalobill.org/

The archway leading to the High Jinks Ranch, built by Dean Prichard in the 1980s. The ranch house was constructed by Buffalo Bill Cody's foster son Johnny Baker. The ranch was the site of a movie production and may contain one of the Campo Bonito mining claims. Campo Bonito is just south of the ranch.

Johnny Baker was well known for his exquisite juniper woodcarvings from cigarette boxes to large coffee tables. Experts at the University were puzzled how Baker acquired local juniper timber because there was a forest fire in the early 1700s that wiped out all vegetation.

Baker didn't want to reveal his source as he was afraid others would rob his supply. He revealed that he found the "underground workings of the Esperanza mine" as named in Harold Bell Wright's book THE MINE WITH THE IRON DOOR. According to this story related by E. Hobart Molson who took over the Campo Bonito properties, Baker had used the "stulls that the padres installed to hold the hanging wall" to make his beautiful juniper wood carvings. [1226]

[1226] Letter from E. Holbart Molson, Molson & Co. Graphite Division, La Jolla, California. February 15, 1974. Molson sent a copy of a map of Campo Bonito and related this story about Baker to the Buffalo Bill Historical Center in Cody, Wyoming.

William Carter stands among the debris from the legendary Lost City in the Santa Catalina Mountains. The spot may have also been built over as the Hartman Homestake mining camp at the turn of the 20th Century. Photo courtesy of William Carter.

Catalina Camp – Marble Peak

Considerable mining activity has been ongoing around Oracle Ridge, at least, for hundreds of years. The portion of the mountain range that extends from Mt. Lemmon and the community of Summerhaven northward toward Marble Peak is rich in copper and other minerals.

For hikers, the Oracle Ridge is a portion of the popular Arizona Trail. It passes the old Oracle Ridge Mine and the former Catalina Camp where E.O. Stratton, Francis Hartman, and others staked numerous claims in the 1880s through the early part of the 20th Century.

The Oracle Ridge Mining District was originally part of the Old Hat or Control Mining District. Dozens of claims around Marble Peak were consolidated into the Phelps Dodge Copper Company in 1910 and the Daily Arizona Copper Company in 1937. The property exchanged hands numerous times over the decades. [1227]

Now this area is so remote it takes horseback or a full day to hike in and out. It is difficult to believe that hundreds of men worked and lived in this desolate area. At one time there were numerous building and a store to support a small community.

Besides being an active mining site, the Oracle Ridge area has had some legends tied to this region, and ruins have been buried deep in the hills that point to earlier inhabitants.

[1227] The Control Mines (1939), Continental Copper, Inc. (1968), Union Mines (1977), South Atlantic Ventures, Southern Copper Corp. (188), Santa Catalina Mining Company (1993), Marble Ventures (2005) and Oracle Ridge Copper Co. (2010). Source: Review of the Oracle Ridge Mine Project for Gold Hawk Resources Inc., prepared by Glenn R. Clark. August 20, 2010. Pages 26-29.

Old Mexican Coin, Artifact Found

Nearby the Catalina Camp is where a 1812 Mexican coin and a rusty old iron pick were discovered in the 1980s by several seasoned hikers. [1228]

The coin was found near a tunnel on the west side of Oracle Ridge. The buried coin may have been from a payment made to a Mexican or early Anglo miner and lost in the dirt. Both items were turned over to the U.S. Forest Service [1229] and reviewed by the Arizona Historical Society. [1230]

Miners could have used the iron pick because the Iron Door legend indicates the mine was so rich, the gold was cut out by a *hacheta* that resembled in shape and size the recovered artifact. [1231]

The 1812 Mexican real discovered at Catalina Camp in 1988. The coin is archived by the U.S. Forest Service. Next page, close up of coin. Photos courtesy of William Carter.

[1228] Reported to the U.S. Forest Service in 1981 by William T. Carter.

[1229] Letter to Mr. William Carter from James A. McDonald, Forest Archeologist, Coronado National Forest, United States Department of Agriculture. November 14, 1994.

[1230] Letter to Mr. William Carter from Mark Santiago, Collections Manager, Arizona Historical Society. July 10, 1995.

[1231] As reported by William Carter.

The copper coin is determined to be an authentic Mexican 1812 two-real piece minted by the Insurgent Government of José Maria Morelos, one of the fathers of Mexican Independence. [1232] It is unlikely it was used as payment for miners because in the mid to late 19th century Americans conducted business mostly in Mexican gold and silver. The iron pick could not be explained either. [1233]

Since there were mining activities in the area during the early to mid-1800s, it could help explain the discovery of an 1812 Mexican coin at nearby Catalina Camp. Prior to the Americans only Mexicans and maybe the Spaniards mined the area.

The rusty iron pick and 1812 Mexican *real* coin dug up near Marble Peak at the Catalina Camp site. Photo courtesy of William Carter.

[1232] Letter to William Carter from Mark Santiago, Collections Manager, the Arizona Historical Society, July 10, 1995.

[1233] Ibid.

1880-1940s: Marble Peak– The Ledge Of Copper

"Marble Peak is the remnant of a synclinal mountain. It is all that is left to use of a great but spreading mass of limestone and of quartzite of marine origin and palaeozoic age…The peak and its marble capping give to us a striking example, or exhibition, of the stupendous amount of erosion and cutting away suffered by the mountains of Arizona in past geologic ages…" [1234]

While mining was taking root during the 1880s in the Cañada del Oro on the northwest side and in the Old Hat District near Oracle on the northeast, another part of the Santa Catalinas was also being explored– Marble Peak.

Marble Peak is located a few miles north of Mt. Lemmon, near the current site of the Oracle Ridge Mine. It was one of the most remote mining locations in the Catalinas.

A large copper belt extended a mile long and a quarter mile wide on the southeast side of Marble Peak. After discovering the copper protrusion, C. A. Wyatt and Pete Dumphrey located their claim in 1880 [1235] on the eastern slope near the Lee and Waldow's trail about ¼ mile south of Marble Peak; they called it the Apache.

On the Apache, a crosscut revealed a fifteen-foot vein of ore that assayed as high as 70 percent copper. The ledge of copper followed the whole one thousand five hundred foot claim. The extension claims, the Midas and St. Nicholas, showed similar results. At that time thirty percent copper ore was worth $60 per ton. At the same time the abundance of yellow pine easily fed a hungry smelter to also produce some quality charcoal. [1236]

[1234] "Santa Catalinas Are Attracting Attention, Hartman's Camp" (Tucson Star), from Weekly Journal Miner, July 7, 1909.

[1235] The History of the Lower San Pedro Valley in Arizona, by Bernard W. Muffley, Thesis for Department of History, Mater of Arts, University of Arizona. 1938. Page 25.

[1236] "Arizona Copper Mines," from the San Francisco Bulletin and reprinted in Arizona Weekly Citizen. March 20, 1881.

By 1881 a 20-ton daily capacity smelter was built at the nearby Apache Camp. Ore for the smelter came from the Hartman, Homestake, Leatherwood, Stratton, Geesman, and other small claims around the mountain. [1237]

Marble boulders are still scattered in the dry creek east of Marble Peak.

[1237] Review of the Oracle Ridge Mine Project for Gold Hawk Resources Inc., August 20, 2010. Pages 26-29.

Emerson Oliver Stratton's old homestead that sits above the old mine, now the east side of the Oracle Ridge mine below the monolith. Photo courtesy of William Carter.

Map of pointing to the Oracle Ridge and Marble Peak site. This area is also the site of the Lost City. Summerhaven is two miles south of Marble Peak.

The San Catarina Copper Company

D r. S. K. Kane, a prominent Tucson physician and surgeon who had several claims in the Catalinas, bought the Dumphrey and Wyatt's Marble Peak claims in the Santa Catarina copper belt in December, 1881. The lode was so promising that a furnace was to be installed. The immense copper ledge was estimated to produce a thousand tons of high-grade copper ore.

The northeast extension of the mine was sold off to Ed Reilly of the Copper Queen for $20,000. An assay showed 33.7 percent copper with silver. Each of the claims had a natural spring nearby to provide sufficient water. [1238] Claims owned on the west side by Moye Wicks, a Tucson attorney, and his company, followed along another vein of copper. Pine and oak timber was in abundant supply along the side of the mountain. [1239]

Although, as of January, 1882, no bullion was produced, Kane's investors [1240] were still pleased with the progress. A furnace and sawmill were in transit to be installed on the property. [1241] On the Midas claim a five-ton boulder was about forty five percent copper and a large percentage of gold and silver. [1242]

An 1882 plat map of the San Catarina Copper Company's Apache lode showed three buildings– a store, bunkhouse, and smelter– on the north side of Rattlesnake Creek in

---

[1238] The claims included the Apache, St. Nicolas and Midas. Also note "Deed of Mill Site, Walter T Marvin to Santa Catarina Copper Company, Apache mill site, October 19, 1881; consideration $1. Consideration of 199,993 shares of stock in said Company: Midas, Apache, St. Nicholas Mines," Arizona Weekly Citizen, Tucson, A.T., December 18, 1881. Pages 1 and 3.

[1239] Claims included the Mermaid, Lord Byron, Santa Claus, Little Buttercup and Everlasting. "From the Old Hat," Arizona Weekly Citizen, Tucson, A.T., December 18, 1881.

[1240] Mr. H. M. Munsell, vice president of Santa Catarina Copper Company, Mr. Baker, a major stockholder, and Mr. Frank Stevens were sent by the New York company to take charge of the books when they went to visit the mines. Stevens planned to become a resident. Arizona Weekly Citizen, Tucson, A.T., January 16, 1882.

[1241] "More Copper Companies," Arizona Weekly Citizen, Tucson, A.T., January 15, 1882.

[1242] Tombstone Epitaph, February 13, 1882. Reported by Mr. Marvin.

addition to an assay office on the south. [1243] On the adjoining Santa Catalina claim, there were a saloon and store that sat along Rattlesnake Creek. [1244] Those eight buildings were still standing through the 1970s not far from the town of Summerhaven. [1245]

Things seemed to be so promising for this new settlement that a stagecoach line was to be established by H. Ashworth from Tucson to the camp on the east portion of Marble Peak. Ashworth also planned to build a hotel for a summer resort to be enjoyed during the hot Tucson summers. [1246]

The Catalina Copper Mining Company of Boston bought up the claims a year later. A mill, smelter, sawmill, and several other buildings were constructed.

Emerson O. Stratton, a rancher who had mining property nearby, built a road from the mine to the San Pedro River, but the venture ceased operations in May, 1882, after only $20,000 worth of ore was recovered. [1247]

The next month James Buell, an attorney, filed a patent application for the Apache Mining Claims and mill site [1248] and a patent for the nearby Saint Nicholas mining claim a month after that. That claim was on the southwest slope about ¼ mile northerly of Rattlesnake Creek. [1249]

A few months after the application, a four-ton "kidney" of copper ore was found. That was a disappointment, as they expected to locate considerably more. [1250] That September,

---

[1243] Survey No. 362 Plat of the Apache Mill Site, March 15, 1882. Maps were also recorded for #363 Saint Nicholas mining claim; #359 Midas claim; #362 Apache claim; and #360 Santa Catalina mill site claim. The San Catarina Copper Co.

[1244] Survey No. 360, Lot 37B Plat of the Santa Catalina mill site, April 24, 1882.

[1245] The surveys were cancelled October 8, 1986. Eight buildings were listed in Mineral Survey 3679 as other improvements to the Daily Extension No. 2, 3 and 4. That survey was conducted May 4, 1974, when the property was owned by the Continental Copper Company from Phoenix.

[1246] Arizona Weekly Citizen, Tucson, A.T., March 5, 1882.

[1247] The History of the Lower San Pedro Valley in Arizona, Page 25. Referenced by, Reminiscences, by E.O. Stratton.

[1248] Application No. 207 and 208 for Patent to the Apache Mining Claims and Apache Mill Site, U.S. Land Office, Tucson, Arizona. Arizona Weekly Citizen, Tucson, A.T., June 11, 1882.

[1249] Application No. 209 for Patent to the Saint Nicholas Mining Claim. U.S. Land Office, Tucson, Arizona. Arizona Weekly Citizen, Tucson, A.T., July 23, 1882.

[1250] Arizona Sentinel, Yuma, A.T., September 9, 1882.

Judge Buell, gave notice in the local newspaper that the "San Catarina Copper Company will pay all just debts against them." [1251] Over the next year the company fought off several lawsuits, eventually Buell lost the claims.

The old San Catarina Copper Company workings were taken over by Mr. Terry and Mr. Mellvaine in 1886. They cleaned out an old tunnel and opened up a four-foot vein of copper that ran from sixty to eighty percent. The smelter and sawmill were up and running again and lumber was being cut for $25 per thousand. While that property was restarting, on the other side of the mountain near Oracle, the American Flag and Southern Belle were producing ore. [1252]

The venture didn't last long and by September, 1887, the property was abandoned until another Tucson lawyer took an interest. [1253]

Tucson attorney Francis M. Hartman did more than just practice law. He also ventured into the mining businesses for several decades. Hartman, an Ohio lawyer, came to Tucson as an attorney for the Southern Pacific in Arizona and New Mexico. In 1901 Hartman was the manager of the newly revived Catalina Copper Mining Company, and he resurrected the abandoned Apache mine on the east slope of Marble Peak.

"Substantial stone houses are being erected and work will begin in a few days on a 100 foot winze," it was reported. [1254] This mine was expected to become the first bullion producer in the Catalina Mountains. The venture, backed by Boston capitalists, brought in Robert Johns as the superintendent to work along the Silver Reef, which was in the center of four older claims of big outcroppings of copper and other minerals. One copper vein was twelve feet wide and was cut by three hundred and twenty feet from the mouth of the tunnel. [1255]

By 1902 the company had fifteen claims and four mill sites in the area and was known as Apache Camp. The claims, spread over three hundred and twenty acres, had names like Big Elephant, St. Charles, Lead King, Congress Street, Silver King, and Silver Reef. The ore carried a good amount of copper, gold, silver, and lead.

[1251] *Arizona Weekly Citizen*, Tucson, A.T., September 17, 1882.

[1252] *Arizona Weekly Citizen*, Tucson, A.T., January 9, 1886.

[1253] *Arizona Weekly Citizen*, Tucson, A.T., September 17, 1887. Called Santa Catalina Copper Company.

[1254] *Arizona Republican*, Phoenix, A.T., October 26, 1901.

[1255] *Arizona Republican*, Phoenix, A.T., November 15, 1901.

The Silver King Claim has been worked on fifty years earlier as a lead and a silver mine, according to Hartman. Several of the claims also had a large percentage of iron. The property had one thousand feet of underground tracks, a boarding house, bunkhouse, and superintendent house built of stone. Robert Leatherwood's Old Hat mines consisted of six claims just east of Oracle and north of Hartman's. The promise of a new railroad that would come within twelve miles of the Leatherwood and Hartman's claims was encouraging to both miners. [1256]

Nearby in July, 1902, E. O. Stratton began to develop the Barnite Group of copper mines, adjoining the Catalina Copper mines. Stratton didn't claim to have any mines, but he said the vein of copper, lime, iron, and porphyry was about sixty feet wide and ran right through the property. [1257]

Hartman had an option on the Catalina Copper property until April 1907 when he bonded his claims, along with Leatherwood and Geesman to Epes Randolph, a railroad mogul. [1258] Randolph, who donated the majority of land for Tucson's mid-town Reid Park was the original namesake for the park formerly called Randolph Park. The name was changed to Reid Park in 1978. [1259]

[1256] The article details the claims, their workings and status. Report of the Governor of Arizona," Catalina Copper Mining Company, by F. M. Hartman. 1903. Pages 109-110. The article is also reprinted in the Annual Report of the Department of the Interior, The Congressional Serial Set, 1903. Page 209-210.

[1257] Bisbee Daily Review, Bisbee, A.T., July 13, 1902.

[1258] "What is the Mining History of the Oracle Ridge Mine, Part 1," by Evaline Aubacher, Copper Area News, Arizona.

[1259] Randolph Golf Course (Park) Origin of name, Tucson Public library, Librarian Files. The park was renamed for Gene Reid, city parks director.

1900: Catalina Camp Deep In The Catalinas

Near the east fork of the canyon where the Cañada del Oro joins the west, the Red Ridge Trail #2 branches off towards the old mining outpost of Catalina Camp.

Owned by a Detroit company, Catalina Camp was another site of major mining activities from the turn of the 1900s through the 1940s. Today the abandoned mining camp is near a small patch of cleared dirt and two outbuildings. [1260] The camp was managed by Francis B Hartman, who also had interests near the head of the canyon and on the eastern side of the Catalina Mountains at Camp Condon. The Catalina Camp closed temporarily in 1901 while they awaited the arrival of heavy machinery. All three areas worked by Hartman were rich in gold, silver, and copper. [1261]

One of the two remote cabins near Catalina Camp may have been built before the turn of the 20th Century where E. O. Stratton mined with his family. Today an inscription above the door of the larger cabin is marked "One Park Place." The nearby shack is named "10 Downing Street." The buildings still stand and are often visited by hikers off the Arizona Trail. A roster for visitors to sign contains hundreds of comments. [1262]

Francis Hartman was also involved in a 1907 silver, carbonate, and sulphide copper mining adventure with pioneer M. G. Samaniego called the Esperanza Copper Co. in the Cañada del Oro. [1263] Samples from the Catalina Camp site averaged .03 ounces of gold, .47 oz. of copper, and .55 oz of silver per ton. [1264]

[1260] Coronado Hiking Trails, Coronado National Forest, Cañada del Oro Trails.

[1261] "Canada del Oro, A Rich Mining District in the Catalina mountains," Arizona Republican, Phoenix, Ariz. A.T., August 31, 1901.

[1262] "Sign In Roster," One Park Place, in possession of William Carter.

[1263] "At Esperanza Mine," Bisbee Daily Review, February 24, 1907.

[1264] Mineral Appraisal of Coronado National Forest, Part 5, 1994. Page A13.

One Park Place, was the Cody building similar to the structure that once stood at the High Jinks Ranch. Nearby are Catalina Camp and several gold and copper mines. Photos courtesy of William Carter.

1902: End Of A Mining Era At Catalina Camp

"Mining in the Catalina Mountains is at a stand still, but if the Phoenix and Eastern railroad is built work will be resumed at Camp Condon, Copper Hill and the Catalina camp. This will, however, have a tendency to hurt rather than to aid Tucson, as the trade from these camps, will then go to Phoenix and Benson." [1265]

The railroad line was never built to the Catalina Camp site. Progress slowed down for a few years while the Old Hat District and Campo Bonito mines endured.

The Reef of Rock is seen towards the left from the nearby Catalina Camp. Photo courtesy of William Carter.

[1265] Bisbee Daily Review, June 26, 1902.

1917: Road Built; Stratton Claims Sold To Wilson

A 15-mile road, from Peppersauce Canyon to the Stratton Camp was completed in January of 1917. [1266] This was the only route to Mount Lemmon, and it took two hours and fifty minutes to get from Tucson to the Stratton Camp. [1267]

Emerson Oliver Stratton built the road from the San Pedro River and took it west toward Marble Peak for access to his mining claims, Condon Camp, and the Daily Group (of Bisbee) who were some of first miners to settle the east side of Marble Peak. When the great Stratton highway was completed in 1917, it reached seven miles from the top of Mt. Lemmon. Later the road was expanded to the top for settlers to access supplies. The original road went through Rattlesnake Pass to the west side of Marble Peak and ended at Stratton's property on the west side of the peak.

Two months later the copper clams of the Stratton Group [1268] were sold for $50,000 to Charles N. Wilson. He owned the claims for thirty years. It was considered to be "one of the most promising mining properties of this section."

Stratton staked the claims while he was a cattle rancher in the San Pedro area. The highly mineralized belt adjoins the Copper Queen and Daily Consolidation mines. Wilson built a road from his mining interests to Mount Lemmon, and for several seasons the only automobile route to Mount Lemmon was through the Stratton camp. Wilson also invested $150,000 in machinery, electric lights, and a water system. Stratton later retired in San Francisco. [1269]

By 1928 there were sixty three patent mining claims that were staked across Marble Peak and flanked both the east and west sides of the range northwest of 'Lemon Mt.' They included the Copper Princess, the Chalcopyrite, the Roosevelt, the Hidden Treasure, and the Homestake. [1270]

[1266] "Great Stratton Road Completed," Arizona Daily Star, January 3, 1917.

[1267] "Repair Stratton Road," Bisbee Daily Review, June 20, 1919.

[1268] USGS: Stratton Mine is a past producer of copper, gold, molybdenum, silver and uranium. MRDS M050643, Deposit ID 10138003.

[1269] "Final Payment On Stratton Claims," Bisbee Daily Review, August 31, 1919.

[1270] 1928 Plat of Township No. 11 South, Range 16 East Gila and Salt River Meridian, Arizona. Department of the Interior General Land Office, July 12, 1928.

1940s: Hartman's Homestake Mines Expands Claim

In the 1940s Tucson attorney and prospector Francis Hartman expanded the Hartman Homestake Mines [1271] on the west flank of the Oracle Ridge.

The Hartman Homestake Fault was one of several cross fault lines in the Santa Catalinas and was exposed near the Hartman Homestake Mines. [1272] Past production from the Hartman site yielded .03 ounces of gold per ton. [1273]

1942: U.S. Closes Gold Mines In War Effort

The official end of mining for gold came in 1942 with Limitation Order No. 208. That mandate switched mining activities to copper and zinc, the raw materials needed to fight in World War II. That effectively shut down many operations, and gold mining went underground.

A mineral survey from the 1970s described eight structures on the southwest portion of Marble Peak, including four cottages, a store and office, boiler and engine room, a garage and a blacksmith shop. Those buildings, owned at the time by the Continental Copper Co., are no longer standing. The cleared area on the mountainside shows some signs of past construction. [1274]

An era of glorious mining in the Santa Catalinas quietly faded. The mountains swallowed up another sign of civilization. William "Flint" Carter has remained one of the last prospectors to retain mining claims in these hills over the past decades.

[1271] USGS: Hartman Homestake Mines is a past producer of copper, lead, silver and zinc, MRDS M051051, Deposit ID 10113593.

[1272] The Geology of the Cañada del Oro Headwaters, Santa Catalina Mountains, Arizona, by Gene Arthur Suemnicht, thesis submitted 1977, University of Arizona Campus Repository. Page 91.

[1273] Ibid, A 18

[1274] Mineral Survey No. 3679 Daily Extension No. 2, 3 and 4. Survey conducted May 4, 1974. Continental Copper Co. Source: Bureau of Land Management.

The Last Prospector

"If I did find a treasure, do you really think I would tell anyone?"

William "Flint" Carter, "Miner's Story Project," 2009. [1275]

One local prospector, William "Flint" Carter, has been mining the Santa Catalina Mountains most of his life.

Now in his mid-60's, he spent the last forty years venturing deep into the mountains to service his mining claims. He is the only prospector with a continuously active mining claim in the Catalina Mountains. [1276]

With the scarcity of ongoing mining projects in the mountains today, he may be the last, lone prospector.

Photo of Flint Carter during a 2014 expedition into the Santa Catalinas. Courtesy of Will Grant.

[1275] "Miners Story Project," The University of Arizona. CD format. August 11, 2009.

[1276] Carter has held 169 mining claims since the 1970s. Bureau of Land Management mining claim records, 2014.

William "Flint" Carter was lured, as hundreds before him, by the prospect of finding the Lost Mine with the Iron Door and the natural occurrence of precious minerals.

After Carter moved to Southern Arizona in the early 1970s, Susan Thurman introduced him to Burton Holly, the man who helped build Hollywood and owned land in the Cañada del Oro. Holly shared with him the legend of the Iron Door Mine.

Holly told Carter that he was sitting on the largest gold mine in the U.S. Later, Carter learned more about the history of the area and about the biggest gold legend in the West. The story of that rich mine was just part of the reason the legend still exists and continues to grow. Carter believed that the largest land treasure in the world, over 100 tons of gold, was partially moved out of the Catalinas and carted a few hundred miles east. "The local legend mentions a treasure, but it is more focused on the lost mine," Carter remarked. [1277]

It was during one exploration of the Catalinas in the 1970s that Carter and his group stumbled upon more than just an old mine deep within the Cañada del Oro. His claim to discover the Lost Iron Door Mine [1278] became overshadowed by the minerals he has been quietly recovering from his claims over the past decades.

In 1972 Carter purchased an acre on the former Samaniego Ranch [1279] from Holly. There was a chicken coop between two old adobe buildings. Carter built a natural stone-incorporated earth shelter with a black sand iron structure from the chicken coop as an alternative solar energy concept. It was documented as Arizona's first solar heated and cooled museum by the Arizona Governor's Office in 1986. No other building had incorporated alternative building designs in the structures at that time. [1280] The building used Paolo Soleri's design of arcology– [1281] a combination of ecology and architecture– allowed the walls inside and out to be farmed, thereby increasing space instead of decreasing it. No fossil fuels were required. The house was to be used as a charging unit to run a vehicle one hundred miles a day, truly non-polluting transportation.

[1277] From a conversation with William Carter, 2014.

[1278] "William 'Flint' Carter hints that he has found the Iron Door Mine," C.T. Revere, *Tucson Citizen*, October 1, 1997.

[1279] "Warranty Deed," November 30, 2006. Official Records of Pinal County Recorder.

[1280] William T. Carter memoirs, 2010. The letter from the Arizona Governor's office by Sam Udall stating it was Arizona's first solar heated and cooled museum.

[1281] Introduction to Arcology, from Arconsanti, https://arcosanti.org/arcology

"At the beginning 1970s, there was a 350-acre man made lake called Golder Dam. I was the only person to buy lake front property and build. The concept was simple. I wanted to be self-sufficient. The house would heat and cool its self while acting as a vehicle charging unit for 100 miles a day travel. But, funding was the major problem." [1282]

The reason Carter became involved in both the hunt for the Iron Door Mine and for minerals was to provide resources for his environmental projects.

A 23-pound boulder nugget of silver and gold veins, marketed today as Cody Stone, from the Santa Catalina Mountains. The value has been placed at $1/4 million. [1283]

In the early 1980s Carter accompanied Mel Fisher on the James Bay to the wreck of the Spanish galleon Atocha where the largest bullion discovery of the century was recovered

---

[1282] According to William Carter.

[1283] In possession of William Carter.

shortly thereafter. In the late 1990s Carter partnered with Jerry Cheatham, the grandson of Doc Noss of the Victorio Peak treasure that was considered to be the largest land treasure in the world with over one hundred tons of gold.

Carter has maintained one active mining claim deep within the Catalinas. With a collection of high-grade ore accumulated from the claim, Carter has cut, polished, and fabricated the stones into jewelry called Cody Stone, which he named after "Buffalo Bill" Cody who owned mines in the Oracle area.

Carter's business, Celebrity Stones only uses materials from the Santa Catalinas. The stones are named for past celebrities that owned the sites where the stones were mined. Cody Stone, Geronimo's Gold, the Wilma Huggett stone, the Esmerelda, and others are just an example of some of the minerals still found in the mountains. These have become extremely rare collectibles. There have been fewer than five hundred pieces recorded. They are from the only known source of gold and silver from Mt. Lemmon.

Refined gold and silver can be purchased almost anywhere, but one hundred precent natural specimens are almost non-existent. Almost anything of value usually goes through the crushers, and only a few pounds remain. The values are placed on each stone by its separate grading.

Cody Stone samples are on display in fourteen museums worldwide, including the Mining Hall of Fame and the Gem Institute of America. For five years during the last half of the 1990s, an educational exhibit at the Tucson Gem and Mineral Show highlighted the history of this epic gold legend.

In 2010 Carter appeared in the motion picture, Buffalo Bill, Beyond the Legend, [1284] to describe Cody's role in the search for the mine with iron door. He is working on a new film that carries the theme of the Iron Door Mine and continues to recover minerals from his mine.

[1284] Buffalo Bill, Beyond the Legend, by Jack Hubbell, Little Bighorn Productions. DVD preview at http://www.littlebighornproductions.com/bb-2.html

Samples of Cody Stone jewelry– silver and gold in quartz designed by Michael Garcia.

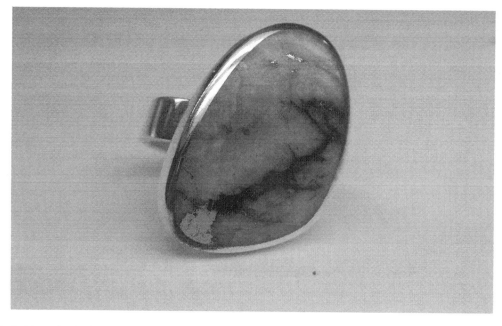

Cody Stone ring designed by Orlando Jewelers, UK. Photos courtesy of William Carter.

"The beautiful yellow metal matrix in hard white quartz is the mark of Cody Stone. Similar to diamonds, the hard quartz provides a strong and timeless durability, protecting the soft, precious, noble metals." [1285]

Cody Stone from the Santa Catalina Mountains has been fabricated into fashion-wear by jewelers such as William T. Carter; Gary Holdcroft; Isaac Hunan; Bisbee Bob; Poncho; Buzz Stringer; Steve Montez; Michael Garcia; AAA Family Jewelers in Tustin, CA; the Navajo nation; Will Dentondale, a Navajo artist; Orlando Jewelers UK, James Svoboda, and Cornelious Hollander.

Although each stone has to be graded individually, it has an established value at $5 per carat for silver content and $25 per carat for gold content.

Polished silver and gold embedded quartz from the Santa Catalinas, today marketed as Cody Stone.

[1285] Source: William T. Carter.

The Legend: Revisited

From this thorough examination of the literature, documents, diaries, personal and newspaper accounts, the multiple legends of the Santa Catalinas can be merged into a more reasonable rendition.

Did the early Spanish discover minerals in the Catalinas, build a mission and a small community? Was there actually a tunnel in the Catalinas where they hid their bullion? Did someone already discover its location and steal away its treasures? Or, is it still covered up by nature or an earthquake? Are there still an abundance of natural minerals still out there? Possible.

After Father Eusebio Kino arrived in the newly acquired land of the Spanish Pimería Alta, there was a reported discovery of gold, silver, or quicksilver possibly near the Santa Catalina Mountains. A combined missionary and military expedition was launched several times beginning in 1698 to seek out the source of the minerals and create new settlements in the region.

One of the military officers who accompanied Kino was Juan Bautista de Escalante. While Kino's mission was to make peace and baptize the natives, the military's role was to provide protection and search for mineral deposits. The diaries of Kino and others reported on vast minerals throughout the Sonoran frontier. Kino was dismayed, however, that his main mission to convert the natives was thwarted by the military's need for slave labor. Spanish records confirm this did happen– and both Kino and an Escalante were involved. And, a legend sprouted.

At this time mining operations were ongoing in the nearby Santa Rita Mountains and near San Xavier, as Kino and others reported. In the early 1700s, the most northern mission, Santa Catalina, was located near Picacho Peak about forty miles northwest of San Xavier.

A decade after Kino died, another Escalante, Francisco Xavier de Escalante, spent his entire career in the Fronteras military during this time wandering the entire Pimería Alta. While this Escalante is not well known, he knew the Santa Catalinas very well.

From 1720 through the 1760s, there was an influx of missionaries into the Santa Cruz Valley. They went to the missions of San Xavier del Bac and *visita* of Santa Catalina, among others. By the 1730s, the Santa Catalina "mission" may have been moved "seven leagues east of San Agustin." This would place it somewhere along the Cañada del Oro in the Catalinas.

If at any time there had been a mission, a mine and a city in the Catalinas, it would have happened during this period. Recently uncovered Old Spanish documents suggest some of this did occur, and, another legend was revealed.

After the 1751 "Pima Indian Uprising," the missions were abandoned for a while. Subsequent attacks by Apache Indians occasionally caused people to flee. After the Jesuits were expelled from New Spain, the missions were again abandoned until the Franciscans took over and tried to reestablish them. After the Franciscans were expelled, all missions and mines were again abandoned, and, the legend was carried on.

During one of those times, one of the mines– maybe a mine operated at one time by a man named Escalante– filled with bullion, was supposedly sealed off with a large door– maybe a door of iron or reinforced with iron. When the Americans arrived, all that was left were the legends. Almost all of the evidence except for some maps and scant records had disappeared from history. But they followed their instincts and directions from the locals to eventually discover a natural wealth of gold, silver, and copper.

The lost treasure may still remain buried somewhere in the canyon of gold– covered over by an earthquake or centuries of mother earth. Or, possibly some lucky prospector may have secretly carted it off.

Whether the treasure existed or not, the enticement of those fabulous riches helped fuel the rush for gold in the Old West.

This is the obvious treasure of the Santa Catalina Mountains. The story behind it is the romance.

Prospecting The
Santa Catalina Mountains Today

T he Santa Catalina Mountains are quiet now. The only sounds heard are wildlife and occasionally aircraft overhead.

Active gold mining clubs and weekend prospectors still regularly travel the dusty roads in the back of the Catalinas to find small nuggets, flakes, and tailings left behind from the heavy mining days.

The remains of the old mining claims in the Old Hat, Marble Peak and Campo Bonito areas are on private patented property or part of the Coronado National Forest Santa Catalina District. These spots barely show any signs of previous activities. The mountains have reclaimed most of the land.

While most of the land is off-limits to mining operations, there are still several places in the mountains where professional activities are quietly being conducted.

Recently mining operations have been revived on Marble Peak near the Oracle Ridge by the Oracle Mining Corp. [1286] known as the Oracle Ridge Copper Company. The underground mining project is in the environmental clearance and permitting process. [1287] The project has a reserve estimate of 24.71 million tons grading 2.33% in copper. The company, which estimated $100 million in capital expenditures to restart production, [1288] received a non-binding term agreement up to $70 million from Credit Suisse for the venture. [1289]

[1286] Oracle Mining Corp. ("Oracle Mining" or the "Corporation") (TSX VENTURE:OMN)(OTCQX:OMCCF)(PINK SHEETS:OMCCF)(XETRA:OMC). Formerly called Gold Hawk (name changed on August 16, 2011.)

[1287] Oracle Ridge Copper Company website. http://www.oracleridgecopper.com

[1288] "Oracle Mining Reports Additional Drill Results from 2014 Drill Program," News, Oracle Ridge Copper. May 22, 2014.

[1289] "Oracle Mining Corp. Enters into a non-binding term sheet with Credit Suisse AG for up to $70 million," Fundamental Research Corp. analysis for investors, April 11, 2012.

Oracle Ridge Copper is expected to employ up to one hundred and eighty people and produce about one hundred and forty tons of concentrate a day. [1290] The company plans the first historic attempt to recover iron from magnetite found in the ores. Substantial copper, silver, and gold recovery is expected based on recent tests where recovery of gold and silver "at times exceed 90%, but averaged 80%-85%." Gold and silver have been historically recovered in copper concentrates from the site. [1291]

The Little Hills Mine [1292] near Oracle has been running for decades, but its main material is now granite.

Prospective recreational mining in the Coronado National Forest is still allowed without a permit as long as the gold is recovered by non-mechanized means, but there are roadblocks that are just as menacing as Indian attacks.

The U.S. Forest Service, however, is concerned about the impact that individual placer activities can have on the environment, especially in the Campo Bonito and Coronado Camp areas. Studies are being conducted to limit motorized access to the mountains and to discourage overuse. These spots favored by amateur gold hunters are vulnerable because of the risk of uprooting, crushing and disrupting vegetation growth. [1293]

Amateur prospectors still roam the mountains searching for that precious gold– and that lost mine.

And the lone prospector traverses the Catalinas each year to claim another load.

[1290] Gold Hawk Resources, Inc. Initiating Coverage; Committed to Exploration and Development of Oracle Ridge Copper Mine Project. http://www.goldhawkresources.com

[1291] Review of the Oracle Ridge Mine Project, effective date April 13, 2012. Prepared by Glenn R. Clark & Associates Limited. Sections 1.0, 13.2 and 7.2.

[1292] Little Hills Mine. T10S, R15E SW 1/4. Discovered in 1885. First gold and silver claims staked in 1962-1965. http://www.mindat.org/loc-68645.html

[1293] Coronado National Forest, Santa Catalina Mountains Ecosystem Management Area Transportation Analysis Plan, revised February 2009. Page 65.

Author: Robert Zucker

"So, now, I am perpetuating the legends."

I have seen the Santa Catalina Mountains almost every day since I was born. [1294]

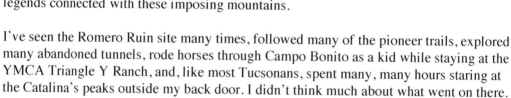

Those ominous mountains have been a constant backdrop my entire life. I have always been allured by their beauty and remoteness.

Although I've explored the Santa Catalina Mountains for many decades and hiked the back trails, I wasn't aware of the extensive history and legends connected with these imposing mountains.

I've seen the Romero Ruin site many times, followed many of the pioneer trails, explored many abandoned tunnels, rode horses through Campo Bonito as a kid while staying at the YMCA Triangle Y Ranch, and, like most Tucsonans, spent many, many hours staring at the Catalina's peaks outside my back door. I didn't think much about what went on there.

After learning more about many obscure legends and stories of the Catalinas from Tucson's last prospector, William "Flint" Carter, I listened with the same doubt as many others over the millennium that considered the legends a fairy tale. I decided to explore the legends and the claims. Just as a prospector would dig through the dirt to get to the

---

[1294] As a Tucson native, I lived here most of my life except for a few years in California. In the late 1970s through mid 1990s, I published several newspaper titles, including Youth Alternatives, Youth Awareness Press, Tucson Teen and Entertainment Magazine. The newspapers are now represented online at EMOL.org, EntertainTucson.com, EntertainmentMagazine.org, AZentertain.com among other domain names. Recently, I authored a couple of other books, "Entertaining Tucson Across the Decades" and Traveling Show, with more titles on the horizon.

Photo of author Robert Zucker at one of the tunnels in Campo Bonito.

bedrock, I dug through thousands of pages of documents to uncover the real story of what happened in those now stoic mountains. Years later, this edition emerged. There are still many loose ends and much more speculation to confirm or dispel.

But, I was able to discover more than the story behind the legends. It became clearer how history– historians and treasure hunters– revealed, and distorted, the mountains' secrets. I also collected a few nice rocks along the way.

There are still more riches to be discovered about the Santa Catalina Mountains. Buried behind centuries of dirt, and stuffed away in some forgotten storage box, those treasures will eventually be revealed.

Anyone with any other information not included in this survey of history and legends, should contact the author. There are still more files, manuscripts, records and dirt to dig through.

And, there will be more stories to be told.

Resources

These are some of the major sources with more information about the history and legends and mineralogy in the Santa Catalina Mountains. Additional resources, manuscripts, letters and books are found in the Bibliography.

Web Site Resources

Most of the newspaper articles, citations and quotations are compiled from the Chronicling America Newspaper Project, National Endowment for the Humanities of the Library of Congress. http://chroniclingamerica.loc.gov/

Other citations and quotations are from library books in and out of print, public domain documents digitized by Google Books and manuscripts archived at https://archive.org/

Treasures in the Santa Catalinas official web site for this book with updated information, sample chapters to read online. http://emol.org/treasurescatalinas/

Flint Carter's web site with examples of Cody Stone, videos and articles about the Iron Door Mine, Lost City and Lost Mission. http://emol.org/flintcarter/

The **Buffalo Bill Museum and Grave**, a facility owned and operated by the City and County of Denver, exists to preserve the memory of William F. "Buffalo Bill" Cody. To this end it maintains the Cody gravesite and related structures on Lookout Mountain Park; and records Cody's ongoing influence on American culture. http://www.buffalobill.org/

Arizona Historical Society, Tucson, Arizona, 929 E. 2nd Street, Tucson, Arizona. http://www.arizonahistoricalsociety.org

Mission 2000: Spanish Mission Records, Tumacacori National Historical Park http://home.nps.gov/applications/tuma/search.cfm

Mineral Appraisal of Coronado National Forest, Part 5, Santa Catalina-Rincon Mountains Unit. Mineral Land Assessment 1994. MLA-25-94. http://mines.az.gov/DigitalLibrary/usbm_mla/USBM_MLA_025-94.pdf

Historical Gold Prices

The price of gold was steady for many decades. The official U.S. Government price for gold has changed only four times from 1792 until a two-tiered pricing system was created in 1968. Since then, the price of gold has been set by the market and has been able to fluctuate. [1295] While the government set the official rate, gold would fetch as much as one was willing to pay.

Year	Average price per ounce
1833-1872	$18.93
1872-1918	between $18.94 and $18.99
1919-1933	between $19.95 and $20.69 when Executive Order 6102 issued.
1934-1968	between $34.69 and $39.31
1968-2011	between $41.28 and $1,571.52

Videos

These YouTube videos are from Flint Carter's video collection of stories, history and tours of the Santa Catalina Mountains.

Lost City in the Santa Catalina Mountains with Flint Carter
http://www.youtube.com/watch?v=93kSR8VoVIA

Santa Catalina Mission with Flint Carter
http://www.youtube.com/watch?v=dqQ9VZFN7Us

Santa Catalina Mission Artifacts
http://www.youtube.com/watch?v=nUI6bjAjIWg
http://www.youtube.com/watch?v=Cgy_t3lP9Iw

Iron Door Mine
http://www.youtube.com/watch?v=Cgy_t3lP9Iw

All photos and art work by Robert Zucker, unless otherwise noted.
Graphics and clip art courtesy of Zedcor, Inc., Tucson, Arizona.

[1295] Historical Gold Prices 1833 to Present (2011). Prices from 1883-1994 from World Gold Council, published in Timothy Green's Historical Gold Price Table. Prices from 1995-2011, kitco.com, based on the London PM fix.

TIME LINE

Early History

First Spanish Conquest

Kino & Escalante

After Kino's Death, Minerals in the Mountains

Expulsion of the Jesuits

Expulsion of the Franciscans and Mexican Independence

The New Arizona Territory– the Rush for Gold

"Buffalo Bill" Cody's Mines in Oracle

Arizona Statehood

Bibliography

CASES

10th Annual Report of the Board of Regents of the Smithsonian Institute, 1856. 88

A Brief History of Mission San Xavier del Bac, from Mission San Xavier del Bac 49

A Field Guide to Shells: Atlantic and Gulf Coasts and the West Indies, by Abbott Morris..............112

A Frontier Documentary: Sonora and Tucson, 1821-1848, by Kieran McCarty 131

A Guide to Tucson's Historic Neighborhoods, by City of Tucson..180

A History of Cochise County, Arizona 99

A History of Mining in AZ," 95

A History of the Precious Metals, from the earliest times to the present, by Alex Del Mar..............98

A Natural and Civil History of California..83, 84, 85, 102, 116

African American Women and the Old West, by Tricia Martineau Wagner.....................................305

All the Western States and Territories, from the Alleghanies to the Pacific, By John Warner 90

American Flag Ranch and Acadia Ranch - The Story of Oracle's Post Offices, ...293

American West Magazine..7

An Old Timers Experiences in Arizona. Pioneer Days of Isaac Goldberg, by Isaac Goldberg 234

Annals of the Spanish Northwest: North Mexican States 104, 106

Annual Report of the Department of Interior for 1899 90

Another New Territory, The M'arthur Democrat, McArthur...219

Antigua California: Mission and Colony on the Peninsular Frontier, by Harry Crosby 104, 124

Anza's California Expedition, Anza's Diary, Herbert Eugene Bolton...158

Apaches and the Mining Menace, 1800-1886, by Hana Samek Norton 234

Aquituni, New Mexico Historic Review...147

Aravaipa: Apache Peoplehood, by Ian Wilson Record 238

Archaeological Survey in Catalina State Park With A Focus On The Romero Ruin.... 45, 49, 60, 61,
    111

Archaeological Testing At Romero Ruin, by Deborah L. Swartz...61

Archaeology in Tucson 26, 68, 69, 93, 282

Archaeology of Southeast Arizona: A Class I Cultural Resource Inventory, by Gordon Bronitsky and
    James D. Merritt. 45

Archaeology of the San Pedro Valley, by Patrick D. Lyon..44

Arizona and New Mexico, 1888, by Hubert Howe Bancroft..213

Arizona and Sonora, by Sylvester Mowry..90, 92

Arizona Gold Placers and Placering, by G.M. Butler 207, 279, 336

Arizona Place Names, by Will C. Barnes..21, 22, 23, 228, 256, 291

Arizona: A Guide to the Grand Canyon State, by the WPA.................................101, 109, 110

Arizona: A State Guide, North American Book Dist LLC 181

Arizona: The Jesuits in Pimería Alta, From American Journeys Collection.................. 105, 114, 140

Arizona: The Nation's Youngest Commonwealth Within A Land of Ancient Culture, by James H.
    McClintock 237

Arizpe, Encyclopedia de los Municipios y Deligaciones de Mexico 132

Auraria, The Story of A Georgia Gold-Mining Town, by E. Merton Coulter 203

Bernardo Middendorf, by Ginny Sphar, Tumacacori National Historic Park...............................153

Books of the Southwest, History of Arizona, VIII...236, 238

Breathing Space: How Allergies Shape Our Lives and Landscapes, by Gregg Mitman 180

Buffalo Bill and his Shoshone Oil 327

Buffalo Bill and His Wild West, by Jospeh G. Rosa and Robin May 305

Illustrations

Index

Other Titles by BZB Publishing, Inc.
Entertaining Tucson Across the Decades, Vol. I: 1950s-1985, by Robert E. Zucker
Entertaining Tucson Across the Decades, Vol. II: 1986- 2000s, by Robert E. Zucker
Traveling Show, by Robert E. Zucker
Searching for Arizona's Buried Treasures, by Ron Quinn
Mysterious Disappearances and Other Strange Tales, by Ron Quinn

Titles can be purchased at Amazon.com and other retail outlets.

Treasures of the Santa Catalina Mountains is published by the
Santa Catalina Historical Preservation Project, a program of Southwest Alternatives
Institute, Inc., a non-profit 501 (c)(3) corporation, through BZB Publishing, Inc.

If there is any additional information to contribute about the history and legends of the
Catalinas or to contact publisher:

Robert Zucker
SAI/BZB Publishing, Inc.
P.O. Box 91317
Tucson, Arizona 85752-1317 USA
520-623-3733

Web: emol.org/treasurescatalinas
Email: *publisher@emol.org*

Made in the USA
San Bernardino, CA
13 September 2015